CASS LIBRARY OF WEST INDIAN STUDIES
No. 26

THE HISTORY OF
BARBADOS

CASS LIBRARY OF WEST INDIAN STUDIES

No. 9. Henry H. Breen

St. Lucia: Historical, Statistical, and Descriptive   (1844).
New Impression

No. 10. Sir Robert Hermann Schomburgk

A Description of British Guiana, Geographical and Statistical; exhibiting its resources and capabilities, together with the present and future condition and prospects of the colony   (1840).
New Impression

No. 11. Richard Ligon

A True and Exact History of the Island of Barbadoes. Illustrated with a Map of the Island, as also the Principal Trees and Plants there, set forth in their due Proportions and Shapes, drawn out by their several respective scales. Together with the Ingenio that makes the Sugar etc., etc.   (18-, 1873).
New Impression of the First Edition

No. 12. Edward Long

The History of Jamaica, or General Survey of the Ancient and Modern State of that Island; with Reflections on its Situation, Settlements, Inhabitants, Climate, Products, Commerce, Laws, and Government   (1774).
With a new introduction by George Metcalf
New Edition

No. 13. E. L. Joseph

History of Trinidad   (1838).
New Impression

No. 14. Alfred Caldecott

The Church in the West Indies   (1898).
New Impression

No. 15. C. S. Salmon

The Caribbean Confederation. A plan for the union of the fifteen British West Indian Colonies, preceded by An Account of the Past and Present Condition of the European and the African Races Inhabiting them, with a true explanation of the Haytian Mystery (1888).
New Impression

No. 16. Lillian M. Penson

The Colonial Agents of the British West Indies; a study in Colonial Administration, mainly in the Eighteenth Century   (1924).
New Impression

THE
HISTORY
OF
B A R B A D O S

FROM THE

FIRST DISCOVERY OF THE ISLAND
IN THE YEAR 1605

TILL THE

ACCESSION OF LORD SEAFORTH
1801

JOHN POYER

FRANK CASS & CO. LTD.
1971

Published by
FRANK CASS AND COMPANY LIMITED
67 Great Russell Street, London WC1B 3BT

First published   1808
New impression   1971

ISBN 0 7146 1945 0

Printed in Great Britain by
Stephen Austin and Sons Ltd., Hertford.

THE

HISTORY

OF

BARBADOS,

FROM THE

FIRST DISCOVERY OF THE ISLAND,

IN THE YEAR 1605,

TILL

THE ACCESSION OF LORD SEAFORTH, 1801.

BY JOHN POYER.

LONDON:

PRINTED FOR J. MAWMAN,

22, POULTRY.

1808.

[J. G. Barnard, Printer, Snow-Hill.]

PREFACE.

THERE is no desire more natural to the mind of civilized man, than that of retracing the transactions of former ages. Curiosity stamps a value on the most trifling records of antiquity, and we attend with pleasure to the recital of occurrences, in which we are no longer interested. Like every other affection of the human soul, this propensity gathers strength, and becomes more ardent, as its energies are more concentrated, and its object is more limited. Hence we pursue, with encreased eagerness, the inquiry which leads to the knowledge of those events that have occurred in the country which we claim as our own. To gratify

this laudable and rational curiosity, is the object of
the present undertaking, in which I have endeavoured to give, with historic fidelity, a Narrative of
the most remarkable Events and Legislative Transactions of my native Country.

It will readily be perceived, that the annals of a
small colony can furnish but few particulars worthy
the attention of the general historian, or the profound politician, whose enlarged views are occupied
with the fate of nations, or the complicated interests
of empires. But, " no period in the history of
one's own country," says a celebrated author, " can
be considered as altogether uninteresting. Such
transactions as tend to illustrate the progress of its
constitution, laws, and manners, merit the utmost
attention. Even remote and minute events are
objects of a curiosity, which, being natural to the
human mind, the gratification of it is attended
with pleasure." Encouraged by this opinion of
Robertson, the first historian of the age, I have
presumed to submit the following Work to the

candour of the public, in the hope that it will not be deemed wholly unimportant, or unworthy of their approbation.

To others, I willingly resign the brilliant meed which crowns the efforts of comprehensive genius, employed in recording the splendid achievements of warriors, the actions of heroes, or the beneficent institutions of statesmen. My ambition soars not beyond the humble task of presenting my country-men with a more complete and impartial History of Barbadoes than has hitherto appeared. In the progress of the work, due notice has been taken of the civil, military, and ecclesiastical establishments of the colony, its laws, and constitution. Their errors and imperfections are illustrated, and the abuses which have crept into the public admini-stration are noted with decent freedom, in which candour has not been forgotten.

In the performance of this delicate and essential part of my plan, I am apprehensive that I shall be thought obnoxious to censure, for having deviated from the strict rules of historical composition. The reflections scattered through the book, and the discussions of political subjects, into which I have occasionally descended, frequently interrupt the narrative, and divert the attention from its proper object. I was not aware of this inconvenience till it was too late to make any alteration in the arrangement. Yet there are many intelligent readers, by whom, I am persuaded, these will be considered the best parts of the work. Fatigued with a tedious narrative of events, which it is feared will not be generally interesting, the mind will repose and unbend itself in these caravanseras of rest and refreshment. Like episodes in an epic poem, they will relieve the attention, and amuse the imagination with their variety. And, even with respect to their utility, if the sentiments of the author should be found worthy of attention, it is presumed that their effect must be increased, by preserving the natural union between the reflection and the fact, by which it was suggested. These digressions are vindicated by an author of the first class in this department of literature; and I may venture to affirm, with Gibbon, that they will be censured only by those readers who are insensible to the importance of laws and manners, while they peruse, with eager curiosity, the transient intrigues of a court, or the accidental event of a battle.

The freedom of my remarks may probably give offence to many respectable persons in high official situations; and I may even be accused of betraying the interests of my country, by the representation which I have drawn of its internal government. But I utterly disclaim the smallest personal allusion whatever. Measures, and not men, where they can be separated, are the objects of reprobation; and in commenting on the errors of our establishment, it is not my intention to wound the feelings of any honest man, to whom the abuses of office have been transmitted through successive generations. Nor is it treachery, but patriotism, which calls the attention of persons in authority to the causes of those abuses which exist in the subordinate departments of the state. The purity of the motive will, I hope, entitle me to the indulgence of the public, and extenuate any imperfection which may be perceptible in the execution of this part of my design.

Had I foreseen the difficulties which I have had to encounter, I must confess, that I should never have engaged in this undertaking. Sensible how little I had to expect from the ordinary sources of information, I flattered myself that, as soon as my design was known, the lovers of literature would have facilitated, by every communication in their power, a Work, the want of which was universally acknowledged. But I have met with discouragement and disappointment, where I expected to have found support and assistance.

Notwithstanding several historical accounts of Barbadoes have been published, its genuine history remains involved in great obscurity. Of these publications, that of Ligon is little more than a journal of his voyage to and from the island, including an account of what happened during the few years he resided in the country. Mr. Hughs's Natural History is entirely barren of events; and the Memoirs of Barbadoes, published in the year 1742, though they contain some valuable information, are too concise to reward the search of the curious inquirer. The best and most copious account of this country extant, is said to have been published by Oldmixon, in his History of the British Empire in America. This publication I have never seen. Anxious to consult every author who had written on the subject, I offered, by public advertisement, any price for the book, but those who had it were not liberal enough to indulge me with the use of it.

This disappointment has been, in a great measure, compensated by the Account of Barbadoes contained in the forty-first volume of the Universal History, which seems to have been compiled from Oldmixon's book. Here I found a sufficient stock of materials to begin with. The outlines of my work were strongly marked, but many of the principal features of the figure were wanting. Many interesting periods are passed over with negligence and rapidity; and the inaccuracy with which many important facts are related, lessens the utility of that publication. It was in vain to seek information from the Short History of Barbadoes. Of that meagre volume there is little that the author can call his own. The greater part of it is a palpable plagiarism, and the adoption is rendered less valuable by the mutilated and imperfect state in which it was sent into the world.

I have thus been compelled to accept the Universal History for my principal guide, from the first settlement of the island to the administration of Mr. Pinfold. Its deficiencies have been supplied, and its errors corrected, by the memoirs already mentioned; and by the acquisition of many well-authenticated facts, extracted from a valuable collection of Essays, published under the title of the Caribbeanna. I have derived much collateral information from an excellent manuscript account of *the First Settlement of Barbadoes*, written by Hall, the editor of the Laws; which was kindly communicated to me by the Honourable Benjamin Hinds, chief justice of a court of common pleas, and treasurer of the island; a gentleman, whose stern political rectitude and integrity are softened by a happy union with the most amiable domestic virtues. Many of the most important transactions of Sir Bevill Granville's and Mr. Crowe's administrations, are detailed from an old journal of the proceedings of the assembly, lent me, with his usual urbanity, by my esteemed and ingenious friend Mr. Abraham Hartle. For many interesting particulars, I am indebted to two valuable manuscripts, which were politely put into my hands by William Eversley, Esq. an eminent attorney, whose integrity and professional knowledge have procured him the confidence and esteem, not only of his clients, but of all who enjoy the pleasure of his acquaintance.

Having, at length, taken leave of all my histo-rical guides, I was left to pursue the trackless waste with nothing to direct my footsteps, but a few fee-ble lights accidentally scattered in my way. The compass by which I might have steered my course, with ease and certainty, was placed beyond my reach. The journals of the colonial parliament, had I been allowed access to them, would have supplied every deficiency, and smoothed the way before me; but this was an advantage which I was not permitted to enjoy. Precluded from this source of information, I had no alternative left but to col-lect the fugitive productions of the press, which contained the minutes of the general assembly pub-lished by authority. Nor was this accomplished without difficulty. And I should have been obliged to relinquish my design, but for the liberal and friendly interposition of the Honourable and Reve-rend Mr. Brome and Judge Hinds, whose endea-vours have been unremittingly employed to pro-cure for me the materials necessary for the comple-tion of my work. To these gentlemen I am proud to acknowledge my obligations. The friendship of such men is a distinction of which I am justly vain, and amply compensates me for the envious malignity which has endeavoured to obstruct my suits.

And now, having surmounted the difficulties and impediments that have lain in my way, I submit to the candour of an enlightened community, with all those tender hopes and fears which are natural to the mind of a man, anxious for the success of a a production on which he has bestowed much time and pains. Conscious of my own deficiencies, I can scarcely expect a favourable reception from the world. Denied the advantages of an academical education, I cannot pretend to those ornaments of style which are necessary to embellish and recommend a work, which, from the nature of the subject, it is apprehended, will prove dry and unentertaining. I have endeavoured, however, to supply the want of learning and talents by diligence and application; and I trust that, as my faults have not been aggravated by presumption, they will not be punished with the severity of literary criticism.

From the lively interest taken by people of every description, in whatever relates to the condition of the enslaved African, it may, perhaps, appear strange that I should have taken no notice of the general state of West Indian slavery. But the subject has been so fully and ably treated, by Mr. Bryan Edwards, the elegant and ingenious historian of the West Indies, as to preclude the necessity of any ulterior discussion. And, as his valuable work is in general circulation, it would be superfluous to repeat what he has advanced with so much greater ability. It has, doubtless, been expected, that I should take notice of the torrent of illiberal invective with which our mistaken, misinformed, transatlantic fellow-subjects continue to overwhelm a peaceful, unoffending community, with whose internal situation they are very imperfectly acquainted; and that I should vindicate the character of my injured country, from the gross calumnies which are daily propagated, concerning the treatment of slaves. But I have forborne to remark upon this unwarrantable abuse, with that honest indignation which a due sense of accumulated injuries and insults, might naturally inspire and excuse, and shall leave the dart to recoil on those by whom it has been so unjustly and unfeelingly thrown. I may, however, be permitted to refer to the candid representations of a few intelligent travellers, for a refutation of the charges of inhumanity, too indiscriminately imputed to the West Indians to be just.

I shall begin with the testimony of the Reverend Mr. Williams, vicar of Exning, in Suffolk. This respectable minister of the gospel, was chaplain of Sir John Jervis's flag-ship, when that celebrated commander and Sir Charles Grey were employed in extending the glory of the British arms in the western hemisphere. While the fleet lay at Barbadoes, he had an opportunity of observing the condition of slaves, and the result of his observations is related with a candour becoming his holy voca-

tion: " During our residence at this island, curiosity led me to be present at a sale of slaves, just
imported from Africa.   As this horrid traffic in
human flesh has been the topic of public investigation for some time past, and much learning and
ingenuity have been displayed on both sides of the
question, I shall not give any opinion on it, but
merely state facts that came within my own knowledge.   The sale is proclaimed by beat of drum,
and is held, at Barbadoes at least, not in the open
air, as I had been taught to believe, but in a commodious house, appointed for that purpose.   As
soon as the planter has fixed on a slave, he retires
with the salesman to another room, there concludes
the bargain, and departs with his purchase to his
plantation, where the new comer, being clothed in
a coarse jacket, and provided with a hat, knife,
and other trifles, is placed with one of the old negroes, by whom he is instructed in his business.
In regard to the severity exercised by the slave-
owners on their slaves, whatever may have been
the case, I am well assured that now there are sel-

dom instances of those cruelties which have been so feelingly described, at least in the islands we visited on this expedition. At Barbadoes, they appeared to be in as comfortable situation as the lower ranks of society generally are; and as the climate is peculiarly favourable to poverty, clothes and firing, the great articles of expense to the poor in other countries, being hardly here required, I may venture to affirm, that the slaves in the West Indies are in a better situation, as to the necessaries of life, than the labouring poor in England, or any other country in Europe*."

On the comparative felicity of the West Indian slaves, we have the candid declaration of another clergyman, the Rev. Mr. Munn, who was sent to Jamaica as a missionary. He acknowledged that he had received, in England, very unfavourable impressions respecting the treatment of slaves; but, from what he had himself witnessed, he saw

---

* Williamson's Campaign in the West Indies, p. 12.

more of the comforts of life among them, more apparent contentment, more happiness, than he had ever seen among the labouring order of people in any part of Europe*.

To these venerable authorities let me add that of Doctor Pinckard. This gentleman was employed in a professional capacity to attend the troops under the command of Sir Ralph Abercrombie, on the expedition to the West Indies, and brought with him all those inveterate prejudices, generated by ignorance and falsehood, and nurtured by humanity, which prevail against the calumniated slave owner. Soon after his arrival, at Barbadoes, he had an opportunity of visiting a slave ship, "to witness," as he explains his design, " the manner of treating those poor beings of sable skin, who are torn from their native home by the iron hand of commerce, to be transported to a home of slavery." After a minute detail of the

* Dallas's History of the Maroons, vol. 2, p. 451.

particulars of this novel sight, the doctor assures his correspondent---" I am most happy to conclude my report, by informing you, that we observed no marks of those horrors and cruelties said to be practiced on board the ships occupied in this sad traffic of human flesh, and which are represented as frightfully augmenting the manifold ills of slavery*." And in a subsequent letter, the doctor adds, " the difference, in point of health, is peculiarly striking, between the troops conveyed in transports from England, and the slaves brought in the Guinea ships from Africa. The slaves are far more crowded than the soldiers, yet far more healthy. I might venture it as an opinion, that a Guinea ship would carry with less danger of disease being generated among them, a cargo of slaves more than thrice as numerous as a transport would carry of soldiers†." No better evidence can be had than this of a gentleman of professional eminence,

---

* Pinckard's Notes on the West Indies, vol. 1, p. 232.
† Ibid, vol. 2, p. 9.

who had a fair opportunity of examining both the transport and slave ships, and whose spontaneous declaration in favour of the latter mode of conveyance proves, that so far from *augmenting*, as had been represented, *the manifold ills of slavery*, it was, in fact, an amelioration of human misery.

In the course of this traveller's peregrinations in this country, he met with, what he is pleased to term, *a happy negro yard.* " We contemplated this spot with much satisfaction, and were gratified in observing the high degree of attention which was here given to the comfort and accommodation of the negroes; who had little cause to lament their removal from the wild woods of Africa to an opposite shore, *and could as little desire to exchange their present lot for the high-rated freedom of European paupers.* No thought have they to provide for their infants or their aged parents, nor have they to seek either food, habitation, or apparel. To each family is allotted a separate home; the necessary food and clothing are issued to them; and they know none of the anxious cares or difficulties of the world. No fearful concern, nor harassing incumbrance, can arise to them, on account of their offspring, who, like themselves, are furnished with all that is needful; and those who have most children, find themselves most valued and esteemed. In sickness, medical attendance is provided for them, and whatever is necessary is administered without thought or anxiety on their own part. Six days labour is demanded from them in the week, but the seventh is given them as a day of rest and relaxation; and from the total absence of care, it is usually spent in unbounded mirth and festivity *." Is there any particular hardship in this species of servitude? To labour, is the common lot of mankind. To eat bread earned by the sweat of his brow, was the sentence pronounced by an incensed God against fallen, disobedient man. And is the sable African less guilty than all the other descendants of Adam, that he alone should be exempted from the operation of Divine law?

---

* Pinckard's Notes on the West Indies, vol. 1, p. 288.

Again, speaking of the slaves on Mr. Dougan's plantations, in Demarara, Doctor Pinckard is forced to acknowledge, " that the labouring poor of Europe can attain no state at all adequate to such slavery; for had they equal comfort, still could they never be equally free from care." And at a fête given by Governor Battenburg, of Berbice, to his slaves, the doctor says, " While looking upon them at this joyous moment, I bent a thought to Europe, and wished that the tattered, indigent sons of liberty could feel as happy. Reflecting, that the peasants of Europe, who toil in freedom for their daily bread, have not within their reach such complete and cheerful relaxation as was procured for these contented slaves, I became fixed in contemplation of the scene before me, until the comforts and advantages had nearly concealed from my mind the bitter ills of slavery*." No condition of human life is exempt from many *bitter ills*; and it were, perhaps, a task as impious as it would

---

* Pinckard's Notes, vol. 2, p. 352.

be vain, to attempt to free .from the common lot of humanity those, who, in a state of slavery, are fulfilling the mysterious dispensations of Providence.

It may possibly be said, that these are a few particular instances of negro felicity, whence no inference can be justly drawn in favour of the system. But I assert, and I do it without the fear of contradiction, that the picture which Dr. Pinckard has drawn of the condition of slaves, is a correct representation of the general state of slavery in Barbadoes. Indeed the point is established by his own confession, " that the slaves of many persons whom he visited in this country might be envied by the poor of nations where freedom is better known*." And, though he has selected Mr. Waith from the group, and held him up to public admiration, I am happy to say, that, among the planters of Barbadoes, there are thousands whose hearts throb with the finest sensibilities of humanity; and who pos-

_____

* Pinckard's Notes, vol. 2, p. 109.

sess as much of the milk of human kindness as any men upon the face of the earth.

I shall conclude with the flattering attestation of an illustrious Prince of the Blood, his Royal Highness the Duke of Clarence; who, in his place, as a peer of the realm, asserted, that he knew, from personal observation on the spot, that the situation of slaves in the West Indies, was more desirable than that of the lower classes of whites in Great Britain. To declarations so explicit, to testimony so unquestionable, it would be impertinent, in one labouring under the opprobrium of a West Indian character, to add one single syllable. If the people of England believe not these, what chance is there, that my feeble voice will command attention amidst the clamour which has been raised by prejudice and perverted philanthropy? The obdurate ear of partial incredulity cannot be penetrated by the distant, unharmonious accents of truth.

Speight's Town,
March 16, 1807.

CONTENTS.

CHAP. I.

CHAP. II.

CHAP. III.

CHAP. IV.

CHAP. V.

CHAP. VI.

CHAP. VII.

CHAP. VIII.

CHAP. IX.

CHAP. X.

CHAP. XI.

CHAP. XII.

CHAP. XIII.

CHAP. XIV.

CHAP. XV.

CONTENTS.

CHAP. XVI.

CHAP. XVII.

CHAP. XVIII.

A LIST OF SUBSCRIBERS.

A.

The Rev. Thomas Allinson.
The Rev. William Alls.
The Hon. John Forster Alleyne.
James Anstie, Esq.
Samuel Applewhaite, Esq.
Mr. Richard Archer.
Mr. Charles Barrington Agard.
Mr. John Agard, Jun.
Mr. John Archer.
Mr. Israel Armstrong.
Mr. Richard Austin.
Doctor Abel Alleyne.
Haynes Gibbes Alleyne, Esq.
Mr. Thomas Gent Armstrong.
Mr Benjamin Armstrong.
Mr. Howard Armstrong.
Mr. Joseph Taitte Agard.
Mr. Edwin Agard.
Mr. Abel Archer.
Robert C. Ashby, Esq.
Mr. William Adamson, Jun.
John Alleyne, Esq.

John P. F. Armstrong, Esq.
Mr. Thomas Agard.
Mr. William Amey.

B.

The Hon. and Rev. John Brome, 3 copies
The Hon. John Beckles, Attorney-General and Speaker of the Assembly.
The Hon. John Alleyne Beckles.
John William Bovell, M. D.
William Bovell, Esq Demerara.
Stephen Blackett, Esq. 2 copies.
Mr. James Bovell.
Mr. Howard Bovell.
Mr. William Ball.
George Barclay, Esq. 2 copies.
William Barton, Esq. Liverpool.
Mr. Jacob Belgrave.
Joseph Bute, Esq. Demerara.
The Hon. Miles Brathwaite.
General Henry Bowyer, 2 copies.
Colonel Pinson Bonham.
The Hon. John Barrow.

LIST OF SUBSCRIBERS.

Mr. Charles Brough.

Mr. John B. Brown.

Mr. James Butcher.

Mr. Thomas Burton.

Mr. Finch Bovell.

Jehu Caudle Bend, Esq.

Mr. Thomas Beard.

Samuel Berrisford, Esq. Berbice.

Francis Shorey Bayley, Esq.

Charles Kyd Bishop, Esq.

Joseph Bayne, Esq.

Mr. William Bosie Baker.

Andrew Boyce, Esq.

Jonathan Boyce, Esq.

John Brathwaite, Esq.

Mr. Matthew Boyce.

Mr. Israel Bowen

Mr. Samuel Boyce.

Mr. Thompson Boyce.

John Bowen, Esq.

John Bowen, Jun. Esq.

Mr. John Birmingham.

Mr. Harbourne Barnwell, Demerara

Mr. Francis A. Barrow.

Mr. J. L. Bynoe.

Mr. Thomas Briggs.

Mr. James Buhot.

Mr. James Thomas Bascom.

Mr. Henry Crofts Baley.

C.

John Cobham, Esq.

The Hon. Thomas Chase.

Mr. Thomas Chase, Breedies.

Mr. R. S. Carter.

William Alleyne Culpeper, Esq.

Mr. John Crichlow.

Ward Cadogan, Esq. 2 copies.

John Carew, Esq.

Hamlet Alexander Chase, Esq.

Jacob Perry Clarke, Esq.

Mr. Samuel Clarke.

Mr. James Clinkett.

Mr. Richard Cock, Jun.

John Charles Coleman, Esq. 2 copies.

Mr. Bernard Conolly.

Mr. Othniel Crane.

Mr. Henry Thomas Crane.

Henry S. Cummins, Esq. 2 copies.

Doctor John Cutting.

James Cummins, Esq.

Mr. George Cragg.

Mr. Christopher F. Carmichael.

Matthew Coulthurst, Esq. Advocate-General, 2 copies.

The Rev. Henry Caddell.

Philip Caddell, Esq.

Philip Crick, Esq.

James Cook, Esq.

Mr. Abel Clinckett

Mr. John Chadderton.

William Cadogan, Esq.

Charles G. Colleton, Esq.

James Cavan, Esq.

Charles Cadogan, Esq.

Mr. Renn P. Collymore.

Mr. John Carter.

LIST OF SUBSCRIBERS.

Nicholas Rice Callender, Esq.
Forster Clark, Esq.
Benjamin Collynns, M. D.
Lawrence T. Cumberbatch, Esq.
Mr. Thomas Connell, Pie Corner.
Mr. John Crone.
Mr. Christopher Chandler.
Thomas Challenor, Esq.
Richard Clement, Esq.
Mr. Michael Corbin.
Mr. George Clinton.
John Cummins, Esq.
Mr. Joseph Crick.
Mr. John Crick.
Mr. W. Ashby Capleman.
Mrs. Anna Maria Clinton.

D.

Allen Dalzell, Esq. 5 copies.
Francis Dixon, Esq.
Thomas Dummett, Esq.
Thomas Dayrell, Esq.
James Douglas, Esq.
Mr. S. H. David.
Thomas Whitaker Drake, Esq.
John Perrott Devonish, Esq.
Mr. William Dowrich, Jun.
Mr. William Drake.
Thomas Daniel, Esq. 2 copies.
John Daniel, Esq.

E.

Grant Ellcock, M. D.
John Gittens Eastmond, Esq.

John William Edward Elder, Esq.
Mr. Samuel Evans.
Mr. Samuel French Edwards.
Nathaniel Evanson, Esq.
Mr. William Grant Ellis.
William Eversley, Esq.

F.

William Foderingham, Esq.
William Newton Firebrace, Esq. Demerara.
Charles Davis Forrester, Esq. Demerara.
Mr. Joseph Farnum.
Mr. John R. Farrell.
Mr. Christopher Forte.
Doctor Nathaniel Forte.
Doctor Samuel Forte.
Doctor Christopher Forte.
Mr. Thomas Carmichael Forte.

G.

The Hon. Joshua Gittens.
The Rev. William Garnett.
Doctor Nicholas R. Garner.
William Gill, Esq.
Mr. Isaac Gittens.
James Grasett, Esq.
Robert Gibbons, Esq. 2 copies.
William Grasett, Esq.
Doctor Parris Greaves.
Mr. Howard Griffith, St. Lucy's.
John Jordan Griffith, Esq.

LIST OF SUBSCRIBERS.

William Griffith, Esq.

Mr. Edward Greenidge.

Mr. Howard Griffith, Speight's Town.

Messrs. John and William Goodridge.

Alexander Graham, Esq.

William Graham, Esq.

John Gay Goding, Esq.

Mr. William Greenidge.

Francis Bell Grant, Esq.

Mr. Thomas Gill.

Jacob Goodridge, Esq. Christ Church.

Mr. John Goring.

Mr. Richard Grannum.

Mr. Robert Manly Gaskin.

H.

The Hon. Benjamin Hinds, 2 copies.

Messrs. David and George Hall, 4 copies.

The Rev. Henry Evans Husbands.

The Hon. Robert Haynes.

Mr. William M. Harris.

M. Jacob Hinds.

Mr. Robert Harris.

Mr. John Hawkesworth.

Mr. John Heyes.

John Higginson, Esq

Mr. Samuel Hinds, Jun.

Richard Hooton, Esq.

Conrade Adams Howell, Esq. 2 copies.

John Humpleby, Esq.

Mr. Daniel Hunte.

Joseph Dotin Husbands, Esq.

The Hon. Rob. Aug. Hyndman.

Thomas Hollingsworth, Esq.

The Hon. William Hinds.

Mr. John Boyce Harris.

Mr. William Hall.

Mr. John Hussey Hendy.

Mr. Richard Hawkesworth

Mrs. Mary Sims Howell.

The Rev. William M. Harte.

John Hamden, Esq.

Mr. Edward J. Henery, Demerara

Mr. William Hallstead, Demerara

J.

Mr. William Jackson.

Samuel Jackman, Esq

Gabriel Jemmett, Esq.

Benjamin Ifill, Esq. 2 copies.

George Irlam, Esq. Liverpool.

Mr. John Ironmonger.

John Johnson, Esq. Demerara.

Mr. John Inniss.

Joseph Johnson, Esq.

Doctor William Howard Jordan.

Mr. Joseph Jordan.

Mr. Joseph Johnson, Jun.

Mr. Nathaniel M. Jemott.

John F. D Jones, M. D.

Benjamin Jones, Esq

Frere Jones, Esq.

Gibbes Walker Jordan, Esq. F. R. S.

LIST OF SUBSCRIBERS.

K.

Mr. Alexander King, Jun.

Mr. Samuel Knight, Jun.

Mr. Samuel Knight.

Mr. Samuel Knight, Jun.

Christopher Knight, Esq. 2 copies.

Mr. James C. Killman.

John Keir, Esq.

Mr. Francis Kirton.

L.

Literary Society of Barbadoes, 2 copies.

Mr. Edward Linton.

Thomas M. Lovell, Esq.

Nathaniel Lucas, Esq.

Capt. Francis Lightbourne.

William Draper Lloyd, Esq. 2 copies.

John Wrong Leacock, Esq.

Mr. Edward Licorish.

Mr. William C. Leslie.

Joseph Leacock, Esq.

Lisle Lloyd, Esq.

Mr. William Licorish.

Mr. Richard Ambrose Layne.

Mr. George Law.

Joseph Lowe, Esq.

John Lewis, Esq.

M.

William Miller, Esq. 2 copies.

James Maxwell, Esq. 6 copies.

John Pollard Mayers, Esq. 3 copies.

David Martindale, Esq.

Mr. John M'Pherson.

Mr. Henry M'Grath.

Mr. William Morris.

Lawrance Mudie, Esq.

John M'Leay, Esq.

William Moore, Esq.

The Hon. George Maynard.

Mr. Francis M'Clure.

Eliezer Montefiori, Esq. 2 copies.

Mr. John Melvin.

Mr. Henry Madden.

Thomas M'Intosh, Esq.

N.

The Rev. Mark Nicholson.

The Rev. James Fowler Neblett.

Nathaniel Nowell, Esq.

Mr. Joshua Nurse.

Mr. Robert Norris.

Mr. Samuel O. Nurse.

Mr. Richard Nurse.

O.

The Rev. Thomas H. Orderson.

Mr. Isaac Williamson Orderson.

Mrs. Isaac W. Orderson.

Arthur Oughterson, Esq.

Mr. William Oxley.

Thomas Whitfoot O'Neale, Esq.

Gera Olton, Esq.

Thomas Ostrehan, Esq.

LIST OF SUBSCRIBERS.

P.

Henry Piggott, Esq.

Mrs. Sarah Poyer.

The Rev. John F. Pilgrim.

Mr. Henry Parkinson.

Mr. Lionel Parks.

Joseph Alleyne Payne, Esq.

Peter Phillips, Esq.

Stephen Phillips, Esq.

Mr. Nathaniel Phillips.

Mr. John Phillips.

Thomas Pierrepont, Esq.

William Hinds Prescod, Esq.

John Hothersal Pinder, Esq.

Francis Ford Pinder, Esq.

Mr. John W. Perch.

John Randall Phillips, Esq.

Thomas Piggott, Esq.

James Scott Payne, Esq.

Mr. James Pairman.

Mr. Conrade Pile.

Joseph Payne, Esq.

Mr. Edward Parris.

R.

George Reed, Esq.

Mr. James Reid.

Hillary Rowe, Esq.

Messrs. Rodie and Shand, Liverpool.

Doctor Charles Straghan Rudder.

Thomas Reese, Esq.

S.

The Hon. John Spooner, President of the Council.

Doctor John William Sober.

The Hon. John Spooner, Jun.

Mr. John Soper.

Thomas Spencer, Esq.

John Straker, Esq.

John C. Straker, Esq.

Mr. John Seed.

Mr. Thomas H. Shepherd.

Thomas Sealy, Jun. Esq.

Henry Sealy, Esq.

Mr. Christopher Saint Hill.

Mr. James R. Sample.

William Shand, Esq. Liverpool.

John Sober, Esq.

John Springer, Esq. Gay's-Cove.

Mr. Horatio Nelson Springer.

George Wallwyn Shepherd, Esq.

Mr. William Springer.

Mr. Richard Smitten.

Mr. John Springer, Jun.

Mr. Thomas Johnson Springer.

Mr. Benjamin Stoute.

Mr. Enos Skinner.

Edward Skeete, Esq.

Jacob Skinner, Esq.

Mr. Richard Stoute, Jun.

Hugh Williams Straghan, Esq.

Richard Skinner, Esq.

LIST OF SUBSCRIBERS.

John Simpson, Esq.
John Sulevan, Esq.
Henry P. Simmons, Esq.
Mrs. Alice Southwell.

T.

Samuel Taylor, Esq.
William Carter Thomas, Esq.
George Toosey, Esq.
Mr. Henry Skeete Thomas.
Mr. Henry Taitte.
Timothy Thornhill, Esq.
The Rev. Anthony K. Thomas.
Mr. John Howell Todd.
Mr. Henry Thorpe.
Thomas Clarke Trotman, Esq.
Dowding Thornhill, Esq.
Henry Thornhill, Esq.
Doctor Joseph Taylor.
Mr. John Taylor.
Henry Trotman, Esq.
Thompson Isly Thorne, Esq.

W.

Mr. William Wilson, Bristol.
Benjamin Walrond, Esq.
John Walton, Esq.
Mr. James Wallcott.
Mr. William Wayne.
Mr. Henry Thomas Ward.
Mr. Samuel Watt.
Capt. Rees Webb.
Capt. William Wilson.

Mr. John Williams.
Mr. Jonas Wilkinson.
Mr. Richard Wall.
Stephen Wallcott, Esq.
Robert James Wallcott, Esq.
Thomas Went, Esq.
Hamlet Wilson, Esq.
Mr. William Welch, London.
Mr. Thomas Williams, St. Joseph's.
Mr. Richard Wood.
William Welch, M. D.
Mr. John Ward, Jun.
Mr. William Wilkinson.
Thomas Williams, Esq. St. Thomas's.
James Thomas Williams, Esq.
Mrs. Elizabeth Williams.
Miss Ruth Whitfoot.
George Williams, Esq.
Mr. Thomas Williams, Jun. St. Thomas's
John Walton, Esq.
Mr. Thomas W. White.

Y.

Thomas Yard, Esq.
Mr. William T. Yearwood.
Mr. Lewis Young.
Mr. Samuel Yearwood.
Mr. James Johnson Yearwood.
Doctor John Kelly Yearwood
Mr. George D. Yonge.
Mr. Howard Griffith Yearwood.

THE

HISTORY

OF

BARBADOES.

CHAP. I.

THE ISLAND DISCOVERED—GRANTED TO THE EARL OF MARLBO-
ROUGH—A SETTLEMENT MADE BY COURTEEN—GRANTED TO
LORD CARLISLE—A SECOND SETTLEMENT MADE BY A COMPANY
OF MERCHANTS—DISPUTES BETWEEN THE SETTLERS—SIR W.
TUFTON APPOINTED GOVERNOR—SUPERSEDED BY HAWLEY—
TUFTON EXECUTED FOR MUTINY—PRUDENT ADMINISTRATION
OF MR. BELL—SUGAR CANE INTRODUCED—AFRICAN SLAVES—
STORY OF INCKLE AND YARICO—A CONSPIRACY AMONG THE
NEGROES.

THE discovery of Barbadoes is involved in greater obscurity than that of any of the adjacent islands. Placed
at the south-eastern extremity of the great American Archipelago, it remained unknown, or unnoticed, for upwards
of a century after the bold and enterprising genius of Colum-

CHAP. I. bus had extended the bounds of the habitable globe, and added a new world to the dominions of Spain. No mention is made of this island in the journals or charts of any European navigator earlier than the year one thousand six hundred. Hence there is reason to believe that it was the last known of all the Caribbees. From its geographical position*, it seems most likely that Barbadoes was first seen and visited by the Portuguese. These adventurers, in their voyages to the coast of Africa, or to their settlements in South America, might have been driven by contrary winds, or adverse currents, within sight of its shores. Curiosity, or the want of refreshment, probably induced their nearer approach; but the rude, uncultivated aspect of the country, which they found without inhabitants, and destitute of every article necessary for human accommodation, was little calculated to induce these travellers to remain long on a spot incapable of yielding those advantages which were then the principal objects of European pursuit in the western hemisphere. Its natural beauties and favourable situation for commercial purposes were overlooked by men whose sordid minds were wholly occupied with the hope of obtaining the immediate possession of gold and silver. To render their discovery, however, in some measure useful to themselves, or to such of their countrymen as should have occasion to touch here, in any of their future voyages, they

---

* In lat. 13 deg. 5. min. N. and longitude 59 deg. 41 min. W.

planted some vegetables, and left a few swine for the purpose of propagation.

From the Portuguese the island obtained the name of *Las Barbadas*; in allusion, as some writers have supposed, to the barbarous, inhospitable state of the country. The learned author of the Natural History of Barbadoes, however, with much greater probability, conjectures this appellation to have signified *the Bearded Island*, from the vast number of Indian fig-trees with which it abounded. The wide spreading branches of this venerable tree send forth innumerable fibres which, by the help of a warm imagination, might, not unreasonably, have been supposed to resemble those luxuriant beards which were so much in vogue in those days*.

---

* Our great English epic-poet represents this tree as affording the first covering made use of by Adam and Eve, after having exchanged their innocence for a consciousness of shame, and thus accurately describes its growth;

> *The fig-tree, not that kind for fruit renown'd,*
> *But such as at this day to Indians known,*
> *In* Malabar *or* Decan *spreads her arms;*
> *Branching so broad and long, that in the ground*
> *The bending twigs take root, and daughters grow*
> *About the mother tree, a pillar'd shade !*
> *High over-arch'd and echoing walks between.*

" It is under this tree that the Brahmins and the devotees of their religion celebrate their rites. The pagodas are usually erected in the neighbourhood of this friendly

Abandoned by its original discoverers, Barbadoes continued unfrequented till the year one thousand six hundred
and five. At that time a vessel, called the Olive, belong-
to Sir Olive Leigh, returning from Guinea, accidentally
put in here, and landed a part of her crew near the spot on
which the Hole-town was afterwards built. Here they
erected a cross, and took possession of the island in the
name of their sovereign ; inscribing these words on a tree
in the vicinity of the place where they landed, " James,
King of England and of this Island." They then proceeded
along the coast until their progress was obstructed by the
stream since called Indian River, from the Indian implements and utensils found there. Here, again, they fixed
some memorial of the title which the right of occupancy
conferred on the crown, to this distant and hitherto neglected territory. But finding no refreshments necessary for
persons in their situation, not even fresh water, (no springs
or reservoirs of that useful element being at that time accessible to strangers) they quitted their new acquisition and
sailed for Saint Christopher's, where the establishment of
a colony had been recently attempted by thirty-three English settlers.

---

shade. It is common for the Indian to take up his abode under this tree, and to remain stretched at his ease in the shade, while every thing, exposed to the rays of the
sun, is scorched with intolerable heat."

                                        Vide PERCEVAL'S ACCOUNT OF CEYLON.

After this visit Barbadoes appears to have been thought of no more, until some Dutch men of war, which had been employed on a secret expedition against the Spaniards, returning home, chanced to stop here*. It may be proper to observe, that this account does not agree with that given by the compilers of the Universal History†; by which it would seem that these vessels were particularly licensed by the Spanish court to trade to Brasil. But, notwithstanding the Spaniards and Portuguese endeavoured to exclude the other nations of Europe from any participation in the commerce with their settlements in the new world, if we may credit the Abbé Raynal, the Dutch had long been engaged in an illicit intercourse with Brasil. At length the West India company, established in Holland, had, about this time, wrested that valuable country from the Spaniards, under whose yoke it had fallen by the subjugation of Portugal. Whether these vessels were fair traders, smugglers, or ships of war, is immaterial. Certain it is, that their crews, having procured some refreshments at Barbadoes, and finding the soil capable of cultivation, were induced, on their return to Europe, to speak of it in the most favourable terms.

These particulars having been communicated to Sir William Courteen, a principal merchant of the city of London, by his correspondent in Zealand, his enterprising ge-

---

* Memoirs of Barbadoes, p. 3.　　　† Univ. Hist. vol. 41. p. 131.

nius was fired with the magnificent project of making an effectual settlement on the island. In this design he was soon confirmed by the arrival of a ship of his own, which returning from Fernambucca, in Brasil, was driven, by stress of weather, on the coast of Barbadoes. The seamen belonging to this vessel, having explored the country, were pleased with the bloom and verdure which every where met their view; and having procured some provisions, probably part of the hogs formerly left here by the Portuguese, they proceeded on their voyage. The representation made by these mariners, on their return to England, of the beauty and fertility of the island, and of its advantageous position for diffusing the commodities and manufactures of Europe among the rising colonies in the Caribbean Sea, made such an impression on the minds of people, that the Earl of Marlborough, afterwards Lord High Treasurer, obtained from James I. a patent for the island, to him and his heirs for ever*.

This grant did not obstruct the execution of Sir William Courteen's design. Persisting in his original intention of making a settlement which promised fair to improve his fortune; and having obtained the sanction of the noble patentee, he fitted out two large ships at his own expence, supplied with men, arms, ammunition, and every thing requisite for establishing a colony, and securing it from in-

---

* Univ. Hist. vol. 41. p. 131.   Edwards's Hist. West. Indies, vol. 1. p. 323.

vasion. Of these ships one only, the John and William, commanded by John Powell, arrived at Barbadoes. Thirty men were immediately landed * on the spot which had been taken possession of nearly twenty years before by the crew of the Olive. Here these adventurers commenced their operations, and laid the foundation of a town, which, in honour of the prince on the throne, they called James Town, since denominated the Hole-town.

In all enterprises, in which numbers are concerned, the necessity of submitting to the guidance and authority of a particular chief, or leader, whose power may control the actions, and whose judgment may direct the efforts of every individual to the advancement of the common good, is a principle of the most obvious utility, whether the association be civil or political. The first step taken by these early colonists was the appointment of a proper person to superintend and govern the infant settlement. For this purpose, William Deane was unanimously chosen and invested with the authority of commander in chief. The British flag was then displayed, and they proceeded to fortify themselves as well as the nature of their circumstances would permit.

In reviewing this early period of our colonial history, every liberal mind must glow with conscious satisfaction

---

* Memoirs of Barbadoes, p. 3. Of these settlers William Arnold was among the first who landed.

on reflecting, that the settlement which we have been contemplating, was quietly effected without the perpetration
of those atrocious acts of cruelty and injustice which
marked the progress of the Europeans in every other part
of the new world. Abandoned by its aboriginal inhabitants, if any such there were, for some cause wholly unknown to us, Barbadoes, according to every principle of
natural law, became the rightful and legitimate property of
the first occupants.

Although the English found the island uninhabited, the
Reverend Mr. Hughes seems very unwilling to relinquish
the idea of its having been formerly occupied by some savage tribes. He has prosecuted the inquiry concerning
these people with much industry, and collected every circumstance that could give weight or add probability to
his opinion. He relies, however, on facts, which, though
indisputable, are by no means conclusive; " that there are
several places in the island called after their names; and
that in these very places there are daily dug up such marks
of their former residence as were peculiar to the Indians*."
But after all the pains which the learned divine has taken,
the proofs that he has collected are insufficient to establish
the point in dispute. They only shew that the neighbouring Caribs occasionally visited this delightful spot for the
purpose of hunting and fishing; and, perhaps, to procure

---

* Natural Hist. of Barbadoes, p. 5 and 7.

suitable clay for manufacturing the various domestic utensils with which, he asserts, the Leeward Islands were supplied from hence. Of this there is the most indubitable evidence.

Ligon, who visited this island about twenty years after the arrival of the first settlers, relates, that the natives of the neighbouring islands, most likely of Saint Vincent and Saint Lucia, from their proximity of situation, frequently came hither in their canoes or periaguas, for the sake of hunting the hogs that had been left here by the Portuguese; which, he observes, furnished them *with flesh of a sweet and exellent flavour.* In these excursions they would sometimes spend a month or longer; and then returning home, leave behind them many tools and other implements, chiefly pots of several sizes, in which they boiled their meat. These pots were made of clay, *so finely tempered and turned with such art,* that our author affirms, *he had not seen any like them, for fineness of mettle and curiosity of turning in England*.

This account of these desultory visits is corroborated by the ingenious natural historian himself, who adds, that their frequent arrivals and departures were always in the wane of the moon, for the benefit of light nights; that when any difference arose between them and the English, the Indians retired to the woods until they were presented with

---

* Ligon's Hist. of Barbadoes, p. 23.

a favourable opportunity of returning home ; and that then, in their way down to their canoes, they would cover themselves with green boughs to elude the search of the English.   During their transient residence in the country, they made the earthen-ware already mentioned ; and, like the ancient idolaters of Europe and Asia, formed, out · of the same materials, sensible representations of the invisible deities whom they adored, and absurdly worshipped the work of their own hands.   Many of these images were seen by Hughes as late as the year one thousand seven hundred and forty-eight.   Among them was one, of which the head alone weighed above sixty pounds*.   Thus it seems easy to account for the number of Indian remains which have been found in different parts of the country, and to reconcile the Indian names still borne by many places with the uninhabited state of the island when first discovered by European navigators.

Some years previous to Courteen's attempt to establish a colony in Barbadoes, Mr. Thomas Warner had engaged in a similar undertaking at St. Christopher's.   This settlement was in a prosperous condition, when the hopes of the planters were suddenly destroyed by a dreadful hurricane, which desolated their plantations.   To repair the injury sustained by this calamity, Warner was obliged to re-

---

* Nat. Hist. of Barbadoes, p. 7.

turn to England to solicit the assistance of his friends. Upon this occasion he applied to James Hay, Earl of Carlisle, who readily patronised the adventurous settler, and, by his powerful support, preserved the colony from ruin.

Warner's application opened a new and splendid prospect to the ambitious peer. He saw very clearly the power and opulence which he might, by prudent management, derive from an extensive establishment in the West Indies ; and, to secure the important advantages thus accidentally thrown in his way, immediately applied to Charles I. who had recently ascended the throne, for a grant of all the Caribbee islands, to be formed into a palatinate, or proprietary government, under the name of Carliola. The unfortunate monarch, to whose want of firmness may be ascribed most of the misfortunes that embittered his reign, readily yielded to the importunity of a powerful favourite, and gave the necessary orders for preparing his patent. This grant was strenuously opposed by the Earl of Marlborough, as affecting his prior right to the island of Barbadoes, and produced a tedious litigation between the two claimants, which was at length compromised, on Lord Carlisle's agreeing to pay to the Lord Treasurer, and his heirs for ever, an annuity of three hundred pounds, in lieu of his claim. This dispute being thus adjusted, the Earl of Carlisle's patent passed the Great Seal on the second day of June, one

CHAP. I.
1626.

thousand six hundred and twenty-seven, and his Lordship became sole proprietor*.

The preamble of this celebrated charter assigns the reason on which it was granted, in these words: " Whereas our well-beloved cousin and counsellor, James Lord Hay, Baron of Sawley, Viscount Doncaster, and Earl of Carlisle, endeavouring, with a laudable and pious design of propagating the Christian religion, and also of the enlargement of the territories of our dominions, hath humbly petitioned us for a certain region of islands in our dominions after-named, lying towards the north part of the world, as yet void and inhabited, in some places, with savages, who have no knowledge of the divine power, commonly called the Caribbee Islands, containing the islands of Saint Christopher, Grenada, Saint Vincent, Saint Lucia, Barbadoes, Martinique, Dominica, Marigalante, Descada, Todosantos, Guadaloupe, Antigua, Montserrat, Redondo, Barbuda, Nevis, Eustatia, Saint Bartholomew, Saint Martin, Anguilla, Sembrera, and Enegada, and many other islands, found out at his great cost and charges, and now brought to that pass to be inhabited by a large and copious colony of English, with certain privileges and jurisdictions belonging to the said government and state of a colony and region to him, his heirs and assigns, to be granted."

---

* Mem. of Barb. p. 4. Edwards's West Indies, Vol. 1. pp. 324, 423. Univ. Hist. Vol. 41, p. 132.

By the succeeding clauses, his Majesty did, by the said grant, for him, his heirs and successors, make, create and constitute the said Earl of Carlisle, his heirs and assigns, absolute proprietor and lord of the said region; reserving still the allegiance due to his Majesty, his heirs and successors. It was then added, " And because we have made and appointed the said James Earl of Carlisle, true lord of all the aforesaid province, as he to whom the right belongeth, know ye, that we have authorized and appointed the said James Earl of Carlisle, and his heirs, of whose fidelity, prudence, justice and wisdom, we have great confidence, for the good and happy government of the said province, or the private utility of every man, to make, erect and set forth; and under his or their signet to publish such laws as he, the said Earl of Carlisle, or his heirs, *with the consent, assent and approbation of the free inhabitants of the said province, or the greater part of them thereunto to be called,* and in such form, and when and as often as he or they, in his or their discretion, shall think fit and best. And these laws must all men, for the time being, that do live within the limits of the said province, observe; whether they be bound to sea or from thence returning to England, or any other of our dominions, or any other place appointed, upon such impositions, penalties, imprisonment, or restraint, that it behoveth, and the quality of the offence requireth; either upon the body, or death itself, to be executed by the said James Earl of Carlisle, and his heirs; or by his or their deputy, judges, magistrates, officers and ministers, according to the tenor and true meaning of these presents, in what case soever; and with such power, as to him, the said James Earl of Carlisle, or his heirs, shall deem best. And to dispose of all offences or riots whatsoever, either by sea or by land, whether before judgment received, or after remitted, freed, pardoned, or forgiven. And to do and perform all and every thing or things, which, to the fulfilling of justice, courts, or manner of proceeding, in their tribunals may or doth belong or appertain, although express mention of them in these presents be not made; yet we have granted full power, by virtue of these presents, them to be made; which laws so absolutely proclaimed, and by strength of right supported, as they are granted, we will enjoin, charge, and command, all and every subject and liege people of us, our heirs and successors, as far as them they do concern, inviolably to keep and observe under the pains therein expressed; *so as*, notwithstanding, *the aforesaid laws be agreeable, and not repugnant unto reason; nor against, but as convenient and agreeable as may be to the laws, statutes, customs, and rights, of our kingdom of England.*"

" And because in the government of so great a province oftentimes sudden occasions do fall out, to which it shall be needful to apply a remedy before the free inhabitants of the said province can be called; and for that it shall not always be needful, in such cases, that all the people be called together, we will and ordain, and by these presents, for us, our heirs and successors, have granted to the said James Earl of Carlisle, and his heirs, that he by himself or his magistrates and officers, in that case lawfully preferred, may make decrees and ordinances both fit and profitable, from time to time, that they may be esteemed, kept, and observed, within the said province, as well for keeping the peace as for the better government of the people there living, so that they may be publicly known to all whom they do concern. Which ordinances we will, within the said provinces, inviolably to be kept, upon pain in them expressed; so that those laws be agreeable to reason, and not repugnant nor against it, but, as far as may be, agreeable to the laws and statutes of our kingdom of England; and so *that those laws extend not to the hurt or discomodity of any person or persons, either to the binding, constraining, burthening, or taking away, either their liberty, goods, or chattles.*"

" We also, of our princely grace, for us, our heirs and successors, will, straightly charge, make and ordain that the said province be of our allegiance, and that all and every subject and liege people of us, our heirs and successors, brought or to be brought, and their children, whether there born, or afterwards to be born, become natives and subjects of us, our heirs and successors, *and be as free as they who were born in England;* and so their inheritance within our kingdom of England, or other our dominions, to seek, receive, take hold, buy and possess, and use and

enjoy them as his own ; and to give, sell, alien and be-
queath them at their pleasure ; *and also freely, quietly, and
peaceably to have and possess, all the liberties, franchises, and
privileges of this kingdom, and them to enjoy as liege people
of England,* whether born or to be born, without impediment, molestation, vexation, injury or trouble of us, our
heirs and successors ; any act or statute to the contrary notwithstanding."

While this business was transacting in England, the
young settlers were diligently prosecuting their enterprise.
In this hazardous undertaking it is easy to imagine, that
they were exposed to innumerable hardships and dangers.
The country, overgrown with thick impenetrable woods,
exhibited the most gloomy prospect that the imagination
can possibly conceive.   No traces of human society cheered
the solitary scene ; no signs of cultivation enlivened the
lurid face of nature.   One immense forest, crowned with
an exuberant foliage, spread itself in every direction.
Within its dark recesses no beasts of burthen were found to
lessen the toil of man, and but few quadrupeds for his
domestic use.

Notwithstanding these discouragements, our adventurers
applied themselves to clearing the woods and planting provisions, with a diligence and perseverance not less commendable than astonishing.   In this necessary employment,
however, they proceeded but slowly and with difficulty.
For, as the trees were in general extremely hard and heavy,

after the laborious task of felling them was accomplished, there was not sufficient strength to remove them; they were, therefore, suffered to remain on the ground; the planters contenting themselves with cultivating in the intermediate spaces, such esculent plants as were necessary for their subsistence*.

Fortunately, the woods afforded lignum vitæ and fustick, which became articles of immediate export to England, and procured, in return, such commodities as were most wanted in the colony. And as the climate, especially at the season of the year in which the first settlers arrived, was mild and pleasant; and the soil appeared to be fertile and well adapted for the cultivation of cotton and tobacco, these enterprising men resolutely persisted in the laudable design of adding so desirable a spot to the comforts of social life. The first fruits of the land were inadequate, both in quantity and quality, to their support. Potatoes, plantains, and Indian corn were little suited to European habits of living; and as their supplies from home were extremely precarious and uncertain, the distresses of the early colonists were proportionably grievous and oppressive. Nor can we sufficiently admire the patience and firmness with which they persisted in combating the various hardships and difficulties incident to their situation.

Flattered with the presages of success, which he re-

---

* Ligon's Hist. Barb. p. 24. Fenning's Geography, vol. 2. p. 702.

CHAP. I.
1627.

ceived from the infant settlement, Sir William Courteen determined to prosecute his scheme with vigour. Deserted, as we have seen, by his former patron, he now sought the protection of the Earl of Pembroke, lord chamberlain of the household. This nobleman, encouraged by the favourable representation made to him of the condition of the new settlement, generously undertook to promote the interest of the worthy citizen, by whom it had been established, by an immediate application to the King*. Charles, who is generally allowed to have had sagacity enough to perceive what was right, though he seldom had resolution to practise it, thought no more of the grant to Lord Carlisle than if it had never existed; and as his lordship was at that moment employed in a diplomatic character abroad, he could give no opposition to an application so repugnant to his prior right. The field being thus left open, the Lord Chamberlain pressed his suit with such

Feb. 25†. successful assiduity, that he soon obtained a grant from his royal master, for the island of Barbadoes, in trust for Sir William Courteen. It is scarcely possible to account for

---

* Mem. of Barb. p. 9. Univ. Hist. vol. 41, p. 132.

† To anticipate any misapprehension concerning the chronology of these early events, it must be remembered, that until the introduction of the new style in 1752, the year was reckoned to commence on the 25th day of March. Hence all transactions between the first of January and the twenty-fourth day of March, are dated as if they had taken place, according to the present computation, one whole year earlier. Thus, for example, the grant mentioned in the text, agreeable to the new style, would bear date, February 25, 1628.

such versatility and inconsistence in the king's conduct, otherwise than by supposing that the opulent merchant might have been able to relieve the wants of his necessitous sovereign. This conjecture will appear the more probable, if we recollect the mean shifts and illegal exactions to which the pecuniary embarrassments of that unfortunate monarch compelled him to resort.

The Earl of Carlisle, soon after the passing of this grant, returned from his embassy; when, being informed of the settlement which had been made upon an island within his province, he determined to adopt such measures as would frustrate the designs of his competitor, and establish a colony of his own! Incensed at the grant which had been so surreptitiously obtained, he complained to the King of the advantage which had been taken of his absence to deprive him of his property. The irresolute Charles, who throughout the whole transaction, was more culpable than any body else, exhibited a fresh instance of his want of firmness; and, to appease the resentment of his irritated favourite, revoked the patent to the Lord Chamberlain, and reinstated the Earl of Carlisle in the possession of the territory of which he had so recently and unjustly deprived him.

Having gained this point, the next steps to be taken by the earl, were to make an effectual settlement on the island, and to concert proper measures for securing to himself the advantages it was capable of yielding. With this view he

contracted with a company of London merchants, consisting of Marmaduke Brandon, William Perkins, Alexander Banister, Robert Wheatly, Edmund Forster, Robert Swinnerton, Henry Wheatly, John Charles, and John Farringdon, for a grant of ten thousand acres of land, on condition of his receiving from each settler forty pounds of cotton annually; and allowing them the privilege of sending out, in quality of governor, a proper person to superintend the settlement and conduct their concerns. For this purpose Charles Wolferstone, a native of Bermuda, was made
choice of, and received a commission from the noble proprietary " empowering him to use, exercise, and put in execution, the office of governor, commander-in-chief, and captain, in doing justice, deciding controversies, keeping his Majesty's peace, and punishing offenders according to the quality of their crimes, and according to the laws of England*."

Armed with these powers, Wolferstone, accompanied by sixty-four persons, arrived in Carlisle-bay, and landed on the twenty-fifth day of July, one thousand six hundred and twenty-eight. Each of these settlers was entitled, on his arrival, to one hundred acres of land†. They fixed their residence in the vicinity of the bay, where they built houses

---

* Mem. Barb. p. 10. Univ. Hist. vol. 41, p. 132.

† Of these adventurers, the names of two only have reached us : S. Bulkley and J. Summers, who established themselves in St. George's parish.

for the reception of their stores; and, for the facility of a communication between the opposite banks of the river, which intersected the ground, they constructed a wooden bridge, whence the new settlement obtained the name of Bridge-Town*.

The Carlisle settlers, to distinguish themselves from those established by Courteen, assumed the appellation of windward-men, while the others were denominated leeward-men. Wolferstone, soon after his arrival, in conformity to his instructions, appointed John Swan to be his lieutenant, and created a council, whom he invested with a portion of legislative and executive authority. Before this tribunal the governor summoned the Pembroke settlers to appear; affirming, that they had no legal title to the lands which they held; and treating their settlement as a palpable encroachment on the rights of his patron. They accordingly made their appearance at the time and place appointed; but not in a temper to listen to any proposals made them by Wolferstone. They utterly disclaimed all dependance on the Earl of Carlisle; and, peremptorily refusing to submit either to his authority or that of his governor, returned home that night.

---

* Ligon's Hist. Barb. p. 25. Hughes, however, is of opinion, that this town derived its denomination from an *Indian* bridge thrown over a narrow neck of the bay by the Caraibs. *Nat. Hist.* p. 6. Hence it is evident, that this capital was always known by the appellation of Bridge-Town; yet in all legislative and judicial proceedings, it is most absurdly called Saint Michael's Town : a name equally unknown to historians and geographers.

Upon this occasion, Deane, who, it seems, was also a Bermudian, deserted them; and having submitted to the governor, was intrusted with the command of a party of armed men, who were detached in order to reduce them to subjection. Abandoned by their faithless leader, the leeward settlers arrayed themselves under the direction of John Powell, son of the mariner who brought them to Barbadoes, and marched out to meet their adversaries. The hostile parties met at Palmeto fort, near the Hole Town; and, prompted by mutual animosity, prepared for action. Happily the effusion of human blood was prevented by the humane interposition of Mr. Kentlane, a pious clergyman, who, rushing between the angry disputants, prevailed on them to suspend their mutual resentment, and refer their differences to the determination of the noble personages, whose opposite interests had occasioned the contest.

Sept. 14.

Peace being thus restored, the Pembroke settlers acknowledged Wolferstone's authority, and Powell became the prisoner of his fortunate rival*. The calm, however, was not of long duration. Henry Powell, soon after this arrangement, arrived, and brought with him a commission from the Earl of Pembroke, appointing John Powell governor of the colony. Wolferstone now, in turn, became the prisoner of his former captive. Taken by surprise, he and the perfidious Deane were conveyed on board ship, loaded

Jan. 14.

* Mem. of Barb. p. 12.

with fetters, and sent to England. Powell enjoyed his triumph but a short time before he experienced the mutability of fortune. Hearing of the disturbances which existed in the colony, Robert Wheatly, one of the merchants concerned in the contract with Lord Carlisle, determined on making a voyage to Barbadoes, accompanied by Captain Henry Hawley, in the hope of being able, by his presence and prudent management, to adjust all differences. This gentleman, artfully concealing his intentions, on his arrival, invited Powell on board his ship, where he was kept under confinement until he could be sent to England to answer for his conduct.

April 9.

Incensed at this injurious treatment, the leeward settlers instantly resumed their arms, with the design of avenging the insult offered them in the person of their chief, and of extirpating the Carlisle settlement*. In this spirited attack, however, they met with such a vigorous resistance as compelled them to a precipitate retreat. For this gallant defence, the windward-men were honoured with the thanks of their noble patron, who farther rewarded their bravery by allowing them their goods free from any charge of storage for the term of seven years.

April 16.

In the mean time, the noble peers, whose opposite claims had produced these contentions, did not remain indifferent spectators of the disputes. They appealed to

---

* Univ. Hist. vol. 41. p. 134.

the King; each complained of the injustice with which he
had been treated, and endeavoured, by plausible objections, to invalidate his competitor's pretensions. Finding
that the Lord Chamberlain's title rested principally on
some informality in the original charter granted to Lord
Carlisle, his Majesty ordered a second patent, made out on
the seventh day of April, correcting and explaining the
errors imputed to the first; and confirming, in the most explicit and unequivocal manner, the former grant to Lord
Carlisle.

The Earl of Carlisle, having thus overcome all opposition,
and rendered himself lord paramount of Barbadoes, thought
now of providing for the security of his subjects. To this
end he gave a commission to Sir William Tufton, appointing him commander-in-chief of the island. This gentleman, accompanied with a sufficient force to reduce the discontented settlers to obedience, arrived at his government
Decem. 21. early in December, and immediately applied himself to
business. The first step taken after his arrival, was the
appointment of a council*, with whom he held a court or
general sessions of the peace. He issued one hundred
and forty grants for nearly sixteen thousand acres of

---

* Curiosity will not, it is presumed, quarrel with us for inserting a list of the
members of this board, in which it is easy to recognise the origin of the second
branch of the legislature; S. Andrews, Captain Talbot, T. Peers, R. Hall, R. Leonard, A. Marbury, H. Brown, Captain Heywood, T. Gibbes, D. Fletcher and W.
Birch.

land, and confirmed those which had been already given. During his short administration many laws were enacted, with the consent of his council; and the part of the country which had first yielded to the arts of cultivation, was divided into the six parishes of Christ Church, of Saint Michael, Saint James, Saint Thomas, Saint Peter, and Saint Lucy*.

The governor was proceeding in the adoption of such measures as appeared to be most essential to the welfare of those over whom he presided, when he was unexpectedly interrupted by the arrival of Henry Hawley, who brought June. with him a power to supersede Tufton and to assume the government. It has been conjectured that Sir William had drawn upon himself the displeasure of the noble proprietary; but, as no cause has been assigned for this dislike, it is highly probable that his removal was not owing to his own misconduct. The fact is, that Hawley, who on his voyage home, the last year, had been captured by the Spaniards, had, on his return to England, procured from Lord Carlisle a grant for a considerable tract of land. In negotiating this business, it is not unlikely that an artful man, such as Hawley appears to have been, should have had recourse to some unfair means to prevail on a nobleman, governed only by his interest, to invest him with the supreme authority over this distant settlement.

---

* Memoirs of Barbadoes, p. 14.

Tufton calmly submitted to the arrangement which deprived him of his employment; but, suspecting that some improper influence had been used to prejudice him, he appears to have cherished a secret resentment against the suspected author of his downfall. Nor was it long before he was furnished with an opportunity of shewing his animosity. About this time the colony suffered very severely from the effects of a long continued drought, which occasioned so great a scarcity of provisions, that the planters were reduced to the utmost extremity. Actuated, as was alleged, by motives of personal enmity to the governor, Sir William prevailed on many of the inhabitants to join in a petition to his excellency, complaining of his withholding from them certain stores, which had been sent out by the Earl of Carlisle for the relief of the sufferers, during the late calamity.

Incensed at this proceeding, Hawley now determined to destroy the man whom he had already injured. A council of twelve persons* had been previously appointed to assist him in framing such ordinances, as should be deemed expedient for the public welfare, and to serve as a court of judicature. Before this tribunal Tufton was arraigned, on a charge of mutiny. Although Sir

---

* These persons, whose names deserve to be remembered with execration, were Sir R. Calvily, T. Peers, T. Gibbes, Edm. Reed, J. Yates, T. Ellis, W. Riley, R. Leonard, W. Kitterich, F. Langdon, Reynold Alleyne, and W. Dolin.

William's conduct was not altogether free from blame, there certainly was not the smallest foundation for the charge exhibited against him. Nevertheless, the servile court, awed into a mean compliance with the sanguinary designs of their arbitrary principal, found the prisoner guilty of the crime with which he stood accused, and condemned him to be shot to death. This iniquitous sentence was suspended until the next month, and then executed without remorse*.

A transaction so cruel and illegal, excited the most lively indignation and discontent throughout the province. The death of this unfortunate gentleman was universally regarded, as an act of the greatest cruelty and injustice. The governor himself was abhorred as a tyrant and a murderer; and in the subsequent fate of the base instruments of his revenge, the superstitious, who, in the dispensations of Providence, always pretend to discern the retributive arm of Omnipotence, were persuaded, that they beheld the Divine justice particularly displayed in the punishment of the guilty judges.

The innumerable emigrations from Europe, added to the natural fecundity of the human species, had, by this time, so increased the population of Barbadoes, that it became

---

* Mem. of Barbadoes, p. 17. Univ. Hist. vol. 41, p. 135. It may, perhaps, be thought strange that, notwithstanding the indisputable authority on which these facts are related, the author of the Short History of Barbadoes, should have passed over these and many other important particulars in total silence.

necessary to establish judicatories for the distribution of justice in civil cases. Accordingly the island was this year divided into four precincts, in each of which a court of common-pleas, consisting of a chief judge and four assistants, was appointed to be holden every month, for the purpose of determining all causes of litigation, not exceeding the value of five hundred pounds of tobacco, subject to an appeal to the supreme court, in which the governor presided in person. In this institution, we may perceive the first rude sketches, though imperfectly defined, of that erroneous judicial system, which has been handed down to the present day, sanctioned rather by the force of deep-rooted prejudices, and the respect due to ancient customs, than to any experience of its wisdom and efficacy.

The supreme court, at present, consists of the governor and council, and takes cognizance of all grievances and erroneous proceedings in the inferior courts. Five members of the council, with the governor, make a quorum for transacting business in their judicial, as in their legislative capacity. They constitute a court of error and equity, in which the governor, though he has the style and title of chancellor, presides only as *primus inter pares* : his vote or opinion being of no greater importance than that of any other member. Some writers on West Indian politics have censured this practice, as a radical imperfection in the constitution of the colonial chancery. They conceive that justice would be more uniformly, promptly and impartially administered, were the governor here, as in most of the other colonies, sole chancellor.

Among the Leeward Islands, the commander in chief is chancellor of each, by virtue of his office. " Attempts have been made at St. Christopher's to join the council with him, but without success; the inhabitants choosing rather to submit to the expence and delay of following the chancellor to Antigua, the seat of government, where the court of chancery is usually held for those islands, than suffer the inconveniency of submitting their suits to the decision of judges, who, from their situation and connexions, may be interested in the event of every cause that should come before them*."

On this subject the sentiments of an ingenious writer on our colonial constitutions merit attention.. " A governor," says he, " has fewer connexions in the country, and is less liable to influence than either of the council, who for the most part are natives. A gentleman who has interest to obtain a government, must be a man of some character and distinction.. He is responsible for his conduct, and has at stake the loss of office. When he sits alone, let his disposition be what it may, he will hardly venture to commit any flagrant act of injustice. But when a dozen counsellors are placed on the bench with him, *defendit numerus*, if they are inclined to do mischief, they keep each other in

---

* Edwards's Hist. of the West Indies, vol. 1, p. 431.

countenance. It very seldom happens that either of these counsellors has been bred to the law, and a governor can have little assistance, and the country little benefit, from twelve gentlemen being placed on the chancery bench, with no knowledge of law. Besides, in small communities, scarce any cause can come on, in which all who sit on the bench are totally disinterested*."

1633.

The clamours of the people, occasioned by the violent and arbitrary proceedings of the Governor, having at length reached the proprietary's ears, Mr. Hawley was called home. Though it was generally expected that he would there meet with the punishment which he so justly deserved, for the murder of Sir William Tufton, he found an unmerited protection under the influence of his patron, who prevented any inquiry into the affair.

April 3.

On the departure of Hawley, his brother-in-law, Richard Peers, assumed the government. Of the deputy-governor's administration nothing is recorded, except, that under his authority two persons were condemned, by a court martial, to suffer death for treasonable practices against the colonial government, and that they were executed pursuant to their sentence.

1634.
April 7.

Hawley returned the next year with fresh powers from the Earl of Carlisle, and particular instructions concerning the issuing of grants for land. He was positively enjoined

---

* Stokes's View of the Constitution of the Colonies, p. 197.

to make no grants for a longer term than seven years; or, on any condition beyond the life of the grantee; reserving to the earl the payment of an annual tribute, and securing to the governor and the clergy their respective dues; otherwise the estate so granted was to determine, and the land to revert to the proprietary. Neglect of cultivation, and omitting to provide a servant for every ten acres, were also declared to be causes of forfeiture*. These particulars are worthy of attention, as they serve to elucidate the nature of the tenure by which the early settlers held their plantations, and to throw some light on the delicate question which occurred on the island's reverting to the crown. By an order of the governor and council, a tax of twenty shillings, for his excellency's use, was imposed on every foreign vessel which should arrive at this island, for trade or refreshment; with an additional duty of seven shillings per cent. ad valorem, on all goods which they should offer for sale, to be applied to the use of the harbour: a judicious application of an impolitic impost.

May 22.

Hawley soon afterwards resigned his authority a second time to Mr. Peers, and returned to England. The administration of this gentleman was again stained with blood. At a general sessions of the peace, William Kitterich, one of Tufton's judges, was convicted of the murder of Captain Birch, and sentenced to be hanged; but, in consider-

Sept. 1.

---

* Mem. of Barbadoes, p. 19.

ation of his having borne arms as an officer, the court mitigated the sentence, and he was ordered to be shot.

Hawley quickly returned to Barbadoes, and, after appointing a new council*, reduced the courts of common pleas to two precincts, extending their jurisdiction to suits not exceeding the value of one thousand pounds of cotton or tobacco; and appointed informers in each parish. The population had now greatly encreased, and of the inhabitants there were seven hundred and sixty-six persons, each of whom possessed ten acres of land or more. Slavery was now countenanced, and a law passed, authorising the sale of negroes and Indians for life.

After issuing many grants for land, Hawley undertook another voyage to England, leaving the government in the hands of his brother William Hawley. Lord Carlisle, about this time, began to estimate the value of Barbadoes highly, and to suspect that the revenue which he drew from it was not proportioned to its rapid advance in numbers and cultivation. Hawley, finding his patron dissatisfied at the management of his colonial concern, privately left the
kingdom and returned to Barbadoes. Sir Henry Hunks was instantly dispatched by the proprietary with a commission to supersede the governor, and to assume the direction of affairs. Hawley, however, unwilling to part with his power,

---

* The new council was composed of R. Peers, J. Holdip, W. Fortescue, T. Gibbes, T. Ellis, W. Hawley, G. Bowyer, W. Sandiford, E. Cranefield, S. Andrews and T. Stevens.

peremptorily refused to submit to the authority of his successor; who, unable to resist the force with which he was opposed, quietly proceeded to Antigua. As soon as Lord Carlisle was made acquainted with these particulars, he appointed five commissioners*, with full power to reduce the refractory governor to obedience. In pursuance of his lordship's commands, Hawley was arrested, sent home prisoner, and his estate confiscated. The commissioners then sent for Hunks, and invested him with the government†.

The short period during which this gentleman exercised the supreme authority seems to have been distinguished by no occurrence worth recording. The power which he acquired with difficulty, he resigned without reluctance; and deputing Philip Bell to be his lieutenant-governor, embarked for Europe. The prudence and moderation of Mr. Bell's conduct in the exercise of this delegated trust, while it engaged him the approbation and esteem of all ranks of people, recommended him in the strongest manner to the proprietary as the properest person to promote the prosperity of the rising colony. He, therefore, sent him a commission as commander in chief.

The civil war, which at this time raged with the utmost violence in England, as well as the religious disputes which preceded, and in a great measure produced it, contributed

---

* These were H. Ashton, P. Hayes, W. Powry, D. Fletcher, and J. Hanmer.
† Mem. Barbadoes, p. 21.

in a considerable degree to the rapid population of the new world. And while the puritans and fanatics, whose principles were inimical to regal power and the established hierarchy, fled to the inhospitable wilds of North America, many respectable families, attached to the royal cause, found in this delightful little spot an asylum from religious persecution and republican tyranny. This emigration of the royalists, and their settlement in this country, may possibly account for that attachment to the parent state, and loyalty to their sovereign, which have ever been the characteristics of Barbadians. And, in justice to my own feelings, while I assign the cause, I hope I may be permitted to exult in the sentiment.

At this calamitous period, when the violence of contending parties threatened the total subversion of the British constitution, and the entire annihilation of the most invaluable distinctions of civil society, it may be readily supposed that the Earl of Carlisle, whose rank and fortune depended upon the issue of the fatal contests between the republicans and the defenders of monarchy and social order, had but little leisure to attend to his less important concerns in this remote quarter of the globe. His authority, therefore, daily lost ground, and was, at length, scarcely recognised in the colony. Barbadoes, thus left to its own councils, enjoyed all the advantages of commercial freedom. To this cause we may properly assign the extraordinary opulence and prosperity which it attained, while Great Britain was desolated by the folly and wickedness of her unnatural sons.

The leeward part of the island seems to have been the first and best settled. Many of the planters had at this time amassed considerable fortunes. Hence the penetrating eye of Mr. Bell perceived the necessity of adopting a more regular and efficacious system than had been hitherto observed. Under the mild and beneficent administration of this prudent chief, a new and auspicious era is presented to our view. His enlarged mind embraced a greater variety of interesting objects than had ever engaged the attention of his predecessors; and it was now that the Barbadians began to enjoy the benefits of equal laws and social order.

Sensible of the influence of religion in harmonising the passions and softening the manners of mankind, Mr. Bell's first care was to provide for the uniformity of common prayer, and the establishment of public worship. Assisted by the advice of a council consisting of ten persons, whose names are not transmitted to us, he divided the island into eleven parishes*, in each of which a church was built and a minister appointed to officiate at the altar. To secure to the people the grand and inestimable privilege of participating, by their representatives, in the business of legislation, a general assembly was instituted, composed of two

---

* St. George's, St. Philip's, St. John's, and St. Andrew's, being now added to the six already mentioned. *Vide ante,* p. 50.

deputies from each parish*, duly elected by a majority of
the freeholders. And, that justice should be brought home
to every man's own door, the island was again divided into
four circuits, in each of which a court of law was duly
constituted.

From the number and utility of the laws passed during this period, Mr. Bell may, with some propriety, be
styled the Barbadian Justinian. Few of his ordinances
have reached the present generation, but no inference
can thence be drawn to their prejudice. Many legislative
acts might then have been necessary and proper, which
from the lapse of time, change of circumstances, and
alteration of manners, would now be useless and inex-
pedient. This enlightened legislator very early saw the
necessity of prescribing some bounds to the rapacity of
public officers, by ascertaining their fees. The law which
passed for this purpose still remains in the statute-book,
as being in full force, though it is disregarded. It is
indeed more than probable that the fees which are
there specified, are inadequate to afford men of talents

---

* This may justly be thought a very unequal representation of the country. In the
present state of population and increase of commerce, it is but reasonable that the
merchants and traders should be allowed a choice distinct from the land-holder;
and that the representatives of the several towns should be proportioned to the number of electors. Such an accession to the popular branch of the legislature might
possibly infuse a fresh portion of strength and vigour into that assembly, and render it
more independent of the executive power.

and respectability a reasonable compensation for their services.

This evil is principally owing to the mischievous policy of bestowing the most lucrative employments in the island on persons resident in England. These offices are executed by deputies, who farm them from the patentees at an annual rent, far exceeding their real value. The remedy is obvious. Were all patent offices executed by their principals, the legal emoluments of each would be a sufficient compensation to an able, upright officer, without resorting to the unjustifiable means now practised; the money, which is now remitted to Great Britain, to pamper the needy minions of a court favourite, would be expended at home; and, in the course of its circulation, replenish the sources from whence it had been drawn. The executive authority would be strengthened, and the country, in general, benefited by the accession of the talents of a number of intelligent men, employed in the various departments of government.

Nor was Mr. Bell inattentive to the means of defending the island against the attempts of an external foe. In the list of expired laws, we find many acts mentioned for fortifying the sea coasts. For this purpose the produce of the excise act was granted to Captain Burrowes for seven years. But the fortifications which he erected, were so unskilfully contrived,

1647.

that they were afterwards demolished by order of a more able engineer, who was appointed to inspect them. The militia was rendered formidable by its numbers, which at this time amounted to a thousand cavalry and ten thousand infantry.

The misfortunes of the mother country contributed materially to the prosperity of the infant colony. Its population had encreased to the amazing extent of fifty thousand persons of both sexes; and the value of land had encreased in proportion to the number of inhabitants. It is asserted by a contemporary historian, that Colonel Modiford, in the course of this year, purchased half of a plantation, containing five hundred acres of land, ninety-nine slaves, and twenty-eight white servants, with the stock and buildings, for seven thousand pounds; which will doubtless be thought a cheap purchase, until it is added, that the same land had been sold, seven years before, for only two thousand pounds*.

The unrestrained intercourse which subsisted between the merchants of Barbadoes and those of Holland, was attended with great advantages to the inhabitants of both countries; but particularly to the Barbadians, who were supplied by the Dutch with the articles required for internal consumption, upon better and cheaper terms than they could have obtained them from home. One

---

* Ligon's Hist. of Barb. p. 22.

inconvenience must have been severely felt—the want of a circulating medium, to facilitate the mercantile transactions of the country. Money, the universal representative of the value of commodities, was so scarce, that both merchants and planters were frequently obliged to barter one commodity for another*. All fees of office, and even the emoluments which the governor derived from his appointment, were, at first, payable in cotton or tobacco, and in later times, in sugar.

At what time the sugar-cane was first introduced into Barbadoes, it is now impossible to ascertain exactly. It could not, however, have been long before the period we are now contemplating; for we are informed by Ligon, that on his arrival here, in 1647, the great business of sugar-making had been recently begun and was but imperfectly understood. An author, whom we have had frequent occasion to quote, speaks of the cane

---

* Of this *Ligon* relates a ludicrous instance. " Neighbour," said one planter to another, " I hear you have lately bought good store of servants out of the last ships from England; and I hear that you want provisions. I would be glad to make an exchange. If you will let me have some of your woman's flesh you shall have some of my hog's flesh." The price fixed upon was a groat a pound for the hog's flesh, and six-pence for the woman's. The scales were set up; the planter had a maid whose name was *Honor*, fat, lazy, and good for nothing. The man brought a great fat sow, and put it into one scale, and *Honor* was put into the other, but when he saw how much the hog outweighed the maid, he broke off the bargain. *Vide Ligon's Hist. Barb. p.* 59.

as having been first brought to this island by Mr. James Holdip, in a ship from Guinea*. But it seems much more likely to have been imported, as is elsewhere asserted, from Fernambucca, in Brasil†.

This valuable plant grew luxuriantly, and was easily propagated. The planters were at first so extremely ignorant of the proper management of the cane and the manufacture of sugar, that it was several years before it became a profitable article of export. It was, however, useful in supplying the means of preparing and fermenting those refreshing beverages, which, in the heat of a tropical climate, were both agreeable and salutary. By perseverance the planters at length acquired sufficient skill to enable them to proceed with greater advantage. For several years the art of sugar-boiling remained a secret, known only to Mr. Drax and a few other gentlemen, who had employed a Dutch planter from Brasil, to superintend their works. The improvements which he introduced in the management of their plantations enriched his employers, and excited an emulation among others, to whom the mystery was yet unknown. Several planters were induced to undergo the hazard and fatigue of a voyage to Brasil, to acquire the best information respecting the treatment of a plant

---

* Mem. of Barb. Appen. p. 1.   † Ligon's Hist. of Barbadoes, p. 85.

which, by proper management, was found capable of producing the most solid benefits. At length, when the Portuguese, after the revolution which placed the Duke of Braganza on the throne of Portugal, had recovered possession of their territories on the southern continent, the Dutch, expelled from Brasil, became our masters in the art of making sugar. Many of these exiles, settling on the island, instructed the Barbadians in the proper culture of the plant, the season of its maturity, and in the construction of works suitable for the manufacture of this valuable staple.

The field thus opened to the industry of the islanders necessarily required an encrease of labourers. European constitutions were found by experience unequal to the laborious occupations of agriculture, in a climate continually exposed to the scorching rays of a vertical sun. Recourse was therefore had, of necessity, to the shocking expedient suggested by the partial humanity of *Las Casas**, who, to preserve the scanty remains of

---

* Bartholomew de las Casas, the benevolent bishop of Chiapa, was a native of Seville, and held a curacy in Cuba; where he was distinguished by his humanity and zeal for the conversion of the Indians. He exerted himself with unremitting assiduity in behalf of that injured and oppressed people. At last the Emperor Charles V. moved by his continual remonstrances, made some laws in favour of the Indians; and, to relieve them from a part of the burthen under which they groaned, granted a patent to certain persons to supply the islands of Hispaniola, Cuba, Porto-Rico, and Jamaica with 4000 negroes annually. The active part taken by the bishop has in-

the aborigines of the American isles from destruction, proposed to the Spaniards the project of supplying their plantations with negroes from Africa. This early apostle of humanity justly conceived that there would be less immorality in employing in the labours of the field, an unfortunate,
but hardy race, who are slaves from their birth, than in
enslaving the effeminate, but free-born sons of America.
Barbadoes was, therefore, obliged to imitate the example
of the French and Spaniards in her neighbourhood, and
to import from Africa those wretched negro labourers,
whom the mysterious dispensations of Providence had
apparently doomed to perpetual slavery.

---

curred unmerited censure. " While he contended," says the great Dr. Robinson,
" for the liberty of the people born in one quarter of the globe, he laboured to enslave
the inhabitants of another region; and in the warmth of his zeal to save the Americans from the yoke, pronounced it to be lawful and expedient to impose one, still
heavier, upon the Africans." " But the conduct of Las Casas," says the elegant historian of the West Indies, " is not fairly stated in the foregoing representation; for
it supposes that each class of people was found in a similar condition and situation of
life; whereas it is notorious, that most of the negroes imported from Africa are born
of enslaved parents; are bred up as slaves themselves, and have been habituated to
slavery from their infancy. On the other hand, the inhabitants of these islands have
been so used to the enjoyment of liberty in a life of plenty and pastime, that the yoke
of servitude is insupportable to them. Las Casas therefore contended reasonably enough,
that men, inured to servitude and drudgery, who could experience no alteration of
circumstances from a change of masters, and who felt not the sentiments which freedom alone inspires, were not so great objects of commiseration as those who having
always enjoyed the sweets of unbounded liberty, were suddenly deprived of it and
urged to tasks of labour, which their strength was unable to perform."

EDWARDS'S HISTORY OF THE WEST INDIES, VOL. 2. p. 39.

But this supply proving inadequate to the effectual culti-vation of the soil, recourse was had to the more cruel and less justifiable practice of kidnapping and enslaving the neighbouring Indians and Caribs. These barbarians, im-patient of subjection, and too indolent to endure the hard-ships of a life of slavery, pined themselves to death, or ex-pired under the rigour of servitude; thus depriving avarice of its reward, and punishing treachery for its deceit and cruelty. These acts of injustice and inhumanity, far from benefiting the cruel perpetrators of them, entailed on the English the perpetual animosity of those savage tribes. A British vessel, engaged in this odious commerce, lying at Dominica, was visited by many of the Caribs, for the pur-pose of exchanging their commodities for such articles as they wanted. The captain, having made them drunk, put to sea with them; but the savages, notwithstanding their intoxication, perceiving his execrable design, leaped over-board, and regained the shore; except two, who were con-fined and afterwards sold for slaves. To avenge this injury, the Caribs, dispersed through the Windward islands, landed upon the English settlements accessible to their canoes, and massacred the unsuspicious inhabitants with the most in-discriminate fury and remorseless vengeance*.

Among the many instances of treachery practised on

---

* Univ. Hist. vol. 41. p. 215.

these wretched victims of European cupidity, there is one mentioned by a contemporary historian, which, as it has employed the elegant and pathetic pen of Addison, and has excited the most lively sentiments of indignation in the breast of the philanthropic Abbe Raynal, ought not to be omitted in this place. I shall, however, divest the affecting narrative of the fanciful embellishments with which it has been decorated by others, and recite it, with historic fidelity, in the words of the original and artless writer by whom the story was first told*. " An English ship having put into a bay, sent some of her men ashore to try what victuals or water they could find ; but the Indians perceiving them to go far into the country, intercepted them on their return and fell upon them, chasing them into a wood, where some were taken, and some killed. A young man, whose name was Inckle, straggling from the rest, was met by an Indian maid, who, upon the first sight, fell in love with him, and hid him close from her countrymen in a cave, and there fed him till they could safely go down to the shore, where the ship lay at anchor, expecting the return of their friends. But at last seeing them upon the shore, the boat was sent for them, took them on board and brought them away. But the youth, when he came to Barbadoes, forgot the kindness of the poor maid, who had ventured her life

---

* Ligon's Hist. of Barb. p. 55.

for his safety, and sold her for a slave. And so poor *Yarico* for her love lost her liberty."

It will readily be perceived, how much this simple tale has been embellished by the creative imagination and descriptive powers of Addison*. And it is painful to add, though it is too obvious to escape observation, that similar artifices and exaggerations have been successfully employed in later times to inflame the passions and prejudice the minds of the credulous misinformed Europeans on the subject of West Indian slavery. It does not, however, appear, that the lady possessed any remarkable share of delicacy, since it is reported by Ligon, who was personally acquainted with her, and received many offices of kindness at her hands, " that she would not be wooed by any means to wear clothes." Nor does she seem to have been much affected by the ingratitude of her perfidious betrayer. " Her excellent shape and colour, which was a pure bright bay; and small breasts, with nipples of porphyrie," were irresistible attractions, and she soon consoled herself in the arms of another lover. In short, "she chanced to be with child by a christian servant, and lodging in an Indian house, amongst the other women of her own country, and being very great with child, so that her time was come to be delivered, she walked down to a wood, and there, by the side

---

* Vide the Spectator, No. 11.

of a pond*, brought herself *a-bed*; and presently washing her child, in three hours time came home with a lusty boy, frolic and lively†." Who could suppose that this is the same unfortunate female, of whom so much has been said and sung by moralists, poets and historians; whose hapless fate has caused such lively sensations in the tender minds of Europe's philanthropic sons? No apology, it is presumed, will be thought necessary for this minute and authentic account of the celebrated *Belle Sauvage*, whose wrongs have been amplified and recorded by the ablest pens; and whose imaginary sorrows have drawn the tear of sympathy from the brightest eyes.

The elegant, though inaccurate, Abbé Raynal, erroneously ascribes a conspiracy among the negroes, which was formed about this time, to a design of avenging the quarrel of this much injured woman. The fact is related, and very differently accounted for, by an eye witness‡, though not in a manner more favourable to the character of the colony. The slaves, lately imported from Africa, whose savage manners and natural ferocity had not yielded to the arts of civilization, nor been softened by the influence of European habits, probably conscious of their superiority of numbers, and groaning under a new and toilsome species

---

* There is a pond in Kindall's plantation, which, from this circumstance, is called, at this day, Yarico's Pond.

† Ligon's Hist. of Barb. pp. 54 and 65.   ‡ Ibid. 54.

of bondage, determined to make an effort to throw off the galling chain. With this view a conspiracy was entered into by the bold and discontented, and a day appointed for a general insurrection; when they proposed to massacre all the white inhabitants, and to make themselves masters of the island. This horrid plot was conducted with such inviolable secrecy, that no doubt was entertained by the conspirators of its successful completion. But on the day preceding the execution of their diabolical design, a servant of Judge Hothersall, filled with horror at the prospect of the dreadful scene which was about to commence, dismayed by the apprehension of a failure, or actuated by gratitude for the kindness with which he had been treated, divulged the fatal secret, with which he had been intrusted, to his master. Proper measures were immediately taken to frustrate the scheme; many of the conspirators being secured, underwent a legal examination; and eighteen of the principal leaders, who were the most turbulent and sanguinary, were condemned to expiate their guilt on a gibbet; an awful example, dictated by the imperious law of self-preservation.

CHAP.

CHAP. II.

LORD WILLOUGHBY SUCCEEDS TO THE GOVERNMENT—RE-
STRAINTS ON TRADE—SIR GEORGE AYSCUE REDUCES THE ISLAND
—RESTORATION—COLONEL MODIFORD APPOINTED GOVERNOR
—SUCCEEDED BY PRESIDENT WALROND—DIGRESSION CONCERN-
ING COURTS OF LAW.

CHAP. II. $\quad$ DURING the fatal disputes between the king and par-
1649. $\quad$ liament, which distracted and desolated the kingdom, the
interest of the proprietary appears to have been entirely
neglected and forgotten in Barbadoes. After the death of
Lord Carlisle, the reputation of its amazing wealth and
prosperity encouraged his son to claim the island under the
original grant made to his father. But the great difficulty
was how to secure the benefits arising from a property so
distant. At length, the noble patentee executed a lease to
Francis Lord Willoughby, of Parham, by which he conveyed to his lordship all his right and title to the colony for
the term of twenty-one years, upon condition that the profits arising from his claim, during the existence of the
contract, should be applied to their mutual advantage. In
consequence of this arrangement, the Earl appointed Lord

Willoughby governor of the whole province of Carliola. But apprehensive that the inhabitants might be inclined to dispute his authority, it was thought necessary, as a prudent precaution, to obtain a commission from the king, confirming his lordship's appointment*. The unhappy posture of the king's affairs, at this critical period, probably suspended the execution of this design. But when the blind fury of an infatuated people had sated itself with the blood of their legitimate, hereditary sovereign, the project was revived and carried into full effect.

Lord Willoughby was a brave and active officer. As a presbyterian, he had been formerly inimical to the royal cause; but disapproving of the violent measures pursued by the republican party, he had renounced their principles; and, after the execution of the unfortunate Charles, disgusted at the infamous conduct of the regicides, he passed over into Holland, and openly espoused the cause of the exiled prince. But as there was no prospect of his being serviceable to his royal master, under his present unfortunate circumstances, he requested the king's permission to assume the government of Barbadoes, in the hope of being more usefully employed in that quarter. The affairs of the illustrious exile now wore so gloomy an aspect, that his most sanguine friends despaired of being ever able to place

---

* Caribbianna, vol. 2. pref. p. vi. Mem. of Barb. p. 27.

him on the throne, which the enemies of his family had subverted. It was deemed an object of great importance to secure even the West Indian settlements in their allegiance to the crown; and for this undertaking no one was better qualified than Lord Willoughby. His Majesty, therefore, readily complied with his desire, and appointed him governor and lieutenant-general of Barbadoes, and all the Caribbee islands. Could the effect of this mission have been accomplished, and the colonies in North America, induced to reject the authority of parliament, it was conjectured, that his Majesty would have retired to that continent, to avoid the dangers and persecutions to which he was continually exposed in Europe*.

May 7.　Lord Willoughby, on his arrival at Barbadoes, found the colony in the most prosperous circumstances; rich, populous, and tranquil. Many of the republicans, who had fled from the rage of civil contention at home, concluding that the interest of the royal party was entirely ruined by the murder of their sovereign, returned to England, allured by the prospect of deriving greater advantages from their friend's accession to power, than they could expect to enjoy in this obscure part of the world, under a proprietary government. This partial emigration afforded a wider field for the royalists, who at this time formed by far the most considerable part of the people. But, as many of the pu-

* Univ. Hist. vol. 41. p. 139.

ritans, or parliamentarians, remained in the island, the two parties had mutually agreed to avoid all political controversy, and live together on terms of reciprocal friendship and good-will.

This harmony and unanimity were, in some measure, interrupted, by the arrival of Lord Willoughby. His excellency was too zealously attached to the royal cause to temporize with the opposite party. The first step taken by his lordship was to proclaim the accession of Charles II. to the crown, and to the sovereignty of all the dominions thereto belonging. His next care was to convene the legislature, who entered into all his lordship's views with ardour and alacrity. An act was immediately passed, acknowledging his majesty's right to the sovereignty of the island, and that of the Earl of Carlisle, derived from his majesty, and transferred to his excellency Lord Willoughby. It also enjoined the unanimous profession of the true religion, and provided for imposing condign punishment on all opposers of the established church. No less than twenty-five laws received the governor's assent in the course of this year; a circumstance which manifests much diligence and attention to business, on the part of the members of the general assembly. Among these laws are many salutary regulations for preserving peace and tranquillity; for training the militia, and fortifying the maritime parts of the island: all of them useful objects, and well worthy the attention of an enlightened administration. Availing himself of the spirit of loyalty which prevailed throughout the country, Lord Willoughby raised a body of men, and equipped several ships, with which he compelled the neighbouring islands, within his commission, to submit to the royal authority.

Meanwhile, Colonel Alleyne, and several other opulent planters, attached to the parliamentary interest, fearing that these strong measures might draw on the colony the resentment of the ruling power on the other side of the Atlantic, removed to England, to escape the storm which they saw gathering; and which they thought themselves unable to withstand. The council of state, which then directed the national concerns, having obtained from these persons the most ample information concerning the state of affairs in the West Indies, immediately determined upon punishing the refractory colonists, and reducing them to obedience. A formidable body of troops was accordingly embarked on board a squadron, under the command of Sir George Ayscue, for the purpose of giving effect to this determination. But this was not enough. Hitherto the colonies had enjoyed the most unbounded freedom of commerce with the Dutch. This furnished the council of state with a favourable opportunity of mortifying and oppressing the obstinate planters, by prohibiting the lucrative intercourse which subsisted between the sugar colonies and the United Provinces; and, at the same time, checking the growing prosperity of those wealthy republicans, the

Dutch. With these views, the long parliament passed an act, which laid the foundation of the celebrated navigation system, to which Great Britain is chiefly indebted for her present opulence, grandeur, and maritime strength*.

By this famous act all ships belonging to any foreign nation, were prohibited from trading with any of the English plantations without a license from the council of state. Though this law was expressed in general terms, the Dutch were most particularly affected by it, because they enjoyed the greatest share of the benefits accruing from the trade to the British West-Indian islands. The merchants of Holland, by whom the injury was most severely felt, presented a memorial to the States General, assembled at the Hague, against this proceeding, complaining, that they should be ruined by a prohibition which destroyed the most lucrative branch of their commerce, and praying their High Mightinesses to expostulate with the British government on a measure so fatal to the interests of the republic. But the approach of hostilities between the two commonwealths, rendered all negociation fruitless and unavailing; though it is asserted by an author of much credit†, that some Dutch merchants had the address to obtain from Cromwell an exclusive indulgence of trading to the West-Indies.

---

* Univ. Hist. vol. 41. pp. 141 and 289. Blackstone's Comment. vol. 1. p. 418.

† Vide Univ. Hist. vol. 41. p. 141.

Nor did the Barbadians remain calm spectators of a measure so hostile and oppressive to themselves. The greatest consternation, mingled with resentment, was raised in the colony by an act, which the people saw very clearly was intended as a punishment for their attachment to their king, and which, in its operation, must prove extremely injurious to the landed and commercial interests of the country. Nevertheless, with a spirit and firmness which nothing but their weakness rendered blameable, they determined to encounter every danger in the maintenance of their rights. The act having been sent out to the colonies, a spirited declaration was drawn up and subscribed by Feb. 18. Lord Willoughby, the members of council and the assembly, stating their objections, and expressing their firm resolution of opposing the act of parliament to the utmost extent of their power.

In this declaration they deny that the island had been settled by the British government, at the expense of the crown. It is certain, they say, that the present inhabitants had, at the manifest hazard of their lives, resorted to this distant and desolate spot, which they had, at their own particular cost and trouble, cleared, settled, and brought to its present prosperous condition. They totally disclaimed the authority of the British parliament, in which they were not represented. To submit to such a jurisdiction, they asserted, would be a species of slavery far exceeding any thing which the nation had yet suffered; and

they affected not to doubt that the courage which had enabled them to sustain the hardships and dangers which they
had encountered in a region remote from their native clime,
would continue to support them in the maintenance of that
freedom, without which life itself would be uncomfortable
and of little value.

They proceed with observing, " that by this act all out-
landish nations are forbidden to hold any correspondence
or traffic with the inhabitants of this island; although all
the ancient inhabitants know very well, how greatly they
have been obliged to those of the Low Countries for their
subsistence; and how difficult it would have been for us,
without their assistance, ever to have inhabited these places,
or to have brought them into order. And we are yet sensible,
what necessary comfort they bring to us daily; and that
they sell their commodities a great deal cheaper than our
own nation will do. But this comfort must be taken from
us by those whose wills are set up as a law for us. But we
declare that we will never be so unthankful to the Nether-
landers for their former help and assistance, as to deny or
forbid them, or any other nation, the freedom of our
harbours and the protection of our laws; by which they may
continue, if they please, in all freedom of commerce and
traffic with us. To perfect and accomplish our intended
slavery, and to make our necks pliable to the yoke, they
forbid our own countrymen to hold any commerce or traffic
with us, nor suffer any one to come to us, but such who have
obtained particular licenses from some persons who are

expressly ordered for that purpose; by whose means it may be brought to pass, that no other goods or merchandise shall be brought hither than such as the licensed persons shall please and think fit to give way to; and that they are to sell the same at such a price as they shall please to impose upon them; and suffer no ships to come hither but their own. As likewise that no inhabitants of the island may send home upon their own account any island goods of this place; but shall be as slaves to the company who shall have the license, just as our negroes are to us, and submit to them the whole advantage of our labour and industry."

" Wherefore, having rightly considered, we declare that as we would not be wanting to use all honest means for the obtaining a continuance of commerce, trade, and good correspondence with our country, so we will not alienate ourselves from those old heroic virtues of true Englishmen, to prostrate our freedom and privileges to which we are born, to the will and opinion of any one. Neither do we think our number so contemptible, nor our resolution, so weak as to be forced or persuaded to so ignoble a submission; and we cannot think that there are any amongst us who are so simple and so unworthily minded, that they would not rather choose a noble death than forsake their old liberties and privileges."*

---

* Grey's Hist. of the Puritan's, vol. 4. Append. 12. Political Register for 1768.

This manifesto was productive of no benefit to the colonies. The council of state had taken effectual measures for reducing them to obedience; and the Barbadians were soon called upon to give more active and indubitable proofs of their loyalty and courage. The sailing of the armament destined for the redution of the West Indies having been delayed beyond the expected time, Sir George Ayscue, to whom the command of the expedition was intrusted, did not reach Barbadoes before the eighteenth day of October, when appearing off Carlisle-Bay, he sent in Captain Peck of the Amity frigate, who captured seventeen Dutch merchant ships, making their officers and crews prisoners of war. Sir George, however, found the enterprise in which he was engaged, attended with greater difficulty and more danger than had been apprehended. Lord Willoughby made such an excellent disposition of the militia under his command, amounting to five thousand men, that the gallant admiral found it impracticable to land his troops. The council and assembly resolved to support the governor with all their strength. They published a loyal and patriotic declaration, in which they expressed their unalterable determination to defend his Majesty's lawful right to the possession of the island; to protect the person of their governor; and to vindicate the liberties and immunites which they had enjoyed under the ancient constitution*.

Nov. 4.

---

* Mem. of Barb. p. 27. Laws of Barb. Hall's Edit. p. 463.

Meeting with an opposition so unexpected, Sir George, having been frustrated in several attempts to effect a landing, endeavoured to obtain, by intrigue, what he could not accomplish by force. To this end, he opened a negotiation with the Barbadians; who, although they would not consent to acknowledge the supremacy of the parliament, proposed that Colonel Alleyne, and the other republican planters, who, in the expectation of subduing the island, had joined the fleet, should resume the peaceable possession of their estates. This proposal was too favourable to be refused by such as were willing to sacrifice their principles to their interest. It was eagerly embraced by all except Alleyne, who having been appointed to conduct the landing of the troops, whenever a favourable opportunity should present itself for that purpose, obstinately adhered to the cause in which he had embarked. Meanwhile, Sir George, finding that his forces were inadequate to the conquest of the island, prudently desisted from any hostile attempt until he should have a better prospect of rendering his efforts successful.

This inaction on the part of that artful commander was calculated to impress the Barbadians with an idea that the danger was over. Whether it produced that effect is now uncertain; but the assembly, on Christmas-day, passed two acts; the first for settling the peace and quiet of the island; the second for returning thanks to the well-affected to his Majesty, who had lately appeared in arms. But though the republican commander had suspended the execution of his enterprise, he had not wholly relinquished his design. He brought his squadron to an anchor off Speight's Town, with a view of availing himself of the first opportunity of disembarking. But the formidable appearance of Lord Willoughby's army disconcerted all his schemes, till the arrival of a fleet from Virginia, by which he pretended he had received a considerable reinforcement.

Profiting by this fortunate conjunction, the admiral made the necessary preparations for landing the troops, amounting to nearly three thousand men. The descent was effected under the direction of Colonel Alleyne, who was killed by a musket ball, before he reached the shore. Notwithstanding the loss of their leader, the republicans advanced with great vivacity, and attacked Lord Willoughby, who lay strongly posted near the fort; after a sharp conflict, his lordship was driven from his intrenchments and the fort was taken possession of by the assailants, with the loss of about sixty of their men*.

Far from being dispirited at this misfortune, Lord Willoughby still kept the field at the head of his brave militia, composed principally of the common people; who, though they have the least to lose, will, on every similar occasion, be found the most firm and steady in the hour of danger. From the example before us, let our legislators learn to ap-

---

* Univer. Hist. vol. 41. p. 142.—Naval Hist. vol. 2. p. 85.

preciate the value of a hardy peasantry; and influenced by every principle of sound policy, encourage a class of people who, in reality, form the physical strength of the country*.

---

* Every man, even of common observation, must be convinced that the decline of the Barbadoes militia, is owing to the disastrous emigration of the lower classes of people. This growing evil requires some legislative remedy. In a country possessed of a population so extensive as this is, and circumscribed within such narrow boundaries, every possible encouragement should be held out to the poor and laborious, to exert their industry and ingenuity in such useful employments as are suited to their humble condition. These men are not only the real effective strength of their country; they would add to its opulence were they placed in a situation to earn a subsistence for their families. But, unfortunately, a different policy prevails among us. Few plantations have a sufficient number of labourers to cultivate their fields, yet many slaves are employed as tradesmen, who would be equally as profitably engaged in agricultural occupations, while the industrious mechanic is destitute of employment. No wonder that, under such discouragements, he is compelled to forego his fond attachment to his native soil, and emigrate to the neighbouring colonies, where his skill and diligence are better rewarded. Thus the physical strength of the country is daily diminished; and the common stock deprived of a due proportion of labour and industry. "The decay of population," according to an eminent political philosopher, "is the greatest evil that a state can suffer; and the improvement of it, the object which ought, in all countries, to be aimed at in preference to every other political purpose whatever. Goldsmith has adorned this sentiment with all the graces of poetry.

> "Ill fares the land to hast'ning ills a prey,
> Where wealth accumulates and men decay;
> Princes and lords may flourish or may fade;
> A breath can make them as a breath has made;
> But a bold peasantry, their country's pride,
> When once destroy'd can never be supply'd."

As the island was completely blockaded by the British squadron, it is more than probable that the governor would

---

To check this alarming decrease of population two things are obviously necessary; first to provide homes for the poor, and employment for the industrious. Among the ancient Romans we find frequent mention of Agrarian laws for the relief of the poor. That wise and politic people thought that it signified but little, if, while the senate and patricians lived in affluence, the veteran soldier pined in want and obscurity. It is not intended to interrupt our modern patricians in the quiet possession of their estates, by recommending this example to their imitation ; but it must be allowed, that there are very few plantations which cannot, without injury to the owner, spare a few acres of indifferent land at their extremities for the accommodation of the tenantry. This unfortunate, but useful class of people, ought to be assisted ; they deserve encouragement. On the scanty glebes which may be assigned to them, they would find rest when their labours were done, and shelter from the *pitiless pelting of the storm.* Here they would toil, and, enjoying the fruits of their industry, become useful members of the community. Sweet, to the mind of the most humble, is the little native cot, under whose lowly roof peace and security dwell. Another important object is, to find employment for the industrious. To effect this grand desideratum, one thing only is necessary, to confine our slaves, by an act of the legislature, to the labours of the field. This will furnish the inferior orders of people with an opportunity of gaining an honest livelihood in the various mechanical professions which luxury and necessity have introduced for the convenience or ornament of society. Were this done, Barbadoes would furnish employ and subsistence for her numerous sons at home; the security of the country would be strengthened by the aggregation of faithful loyal subjects; the community would enjoy the advantages of a general circulation of the wages of industry ; and our planters would no longer require fresh importations of Africans for the cultivation of the land. Perfectly aware of the objections to the execution of this plan, I can only lament the invincible obstacles which deep-rooted prejudices and mistaken avarice have raised to oppose its accomplishment : for I feel the strongest conviction that the day is not far distant, when the proposed regulations, had they been early adopted, would have proved the salvation of the country.

have been eventually reduced to the necessity of capitulating; yet it is evident, from every account of this affair, that the parliamentary forces could have made no effectual impression on the Barbadians had they continued united firmly among themselves. Sensible of this truth, and impatient of delay, Sir George Ayscue adopted the only plan which, in his circumstances, was likely to prove successful. His troops, which were quartered at Speight's Town, under the command of Captain Morrice, made frequent incursions into the adjacent parts of the country; plundering and destroying the neighbouring plantations; a species of warfare, which soon produced the desired effect. Many of the principal royalists, who were less solicitous about their king and constitution than anxious for the preservation of their estates, despairing of a successful termination of the contest, and intimidated by the prospect of impending ruin, entered into a secret correspondence with the admiral. The negociation on the part of the Barbadians, was conducted by Colonel Modiford, who engaged, in case Lord Willoughby should continue to reject all overtures of accommodation, that he and all his friends would join the leader of the republican forces, and compel his lordship to surrender on fair and equitable conditions. Lord Willoughby, finding himself abandoned by those from whom he expected the most powerful support, had no alternative left. He was compelled to agree to a cessation of hostilities, and to appoint commissioners to arrange articles of capitulation*.

The circumstances which led to this pacification are variously related by different authors. Ludlow, who had certainly the best opportunities of collecting correct information, though his veracity is rendered liable to suspicion from his connexion with Cromwell, relates, that Lord Willoughby had intended to make one bold effort to terminate the dispute, by charging his adversaries with a body of horse, in which he was greatly superior, had not a cannon-ball, fired at random, beaten open the door of a room where he and his council of war were sitting; which, taking off the head of the centinel who was placed at the door, so alarmed the governor, that he changed his design, and retreated to a distance of two miles from the harbour. And, on the republican army marching towards him, he proposed to treat for the surrender of the island†.

The commissioners appointed by Lord Willoughby were Sir Richard Peers, Charles Pym, Colonel Ellis, and Major Byham. Those on the part of the Admiral were Captain Peck, Mr. Searl, Colonel Modiford, and James Colleton; all of whom, excepting Peck, were opulent landholders on the island. These commissioners met on the seventeenth day of January, and proceeded to adjust the points referred

---

* Univ. Hist. vol. 41. p. 142. Naval Hist. vol. 2. p. 86.

† Ludlow's Memoirs, vol. 1, p. 385. Campbell's Lives of the Admirals, vol. 2, p. 269.

to their determination, with great temper and moderation. The terms were soon settled by persons so much inclined to mutual concession and accommodation; and were certainly as favourable to the governor and his adherents as could have been expected. It was agreed, that the island should be delivered up to Sir George Ayscue, in behalf of the commonwealth of England; that the government should consist of a governor, council and assembly, according to the ancient custom; the assembly to be chosen by a free and voluntary election of the freeholders in the several parishes. That no taxes, imposts, customs, loans or excise, should be laid on the inhabitants of the island without their own consent in general assembly; and that all laws which had been made by former general assemblies, not repugnant to the laws of England, should still be valid. It was also stipulated, that both parties should continue in the uninterrupted enjoyment of liberty and property[*].

But, whatever eulogies might have been bestowed on the mildness and equity of the terms prescribed or granted by the conquerors, it is evident that, after their accession to power, they assumed a much harsher and more imperious tone. Two months had not elapsed from the signing of the treaty, which, as he imagined, granted him indemnity,

---

[*] Univ. Hist. vol. 41, p. 142. Mem. of Barb. p. 28. Edwards's West Indies, vol. 1. p. 343. Campbell's Lives of the Admirals, vol. 2. p. 269.

freedom of person, and security of property, when Lord Willoughby was banished for life, by an act of the legislature; and Colonel Humphrey Walrond, with several other eminent loyalists, was exiled for one year*.

1651.
March 4.

After the reduction of Barbadoes, the reins of government were placed in the hands of Sir George Ayscue. He, however, soon relinquished them, and proceeded to the conquest of the other colonies, which had maintained their allegiance to the crown. Before his departure, he caused the passing of several laws, by one of which Daniel Searle was appointed deputy-governor. Under this gentleman's auspices the legislative councils were actively employed in providing for the public safety. The statute book contains a long list of laws enacted during his administration, which, having passed under the usurper's authority, were afterwards declared null and void, except a few particular acts, which appearing to be of superior utility, were, for that reason, confirmed after the restoration.

1652.
March 29.

1655.

The inordinate ambition of Cromwell having prompted him to assume the government of the kingdom, under the title of lord protector, the politics of Europe received a new direction. The great continental powers acknowledged his authority, and courted his alliance; but the policy of the ambitious usurper soon plunged him into a war with Spain. All the English historical writers concur in condemning this

---

* Vide Hall's Laws of Barbadoes, p. 464.

measure as unjust, dishonourable, piratical, and an open violation of the most solemn treaties. The elegant historian of the West Indies* alone vindicates the conduct of Cromwell; and proves, by the most unquestionable evidence, that he was principally induced to undertake the war for the purpose of chastising the Spaniards, for the cruelties which they were daily committing on the subjects of Britain in the western hemisphere.

Be this as it may, the Protector, having determined on war, lost no time in equipping a strong squadron, under the command of Admiral Penn, with the design of attacking the enemy in that quarter, whence he expected to obtain the greatest advantages; and in which the Spaniards had perpetrated the greatest enormities on the English settlers. This fleet, in its passage to Hispaniola, touched at Barbadoes, where the troops, under Colonel Venables, were strengthened with a reinforcement of three thousand five hundred effective men; an incontestible proof of the immense population of the country at that time. The attack on Hispaniola having failed, the British commanders turned their arms against Jamaica, where their operations were more successful. The conquest of that island, while it opened a wider field for speculation and the exercise of industry, served to lessen the population of Barbadoes in no inconsiderable degree. Allured by the prospect of greater

---

* Bryan Edward's, vol. 1, p. 142.

advantages on a theatre so much more extensive, many opulent planters and other adventurers removed to Jamaica,
where land could be procured in greater plenty, cheaper,
and with less difficulty.

After the death of Cromwell, and the deposition of his
pusillanimous son, the committee of public safety, who
assumed the management of the national concerns, appointed
Colonel Thomas Modiford, governor of Barbadoes. This
gentleman is represented as a steady adherent to the royal
cause; but the prudence and moderation of his conduct
had, it seems, recommended him to the confidence of the
persons then in power. His administration, however, was
short and unproductive of any interesting occurrence.
The only law which received his sanction was an act limiting the existence of the general assembly to one year;
a term much too short for the dispatch of public business.
The annual dissolution of the popular branch of the legislature has been often found prejudicial to the public, by
impeding the progress of many salutary laws for the security and welfare of the community; yet the evil remains
unredressed; the members fearing to begin the necessary
reform, lest they should incur the resentment of their constituents, for attempting to render the representative body
less dependant on the elective.

The infatuation which had long blinded the English, having
gradually subsided, Charles II. ascended the throne amidst
the acclamations of the very people who had led his father

to the block.   This happy event was soon followed by some important changes in the government of Barbadoes.   Lord Willoughby, by virtue of the authority which he derived from his contract with the Earl of Carlisle, immediately ap-pointed his friend, Colonel Humphrey Walrond, the faith-ful old royalist, who had been banished for his loyalty, de-puty-governor of Barbadoes.   To strengthen this commis-sion, he obtained from the king a mandamus, appointing Walrond, president of the council, with directions to su-

Dec. 17.
persede Colonel Modiford, who, after a short reign of three months, calmly resigned his authority to his successor.

Modiford, who had made a large fortune in Barbadoes, now went to Jamaica, where he found an ample field for employing his capital, talents, and industry.   The people of that country, addicted to a military life, and animated by the piratical spirit of buccaneering, had attended but little to commerce and agriculture.   But as Modiford tho-roughly understood the true interest of the colonies, he in-troduced the arts of civilization, and instructed the inhabit-ants of Jamaica in the proper culture and management of pimento, or allspice; in the manner of making sugar; of planting cocoa groves, and erecting salt works*; so that in a short time the arts of industry began to prevail over the fierce and immoral habits of the islanders; and Modiford, as a just reward for his services, was created an English

---

* Univ. Hist. vol. 41, p. 352. Raynal's Philos. Hist. vol. 6, p. 332.

baronet, and promoted to the government of the island, which he had civilized and improved.

While Sir Thomas Modiford was thus nobly employed in diffusing the blessings of social life in one part of the empire, President Walrond was no less attentive to the means of providing for the security of the country, and promoting the peace and happiness of the people committed to his care. Some of the laws which were passed under his presidency appear to have been founded on the purest principles of justice and patriotism; though, as is too often the case, the means were not exactly proportioned to the end. Among the most important of these laws is " An act for establishing courts of common pleas, and regulating the manner of proceeding in all civil causes." By this act, the island is divided into five precincts, in each of which a chief judge, and four assistants, appointed by the governor, *durante bene placito*, are empowered to hold courts, once in every four weeks, from the last Monday in January to the twenty-fifth day of September, for the decision of all controversies concerning property and other matters of litigation, not cognizable by the criminal judicature*.

---

* It has been observed by a learned writer, who had been himself a provincial chief justice, that " It is absurd to have many distinct superior courts in an island so small. Had there been but one established in the centre of it, for the whole island, five gentlemen, who had some experience in the law, might have been found to fill the office of judges: but it is not conceivable, that such a small island can afford to pay proper

Among the blessings of civil society, the pure and impartial administration of justice is certainly one of the most important. The security of property, which is enjoyed under the protection of just and equal laws, faithfully and impartially administered, is the strongest link in the social chain; and the facility of obtaining a speedy reparation of injuries, is the most effectual means of reconciling the subject to a cheerful submission to the restraints of civil polity. But, unfortunately, the legal institutions of Barbadoes are not calculated to advance the attainment of these objects. The laws by which our judicial tribunals were first established, and their proceedings have been since regulated, are, in many instances partial, absurd, unjust and oppressive; particularly the act above alluded to, which, in many material points, is fundamentally bad. The first thing obnoxious to censure is the extraordinary number of judges which it establishes; who compose a legal corps more than twice as numerous as the whole judicature of England. In the appointment of these gentlemen, little regard is paid to the mental qualifications, or scientific acquirements of the different candidates for preferment. Though the solemn office of a dispenser of justice is generally filled by a man of character

---

salaries to twenty-five judges; by which means none but a man who has little knowledge, and much vanity, will accept an office which is attended with little or no profit." STOKES'S VIEW OF THE CONSTITUTION OF THE COLONIES, p. 256.

and fortune, it is sometimes bestowed as a douceur to secure to the commander in chief an undue influence over the public councils, or as a genteel establishment for some relative or dependant.

Less caution is used in the choice of assistants. The appointment of these is claimed as the privilege of the chief judge, who does not always exercise the delegated power with becoming discretion ; but frequently makes his election as chance, caprice, or personal favour may suggest. These puisne judges, possessed of an office without power or profit, are little more than cyphers on the bench; and, however respectable they may be as private gentlemen, few of them are qualified, by their learning or abilities, to determine abstruse points of law, involving, perhaps, the ruin of families in their decision*.

Thus a judicature is formed of men possessing neither legal erudition, nor forensic knowledge; who suspend the golden balance with timid hands, and wield the sword of justice with trembling nerves. No wonder then that the administration of justice should be irregular, precarious,

---

* " Whenever judicial commissions are rendered so cheap and common, they begin to lose much of their dignity and value in the eyes of many, even among the wiser planters ; and, by this means, very unworthy and illiterate persons may presume to aspire to them, and thus make the office of an assistant disgraceful and useless." LONG'S HIST. OF JAMAICA, vol. 1, p. 74.

and uncertain. Unacquainted with the principles of civil jurisprudence; ignorant of their power, and conscious of their deficiencies, the judges are thrown into a servile dependance on the gentlemen of the bar, and even the more humble retainers of the law, who are thus enabled to clog the streams of justice, and obstruct their course. No imputation is intended to be thrown on the common sense, or the integrity of the magistrates who preside in our courts. The censure is levelled at the *constitution* of the public tribunals, and not at the morality of the judge. Were integrity all that was required, no men in the world would be better qualified to sit in judgment than the judges of Barbadoes. But, with every allowance for probity and moral honesty, it cannot be doubted that they often fall into error, from an inability to discern what is legally right. Nor let it be said that it matters not, whether the judge be wise or simple, learned or illiterate, since the point at issue is to be determined ultimately by a jury. It is the peculiar province, the bounden duty of the judge, in all cases, civil and criminal, to sum up the evidence, explain the law, and instruct the jury, in the verdict which they are to return*. But our juries have no such assistance. In civil cases they

---

* " The judge imparts to the jury the benefit of his experience and erudition : the jury, by their disinterestedness, check any corrupt partialities, which previous application may have produced in the judge."   PALEY's PHILOSOPHY, vol. 2, p. 241.

are left to form the best judgment which they can on the most abstruse points of law; puzzled and perplexed by the contradictory opinions and turbulent eloquence of venal advocates; with no other guide to lead them through the mazy labyrinths of descents and conveyances, than the feeble light of uninformed reason and the dictates of a good conscience.

A thorough reform in the constitution of our courts of law is absolutely necessary, to correct the evils which are now obvious to the most superficial observer; to promote the regular distribution of justice, and to support the dignity of the public tribunals. Few precincts have business enough to require a separate jurisdiction; and in none, that of Saint Michael's excepted, are the emoluments of the office sufficient to encourage the judge to a punctual attendance on his duty. It cannot, therefore, be doubted, that the progress of justice would be accelerated by reducing the number of courts to two*. But this alone would not be sufficient. The assistant judges should be selected from among gentlemen of liberal edu-

---

* "Whenever there is in any country a number of courts independent of each other, the rule of decision is not uniform; and where there are many judges in a colony, scarce any question can come on but some of them are interested in the decision, as friends or relations to one of the parties."

VIDE STOKES'S CONSTITUTION OF THE COLONIES, p. 26.

cation, distinguished abilities, and known integrity. As a recompence for their time and trouble, they may be allowed the customary fees on probates and the examination of *femmes-couvertes*. The office of chief justice should be conferred on some able barrister of probity, study and experience, or reserved to reward either of the inferior judges, whose diligence and learning may entitle him to promotion; with permanent salaries, sufficiently liberal to render the appointment respectable and lucrative.

A laudable ambition would thus be excited in men of rank and professional eminence to devote their time and talents to the public service. The ingenuous youth of the island may then be induced to apply themselves to the study of the laws and constitution of their country, by which they may acquire both honour and profit. " It has been urged," says an enlightened historian, " that a gentleman, liberally educated in England, and bred to the bar, who comes hither to earn a subsistence by his profession, and by merit is advanced in time to the office of chief justice, cannot be suspected of any undue partiality arising from family connections; nor be so little skilled in the practice of a court of law as a gentleman born and educated in the island; that the making this post an object of emulation and pursuit, to able, honest and experienced lawyers, may prove an encouragement

for such to come over and practice here ; by which means
the supreme court of justice will always be supplied with
men learned in the science, whose knowledge will be an
acquisition to the public stock, and redound greatly to the
credit and advantage of the island*."

---

* Long's History of Jamaica, vol. 1, p. 76.

CHAP.

CHAP. III.

DISCONTENTS OF THE BARBADIANS—ORIGIN OF THE FOUR AND
A HALF DUTY—LORD WILLOUGHBY RESUMES THE GOVERNMENT
—THE ASSEMBLY GRANT A REVENUE TO THE CROWN—MR.
FARMER'S SPIRITED CONDUCT—HOSTILE DESIGNS OF THE
DUTCH—LORD WILLOUGHBY PERISHES AT SEA—SUCCEEDED BY
HIS BROTHER—PRESIDENCY OF MR. CODRINGTON—SIR JOHN AT-
KINS GOVERNOR—DREADFUL HURRICANE—REMARKS ON FORE-
STALLING—BARBADIANS GRIEVOUSLY OPPRESSED.

CHAP. III.
1661.

THOUGH Mr. Walrond was advanced to the presidency, on the restoration, as a reward for his zeal and fidelity
to the king, the royal favour was not confined to him alone.

Feb. 18.

His Majesty was pleased to confer the dignity of knight-
hood on thirteen gentlemen of the island*, in consideration
of the difficulties and hardships to which they had been
exposed by their loyalty and attachment to his family and
person.   But these honours and distinctions were not suf-

---

* These were Sir John Colleton, Sir Thomas Modiford, Sir James Drax, Sir Ro-
bert Davers, Sir R. Hackett, Sir John Yeamans, Sir Timothy Thornhill, Sir John
Witham, Sir Robert Le Gard, Sir John Worsum, Sir John Rawdon, Sir Edwin
Stede, and Sir Willoughby Chamberlayne.

ficient to reconcile the Barbadians to the measures which were soon after pursued by the court.

The rudiments of the navigation act, as has been already related, were first formed by Cromwell, during the usurpation. The benefits resulting from a system, which accident or resentment, rather than any just ideas of true policy, had suggested to the mind of that bold usurper, had become so manifest, that the ministers of Charles hesitated not to adopt so judicious a plan, for promoting the national prosperity, though invented by their enemies. Notwithstanding the rigorous prohibitions imposed by the English government on the trade of the colonies, the Barbadians had still contrived to maintain a very friendly and beneficial intercourse with the Dutch; which, from motives of policy, had been connived at by Searl, who then held the reins of government in Barbadoes.

This intercourse, it must be confessed, had greatly contributed to the wealth and opulence of the country; and the inhabitants, who had formerly considered the interruption of their commerce as a punishment inflicted on them for disowning the authority of the Lord Protector, were filled with consternation and resentment, on finding a measure so fatal to their interest, confirmed and adopted by their Sovereign on his restoration. They complained of the hardship and injustice of fettering their commerce with such arbitrary restraints, and deprecated the ruin to which they would be exposed by the operation of the double monopoly of import and export, claimed by Great Britain. But these complaints were unavailing. The objects contended for were of two much importance to be abandoned; nor was it reasonable to expect, that the parent state, in compliance with the wayward whims and sinister desires of selfish individuals, or from a regard to the petty interests of the colonies, should consent to relinquish the solid and permanent advantages of an exclusive commerce with her West Indian settlements.

1662.

From reflecting on this calamity, the Barbadians were soon called to the contemplation of new and greater ills. The minds of the planters were at this time perplexed and agitated with doubts respecting the legality of the tenures by which they held their estates. Lord Willoughby, whose lease from the Earl of Carlisle had eight or nine years yet to run, applied to the King for a renewal of his commission as governor of Barbadoes, intending to return to the island, for the purpose of enforcing his claims under the proprietary grant. As his lordship's views in making this application were generally known, the planters saw very clearly that they were regarded by these powerful noblemen as mere tenants at will. This opinion seems to have been entertained by the great Lord Clarendon himself; who affirms, that " these adventurers had, during the civil wars, planted, without any body's leave, and without opposition or contradiction."

Nor were the planters themselves free from apprehensions of this sort, as is evident from the precautions which were taken, at different times, to strengthen and confirm their titles.   Under the administration of Mr. Bell, an act had been passed for settling the estates and titles of the inhabitants of this island, to their possessions in their plantations.   And, again, five years afterwards, another law was enacted, with this title, " An act importing the customs imposed and granted by the council and assembly to the Right Honourable Francis Lord Willoughby, lord lieutenant-general of the province of Carliola, and governor of Barbadoes; as also his lordship's confirmation of the rights of the people of this island to their several estates, with the *tenure and rent* thereon created*."

But, from the calamitous æra in which the former of these laws was passed, and the peculiar circumstances which accompanied the passing of the latter, their validity might have been disputable.   It might have been insisted, that these acts had not been sanctioned, nor confirmed, by legal authority.   To remove all doubt on a point so interesting to themselves and their posterity, the inhabitants appealed to the King, humbly beseeching his Majesty to take the colony under his immediate protection.   They stated, that as subjects of Great Britain they had repaired to Barbadoes, which they found desolate and uncultivated;

---

* Laws of Barbadoes, Hall's Edition, pp. 12 and 462.

where, nevertheless, by patient industry, they had not only obtained the means of rendering life comfortable, when they could not, with a safe conscience, have remained in England; but had also brought it to a state of cultivation and improvement, by which it was rendered of high importance to the mother country, on account of its productions, commerce, and the customs annually paid to the crown. If they were now left, they said, to ransom themselves, and compound for their estates, rather than submit to the impositions and exactions of the proprietary, they should be compelled to abandon the settlement; and, of course, the plantation would be destroyed, to the manifest injury of his Majesty's revenue. The grant to the Earl of Carlisle, they insisted, had been surreptitiously obtained, under a pretence, notoriously false, that the island had been settled at his own cost and hazard; whereas they had, in fact, sustained the whole weight of labour and expence of establishing the colony, without any assistance whatever from the patentee. They concluded with proposing, that his Majesty would permit them to commence a suit, in his name, but at their own expence, in the Court of Exchequer, to set aside the grant made to the Earl of Carlisle; or that he would resume the sovereignty of the island, and leave the claimants, under that grant, to seek their remedy against the planters by due course of law*. These propo-

---

* Mem. of Barb. p. 30. Caribbeana, vol. 2. pref. p. ix. Edwards's Hist. of the West Indies, vol. 1. p. 332.

sals were fair and reasonable; but the king, unwilling to act precipitately, or unadvisedly in a case of so much moment, determined to refer the matter to the consideration of a committee of the lords of the privy council.

Upon a full and candid investigation of the claims and allegations of the opposite parties it appeared, that the Earl of Carlisle's patent had been obtained by a misrepresentation of facts, and was, therefore, pronounced to be null and void; and, in order to quiet the minds of the people, and secure them in the possession of their estates, the lords of the council advised his Majesty to revoke the grant. But the king declared his resolution of receiving no emolument from it until all claims, affecting the property in dispute, should be satisfied; and that he would make no other use of annulling the charter than to dispose of the profits of the plantation to those who, in law and equity, were entitled to receive them*.

The Earl of Carlisle, dying in the interim, bequeathed his property in the West Indies to his kinsman, the Earl of Kinnoul; and his creditors brought forward demands to the amount of eighty thousand pounds, which could only be paid by the profits arising from those distant possessions. The heirs of the Earl of Marlborough, as has been already mentioned, were entitled to a perpetual annuity from the same quarter, on which no inconsiderable arrears were due. Lord

---

* Caribbeana, vol. 2, pref. p. x.

CHAP. III. Willoughby demanded one moiety of the profits which
1662. should accrue during the unexpired term of his lease; and
the other moiety was claimed by Lord Kinnoul, who naturally expected an equivalent for relinquishing his right to
the whole in reversion. To satisfy these claims, and to induce the King to assume the entire sovereignty of the
island, it was proposed by Mr. Kendall, on the part of the
Barbadians, to lay an internal duty of four and a half per
cent. on all commodities of the native growth and produce
of the country, on exportation; which it was supposed
would raise an ample fund for the support of the colonial
government, and leave a large surplus to be disposed of at
the King's pleasure. Charles, who was never able to reconcile himself to an entire dependance on a parliament but
little inclined to indulge his extravagant disposition, received the proposal with unaffected satisfaction. And the
first care of the committee, according to Lord Chancellor
Clarendon, who assisted on the occasion, was to ascertain, as
nearly as possible, the probable amount of the revenue that
might be raised by this impost.

But when the planters of Barbadoes, resident in England, were called upon to confirm the proposal, they peremptorily refused to make any specific agreement; insisting, that Mr. Kendall was not authorized to enter into any
such engagement for them, or the other inhabitants of the
island. They declared that the island was unable to bear
the weight of so heavy an impost; which, they calculated,

would amount to the enormous sum of ten thousand pounds annually; and would operate as a perpetual rent charge of at least ten per cent. on the profits of their plantations. Were any settlement, they said, to be made, it could be done only by an act of the colonial legislature; who alone, they contended, were competent to determine a question of so much importance, and to assess the sum to be granted. They, however, agreed to use their endeavours to prevail on their friends in Barbadoes to consent to such a plan of raising a revenue for the use of the crown as should appear to them consistent with the public service, and the real circumstances of the country.

To accomplish this desirable object, Lord Willoughby was ordered instantly to repair to Barbadoes, and endeavour to obtain from the assembly such an impost on their native commodities as " should be reasonable, in consideration of the great benefits they would enjoy in being continued in the possession of their plantations, of which, as yet, *they were but tenants at will*.*" It was agreed by the Lords of the committee, that this fund should be applied towards providing a sufficient compensation to the Earl of Kinnoul, for surrendering his right to the Carlisle Charter; and to provide for discharging the Earl of Marlborough's annuity. One moiety of the surplus was directed to be paid to Lord

---

* Caribbeana, vol. 2, pref. p. xii.

Willoughby, for the remainder of his lease; the other moiety to be paid to the creditors of Lord Carlisle, until the expiration of Lord Willoughby's contract; when, after providing for the payment of a salary of twelve hundred pounds a year to the future governor of Barbadoes, the creditors of the Earl of Carlisle were to receive the entire balance until their demands were completely liquidated. With this arrangement all parties were perfectly satisfied. The proprietary government was accordingly dissolved, and the sovereignty of the island annexed to the crown. Lord Willoughby soon after received the King's commission, appointing him captain-general, and governor of Barbadoes and all the English Caribbee islands, for the term of seven years, reserving to his Majesty a negative on all future acts of the legislature.

Aug. 18.   Lord Willoughby found the people of Barbadoes but little disposed to concur in a proposition, by which they were required, in their own acceptation of the measure, to forge chains for themselves and their latest posterity. Those who had suffered in their persons or fortunes, for their attachment to the family on the throne, considered it as an ungrateful return for their fidelity and services; and those of opposite political principles, represented the proposed tax as an arbitrary and oppressive imposition which ought to be resisted. The murmurs and objections of the people, however, were as fruitless and unavailing as they were reasonable and just. Government had, in fact, gone too far to recede. The project of a perpetual revenue, though small, was too alluring to be rescinded ; and Lord Willoughby himself was too deeply interested in the event to remit his exertions for securing the final accomplishment of the plan. In his zeal for attaining the grand object of his mission he neglected to call a new assembly ; but submitted his proposals to the one which he found sitting, by virtue of writs issued under the proprietary authority. No arts of persuasion were spared to prevail on those members whose concurrence could be obtained by argument or entreaty ; nor were menaces omitted to influence such as might be awed into a compliance by the frown of power. Such means could not fail of producing their wonted effect ; and the assembly, after much hesitation, passed the memorable act for settling an impost on the commodities of the island, by which they granted to the king, his heirs and successors, a duty of four and a half per cent. on all the dead commodities of the growth or produce of the country, to be paid in specie, on exportation.

To this measure the most strenuous opposition was given by Colonel Farmer, a gentleman of large property and extensive influence ; and so general was the disapprobation occasioned by the act, that Lord Willoughby appears to have entertained the most serious apprehensions of some violent popular commotion. To preserve the public tranquillity, his lordship had recourse to a measure as cruel and unjust, as it was illegal and unconstitutional. He caused

Farmer to be arrested on a charge of sedition, and conveyed to England as a state prisoner; recommending that
he should not be permitted to return till the inhabitants
could be brought into a better temper.   This arbitrary step
was equally rigorous and unjustifiable.   Had Farmer been
actually guilty of the crime imputed to him he ought to
have been tried in his own country, by a jury of his peers.
But thus to exile him from his home, his family and connections, and expose him to a trial before an unknown tribunal, was contrary to every principle of criminal jurisprudence; it was, in fact, to condemn him unheard, and to
punish him before conviction.

Farmer, on his arrival in England, was carried before
the king in council, where he asserted the rights of an Englishman with manly freedom.   He contended that his conduct had been strictly loyal and constitutional; and that,
as a British subject, he was warranted in opposing any
measure inimical to the interests of his country.   Whatever truth there might have been in these assertions, it is
more than probable that Mr. Farmer behaved not with that
modesty and decorum which were proper upon such an oc-
sion; since so great and good a man as the Earl of Clarendon declared, that his behaviour was insolent and presumptuous; and that he ought to be committed until he could
be sent back to Barbadoes to be proceeded against in the
colonial criminal court.   He was accordingly remanded to
prison; nor did he regain his liberty till after a long and
tedious con..nement.

Notwithstanding the previous arrangements made by the lords of the privy council, it is evident, from the words of the statute, that the representatives of the people could not be prevailed upon to burthen their constituents with the payment of so heavy an impost, for the purposes already mentioned. Their views were very different from those of the British ministry, and are best explained by themselves in the preamble to the clause by which the duty was imposed. It is there expressly declared, that " forasmuch as nothing conduceth more to the peace and prosperity of any place, and the protection of every person therein, than that the public revenue thereof may be, in some measure, proportioned to the public charges and expences ; and also well weighing the great charges that there must be of necessity in maintaining the dignity and honour of his Majesty's authority here ; the public meeting of the sessions ; the often attendance of the council ; the reparation of the forts ; the building of a sessions-house and prison ; and all other charges incumbent on the government ; we do, in consideration thereof, give and grant unto his Majesty, his heirs, and successors, upon all dead commodities that shall be shipped off the same, four and a half, in specie, for every five score*."

This enormous duty on the produce of the country has

---

* Laws of Barb. Hall's edit. p. 56.

been generally condemned by every historian who has treated of our colonial concerns; and from its first imposition to the present moment, it has ever been a favourite theme of declamation with all West Indian patriots. To authorities so respectable the utmost deference and submission are certainly due. But different men will sometimes view the same object through different mediums. The understanding is often darkened by partiality, prejudice, or misconception; and it seldom happens that men will, or indeed can, calmly and dispassionately examine both sides of a question which involves their interest, when the result may prove disagreeable or injurious. In such cases, it becomes the duty of the candid historical inquirer, to dispel the mists of prejudice, and, by a faithful narration of facts, enable the unbiassed mind to form a right judgment. And now, when after repeated unsuccessful endeavours to obtain the repeal of this odious tax, the planter is precluded from every hope of relief from the galling chain, the author presumes, that he shall escape the imputation of betraying the interests of his native country, if, in expressing his own sentiments on this momentous subject, he should suggest a few considerations which may induce the Barbadian reader to submit, with patience, to the load which he is unable to remove.

According to the laws and usage of all civilized nations, the soil, in every newly discovered, or conquered country, becomes the property of the Sovereign by whose subjects

the discovery, or conquest was made; and he has an indubitable right to grant or dispose of the land thus acquired,
on what terms and conditions he thinks proper. Pursuant
to this right, Charles I. granted the island of Barbadoes
to the Earl of Carlisle, who thence became entitled to an
absolute dominion, as proprietor over the soil; to be disposed of in like manner, as he should find most convenient or advantageous. If we look into the preamble of the
act, where alone we can expect to find the reasons which
induced the legislature to consent to lay such an extraordinary impost on the produce of their estates, we shall soon
perceive that, "by virtue of the Earl of Carlisle's patent,
divers governors and agents, properly authorized for that
purpose, had laid out, granted, or conveyed in parcels, the
lands in this island to different persons *many of whom had
lost their grants, warrants, and other evidences of their titles;*
others, from the ignorance of the times, *wanted sufficient
words to create an inheritable right to their estates;* others
had never recorded their warrants or grants; *and others,
again, never had any warrants or grants to record,* for the
lands which they occupied*."

To supply these defects it was enacted, "that all rigthful
possessors of lands, tenements, or hereditaments, within
the island," should be confirmed in the full and peaceable

---

* Hall's Laws of Barb. p. 56.

CHAP. III.
1663.

enjoyment of their several estates; and that they should be released from the annual capitation tribute of forty pounds of cotton, to which they had been hitherto subject; and all other duties, rents, or arrears of rents to which they were liable. Hence the act appears in the light of a contract between the King and the people; by which, in consideration of his Majesty's having confirmed their doubtful and uncertain titles to their plantations, and released them from the payment of other accustomed duties, they agree to raise a perpetual revenue *applicable, however, to the internal expences of government.* The only reasonable ground of complaint, therefore, is to the misapplication of this fund; no part of which has been appropriated to the uses for which it was granted, except the sum of two thousand pounds sterling, annually paid to the governor as a salary from the crown; and one hundred pounds currency, directed to be paid, every six months, out of the King's casual revenue, arising within the island, for defraying the expences attending the Court of Grand Sessions. This must ever be considered as a flagrant violation of the engagement entered into on the part of the crown.

1664.

The commercial rivalry and national jealousy which, at this juncture, subsisted between Great Britain and the United Provinces, had so inflamed the minds of the English against their old allies the Dutch, that Charles II. was forced, in compliance with the wishes of his people, to declare war against those friends who had hospitably entertained him in the hour of distress. The States General, sensible of the value of Barbadoes, delayed not to dispatch a squadron, commanded by the celebrated De Ruyter, with a view of subduing the island. But Lord Willoughby, having taken the field at the head of the militia, made such a judicious arrangement of the forces under his direction, that the gallant admiral, after an ineffectual attempt on the forts which guarded Carlisle Bay, abandoned the enterprize*.

Notwithstanding the florid declamations of modern, parsimonious politicians, concerning the inutility of the militia, and the expence of maintaining the fortifications, we have here a second instance, in the short space of thirteen years, of the usefulness of those forts, which it is now the fashion to decry; and of the real importance of a well-regulated militia. And, although, on the former memorable occasion, the spirited resistance of the militia was not crowned with success, it should be remembered, that the failure was more owing to the intrigues and dissentions of a sinister party within, than to the superior strength of the adversary who assailed them from without.

Lord Willoughby soon resolved to return this visit; and accordingly prepared an expedition for the purpose of taking vengeance on the enemies of his country. The French

1666.

---

* Hume's Hist. of England, vol. 7, p. 409. Univ. Hist. vol. 41, p. 148.

about this time had committed frequent depredations on the British Caribbee Islands. They had dispossessed the English of the small colony of the Saints, carrying the settlers prisoners to Guadaloupe; and, in conjunction with the Dutch, had expelled them from their plantations in Saint Christopher's. These outrages, committed within his government, determined Lord Willoughby to go, in person, and chastise the aggressors. With this view he resigned the government of Barbadoes into the hands of Henry Willoughby, Henry Hawley, and Samuel Barwick, whom his Majesty had appointed joint commissioners to execute the office of commander in chief, in his lordship's absence. The first attack was made on Saint Lucia, the English inhabitants of which, reduced by various casualties to eighty-nine persons, had been forced to evacuate their settlement; nevertheless, Lord Willoughby took possession of the island in the name of his Britannic Majesty. He then proceeded to the small islands of the Saints, which having retaken, he sailed for Saint Christopher's; but, encountering a hurricane, he perished at sea in the streight between Guadaloupe and the Saints*.

Notwithstanding the prejudices entertained against this nobleman, for the active part taken by him in procuring the settlement of an internal revenue on the crown, except the severity and illegality of his proceedings against the patriotic

---

* Univer. Hist. vol. 41. pp. 218 and 257.

Mr. Farmer, it must be confessed, that his conduct was prudent, mild and equitable. Throughout the whole of his administration, Lord Willoughby manifested the warmest zeal for the security of the island, and the most sedulous attention to the administration of justice. Many ordinances, were framed by him and his councils for regulating the courts of law and equity. One of these, for reducing the Courts of Common Pleas to two precincts, seems to have occasioned some dissatisfaction; but, the people no sooner remonstrated against the innovation, than his excellency rescinded the ordinance, and again divided the island into four precincts; appointing, however, but two judges; one of whom, with his assistants, was empowered to preside in the courts at Bridge Town and Oistin's*; and the jurisdiction of the other extended equally to Speight's and James Town.

These ordinances having been made without the participation or concurrence of the representatives of the people, we are left to conjecture, that Lord Willoughby, after prevailing with the assembly to shackle their constituents with the four and half per cent. duty, had neglected to convene that branch of the legislature as long as he could do without them. But finding their assistance necessary to grant

---

* This town was originally called Austin's, not in commemoration of the saint of that name, but of a wild, drunken fellow, whose lewd, dissipated conduct has damned him to everlasting fame.   LIGON'S BARB. p. 25.

supplies for the public service, he summoned a meeting of the General Assembly, early in the present year, when they passed an act for collecting five hundred thousand pounds of sugar, to defray the expence of fortifying the island. Thus, in little more than two years, the mask was thrown aside : and the representatives of the people had scarcely rivetted the chain before they were called upon to impose fresh burthens on their constituents, to answer one of the very purposes for which the former heavy duty had been expressly voted.

1667.

While the executive power was administered by commissioners, a very necessary and useful work was undertaken. In every community it is of the highest importance that the laws, which are prescribed as rules of civil conduct, should be accurately defined and duly promulgated, that the people, who are bound to obey them, may be apprized of what they are enjoined to perform, or what they are prohibited from doing. Those of Barbadoes are become extremely voluminous ; many of the original records had been destroyed by various accidents : and, in the several revolutions of government which the island had experienced, many public acts were rendered, at least of dubious authority. It became necessary, therefore, to collect and arrange them, in order to separate those that were valid and beneficial, from those that were obsolete, void, or no longer useful. Commissioners were accordingly appointed by an act of the legislature, with directions to revise and compile all the laws and statutes then in force. Proceeding on their task with becoming diligence and as-siduity, they soon accomplished the business; and, having fairly transcribed all those which were thought worthy of preservation, the commissioners reported them as laws pro-per to be observed.

But they could not let this opportunity pass without mak-ing one feeble effort to relieve their country from the bur-then laid on its staple productions, by declaring that the assembly, who had consented to the four and a half per cent. duty, was not equally convened at the time the act passed for that purpose. This objection, which was specious and ingenious, was founded on the circumstance that Lord Willoughby had neglected, on the dissolution of the proprietary government, to summon a new assembly under the royal authority, and had accepted the grant from the assembly which had been convened under the presidency of Mr. Walrond. It may, however, be observed, that the convention parliament, by whom the restoration of Charles II. was accomplished, met without any legal authority above a month before the King's return, and continued sit-ting several months afterwards. Hence many eminent law-yers doubted whether it was a good parliament. But ac-cording to Justice Blackstone, this was too nice a scruple ; for the necessity of the thing justified the irregularity of the proceeding.

Again, the convention which placed the British sceptre in the hands of the Prince of Orange, was composed of the remnant of several parliaments assembled in the reign of Charles II. convened, without any constitutional authority*; yet their legislative acts have been confirmed, and we enjoy the benefits of them to this day. But the objection started by the commissioners, whatever might have been its intrinsic value, was wholly disregarded; and the reason assigned by the learned commentator on the laws of England, in the memorable cases just mentioned, may be applied with equal propriety in the present instance; " As the royal prerogative was chiefly wounded by their so meeting, and as the King himself, who alone had a right to object, consented to wave the objection, this cannot be drawn into an example in prejudice of the rights of the crown."

An account of the death of Francis Lord Willoughby having reached England, the King bestowed the vacant government on his brother William Lord Willoughby. His excellency was accompanied to Barbadoes by a regiment, under the command of Sir Tobias Bridge. This circumstance seems to have been misunderstood by former

Jan. 3.

---

* Hume's Hist. of England, vol. 7, pp. 329 and 360. vol. 8, p. 298. Smollet's Continuation, vol. 1, p. 7. Blackstone's Comment. vol. 1, p. 151.

colonial historians. One* supposes it to have been occasioned by some distrust of the loyalty and attachment of the inhabitants. Another † affects not to know " how they were destined, or of what use they were to the country." The fact is, that the nation was then at war with Holland, and that these troops were sent out for the protection of the colony, and to act against the enemies of their country in this quarter of the globe. This detachment, during a long stay in the island, was provided for at a considerable expence to the people ‡. It was at length employed in making a descent on Tobago, then in the possession of the Dutch: and, notwithstanding the place was strongly fortified, the British troops plundered the inhabitants, and carried off four hundred prisoners ‖.

Soon after Lord Willoughby's arrival, the House of Assembly liberally appropriated a considerable part of the excise duty to the purchase of a set of jewels to be presented to his lady, as a testimony of their esteem for her ladyship, and as a mark of the pleasure which they derived from her residence among them.

The fortifications seem to have occupied no inconsiderable portion of the governor's attention; nor does his lordship appear to have been negligent in respect to the administration of justice, and the regulation of the police.

---

* Universal Hist. vol. 41, p. 149. † Frere's Short History of Barb. p. 31.
‡ Hall's Laws of Barb. p. 475. ‖ Fenning's Geography, fol. edit. vol. 2. p. 703.

CHAP. III.
1668.

Many of the laws which were passed at that period have been continued down to the present day.

Lord Willoughby had been merely appointed to the government for the remainder of his brother's term; and as that was near expiring, he determined to return to England, probably intending to solicit a renewal of his commission. He, therefore, resigned the administration to Colonel Christopher Codrington, as deputy-governor, and embarked for Europe. But as the English colony at Dominica had been lately much annoyed by the French, his lordship resolved to visit that island in his way home with a sufficient force to redress the injuries which the inhabitants had sustained. This vigorous measure produced the desired effect, and his lordship procured from the Caraibs a formal surrender of the island to his Britannic Majesty*.

November.

1669.

Mr. Codrington continued to act under Lord Willoughby's appointment, until the expiration of his lordship's contract, as heir to his brother, with Lord Carlisle, which determined his authority under the royal commission. But no new appointment being made, the legislature met, and, by an act passed for settling the government, declared themselves to be Governor, Council and Assembly, until his Majesty's pleasure should be known†. Lord Willoughby soon afterwards arrived with a new commission, appointing

Dec. 23.

* Univ. Hist. vol. 41. p. 285.   † Memb. of Barb. p. 42.

him governor of Barbadoes, and all the Caribbee islands to windward of Guadaloupe. The Leeward Islands were now, for the first time, formed into a distinct government, and the command given to Sir William Stapleton. Hence comes the distinction of Windward and Leeward Islands; Guadaloupe being the point of demarcation.

Lord Willoughby remained but a short time in Barbadoes before he again resolved on recrossing the Atlantic, leaving Mr. Codrington, a second time, commander in chief. The administration of this illustrious West Indian is distinguished by his vigilance, circumspection, and prudent attention to the duties of his exalted station. He considered the power with which he was invested as a sacred deposit, to be employed for the benefit of the people; and the many salutary laws which were passed under his administration, evince the rectitude and propriety of his conduct. This enlightened statesman early saw the necessity of checking the rapacity and collusive practices of the lawyers; and readily assented to an " Act for preventing the abuses of lawyers and the multiplicity of law-suits."

After an absence of more than two years, Lord Willoughby returned to Barbadoes. On this occasion, the King nominated the persons who were to compose the second branch of the legislature, honouring them with the title of *His Majesty's Council;* and directing, in case of the death or absence of the governor, that they should exercise the whole executive authority. By his commission

CHAP. III.   the governor was required to transmit to England all laws,
1672.   within three months after their passing, for the royal approbation or rejection; and, although they were allowed
to be in force until the King's pleasure was known, his
excellency was forbidden to give his assent to any act of
the legislature to continue in force longer than three years,
unless it should receive his Majesty's confirmation within
that time. As some compensation, perhaps, for this
abridgment of legislative authority, the executive power
became more enlarged. The governor, besides being
appointed ordinary and vice-admiral, was authorized to
remit all fines or forfeitures, *before* or after sentence given,
if the persons were proper objects of mercy; treason, and
wilful murder, excepted; and in these cases he was allowed
to reprieve, until the result of an application to the throne*
was ascertained.

1673.   The impaired state of his health rendering him incapable
April 2.   of attending to the arduous duties of government, Lord
Willoughby finally resigned his authority into the hands of
Sir Peter Colleton, senior member of the council, having, for
some reason, not now known, removed Colonel Codrington
from that board, and returned to England, where his
lordship died the ensuing year.

1674.   After the governor's departure, the council, pursuant to
the royal instruction, assumed the direction of the public

---

* Hall's First Settlement of Barbadoes, p. 28. Mem. of Barb. p. 42.

concerns, appointing Sir Peter Colleton captain-general of
the militia. This is the account given by the author of the
Memoirs of Barbadoes. But it is evident, from the statute
book, that Sir Peter's authority was not confined to the
military department; he continued to exercise the constitutional functions of first magistrate, until he was superseded by the arrival of Sir Jonathan Atkins, who was
appointed by his Majesty to the government of Barbadoes
and the Windward Islands.

The new governor fixed the seat of government at Fontabelle; but he had not enjoyed this situation long, when
the country was almost laid waste by one of the most
tremendous hurricanes that ever scourged a guilty land.
Neither the palace, nor the cot, escaped the destructive
violence of this awful visitation. Neither tree, nor house,
was left standing, except the few which were sheltered by
some neighbouring hill or clift. The face of the country
exhibited one continued scene of desolation. So complete
was the destruction of the sugar works, on the several
plantations, that it was nearly two years before they could
be repaired, or put into a condition to renew the business
of sugar making. Nor was the crop of provisions spared
from the general devastation; and, to add to the calamity,
eight valuable ships, laden with the produce of the country,
were sunk or stranded, in Carlisle Bay. In Speight's Town
every house was either blown down or materially injured.
Several families were buried in the ruins of their fallen

habitations; and there was scarcely one but lamented some relation, friend, or acquaintance, swept to an untimely grave*. Amidst this scene of ruin and misery, the fate of Major Streate and his fair bride deserves to be remembered for its whimsical singularity They had been married that evening, at the plantation called Anderson's, but the pitiless storm, regardless of the sanctity of the marriage bed, blew them from their bridal chamber; and, with relentless fury, lodged them in a pimploe hedge. In this bed of thorns they were found the next morning, incapable of manifesting those tender attentions which their new-formed relation demanded, or affording each other the assistance which their comfortless condition required.

This calamity called for the most prudent counsels to avert the consequences which were expected to result from a disaster so fatal. It was apprehended that the property which had been saved from the fury of the elements, would be wrested from the half-ruined planters, by the rapaciousness of their creditors; and that many of them, to avoid such a consummation of their misfortunes, would leave the island, with their effects, exposed to all the horrors and dangers of insurrection. Filled with these gloomy apprehensions, the governor convened the council and assembly, and stated to them his sentiments on the posture of affairs, and recommended them to devise some means of guarding

---

* Hughes's Nat. Hist. p. 25

against the evils to which they would be exposed, in case of any considerable emigration of the white inhabitants, who, partly destitute of commodious habitations, should be induced to seek an asylum elsewhere. But whatever ground there might have been for these apprehensions, no measures were taken to remove or obviate them.

A considerable quantity of sugar, which had been shipped on board the vessels in the harbour, having been lost in the late storm, and the custom-house officers refusing to admit sugar to the same amount to be exported, duty free, the assembly passed an " Act for allowing a second free entry of the dead productions of the Island, lost or taken." The season of distress was thought to be a favourable moment for endeavouring to obtain relief from the odious and oppressive impost on the merchantable commodities of the country. An humble and pathetic address was accordingly presented to the King, describing the deplorable condition to which the colony was reduced by the late destructive tempest; and stating that the entire remission of the four and a half per cent. duty, was the only means of saving the planters from impending ruin. But the pecuniary embarrassments of the extravagant, dissolute monarch, rendered him deaf to the complaints and entreaties of his injured and oppressed subjects. So far from granting the solicited immunity, the partial relief which they sought to obtain, was denied them; and the act, which had been passed for that purpose, was repealed by his Majesty's positive orders.

The situation of the Barbadians, at this juncture, was, in the highest degree, calamitous and deplorable. Their habitations were levelled with the earth; and the owners, unable to rebuild them, or dismayed at the destruction they had recently escaped; and afraid to venture their persons in houses under whose ruins they might be again overwhelmed, lived many months under no better shelter than that of huts lightly and hastily constructed. Artful and designing traders, taking advantage of the general calamity, monopolized what provisions were brought to market, and heightened the distresses of their unfortunate fellow-sufferers, by their unconscionable and villainous exactions. To repress this dangerous and iniquitous practice, the legislature inconsiderately enacted an absurd and impolitic law to prevent *forestalling, engrossing, and regrating;* a short-sighted precaution, which, however, apparently calculated to afford immediate relief, would, if strictly enforced, inevitably produce the scarcity it was intended to prevent. By this curious law none were allowed to sell or barter any foreign provisions whatever, but those to whom they were *bona fide* consigned; or who had imported them at their own risk, and upon their proper account. Thus no merchant, or shop-keeper, was permitted to purchase cargoes from the importers, for the purpose of selling them again, without incurring the heavy punishment attached to the crime of forestalling.

To check the nefarious practices of forestallers and monopolizers; to diffuse the blessings of plenty, and to avert the horrors of famine; or even to guard against the distresses attending a partial failure of the means of subsistence, are undertakings of so much humanity and beneficence, that any proposal for effecting them will readily meet the approbation of benevolent minds, and gain the applause of those superficial thinkers who compose the bulk of mankind. But these important objects are not to be attained by arbitrary prohibitions. Commerce visits only those climes in which it is cherished by the genius of liberty. Trade, like water, should be left to form its own level; and, although many moderate and sensible men may object to this maxim, as affording too great latitude to commercial monopoly, there certainly is less danger in leaving the merchant to exercise his own discretion, than in cramping and depressing the spirit of mercantile speculation, by rigorous and injudicious restrictions. High prices, and a scarcity of provisions, will be the fatal consequences of destroying or discouraging a competition in the market, by prohibitory regulations. The mutual wants of mankind, form the active principle which gives life to commerce, and by which alone it can be safely regulated.

The traders of Barbadoes may be divided into three distinct classes; the importer, the retailer, and the huckster; all of whom are useful in their several vocations. Through them, the commodities imported from abroad are dispersed among the people, in such quantities, and upon such terms, as are best suited to the necessities and conveniencies of the consumers. The two former classes are not infrequently united in the same person. They ought, however, to be considered separate. The merchant, who is engaged ni extensive concerns, and imports large cargoes of provisions, generally finds it more convenient and advantageous to dispose of his commodities to the retailer, in large quantities, and at a proportionable reduction of price, than to await the tedious and precarious sale of them to the consumer. Sometimes the case may be different; at any rate, it would be tyrannical and unjust to deprive him of the option.

The retailer, again, confined to an inland traffic, by the smallness of his capital, or a timidity to adventure, derives an advantage in buying the articles in which he deals by wholesale, and revending them at an advance, which yet exceeds not the prices at which they might have been bought from the importer, had he retailed them. His profits consist in the difference between the wholesale and retail prices. This excess is commonly less in Barbadoes than in any other part of the new World, evidently owing to the competition which prevails among that description of people in this island: a circumstance that will ever prove the most effectual counterpoise to combinations among forestallers and regrators, and is the main spring by which trade will correct its own aberrations.

To elucidate this doctrine, let us advert to a case which frequently happens. During a general scarcity of articles of the first necessity, a vessel laden with corn and flour arrives with a supercargo on board. It may not be conformable to the orders, nor suit the convenience of this factor to retail his cargo. Dispatch is the life of business, and the vessel may be required to discharge her cargo, and to return without delay; yet, were the absurd laws against monopolizing, executed with a spirit equal to that which dictated them, no merchant could venture to purchase the whole, or any part of the cargo, by wholesale to revend; because, in so doing, he would render himself obnoxious to punishment as a forestaller. The consequence is obvious; the vessel, by a ridiculous policy, is driven from our ports, and the people, in a state of *tantalism*, continue in want of those supplies which, but a moment before, had been within their reach. Or suppose the market should be sufficiently tempting to induce the supercargo to land his goods; to compensate himself for his trouble, expense, and detention, he will sell them at the highest retail prices. Thus a stranger will enjoy those lucrative advantages which, under a wiser and more equitable system, would have centered among our own countrymen.

This species of traffic which the law, under the specious pretext of preventing forestalling and regrating, most unwisely discountenances, far from being detrimental, is, in fact, highly beneficial to the public. A large capital is thus employed, which, in so small a community, would otherwise remain inactive and useless; the importer is accommodated and benefited by facilitating his sales; it gives energy to industry; affords bread to a considerable number of useful citizens; and furnishes the consumer with the articles of domestic accommodation in more convenient quantities, and as cheap as he could have purchased them from the original importer. It sometimes happens that the value of the merchandise is enhanced after getting into this intermediate channel of diffusion; but this is not so much owing to any radical defect in the system for which I contend, as to the intervention of casualties to which mercantile affairs are peculiarly liable. The prices of goods are augmented by various causes independant of monopolizers. Supplies from abroad may be intercepted by the enemy, or may experience a temporary suspension from opposing elements, and other disastrous means. In all these cases the holders of provisions will, unquestionably, embrace the favourable opportunity of reimbursing themselves for the losses which both importer and retailer too often sustain from accidents, which no human sagacity can foresee, nor human judgment prevent. And where is the harm in this? The planter strives to obtain the best price that he can get for the produce of his fields, and surely the merchant is entitled to the same privilege in the disposal of his commodities.

The distresses and difficulties under which, as we have seen, the Barbadians were, at this time, struggling, were sufficient to have affected the feelings of the most obdurate heart, but the measure of their misfortunes was not yet full. Scarcely had they recovered from the consternation into which they had been thrown by the late awful visitation of Providence, and begun to recover from their losses; to rebuild their houses; to repair their fortifications, and to provide for the security of the country before they were compelled to submit to the relentless gripe of power. The principles of commerce, until lately, had been but very imperfectly understood in England. Before the restoration, the important objects which occupied the thoughts of both King and parliament, afforded either but little leisure for attending to the minor considerations of colonial affairs. From the freedom of trade which Barbadoes, thus left to herself, was permitted to enjoy, she attained a degree of prosperity almost unparalleled in the annals of mankind. The commencement of the Navigation Act, however essential to the interests of the empire at large, is the memorable epoch whence we may date the rapid decline of her population, and consequently of her strength and opulence.

After the restoration, the ministers of Charles, sensible of the value of the colonies, prudently determined to act upon Cromwell's plan with regard to navigation and trade. Great Britain now began to perceive the advantages arising from the exclusive right of colonial supply; and, in the same spirit which dictated the navigation laws, sought to

CHAP. III. draw into her own bosom the important benefits of the
1678.   African trade; but absurdly confined to the Royal African
Company, established under the patronage of the Duke of
York, the emoluments of this lucrative branch of commerce, which, according to every principle of true policy,
ought to have been laid open to the nation at large. The
exclusive charter granted to this company for supplying the
West Indies with negroes, operated most powerfully against
the interest of the Barbadians, and accomplished the ruin
of many who were recovering from their recent losses. They
were no longer allowed to import their own slaves, or to
purchase them from the Dutch ; but were compelled to submit to the rapacious and exorbitant demands of the new
association.

Sir Jonathan Atkins received the most positive orders to
seize and confiscate all vessels, with their cargoes, belonging to private adventurers, engaged in this prohibited traffic. In addition to these directions, the Warwick man of
war was constantly stationed at Barbadoes for the express
purpose of seizing all interlopers, as they were called, in
the trade to Guinea. These rigorous orders were executed
with equal accuracy and severity. All vessels belonging to
private merchants met with on the coast of Africa, or found
in the West Indies with slaves on board, were captured
with as little hesitation as if they had been the property of
open enemies ; and were condemned with as little ceremony

and reluctance, in the court of Vice-admiralty, in which the governor acted in the double capacity of prosecutor and of judge*. By these arbitrary proceedings, many opulent families were reduced to a state of indigence; and each succeeding day produced fresh bankruptcies among the merchants. At length the grievance became so intolerable, that Sir Jonathan Atkins, shocked at the injustice and oppression under which the people groaned, and to which, in obedience to his orders, he was forced to contribute, requested permission to resign his government and return to England.

Notwithstanding these accumulated misfortunes and oppressions, the attainment of Barbadoes to her natural parent remained firm and unshaken. Under all their injuries and distresses, the legislature exerted a laudable spirit in rebuilding their dismantled fortifications; though, in the prosecution of this commendable design, they were under the painful necessity of imposing additional burthens of sugar and negro labour, on the people, to defray the charges incident to the undertaking.

In religion, as in politics, the sentiments of the Barbadians borrowed their tone from the doctrines and opinions which prevailed among their transatlantic fellow subjects. The discontents and apprehensions which agitated the pub-

---

* Univ. Hist. vol. 41, p. 152.

lic mind in England, concerning the King's prepossession for the Romish communion, and the inconsiderate bigotry of the Duke of York, produced correspondent sensations in Barbadoes. On the discovery made by Titus Oates, and other miscreants, of the pretended plot formed by the Roman Catholics for the subversion of the Protestant religion, the Barbadians, not to be behind hand in suitable endeavours to guard the constitution, both civil and ecclesiastical, from the dangers which threatened them, passed an act to enforce the statute of Great Britain, for preventing the dangers which may happen from Popish rescuants. Their zeal for the true faith was not confined to this attempt to repress the errors of popery. The Quakers had been assiduously endeavouring to convert the negroes; but, as it was apprehended that the promulgation of their pacific tenets might endanger the safety of a colony exposed to invasion, the legislature prohibited, by law, the attendance of slaves on the meetings of that mild and inoffensive society. To preserve the minds of the rising generation from improper impressions, a clause was added, restricting the keeping of schools for the instruction of youth, to such persons only as should take the state oaths, and be duly licensed by the commander in chief. This, says an eminent historian*, was a precaution not quite impolitic among

---

* Vide Univ. Hist. vol. 41, p. 152.

planters, to whom labour was of more utility than learning. But it should be observed, that the object of the law was not discouragement of learning, but to take the business of education out of the hands of those dissenters, whose principles were supposed to be hostile to the establishments of government in church and state.

While other religious sects were thus restrained, the civil rights of the Jews were very properly extended. This extraordinary people, once the most favoured nation of the only true God; at one time groaning under the cruelty and oppression of their Egyptian task-masters, then desolating the kingdoms that lay in their way to the land of promise; alternately abject in slavery and tyrannical in authority; once a powerful nation, now a tribe of fugitives, wandering from pole to pole; in all their migrations honourably distinguished by their invincible attachment to the religion of their forefathers; in all their changes affording the most irrefragable evidence of the Divine truths, which sceptics vainly oppose; here sought an asylum from the odium and detestation which universally, though unjustly, pursued them whithersoever they travelled. Here, too, these unfortunate victims of bigotry and intolerance, were persecuted and oppressed. Their testimony had long been rejected in the courts of law; but a more enlightened policy prevailing over an unjust prejudice, they were now admitted, by a law which was passed for that purpose, to

CHAP. III. give their testimony in all civil suits, and not otherwise,
~
1680.   upon oath, on the five books of Moses, according to the
tenets of their religion*.

---

* The Abbé Raynal relates, that the Jews of Jamaica wholly disregarded the
solemn obligation of an oath thus administered. " A magistrate imagined, that
this evil might arise from the circumstance of the Bible, which was presented to
them, being in English. It was then determined, that they should, in future, take
their oaths upon the Hebrew text, and after this precaution perjuries became infinitely less frequent." HIST. OF THE EAST AND WEST INDIES, vol. 6, p. 322. This
was a species of casuistry worthy only of the most profligate of mankind.

CHAP.

CHAP. IV.

SIR RICHARD DUTTON'S TYRANNICAL ADMINISTRATION—AP-
POINTS SIR JOHN WITHAM, DEPUTY GOVERNOR—NEW DUTY ON
SUGAR—DISPUTES BETWEEN DUTTON AND WITHAM—GOVERNOR
RECALLED—SUCCEEDED BY EDWIN STEDE—A CONSPIRACY
AMONG THE SLAVES—A REVIEW OF THE SLAVE LAWS.

CHARLES II. having formed the dangerous design of
subverting the constitution in church and state, and of
establishing Popery and despotism on the ruins of civil liberty and rational religion, Sir Richard Dutton, an abject
minion of the court, was selected as a proper instrument
for effecting the purpose of the royal brothers, and was,
therefore, appointed to the government of Barbadoes. The
names of the members of his Majesty's council were now,
for the second time, inserted in the governor's commission* ;
with directions, in case of the death or absence of his excellency, that the government should devolve on the senior
member of that board. Sir Richard arrived at Barbadoes.

CHAP. IV.
1680.

---

* These were Henry Walrond, J. Reid, Sir T. Thornhill, J. Gibbes, Francis Bond,
John Farmer, George Lillington, G. Andrews, W. Sharpe, Tobias Frere, Michael
Terril, and the Rev. William Walker.

CHAP. IV.
1681.

on the seventh day of March, and was received with the most lively expressions of loyalty and satisfaction; which, as is very common, produced no adequate return of gratitude. He immediately issued writs for a general election; and, on the meeting of the new assembly*, prevailed on the house to insert a clause in the militia law, requiring the men to wear scarlet uniforms. With such trifling innovations were men then displeased, that this was generally complained of as an unnecessary and expensive regulation.

The annals of this period are barren of any interesting particulars respecting the public concerns of the colony. It is briefly stated, that the conduct of Governor Dutton was so extremely tyrannical and oppressive, that many families, unable to endure the rigour of his administration, abandoned the country, and sought elsewhere an asylum from the persecution which they suffered at home. This disastrous emigration required legislative interposition to check the consequent decline of population; an act was therefore passed, to regulate the issuing of tickets for persons intending to leave the island.

---

* The members present on the return of the writs were, for *St. Michael's*, George Peers, William Wheeler; *Christ Church*, T. Maxwell, Daniel Hooper; *St. Philip's*, W. Fortescue, H. Markland; *St. John's*, John Leslie, James Colleton; *St. George's*, Richard Salter, Miles Toppin; *St. Joseph's*, John Holder, Henry Gallop; *St. Andrew's*, William Dotin, Richard Walter; *St. Thomas's*, Jonathan Downes, T. Sadlier; *St. James's*, Abel Alleyne, W. Holder; *St. Peter's*, Samuel Maynard, Robert Harrison; *St. Lucy's*, T. Merrick, John Gibbes.

Charles II. was, at this time, much perplexed with the number of petitions presented to him from all parts of the kingdom, insisting on a new session of parliament; complaining of the increase of popery; and deprecating the dangers apprehended from plots continually forming by persons of the Romish communion. Unable to withstand or to elude these importunate, and, as they were termed, disrespectful solicitations, the court party had recourse to counter-addresses, professing the utmost abhorrence of those who presumptuously endeavoured to encroach on the royal prerogative, by an improper interference in public measures. Dutton, to manifest his zeal in the service of the crown, prevailed on the assembly of Barbadoes to transmit one of these *abhorring* addresses to the throne; which was honoured by his Majesty with the most particular marks of approbation.

The favourable reception with which this address was distinguished, encouraged the grand-jury to emulate the loyal example of the assembly. They accordingly prepared a pompous address to the King, in which his Majesty was congratulated on the vigour and prudence of his representative *in stifling and suppressing faction and fanaticism in embryo.* The history of the British colonies affords many instances of the facility with which similar addresses are obtained from the contemptible sycophants, who wish to raise themselves to a temporary distinction on the ruin of their country, by flattering the most weak and profligate

men who ever swayed the rod of power. The jury proceeded to inform his Majesty, " that their minds had been infinitely ruffled and disturbed at the notice which they had received of the many attempts and offers lately made by the *rebellious heat of some spirits hatched in hell*, to shake his Majesty's throne ;" and concluded with declaring themselves " *hearty lovers and warm admirers of his dearest brother*.*"   Sir Richard Dutton's affairs requiring his presence
May 3.   in England, this notable address, on his leaving the island, was committed to his care.   Previous to his departure, and in direct opposition to the royal instruction concerning the succession to the government, Dutton appointed Sir John Witham, deputy-governor; restricting him from enacting any new laws, or even from calling an assembly †.

1684.   The governor returned the next year, and endeavoured
Sept. 10.   to acquire an ill-founded popularity, by assuring the assembly, that the King, ever willing to lessen the burthens of his faithful subjects, was ready to commute the four and a half per cent. duty, on fair and equal terms of mutual accommodation.   Rejoiced at the prospect of even a partial relief from this hateful and oppressive impost, the council and assembly proposed to farm the duty at six thousand pounds sterling a year.   For this purpose, they passed a bill, laying a tax of twenty-one pence an acre on all

---

* Univ. Hist. vol. 41, p. 153.   † Mem. of Barb. p. 44.

land belonging to persons possessed of not less than ten
acres, and appointed John Codrington, treasurer, to collect
the money, and remit the stipulated sum to England.   But
the pleasing illusion soon vanished.   On the act being sent
home, for his Majesty's confirmation, the lords of the committee for trade and plantations, to whose consideration it
was referred, reported that the commissioners were then
incapable of making an accurate estimate of the annual
produce of the duty ; but, from the best information which
they could obtain, they were of opinion that it was worth
from eight to ten thousand pounds sterling, at least, clear
of all expense attending the collection.   The offer of the
legislature was therefore rejected; and the bill which had
passed the two houses was repealed by order of the King.

James II. having, on the death of his brother, succeeded
to the throne, his accession was celebrated by Sir Richard
Dutton with unusual pomp and magnificence.   But all the
demonstrations of joy with which the news of this event
was received in Barbadoes, were insufficient to conciliate
the favour of government.   The wealth acquired by the
West Indians, with which they made then no small parade
in England, attracted the notice, and probably the envy,
of people in power; and the produce of their plantations
was deemed a legitimate object of taxation.   Sugar, being
a luxury of life, was supposed able to bear additional burthens with least inconvenience to the consumers ; while,
from its general use, the tax was likely to be more produc-

tive than any other that could be proposed. Parliament, therefore, laid a duty of two shillings and four-pence upon every hundred weight of Muscovado sugar, and seven shillings upon refined. Thus was laid the foundation of a mode of taxation, on which succeeding ministers have reared a fabric of colonial oppression, as ruinous, in the apprehension of the best-informed West Indians, as it is partial and unjust.

The Barbadians were far from beholding, with indifference, a measure, which, by lessening the value of their staple products, would ultimately depreciate that of their estates. They remonstrated against this new grievance, but with no better success than that which attended their former complaints. If new taxes were absolutely necessary for the support of government, it was contended that such imposts ought to be preferred as would equally affect all commodities; that a small advance upon the customs would be equally productive, and less oppressive, than a heavy impost upon any particular article, as the general participation, in that case, would render the tax comparatively easy; and, however unnecessary, its operation would be less insupportable than when confined to the cane planters alone. But all reasoning, or complaining, was precluded by the predilection which the ministry betrayed for their project. They could only be prevailed on to promise, in his Majesty's name, that if the tax should be found oppressive to the planters, it should be taken off. But when the planters claimed the performance of this engagement, and endeavoured to prove the injustice and impolicy of an impost so disproportioned to their ability, and the circumstances of the country, they were briefly told, " That it was very indecent, not to say undutiful, to tax the King with his promise*.

Sir Richard Dutton seems, upon all occasions, to have encouraged every proposal for burthening and distressing the people placed under his care; and, although his administration has been generally reputed grievous and oppressive, the House of Assembly, on his late return from England, voted Captain Jones, of the Diamond frigate, a present of one hundred pounds, for having brought over the governor†; a circumstance which, considering the character of the man, is scarcely credible, if, besides positive evidence, the fact were not corroborated by many later instances, of the respect and adulation with which the worst rulers are treated by men whose rank and station, in the community, ought to place them above every sinister consideration of hope or fear, and render them the faithful, as they are the delegated, guardians of their country's rights.

Upon Sir Richard Dutton's late return to England, his Majesty was pleased to order, that one-half the salary and perquisites, during his absence, should be paid to the de-

---

* Univ. Hist. vol. 41. p. 154.   † Hall's Laws of Barb. p. 484.

puty-governor. Such an arrangement was by no means agreeable to his excellency's mercenary disposition; and With m, who was little disposed to relinquish the reward of his services, incurred the enmity of his chief, by insisting on a strict compliance with his Majesty's favourable intention towards him. Nor was Dutton long at a loss for a pretext to evade the payment of the money. He accused Witham of mal-administration; that he had omitted to take the usual oath for observing trade and navigation; that he had assumed the title of lieutenant-governor; and altered decrees of the Court of Chancery in his chamber. Upon these frivolous charges, Witham was committed to prison, by an order of council*, and bound to appear at the next court of grand sessions, where he was tried on three sepa-

---

* It is now clearly ascertained, that the council do not possess this power over the liberties of their fellow-subjects. " Commitments of the subject for arbitrary causes and contempts of their board, which they were suffered to order till very lately, are now entirely at an end. The privy council of Great Britain is found to possess no greater authority in this case than a common justice of the peace, with this further limitation, that the persons they commit cannot legally be apprehended, in the first instance, by their warrant, except for treasonable practices, or designs against the state, either violently presumed, or actually charged upon oath. For the explication of this we are indebted to Lord Camden, in the case of Wilkes. In the case of Mr. Douglas, *of Jamaica,* who was imprisoned by a warrant of the privy-council of that island, and released by the chief justice, on his writ of *habeas corpus,* they were adjudged, by the supreme court, to have no right of restraining public liberty, vested in them by the laws and constitution of their country."

LONG's HIST. OF JAMAICA, vol. 1. p. 174.

rate indictments, convicted, and condemned to pay a fine of eleven hundred pounds sterling. From this sentence Witham appealed to the justice of his sovereign; and the governor, with Mr. Henry Walrond, chief justice of the court of grand sessions, were immediately ordered home to vindicate their conduct. Upon a full investigation of the affair before the King and council, the sentence of the court was annulled, and the fine remitted.

Witham, not satisfied with this victory, immediately commenced a prosecution against Dutton and Walrond, as president of the council, for an assault and false imprisonment. The governor, in his defence, alledged, that the plaintiff's incarceration had been inflicted, with the concurrence of the council, for malversation in the execution of his office as deputy-governor. The council, it was contended, were competent to commit for offences proved to their satisfaction; and that the inhabitants of Barbadoes were not entitled to the benefit of any particular statute, or even of the common law of England; but that they might be governed by any rule or ordinance that his Majesty should think proper to direct*. To this it was re-

---

* " At a committee of the lords of council, March 11, 1680, their lordships referred this question to the attorney and solicitor general; whether his Majesty's subjects inhabiting and trading to Jamaica, had a right to the laws of England as Englishmen? To which it was answered, The people of Jamaica have no right to be go-

plied, that Sir John was responsible to his Sovereign alone for any misdemeanour of which he might have been guilty in his government: that after the King had given to any people under his allegiance, or subjection, a constitution of their own, no succeeding monarch had a right to alter it without an act of parliament; and, therefore, as the inhabitants of Barbadoes were, by the charter granted to the Earl of Carlisle, invested with all the rights, privileges and franchises of British subjects, they were not to be governed by the laws of England, but by their own particular laws and customs. The court concurring in this reasoning, judgment was given for Sir John Witham; but it was afterwards, in the 5th of William and Mary, reversed by the House of Peers. President Walrond was yet more unfortunate; for although a verdict of only thirty pounds damages was given against him, the suit terminated in his ruin. His long detention from home, the expences of the suit and other charges incident to an European voyage, proved a load too heavy for his fortune to bear. As some reparation for the injury he had sustained, and as a tribute of gratitude for his former meritorious services, the assembly, on his return, voted him a present of five hundred pounds; and added their testimony to the integrity and rectitude of his

---

verned by the laws of England, but by such laws as are made there and established by his Majesty's authority."

EDWARDS'S HIST. OF THE WEST INDIES, vol. 1, p. 304.

conduct in the particular affair which had drawn on him the prosecution that had ended so fatally*.

Notwithstanding the King's order that the executive authority, in case of the Governor's death or absence, should devolve on the senior member of council, Sir Richard, as a fresh proof of his hostility to the interests of the country, on his being recalled, appointed Mr. Edwin Stede, deputy-governor. This gentleman had officiated in the several characters of his Majesty's casual receiver, the governor's secretary, a commissioner for collecting the duty of four and a half per cent. and agent for the African company, whose measures had been so inimical to the prosperity of Barbadoes. To complete the climax, he was soon confirmed in his present situation by a commission from his Majesty, constituting him commander in chief.

July 15.

The rash and ill-concerted enterprise against James II.

---

* Univ. Hist. vol. 41, p. 154. Mem. of Barb. p. 44. This transaction is very incorrectly related by the compilers of the Universal History. They assert, contrary to the plain matter of fact, that Colonel Walrond, who had been left deputy-governor by Dutton, fell under his displeasure, and was sent to England to answer a charge against him, on account of a trial before a court of oyer and terminer, in which Walrond presided. This inconsistent story is implicitly adopted by the author of the *Short History*, p. 37, who asserts, that Walrond's prosecutor was vigorously supported by the governor. Strange that Dutton should have supported his bitterest enemy in a prosecution against the man who had promoted his views! I have been enabled to correct these misstatements on the authority of Hall, the editor of the laws, who, in his manuscript account of the first settlement of Barbadoes, gives the relation of this affair, which I have adopted as the most accurate and consistent.

CHAP. IV.
1680.

which terminated in the destruction of the Duke of Monmouth and his adherents, having been frustrated by the bravery and activity of the king's troops, many of the wretched victims of ambition and tyranny were transported to Barbadoes. Anxious to display their zeal and loyalty, the assembly passed a law for governing and retaining within the island all such rebel convicts as, by his Majesty's most sacred order, have been, or shall be, transported to this place*." By the rigorous provisions of this statute, the condition of these men, whose only crime was prematurely attempting to do that which, in three short years afterwards, was happily accomplished by the Prince of Orange, with the approbation and assistance of a large majority of the nation, was rendered scarcely less miserable than that of the plantation slaves.

Notwithstanding the appearance of attachment to the Prince on the throne, the sentiments of some of the principal men in the country were, in reality, extremely inimical to the existing government, both in England and Barbadoes. Among these, Sir Timothy Thornhill, a member of council, and major-general of the militia; a gentleman most deservedly possessed of great popularity, having expressed his opinion on the state of public affairs with more

---

* Hall's Laws, p. 484. This act was repealed after the revolution, by an order from his Majesty, for the enlargement of the rebels transported to Barbadoes.

warmth than discretion, was prosecuted by order of the governor for sedition, and condemned to pay a fine of five hundred pounds to the king, and fifteen hundred pounds to his excellency. Thornhill appealed to the King in council, but without success: the judgment of the court was affirmed*.

Mr. Stede had enjoyed the honour of his appointment nearly two years, as all his predecessors had done, without receiving any substantial reward from the country; but at length he had the address to ingratiate himself with the council and assembly, who generously made him a present of one thousand pounds sterling, which act of generosity was successively repeated in the latter years of his administration. A precedent was thus established, pregnant with much future mischief and internal dissension. The Barbadians can, with little propriety, complain that none of the patriotic purposes for which the four and a half duty was imposed, have been complied with, since they so eagerly contribute to the abuse of the grant, by providing otherwise for the service to which it ought to be applied. This seasonable donative enabled Mr. Stede to support the dignity of his station with suitable splendour; and was the more acceptable, as he soon had occasion to make a grand display of hospitality. The Duke of Albemarle, on his pas-

1687.

---

* Hall's first settlement of Barb. p. 30. M.S.

sage to Jamaica, of which he had been recently appointed governor*, having stopped at Barbadoes, was received at Fontabelle with all the honours due to his rank and quality; and was entertained by the governor several days with great pomp and magnificence.

1688.
The island was the next year alarmed by the report of a conspiracy among the slaves, to make themselves masters of the country, by murdering all the male inhabitants, or reducing them to slavery, and reserving the women for the gratification of their brutal appetites. The accomplishment of this dreadful design was happily prevented by the timely discovery of the plot; and about twenty of the most daring conspirators were sacrificed to the public safety. The calamity from which the people had been thus providentially delivered seems to have awakened the legislature to a sense of their danger, and the necessity of encouraging the population of the country. To this end they

---

* This nobleman affords a remarkable instance of the mutability of fortune, the vanity of human grandeur, and the fatal effects of vicious habits and profligate manners. He was the only son of General Monk, the principal agent in the restoration of Charles II. The services performed by his father were rewarded with a dukedom, the garter, and a princely fortune; but the son, reduced to indigence by extravagance and debauchery, was compelled to solicit bread from James II. who, to be freed from his importunities, bestowed on him the government of Jamaica, where, dying without issue, the title became extinct; and the honours acquired by the virtue of the father, were lost by the vices of the degenerate son.

enacted a law " to encourage the importation of Christian servants, and for retaining them within the island." Whatever might have been the advantages proposed by this plan it was far from affording an effectual counterpoise to that preponderance which the negroes must necessarily possess in the scale of numbers.

To provide a remedy suitable to the magnitude of this evil, the best policy which could be adopted in a country where slavery prevails, is to hold out every possible encouragement to that hardy and useful, though humble, class of people, known by the colonial appellation of the tenantry. The only legitimate aim of human politic is the extension of human felicity; and this cannot be effected except by the encrease of numbers, provided with the comfortable means of subsistence*. To acquire and maintain an extent of population essential to the security and prosperity of the country, the rich, whose individu interest is inseparably connected with the public welfare, should be made to yield, in some means, to the support and accommodation of the poor. The proprietors of plantations may be compelled, by the militia law, instead of billetted men, to furnish tenants, in proportion to their quantity of land, who should be legally confirmed in the unmo-

---

* Vide Paley's Philosophy, vol. 2, p. 345.

CHAP. IV.
1688.

lested enjoyment of their little tenements*. It was the wish of Henry IV. of France, surnamed the Father of his People, that he might live to see a fowl in the pot of every peasant in his kingdom.   Let it be the aim of every Barbadian, emulous of the same glorious appellation, to erect a cottage over the head of every peasant in Barbadoes, and gratitude will invigorate the arm under which the lordly possessor will find his best security in the hour of danger. The trifling property thus bestowed on the humble husbandman, the lowly roof endeared to him by the society of a wife and children, the partners of his toils and the solace of his days, would bind him, by the most invincible ties to his native soil; and impel him, when led on by his generous landlord, to risque his life with ardour, in defence of a country to which he is attached by the most indissoluble connexions.

---

* The present militia law has made some provisions for tenants; but it seems to have been ineffectual. They either eluded with facility, or violated with impunity. On some plantations, without regard justice, policy, or humanity, the tenants have been wantonly and cruelly driven from their and sham leases given to the white servants for the vacant tenements. In others, the poor tenant, besides his personal services, is compelled to provide himself with uniform, arms, and ammunition, at his own cost, which is more, in many instances, than the rent of the barren heath which he occupies is worth. Some men have a strange propension to evade the legal institutes of their country, merely to shew their superior cunning and dexterity. But what minds must these men possess, who can find satisfaction in such pitiful evasions; who, while they waste thousands in riot and debauchery, deny bread to the labourer, and refuse rest and shelter to the houseless wanderer?

These are the men on whose strength and courage we may rely with confidence to defend us from all attempts of our enemies, foreign or domestic. Their humility renders them more tractable and obedient, under the restraints of military discipline, than the wealthy or luxurious, whose false, mistaken pride, cannot submit to the subordination necessary in the field or the camp; and whose effeminacy renders them incapable of martial exercises. It is not enough to permit the poor to erect their temperary habitations on useless skirts of barren land. They should be encouraged to work, and punctually paid for their labour. Slaves should no longer be employed in mechanical occupations; those employments should be reserved for poor freemen, whence they might derive the means of subsistence, and the public enjoy the benefit arising from a general diffusion of the wages of industry. In Jamaica there exists a law to oblige all owners of negroes to employ one white servant for every thirty slaves; one to every hundred and fifty head of cattle; one to every tavern; and a like proportion for every boat, wherry, and canoe*. This law,

---

* This law is justly commended by a judicious historian, thoroughly acquainted with the true interests of the colonies. *Vide Long's Hist. of Jamaica, vol. 1, p 310.* His remarks on this subject are too diffuse to be inserted in a note. I can only, therefore, recommend his book to the perusal of my reader, as a performance which, though less elegant than Edwards's splendid History of the West Indies, contains more useful information on colonial politics, than any other work which has come within my observation.

though perverted into a mere regulation of finance, is admirably calculated to preserve the legitimate population of the country ; and, under the present circumstances of Barbadoes, may, perhaps, be thought worthy of adoption, with a penalty sufficient to enforce its observance.

It was at this juncture, and upon this occasion, that the legislature of Barbadoes enacted that famous statute, Number Eighty-two, for the government of negroes, which has of late years become a popular theme of declamation in England; and subjected the peaceable, unoffending West Indians, to the most illiberal invectives and the most virulent abuse. By this law, among many provisions made for the prevention of crimes and the punishment of offences; which, to the honour of the people, are executed with a spirit as mild and lenient as the object is just and laudable, it was ordained, " That if any slave, under punishment by his master, or his order, shall suffer in life or member, no one shall be liable to any fine for it. But if any person wantonly or cruelly kill his own slave, he shall pay into the public treasury fifteen pounds*. If he intentionally kill the slave of another, besides paying the owner double the value,

* Though the punishment here prescribed, may appear disproportioned to the enormity of the crime, it should be remembered, that in a country where slaves compose the principal part of the property of the inhabitants : and where their labour, or hire, is, in many cases, the only means of their owner's support; the loss of a slave is, of itself, a very heavy forfeiture, without any additional penalty. It never once entered into the imagination of the legislature, that any reasonable being,

and twenty-five pounds to the treasurer, he shall be bound to his good behaviour, during the pleasure of the governor and council. And if any person kill another man's slave by accident, he shall only be liable to the owner's action at law*. But if any person kill a negro, by night, out of the road, stealing or attempting to steal his provisions or other goods, he shall not be accountable for it†."

The lenity of this law has been generally condemned with indecent asperity by the humane, mistaken, and misinformed Europeans, for its reputed insufficiency to afford protection to a hapless race of beings. Nor is it surprising

---

governed by those considerations of interest which commonly influence mankind, would wilfully sacrifice the life of a valuable slave. People abroad may indulge their talents for conjecture, and reason hypothetically concerning the reputed inhumanity of the West Indians ; but, happily, such instances of extreme cruelty are unknown in Barbadoes.

* A sufficient punishment, surely, for accidental homicide! "This homicide is not felony, because it is not accompanied with a felonious intent, which is necessary in every felony." (1 *Hawkins* 75.) "But in all cases of homicide, by misadventure, it is nevertheless a tresspass, and the person hurt shall recover his damages ; for though the chance excuse from felony, yet it excuseth not from trespass." (1 *Hale's Hist.* 472.) *Burn's Justice, v. 2. p. 505.*

† "If a thief be found breaking up, and he be smitten, that he die, there shall no blood be spilt for him." *Exodus, c.* xxii. *v.* 2. "If any evil disposed person shall feloniously attempt to *rob,* or murder, any person, in any dwelling-house or *highway,* or feloniously attempt to break any dwelling-house *in the night time,* and shall happen in such felonious attempt to be slain, the slayer shall be discharged, and forfeit no lands or goods." *Burn's Justice, v.* 2. *p.* 502.

that a nation, habituated to the contemplation of public executions, without perceiving that crimes are not diminished by excessive severity, should erroneously conclude that no punishment, short of death, is capable of restraining the violence and impetuosity of turbulent, licentious man. But the children of the sun, incapable of those deliberate acts of cruelty, injustice, and treachery, which are frequently perpetrated by the gloomy phlegmatic inhabitants of more northern climates, have found a milder system of jurisprudence, sufficiently efficacious in promoting the ultimate object of all penal laws, the prevention of crimes.

It is not pretended that no murders whatever have been committed. I only mean to assert, and I do it with confidence and exultation, that they are less frequent in Barbadoes than in any county of Great Britain, or, perhaps, in any part of the world, where they are capitally punished. The population of Barbadoes consists of seventy-five thousand blacks, and fifteen thousand white inhabitants; consequently, allowing the provocations offered by both classes to be equal, the number of negro homicides committed by freemen, compared with those of the white, should be in the proportion of five to one. But, however incredible it may appear to our European calumniators, it is an indisputable fact, that homicide among the white inhabitants, though far from being a common occurrence, and notwithstanding it is usually punished here in the same exemplary manner as at the Old Bailey, is yet a much more frequent offence than the murder of a slave by a free man.

In a period of thirty-four years, there have been no authentic accounts of more than *sixteen* negroes killed by white men, and of these only six come within the legal description of that species of homicide which even the English criminal judicature would punish with death. Lord Seaforth, during his administration, instituted a minute inquiry into offences of this sort; and, though he employed no ordinary degree of industry in pursuing the inquisition, *three* instances of extreme cruelty were all that he could ascertain to have been committed for several years. Now let the candid and impartial reader take these facts into consideration, and then let him say in what happy region of the habitable globe it is possible to meet with so few instances of criminality, in the same space of time, among a people so numerous. Such is the lamentable frailty of imperfect man, that in every society, composed of such fallible beings, whether under the rigour of the British criminal code, or the milder influence of West Indian policy, offences *must come*. That they are punished, implies but little merit in the system of legislation by which the punishment is sanctioned, if they are not prevented; or, at least, rendered comparatively few.

But all discussion on this subject is now at an end. The legislature have passed a law to punish the wilful murder of a slave with death. Nor was it from any want of humanity, or regard for justice, that this measure has been so long delayed. The infrequency of the crime proved the efficiency of the existing law, in restraining the hand of violence as effectually as could have been done by a more sanguinary mode of punishment. Barbadians require not the terror of capital inflictions to restrain them from those atrocities which disturb the domestic peace and happiness of private society, in nations who extol the perfection of their criminal code. In the natural mildness and benignity of their tempers, the weak and defenseless find security and protection from violence and injustice.

In a review of this memorable law, the cruelty and injustice of some sections cannot escape observation. The negro is here denied the natural right of defending himself against the attacks of his fellow slave. In assaults and affrays the innocent and the guilty are equally liable to punishment; and in homicide here are no legal gradations of guilt. The slave, who kills another, shall surely die. Self-preservation is nature's primary law. When God bestowed existence upon man, he gave him the right of self-defence; and no human jurisdiction has a legitimate power to deprive him of this sacred privilege. This law of nature, being coeval with mankind, and dictated by God himself, is of superior obligation to any other. No human laws are of any validity, if contrary to this*. Such a law is an

---

* Blackstone's Comm. vol. 1. p. 40. Lord Chief Justice Hobart declares, that even an act of parliament, made contrary to natural justice, is void in itself.

outrage on the natural feelings of mankind, and repugnant to every principle of natural and political justice.

It cannot be dissembled, that some other clauses of the statute evince a harshness and severity unworthy of a christian legislature. Capital offences are created with a facility and heedlessness highly culpable, and the most shocking and immoderate punishments are annexed to trivial offences. It is enacted, That if any slave strike a christian, he shall, for the first offence, be severely whipped, by order of the justice of the peace to whom the complaint shall have been made *upon oath;* and for the second offence he shall, besides being whipped, have his nose slit, and be burned in the face with an hot iron. This clause breathes the sanguinary spirit of a Nero or Domitian; but let me add, with conscious exultation, that it is enforced with the mildness and clemency of a Titus. A single instance of the horrid infliction prescribed for the second offence, is unknown to the oldest inhabitant of the country. It is admitted even by an enemy*, that the present race of Barbadians is more humane, and incomparably more enlightened, than their ancestors. The generous natives of the torrid Zone, whose hearts are as warm as the atmosphere

---

* Dickson, vide Letters on Slavery, p. 145.

CHAP. IV.
1688.

in which they breathe, disdain to oppress the sable labourer who contributes to their luxury, or provides for their subsistence. But this is not enough. It is not enough that this barbarous law should be neglected; it ought to be expunged from the statute book. But while, from the purest motives of humanity, I reprobate this sanguinary clause, with what propriety, may I be permitted to ask, can those condemn it, who, in a land of freedom, sanction and practise punishments more severe for offences not more atrocious? Is the soldier, who fights the battles of his country, and lifts his hand against his commanding officer, more criminal, or punished with less severity, than the audacious slave who strikes his master? Is the gallant sailor, who upholds the nation's glory, and protects it by his valour and prowess, subject to a milder punishment, if, in a moment of unguarded resentment, he should strike the officer whose orders he is bound to obey? No, an ignominious death awaits the rash offender: his former services are forgotten, and he is consigned to a premature grave for his temerity, while the slave lives to repeat his crime and exult in his audacity.

Of the mode of proceeding on the trial of slaves, it may be proper to take some notice in this place. In all common cases, a justice of the peace is empowered to hear the complaint, and proceed to judgment; and, on the most ordinary and trivial aggressions, the evidence of the first gentleman in Barbadoes, against the worst negro, *is given on oath.* But in cases of felony, two justices of the peace are required to take cognizance of the offence, and to summon a jury of three freeholders; not merely of the vicinity, lest any partiality should be used in the selection, but who are nearest to the spot were the felonious act was committed. Here the same formality is practised as in all other judicial proceedings. The accused is confronted with his accuser and the witnesses; he has counsel assigned him at the expense of his master, and every means known to the courts at Westminster Hall, are employed in the full and fair investigation of the charge. When the evidence is closed, the magistrates and the jury, collectively, are left to decide; and a single dissentient absolves the prisoner from guilt. If he is convicted, there yet remains another chance of saving him from the sentence of the law, the right of appeal to the governor and council; a right which is usually exercised, whenever there is the least prospect of its being successful.

To this form of trial, the only objection which can possibly exist, is to the number of the jury; and certainly it would be more conformable to the principles of English jurisprudence, were the jury, on these occasions, composed of the same number of freeholders as in other cases. Yet no inconvenience has ever been experienced from this colonial deviation from this fundamental rule of criminal judicature. Infallibility is not the property of any precise number of persons. Truth may be as thoroughly investigated, and justice as faithfully administered, by five as by twelve. Let me not be misunderstood. I mean not to speak lightly, nor irreverently, of the established mode of trial by jury. With enthusiastic veneration, I regard it as the palladium of all our civil and political rights. These remarks are merely intended to establish this position, that the form prescribed by the colonial law, for the trial of slaves, is, in all respects, competent to the regular and impartial administration of justice; and candid men may probably think, that a tribunal, consisting of two magistrates and three jurymen, may be as capable of deciding justly, as the military and naval courts martial, which are allowed to decide upon the lives of freemen.

To the efficiency of the code of Barbadoes for the protection of slaves it is objected, that it allows not the evidence of coloured people, in any cause of complaint against the white inhabitants. Even the advocates for the admission of such testimony seem startled at the extravagance of their own proposition, and suggest, by way of modification, that the testimony of two or more negroes should be made equivalent to that of one white person, and that such as profess christianity might be sworn on the Evangelists. God forbid that such a direful calamity should befall this happy land. The avenging sword of the conqueror; the famine that spreads desolation in its progress; or the pestilence that precipitates thousands to eternity, is scarcely more terrible to the imagination than the idea of admitting seventy or eighty thousand heathen slaves to bear witness against their christian masters. A proposal so preposterous can originate only in the most consummate ignorance of the character of the negroes.

They are pagans in the most extensive signification of that opprobrious appellative. Without even the advantage of idolatry, they have no system of morality, no sense of religion, nor faith in its doctrines; their creed is witchcraft, and their only religious rite the practice of Obeah. Travellers report, that the Africans are believers in the Supreme being; that they have modes of worship, and many religious ceremonies. But those who have been brought to Barbadoes seem to have left their national faith and household goods behind; and, what is far more unfortunate, they have adopted no others in their stead. Some, indeed, profess Christianity, that is, they have been baptized, but their hearts are as void of any religious impressions as if they had continued in the wilds of Africa. Frequent attempts have been made by some humane owners to convert their favourite slaves to Christianity, and though many of them are treated with parental fondness and indulgence, no benefits have been derived from the pious endeavours to effect their conversion.

It was laid down by Lord Coke, that an infidel cannot be received as a witness; and in a suit for a divorce in Doctor's Commons, the evidence of a negro, in much later times, was rejected, because he was not of the Christian religion. Again, in the case of Admiral Matthews against the India Company, in the Exchequer, the testimony of Orangee, a black man, was rejected, by the advice of the Court of King's Bench, upon the same principle. It seems, however, to be generally admitted, that heathens and idolaters may be sworn upon what they consider the most sacred parts of their religion. This point was not long since elaborately argued in Chancery, by some of the most eminent lawyers in England; and it was finally decided by Lord Hardwicke, assisted by Chief Baron Parker, and the Chief Justices of the King's Bench and the Court of Common Pleas, that the testimony of witnesses of the Gentoo religion, sworn according to their particular ceremonies, should be received*. But then it was proved to their Lordship's entire satisfaction that the Gentoos believe in God, the creator of the universe, and in the doctrine of future retribution. Upon this occasion, Lord Chief Justice Willis, in delivering his opinion, said, " though I am of opinion that infidels, who believe a God

---

* Atkins's Reports, Omychund v. Barker.

and future rewards and punishments, may be witnesses; yet I am as clearly of opinion, that if they do not believe in God, or future rewards and punishments, they ought not to be admitted as witnesses: neither ought the same credit to be given to the evidence of an infidel as of a Christian, because he is not under the same obligation."

I have already shewn that the negroes are not possessed of those religious sentiments which can inspire them with a just sense of the sacred obligation of an oath. Besides an obvious distinction presents itself to the mind, between the testimony of infidel witnesses, in particular cases, and that of slaves admitted generally against their masters. The admission of such testimony, in special cases, in Europe, can be attended with no material inconvenience to the people. With us there is a difference; and it would be almost madness to expose the lives, the liberties, and properties, of the West Indians, to a savage multitude, who have not the fear of God before their eyes to restrain them as witnesses, from glutting their revenge by the most horrid perjuries. Were the testimony of slaves once allowed, Barbadoes would be no place of abode for any honest man who had a regard for his reputation, his interest, or his personal safety. No innocence of life, no integrity of heart, would afford security from criminal prosecutions, supported by such evidence. If in civilized society, in the most polished provinces of Europe, the most barefaced perjuries are daily committed by men educated in the principles of Christianity, it is easy to foresee what must be the fatal consequences of legalising the testimony of an ignorant, superstitious, vindictive race, whom no religious nor moral obligation can bind to speak the truth.

CHAP

CHAP. V.

SIR TIMOTHY THORNHILL'S GALLANT EXPLOITS—COLONEL KEN-
DALL APPOINTED GOVERNOR—THE COUNTRY SUFFERS FROM
AN EPIDEMIC DISEASE—A NEW PLOT AMONG THE NEGROES—
UNSUCCESSFUL ATTACK ON MARTINICO—COLONEL RUSSEL SUC-
CEEDS TO THE GOVERNMENT—HIS DEATH.

IN the course of this year an event had taken place in
England which diffused a general, though short-lived, satisfaction among the King's friends. The royal consort, to
the inexpressible joy of the court and the Roman Catholics,
both at home and abroad, was safely delivered of a son.
The birth of a Prince of Wales, it was vainly hoped,
would give stability to the tottering throne. An occurrence
of so much importance did not fail to draw forth the most
lively demonstrations of joy in Barbadoes. But the public rejoicings on this occasion had scarcely ceased before
the Revolution placed the Crown of Great Britain on the
heads of William and Mary, Prince and Princess of Orange.
Mr. Stede's principles of loyalty and fidelity readily accommodated themselves to this change of circumstances, and
he chearfully proclaimed the accession of the new sovereigns; observing, that if they were King and Queen at

CHAP. V.

1688.

Whitehall, they ought to be so here. For this service his excellency had the honour of having his commission renewed, in due form, by King William.

This event soon presented the Barbadians with an opportunity of displaying their zeal and spirit in defence of his Majesty's rights in the western hemisphere. The French, who were professedly the friends and protectors of the unfortunate family of the Stuarts during their exile, in conjunction with some Irish Roman Catholics, attacked the English settlers at St. Christopher's, immediately after the abdication of James. This hostile proceeding, which was afterwards extended to the other British plantations, was conducted with such an unusual degree of animosity and savage barbarity, that General Codrington, who had been recently appointed by King William to the government of the Leeward Islands, was forced to apply to Barbadoes for succour, to enable him to repel these daring acts of aggression.

The Barbadians, generously participating in the resentment of their injured fellow subjects, consented, without hesitation, to contribute their assistance. Sir Timothy Thornhill, major-general of the militia, gallantly volunteered his services, and quickly raised a regiment of seven hundred men, who were accoutered, armed and embarked at the public expence. This expedition sailed from Carlisle-bay, on the first day of August; and arrived at Antigua on the fifth of the same month. Here Sir Timothy had

the mortification to learn that the people of St. Christopher's had been obliged to capitulate two days before he left Barbadoes, on condition of their being transported to Nevis. His force being insufficient to attempt the recovery of the island, General Codrington and himself determined to await the arrival of a fleet from England, which was daily expected with troops for the defence of the islands. But this reinforcement not arriving at the time it was expected, these spirited commanders embarked a part of the Barbadian militia on board some small sloops, and dispatched them to Anquilla, whence they brought off the remains of that small colony, which had suffered greatly from the cruelty and rapacity of the French and Irish Catholics. November.
After this, Thornhill proceeded with his regiment to Nevis, which was menaced by the enemy, but the timely arrival of this reinforcement effectually relieved the inhabitants from their fear of invasion.

General Codrington, finding the posture of affairs would admit of no delay, hastened after him; and, though the armament from Europe had not arrived, these brave and active officers soon planned an expedition, in which their combined forces might be usefully employed. Pursuant to this plan, Thornhill, with a detachment of three hundred Dec. 15. Barbadian, and two hundred Nevisans, sailed to the attack of Saint Bartholomew's. Having landed his men, he pushed forward with such alacrity that in four days time the island surrendered to his victorious arms. This acquisition was obtained with the loss of only ten men killed and wounded. On this occasion the general does not appear to have acted with becoming moderation. The prisoners, to the amount of nearly seven hundred men, with their negroes, live stock and other effects, were conveyed to Nevis, while the unhappy women and children, torn from the embraces of their husbands and fathers, were sent to Saint Christopher's. This unnecessary cruelty was severely reprobated in England, and the inhabitants were restored to the possession of their property as British subjects*.

Flushed with victory, Sir Timothy next attempted the reduction of Saint Martin's; where, though he was ultimately unsuccessful, he gained fresh laurels. The descent was effected without opposition; but his progress was impeded by greater difficulties than had been foreseen. He nevertheless succeeded in destroying the principal fortifications, and was prevented from accomplishing the conquest of the island only by the unexpected arrival of M. du Casse, the French admiral, with a strong armament, from St. Christopher's. Thornhill was now compelled to contract his posts, and to concert proper measures for his own safety. General Codrington, apprized of his critical situation, immediately detached Colonel Hewitson, to Saint Martin's, with two hundred men, under the convoy of

---

* Universal Hist. vol. 41, p. 155, 259, 273, 290, 304.

three sloops of war. After a smart action between the hostile squadrons, which terminated in favour of the British, Thornhill conveyed all his artillery, baggage, and plunder, on board the fleet; and then, ordering his tents to be struck, began his march to a convenient place for embarking his troops; but the enemy, perceiving his design, commenced a furious attack upon him, in which, however, they were beaten back to the woods. The general having made good his retreat, with a trifling loss, reimbarked his gallant little army, and returned to Nevis, where he was joined by General Codrington, with twelve hundred men.

The ardour of these congenial spirits urged them to the most vigorous operations against the enemy; nor was it long before they were enabled to accomplish the grand object of their wishes. Commodore Wright having at length arrived with the long expected succours from England, Codrington, who was appointed commander in chief of the troops, immediately sailed from Nevis for the attack of Saint Christopher's. The descent was conducted by General Thornhill, who, at the head of his own regiment, strengthened by one hundred and fifty men, drawn from the others, landed at the foot of a hill, which the French, deeming inaccessible, had left unguarded. Sensible of the importance of this post, Thornhill, with his usual vivacity, proceeded to take possession of the height; but this was not effected without much danger and some bloodshed. When he had gained the summit, unexpectedly eucountering a detachment of the enemy, his corps sustained an arduous conflict, with great firmness, till the arrival of Colonel Holt, with the Duke of Bolton's regiment, when the French were driven, in the utmost confusion, from their trenches. In this engagement, Thornhill was so grievously wounded, that he was forced to retire on board one of the ships. The command of his regiment, after this accident, devolved on Colonel Thomas, who was ordered to penetrate into the country, supported by Colonel Williams, at the head of a regiment of Antegonians. On this service the Barbadians were exposed to a spirited attack from a superior body of the enemy, and, from their imprudence in advancing with too great temerity, must have been inevitably cut off, but for the seasonable advance of Williams's reserve. The timely approach of their friends inspired the Barbadians with fresh courage, and the enemy were soon compelled to take refuge in the woods, and other strong holds. Sir Timothy Thornhill, having sufficiently recovered of his wounds, soon after resumed the command of his regiment, and contributed materially, by his bravery and conduct, to the reduction of the island, which at length capitulated to General Codrington, as commander in chief.

July 12.

After the conquest of Saint Christopher's, Thornhill proceeded with the marines and his own regiment to Saint Eustatius, whence the Dutch had been recently expelled by the French. With the trifling loss of no more than eight men, he stormed the principal fort, a place of considerable strength, mounting sixteen guns, drove out the French and restored the island to its former proprietors. This victory closed Sir Timothy Thornhill's brilliant career. Finding that he could be of no farther use in the Leeward Islands he embarked his troops and returned to Barbadoes.

These enterprizes were so judiciously planned and conducted with such consummate prudence and courage, that they reflected the highest honour on the character of the West Indians in general, but more particularly on the illustrious patriot, General Codrington, and the intrepid hero, Sir Timothy Thornhill, by whom they had been disinterestedly undertaken and gallantly performed. These transactions have been 'the more circumstantially detailed, because, independent of the gratification resulting from recording the gallant exploits of a meritorious officer, and a countryman, they serve to correct a popular error into which many economical politicians have fallen with respect to the expence of maintaining the militia; which, in their apprehension, is inadequate to the purposes of effectual defence. We have before us the most indubitable evidence, not only of the courage of the West Indians, but of their having been successfully employed in offensive operations against their enemies abroad. As in this service, attended with no inconsiderable difficulty and danger, they acquitted themselves with a firmness and discipline equal to veteran troops, we may, with a well-grounded confidence, expect no less spirited exertions, when called on to defend their country, their liberty and property.

On Thornhill's return to his native country, the legislature, impressed with a just sense of his extraordinary merit, voted him a present of one thousand pounds, in consideration of the courage, skill and address, which he had displayed in his late command against their Majesties' enemies, and for his services in the care and discipline of the militia. Sir Timothy had the further satisfaction to find, that, during his absence, his implacable enemy, Mr. Stede, had been superseded by Colonel James Kendal, a native of Barbadoes, who had been promoted by his Sovereign to the government of the island.

The appointment of this gentleman seems to have been no less acceptable to his countrymen than beneficial to the colony. By his candid representation of the loyalty and quiet disposition of the people, he effectually removed the prejudice which had been excited against them on the other side of the Atlantic, by the partial and unjust accounts transmitted by his predecessors; and several members of council, who had been suspended in consequence of the misrepresentations which had been made to the crown, were now restored to their former rank and dignity. The legislature, as a testimony of their respect for the person and character of their new governor, within two months after his arrival, voted him a present of fifteen hundred pounds. This liberality was occasionally repeated during his subsequent administration; the assembly manifesting their esteem for him by an annual, though irregular, donative; which fluctuated, according to the humour of the day, or the circumstances of the country, from five hundred pounds currency, to two thousand pounds sterling.

All our colonial historians agree, that Barbadoes had now attained the zenith of prosperity; whence she was to descend by a gradual but certain decline. Rich, powerful, and populous, she possessed all that could make her happy at home and respected abroad. But the pleasing scene was soon overcast with the clouds of calamity, that, louring over her head, obscured the gay sunshine which illumined the horizon. Notwithstanding the success which attended the military operations of the West Indians, the inhabitants of Barbadoes suffered severely from the depredations committed on their commerce. Commodore Wright, who seems to have possessed neither the courage nor the conduct essential to the character of a naval commander, adopted no measures for the protection of trade, while the French remained masters of the sea, and daily intercepted the supplies designed for the support of the plantations. The Barbadians, thus left to defend themselves, were under the necessity of fitting out two large ships, at their own cost, to guard their shores, and afford a feeble security to the remains of their almost ruined commerce. These disasters were aggravated by the avarice of the ship-owners, who, availing themselves of the want of vessels to transport the produce of the island to Europe, demanded the most exorbitant prices for the carriage of sugar and other commodities. To check this evil, it was deemed expedient to pass a law, ascertaining the freight of sugar, cotton, and ginger. This regulation naturally failed to produce the intended effect. The ship-masters, who could not be compelled to send their vessels to Barbadoes, or to receive freight upon the terms prescribed by the act, went to other ports, where they were liable to no restrictions; and the planters suffered more from the operation of the remedy than from the evil which they had vainly sought to redress; a convincing proof that trade will not be bound nor confined by arbitrary restraints. The folly and expediency of the law having been thus demonstrated, it was soon repealed.

The calamities of war were now accompanied by the ravages of pestilence. An epidemic disease, supposed to have been introduced by the troops from Europe, but which was more probably, imported with the negroes from Africa, raged throughout the island with such fury that the number of burials in Bridge-town alone were commonly twenty in a day*. The soil, deprived of a considerable portion of the labour required for its due cultivation, no longer yielded its fruits with its accustomed liberality; and a total failure of the crop added to the general misfortune. To complete

---

* European Settlements in America, vol. 2.

the climax of ills with which the Barbadians were afflicted, the horrors of insurrection seemed ready to overwhelm them.

Encouraged by the public distress, the discontented slaves entered into a well concerted plan for exterminating the white inhabitants, whose numbers were considerably diminished by the contagious distemper which prevailed. This conspiracy appears to have been planned with more judgment than had been hitherto displayed by these ignorant, infatuated creatures, in any of their former criminal attempts. A particular day was appointed for a general revolt of the slaves throughout the island ; those on each plantation were, at a certain hour, to massacre their masters and all the white servants. The carnage was to have commenced with the governor; the store-keeper was to have been assassinated by his waiting-man, who, after perpetrating the atrocious deed, was to supply the conspirators with arms and ammunition from the public magazine. Proper officers were appointed, under whose conduct the insurgents proposed surprising the forts which commanded Carlisle-bay, whence they might have been enabled to secure the shipping.

The project was nearly ripe for execution, when that gracious Providence, which wisely governs all things, miraculously interposed to save the unconscious Barbadians from the destruction just ready to burst on their heads. Two of the principal conspirators, in a state of fancied security, were accidentally overheard, conversing on their diabolical scheme. These wretches were instantly arrested; but, expecting that their confederates would make an effort for their relief, they obstinately refused to make any confession which might implicate their friends; and, with a firmness worthy of a better cause, submitted to be hung in chains four days, without meat or drink; when, finding all hopes of a rescue vain, they offered to impeach their accomplices, on consideration of receiving a full pardon for themselves. This proposal being acceded to, they made an unreserved discovery of the whole plot. Their confederates were immediately apprehended, and put upon their trial; and, upon the most incontestible evidence of their guilt; many of them, to the great injury of their owners, were condemned to suffer death.

The next object of the public attention was to provide some effectual security against the recurrence of the danger from which they had been most providentially delivered. But this seems rather to have been an object of deep-felt solicitude than of easy or perfect attainment. It is scarcely possible, in a country where slavery subsists, to guard against the dark designs of secret treachery, or the more daring attacks of open violence. In every dispute between parties of whom neither possess the advantages of military discipline, numbers must finally prevail. This single consideration is sufficient to convince our colonial statesmen of the imperious necessity of a strict attention to the maintenance of a well-regulated militia, and of the folly of putting arms into the hands of those, who, at no distant period of time, may employ them in the destruction of their unwise rulers.

Whether the legislature of that day overlooked these important points, is now difficult to determine; it is, however, certain that they contented themselves with passing two laws, offering indemnity and emancipation to the slave, who should give information of any conspiracy among the negroes; the other prohibiting the selling of rum, or any kind of strong liquor, to any negro or other slave. The policy of this latter law, was founded on a supposition that plots and conspiracies were commonly entered into upon occasions of negro festivity, and were facilitated by the power of intoxication. But, whatever might then have been the opinion entertained of the propriety and efficacy of this prohibition, it is now suffered to slumber in oblivion. The utility of this particular act is at last extremely doubtful; for, exclusive of the absurdity of formally prohibiting what is still openly permitted; and was, perhaps, never intended to have been entirely prevented, it would be cruel to deny the servile labourer the use of the care-drowning draught, the opiate of affliction; which, taken in moderation, enlivens the heavy hours that roll over his head; obtunds the sense of pain, reanimates the spirits exhausted by fatigue, and invigorates the constitution exposed to the vicissitudes of a rigorous and variable climate.

Far from being disheartened by misfortunes, the Barbadians considered every new calamity as an additional motive for vigorous exertion. The naval superiority of the French, in the West Indies, filled them with the most serious apprehensions of invasion. Under this impression, they wasted no time in fruitless discussions concerning the misapplication of the duty on their staple commodities, nor involved themselves in unavailing disputes with the ministers of the crown, on the injustice of diverting the produce of that impost to purposes foreign from those for which it was granted; but with a truly patriotic spirit, they prudently determined to employ what means were in their power, in providing for the safety of their country. With this view, the old fortifications were repaired, and new ones erected wherever they were required. Two armed ships were equipped, at the public expense, for the protection of trade; and their agents*, in England, were directed to apply to the ministry for a regiment to be stationed on the island for its defence. This request was readily complied with, and the troops on their arrival were quartered on such of the inhabitants as were deficient of men to serve in the militia. Each soldier was allowed, by the person on whom he was quartered, six pounds of salt

---

* Edward Littleton and William Bridges were appointed agents for the colony in September 1691. They were the first persons employed in that character, and had each of them, a salary of two hundred and fifty pounds a year allowed them.

meat or fish, each week, besides plantation provisions ready prest, and comfortable lodgings* .

All these precautions were deemed inadequate to the safety of the island, while the French remained in possesions of Martinico. The proximity of such formidable neighbours, necessarily occasioned continual alarm; the British ministry, therefore, determined to annihilate the power of France in the West Indies. But as a sufficient force could not be spared from England, the colonies were required to contribute a proportion of troops for the service; the contingent demanded of Barbadoes, was one thousand men. The Barbadians entered into the scheme with alacrity. Independent of every other consideration, their resentment against the French was sharpened by recent injuries, and particularly by the more than probable opinion that the late insurrection among the blacks had been contrived and promoted by emissaries from Martinico. Two regiments, consisting of five hundred men each, were accordingly raised, and the command given to Colonel September. Salter and Colonel Boteler, two gentlemen of distinguished rank and fortune in the country. The expense of this undertaking amounted to the sum of thirty thousand pounds; a burthen too great to be borne by a small colony, already labouring under a heavy load of taxes, for the support of government.

---

* Hall's Laws of Barb. p. 486.

The armament which Great Britain allotted for the expedition against Martinico, consisted of eight ships of the line and four frigates, under the command of Sir Francis Wheeler, an officer of high reputation in the navy, with eighteen transports, having on board fifteen hundred troops, commanded by Colonel Foulk. These, on their arrival at Barbadoes, were joined by two regiments raised within the island, and four hundred volunteers, who gallantly offered their services on the occasion. No unnecessary delays were suffered to impede the sailing of the squadron, which left Carlisle Bay on the thirtieth day of March, and arrived at Martinico two days afterwards. The fleet came to an anchor in the Cul de sac Royale; and, after some time spent in making the necessary preparations, Colonel Foulk

April 12. made a descent with fifteen hundred men, whom he employed in destroying some defenceless houses and deserted batteries. Having spent one entire day in these acts of wanton cruelty and useless hostility, against an unresisting enemy, he reimbarked his troops, and took no farther share in the operations of the army. The commodore, at the head of five hundred seamen, now landed, at Diamond Bay, and pursued the work of destruction; burning and destroying several plantations in that neighbourhood, and driving the unarmed, dismayed inhabitants, into the woods. Another detachment, led by Colonel Lillington, penetrated the open country, which they ravaged without oppo-

sition and returned without performing any essential service*.

The army was now reinforced, by the arrival of General
Codrington, with Lloyd's regiment, from Antigua, and a
body of troops raised within his government. This accession of strength was deemed sufficient to enable the
British commander to attempt the reduction of the capital
of Martinico. Sir Francis Wheeler accordingly proceeded
with the fleet to Saint Pierre's, and resolutely anchored
within musket shot of the shore. Here the Barbadians,
supported by the troops from the Leeward Islands, eminently distinguished themselves. Having effected a landing, they immediately occupied an eminence which commanded the town; they scoured the country, drove the
enemy from all their advanced posts, and compelled them
to seek security within their entrenchments. The garrison
made one effort, by a vigorous sortie, to dislodge the
assailants, but they were repulsed, and retired under shelter of their cannon.

While the troops were thus employed on shore, most of
the principal officers of the army remained on board the
ships, where they died ingloriously of pestilential diseases.
Victory, however, seemed ready to crown the invaders with
success, and to reward them with the possession of Saint
Pierre's, when the attack was most unaccountably aban-

---

* Univ. Hist. vol. 1. p. 160. Campbell's Lives of the Admirals, vol. 2. p. 447.

doned. A council of war having met, they resolved, that in the sickly condition of the army and navy, and from many unforeseen difficulties which must be encountered in the progress of the siege, the conquest of the place was impracticable. In consequence of this resolution, the troops and artillery were immediately reimbarked; and thus, under the most encouraging prospects of success, ended an expedition which nothing could have defeated, but the flagrant misconduct of those to whom it was intrusted. Many of the officers were Irish Roman Catholics, notoriously disaffected to the family on the throne, and were employed on this service merely as a pretext for sending them out of the kingdom. To the honour of the West Indians, it is generally allowed, that if the European troops had behaved as well as *they* did, not only Martinico, but all the French islands must have fallen into the hands of the British*.

1694.   Upon the change of ministry in England, Colonel Francis Russel, brother to the Earl of Orford, was appointed to the government of Barbadoes, and his regiment ordered to be stationed there. Mr. Kendall, by a particular order from the King, took his seat at the council, as president of that board†, but was soon after recalled, and made one of the commissioners of the admiralty. The new governor

---

* Univ. Hist. vol. 41. p. 160.   † Hall's First Settlem. of Barb. p. 29. MS.

was received with the usual demonstrations of respect; and notwithstanding the accumulated distresses of the people, the assembly voted him a present of two thousand pounds. Precedents, though dangerous, are easily established; and attempts are sometimes made to justify the worst measures by cases originally innocent and commendable. Thus the liberal largesses bestowed on former governors, under circumstances widely different, had formed a precedent from which the legislature could not depart, without making an invidious distinction to the disadvantage of their present commander in chief. But Colonel Russel was to be distinguished by a munificence which none of his predecessors had ever enjoyed. Though the country was impoverished by a succession of calamities, it was resolved to provide his regiment with quarters at the public charge. The soldiers, by an act of the legislature, were quartered on the plantations, to serve in the militia, and were entitled to receive from each person, for whom they served, the same rations as were allowed during the late administration. The inhabitants received ninepence a day from the treasury, for each soldier quartered on them; and in lieu of provisions, it was optional with the landlord to pay the soldiers, while on duty, one shilling a day.

The next year was marked with acts of still greater generosity. In addition to another benevolence of two thousand pounds, his excellency was presented with three hundred pounds sterling, for the purpose of replenishing his cellars; and, by an extraordinary stretch of complaisance, another act was soon after passed, for supplying the commissioned officers of his regiment with provisions at the public expense. For this purpose, the major was allowed four shillings a day, each captain two shillings and sixpence, the lieutenants, quarter-master, and surgeon, each two shillings, to be paid out of the treasury. The bulk of the people were extremely discontented at this excessive profusion. Their complaints were, however, but little regarded by the parasites who wished to ingratiate themselves with the governor, and to bask in the sun-shine of court favour. Those who hold the strings of the public purse, seldom reflect on the condition of the lower classes of people. Clad with authority, and indulging in the pleasures of affluence, they are strangers to the misery of those from whom they exact the last shilling, to pamper their own luxurious appetites, or to promote their schemes of ambition. They can well afford to gratify the liberality of their tempers, whose extravagance is supported by a whole community; and to purchase the patronage of a venal chief, when the price is paid out of the public treasury. A few leading members of the legislature enjoy all the merit, and receive the exclusive reward of their munificence, while the poor labourer, and the humble householder, from whose starving mouth the scanty morsel is snatched, and from whose shivering limbs the tattered weed is torn, are insulted and despised by the proud, unfeeling great, whom they contribute to support.

The extraordinary generosity of the Barbadians procured them no favour nor indulgence. Indeed, any expectation of conciliating the friendship of government, by such means, will ever terminate in disappointment. The readiness with which the colonial assemblies dispose of the money belonging to their constituents, is generally considered as an evidence of their wealth, rather than of the liberality of their minds; and the demands, on their generosity, will always be proportioned to the facility with which they are granted.

The epidemic disease, already mentioned, still continued to spread desolation throughout the island. On board the men of war, the mortality was so great, that the legislature, notwithstanding the enormous expense which they had lately incurred, were obliged to fit out the Marigold brig, to bring home a part of the troops employed on the late unsuccessful expedition against Martinico, which had been left at Antigua, by Commodore Wheeler. They granted the sum of fourteen hundred and eighty-four pounds sterling, for victualling and manning the Bristol frigate, and the Playfair prize, to cruise against the enemy*, and were under the necessity of paying the very ships appointed to convoy their trade to Europe. Yet so little attention was

---

* Hall's Laws of Barb. p. 488, 489.

CHAP. V. shewn to the security of the island, that on the appearance

1696.   of a French fleet, bound for Carthagena, there were not
seven rounds of powder in all the forts upon the island*.
In this state of things, the governor, who was much addicted to the pleasures of the table, was seized with a fever,
generated by intemperance, which soon put a period to
his existence†.

---

* Univ. Hist, vol, 41. p. 161.   † Memoirs of Barb. p. 46.

CHAP. VI.

PRESIDENCY OF MR. BOND—ARRIVAL OF GOVERNOR GREY—HE
RESIGNS THE GOVERNMENT—MR. FARMER PRESIDENT—A CON-
SPIRACY OF THE SLAVES—SIR BEVILLE GRANVILLE APPOINTED
GOVERNOR—COUNTRY DIVIDED BY FACTION—ATTEMPT ON THE
GOVERNOR'S LIFE—MR. LILLINGTON PROSECUTED—MEMORIAL
AGAINST THE GOVERNOR—SEVERAL MEMBERS OF THE ASSEMBLY
EXPELLED—A BANK ESTABLISHED—DEPARTURE OF THE GO-
VERNOR.

UPON the death of Colonel Russel, the executive autho- CHAP. VI.
rity devolved on the Honourable Francis Bond, senior 1696.
member of council, resident on the island. The Barba- August.
dians appear to have exhausted their whole stock of generosity on their late governor, and to have reserved nothing
to bestow on the president, to whom they gave neither
salary nor present.

Under the auspices of Mr. Bond, the assembly ventured 1697.
to encroach on the prerogative of the crown. They passed
an act, laying an impost of powder on the tonnage of
vessels, in which they assumed the annual right of nominating a store-keeper of the magazine, allowing to the

other branches of the legislature the power only of confirming or rejecting their choice. Whether the appointment of public officers is more beneficially exercised by the representatives of the people, than by the representative of the crown, is a question which admits not of an easy solution. One thing, however, is certain, that the assembly have, in this instance, violated the Sovereign's constitutional right of appointing to all offices, in the state, civil and military.

The presidency of Mr. Bond was productive of no interesting event, though many salutary measures were adopted during his administration. Hence, a colonial historian*, who afterwards sustained, on his own shoulders, the weight of government, takes occasion to remark, "That a man who has an interest in a country, and is a native thereof, will be more concerned for the good government of it, and more attentive to its prosperity, than one who considers it as a temporary dwelling, whither he has procured himself to be sent to raise a fortune, or to patch up one going to decay." This is one of the many plausible theories, whose fallacy is demonstrated by experience. The reasoning by which it is supported is specious, but candour must acknowledge, that the security and prosperity of the country have been seldom more neglected than when the administration of public affairs has been confided to a na-

---

* Mr. Frere.—Short Hist. of Barb. p. 45.

tive, possessing an interest in it. Self-love and social are not here the same: many persons of rank and fortune conceive that they have an interest distinct from the public good, and often sacrifice the welfare of their country to their private emolument, the fleeting breath of popularity, or the gratification of their ambition. It is not, however, intended to detract from the particular merit of Mr. Bond, who, to his own honour, and the satisfaction of his countrymen, held the reins of government for the term of two years. And happy would it have been for Barbadoes if many succeeding presidents had acquitted themselves in the same high trust with equal reputation and fidelity.

The Honourable Ralph Grey, brother to the Earl of Tankerville, having been appointed governor of all the Windward Islands, arrived at Barbadoes, on the twenty-sixth day of July. His excellency found the country suffering under the accumulated evils of tempest, pestilence and war. The epidemic disease, formerly mentioned, though somewhat abated, continued to rage with considerable violence; and many valuable plantations were destroyed by a hurricane. The enormous expense, injudiciously incurred on account of the late unsuccessful expedition against Martinico, and other expensive measures which the inhabitants, wholly neglected by the parent state, had been compelled to adopt for their internal safety, had been defrayed by such oppressive taxes, that many principal planters were entirely ruined, or at least rendered incapable of supporting their plantations. Above forty sugar works were totally abandoned, and land, to a considerable extent, lay waste and unproductive for the want of labourers to cultivate it. Yet, under all these discouragements, the Barbadians maintained the dignity of their government with great spirit and constancy.

The governor was received with every possible mark of respect. Mr. Maxwell, the speaker of the assembly, in an appropriate speech, offered him the congratulations of the house on his safe arrival; and the legislature readily furnished his excellency with much more substantial proofs of their regard. Fontabelle had been hitherto leased by the public for the residence of the first magistrate; but in their solicitude for the safety and accommodation of their new commander in chief, the assembly now discovered that the government-house was not only much out of repair, but that, from its proximity to the sea, it was exposed to the depredations of privateers: five hundred pounds a year was therefore settled on Mr. Grey, for the purpose of providing him with a more eligible and commodious mansion. Though his excellency had a salary of twelve hundred pounds sterling allowed him by the Crown, out of the four and a half per cent. duty, to be paid on the spot by the collector of the customs, the assembly, within two months after his ar-

Sept. 7. rival, made him a present of two thousand pounds to defray the expenses of his voyage.

Mr. Grey was particularly directed by his Majesty's instructions not to suffer any money, or value of money, " to be given or granted by any act or order of the assembly, to any governor or commander in chief, which shall not, according to the style of the acts of parliament in England, be mentioned to be given or granted unto us, with the humble desire of such assembly, that the same be applied to the use of such governor, if we shall think fit. Or if we shall not approve of such gift or application, that the said money, or value of money, be then disposed of and appropriated to such other uses as in the said act, or order shall be mentioned."

His excellency was also instructed " not to suffer any public money whatsoever to be issued or disposed of, otherwise than by warrant, under his hand, by and with the advice and consent of the council. But the assembly may, nevertheless, be permitted, from time to time, to view and examine all accounts of money or value of money disposed of by virtue of such laws as they shall make," which he was directed to signify to them as occasion should offer*.

This year is rendered particularly remarkable by the establishment of the first patent office in Barbadoes. The person selected for this distinction was a Mr. Skene, who was honoured with his Majesty's letters patent, appointing him secretary of the island, and private secretary to the governor. This appointment occasioned a dispute between

---

* Mem. of Barb. p. 47.

his excellency and the new secretary, on the score of fees. As most of the papers issued from that office required the governor's sign manual, either as chancellor or ordinary, former commanders in chief, to expedite the business of those departments, had appointed private secretaries of their own, who were usually recompensed with gratuitous fees for their trouble and attendance. These fees, from the increase of business, soon became an object of attention to the governor himself, who demanded an annual sum from the secretary, as his share of the profits. But Mr. Skene, holding his appointment under the crown, demanded these fees, which had been established only by common consent, as the legal perquisites of his office. The governor opposed this claim, and insisted upon his right to nominate his own private secretary. An appeal to the Crown was the natural consequence of this misunderstanding, but the events which soon after took place prevented the matter from being brought to an issue.

The administration of Mr. Grey was rendered extremely popular by the generosity of his temper and the suavity of his manners. These qualities, whether they soften the austerity of office, or sweeten the social intercourse which subsists between men in the sequestered walks of private life, will ever engage the esteem of mankind. Of a disposition liberal and disinterested, he sought not to enrich himself by the spoil of those whom he was sent to protect; but sedulously endeavoured to promote their prosperity; and, by

the firm but temperate exercise of authority, gained the
hearts of the people whom he governed. Nor were they
deficient in gratitude. In each successive year of his mild
and equitable administration, the representatives of the
people testified their esteem for his virtues by a liberal
gratuity of two thousand pounds. At length, having succeeded to the barony of Werke, on the death of his brother, and finding his health declining, he resigned the ensigns of authority into the hands of John Farmer, son to
the patriotic opponent of Lord Willoughby, and returned
to England.

Soon after the governor's departure, Mr. Farmer received
official information of the King's death, and of the accession of Queen Anne. These events were celebrated with
the usual ceremonies, and the assembly, with the concurrence of the council, transmitted a loyal and dutiful address of condolence to her Majesty on the death of her august relative, and of congratulation on her joyful accession
to the throne of her ancestors, which was prevented by the
late governor, now Lord Grey.

Upon the commencement of hostilities between France
and Great Britain, Commodore Walker was dispatche dto
the West Indies with six ships of the line, having four regiments on board. Their arrival in Carlisle Bay was greeted by
an act of the general assembly for the accommodation of the
troops. They were billetted on the inhabitants for two
months, each man to be allowed six pounds of salted

meat or fish, a week, with plantation provisions and beds of plantain leaves, or in lieu of food, to receive sixpence per day, at the option of the landlord.   Walker soon afterwards sailed for Antigua, where he was joined by Colonel Codrington, with some troops collected among the islands, and proceeded to the invasion of Guadaloupe; but, in consequence of some misunderstanding between the commanding officers, the enterprise was abandoned, after demolishing the fort, burning the town, and ravaging the country.

The Barbadians, recovering from their misfortunes, now entered deeply into schemes of privateering. A fleet of sixteen of their armed vessels, cruizing off Guadaloupe, emboldened by the defenceless state of the island, landed their crews, and, after destroying many plantations, brought away a considerable number of slaves*.   But their attention was soon called off to the means of providing for their internal security.   The turbulent, licentious blacks, entered into a fresh conspiracy for throwing off the yoke of slavery, and getting possession of the forts.   But their diabolical scheme was again frustrated by the interposition of Providence, and many of the infatuated wretches suffered the dreadful punishment incurred by their criminal designs.

1703.
When Lord Grey resigned the government of Barbadoes, the king appointed Mitford Crowe, an opulent London merchant, to be his successor; but, on the death of his

---

* Univ. Hist. vol. 41, p. 104.

Majesty, Queen Anne, to the great disappointment of the Barbadians, committed the important trust to Major-General Sir Bevill Granville. During the whole reign of that illustrious princess the affairs of the colonies were regarded with greater attention than at any former period. Her Majesty, upon every occasion, seems to have manifested the most maternal solicitude for the happiness of her subjects in this remote part of the empire, and an anxiety to relieve them, as much as possible, from the heavy burthens which had been imposed upon them. A petition had been presented to the House of Commons by several merchants and planters of Barbadoes, praying that the money arising from the four and a half per cent. duty, might be applied to the uses for which it had been granted. The petition being referred to a committee, an address was presented to her Majesty, recommending her to comply with the wishes of the Barbadians; and she was accordingly graciously pleased to order, that the produce of the duty should be appropriated to the repairing and erecting of fortifications for the safety of the island; and that an annual account of the expenditure should be laid before parliament.

The next proof which her Majesty gave of her benignant disposition was an attempt to relieve the island from the distresses occasioned by the usual presents to governors. Sir Bevill Granville was strictly prohibited, by his instructions, from receiving any gift or present from the assembly, upon any account, or in manner, whatever, on pain of incurring her Majesty's highest displeasure, and of being re-called from the government. To provide a competent maintenance for the governor, her Majesty was graciously pleased to augment his excellency's salary to two thousand pounds sterling, payable out of the duty of four and a half per cent. " according to the meaning of the act of the assembly, whereby the same is granted for maintaining the honour and dignity of the government, and for other public uses*."

Notwithstanding these liberal concessions on the part of the Crown, the public mind was kept in a continual state of agitation during the whole time of General Granville's administration. In the face of the royal order, the assembly settled five hundred pounds per annum on the governor; and it is generally allowed that his friends contrived, under various pretences, to appropriate several large sums of the public money to his use. They erected an elegant house for him on a small plantation above Bridge-town, called Pilgrim, containing about twenty acres of land, which they leased for twenty-one years, at the annual rent of one hundred and twenty pounds. And, by an extraordinary exercise of complaisance, they nominated his brother-in-law, Sir John Stanley, one of their agents in London. It was certainly highly reprehensible thus to trifle with an employment of so much real importance. Among the many quali-

---

* Mem of Barb. p. 50.   Univ. Hist. vol. 41. p. 64.   Hall's First Settle. of Barb.

fications necessary in a candidate for the colonial agency, it is not one of the least that he should be thoroughly acquainted with the internal policy and general interests of the island which he represents. Yet these were points with which Sir John, as a stranger to the West Indies, must have been very imperfectly acquainted, if not wholly ignorant. On the other hand, it may be said, the honourable Baronet's incompetence could not have been very prejudicial to the interest of his employers, since they had at that time the benefit of the wisdom and diligence of no less than four agents at once.

This amicable disposition unfortunately was not of long continuance. Sir Bevill's tory principles and supercilious behaviour rendered him extremely unpopular; an effect to which it is more than probable the measures that he thought proper to take for the safety of the country might greatly have contributed. Under the apprehensions of invasion, the governor called out the militia and employed them on the tedious and irksome duty of guarding the accessible parts of the coast. This was a strong measure, which nothing could justify but absolute necessity, and it diffused a spirit of discontent throughout the country. To relieve the body of the people from the hardships and fatigue of this species of servitude, which fell heaviest upon those who were least able to bear them, a bill was introduced into

the house of assembly*, to empower his excellency to embody two companies of grenadiers at the public expense,
to be employed on this particular service. The measure
was strenuously opposed by some factious members, from an
objection to the expense, and from apprehension that part
of the money to be raised for the pay and subsistence of the
men would be converted to the governor's private emolument. Finding that a majority of the assembly were favourable to the bill, the members in opposition seceded,
expecting their absence would effectually obstruct its progress by the difficulty of making a house, as fifteen members, at that time, constituted a quorum. The defection
of nearly one-third of the representative body necessarily
impeded the proceedings of the legislature, and occasioned
an entire stagnation of public business. The governor expostulated warmly with the assembly on such a dereliction
of the trust reposed in them, and cautioned them against
the consequences of a conduct so comtumacious and dishonourable. At length, finding all milder expedients ineffectual, he dismissed the seceders from all their civil and

---

* The assembly was composed of the following members; G. Peers and C. Tho-
mas, *St. Michael's*; A. Walker and S. Maynard, *St. Peter's*; W. Allamby and G.
Harper, *St. Thomas's*; J. Leslie and C. Estwick, *St. John's*; P. Kirton and T. Max-
well, *Christchurch*; T. Maycock and W. Terrill, *St. Lucy's*; W. Holder and R.
Wayte, *St. James's*; T. Ince and Enoch Gretton, *St. Philip's*; Rob. Morris and Reyn.
Alleyne, *St. Andrew's*; Paul Lyte and H. Harding, *St. George's*; John Holder and
W. Grant, *St. Joseph's.*

military employments under the crown, and dissolved the assembly*.

The spirit of discord was not confined to the popular branch of the legislature alone; the most violent dissentions prevailed in the council chamber. Here the evil was more immediately within the sphere of the governor's observation and controul; nor did he hesitate long to apply the proper remedy. Availing himself of his prerogative, he suspended the four most turbulent members, George Lillington, David Ramsay, Benjamin Cryer, and Michael Terril. These acts of resentment were not calculated to appease the popular discontent; and in the midst of these feuds and dissentions, an attempt to assassinate the governor was made by some unknown person, in the road, firing a pistol at his excellency as he sat in a window at Pilgrim. Upon this occasion, the assembly presented a respectful address to the governor, declaring their *utter abhorrence of an act so stupendously villainous as that of attempting, through his excellency's sides, to wound and destroy her Majesty's regality here.*

June.

Of this offence Mr. Lillington was accused, and endured, notwithstanding his ill-health, a long and rigorous confinement. He was at length indicted at the court of grand ses-

---

* Many of the most important transactions of this period I am enabled to detail, on the authority of the manuscript journal, of the proceedings of the assembly, mentioned in the preface.

CHAP. VI.   sions, and sentenced to pay a fine of two thousand pounds.
~~~~~   Of the justice of this sentence it is impossible to speak with
1704.   certainty.   No evidence of his innocence, or his guilt, can
now be found, and little confidence is due to the contradictory representations of opposite parties.   The Honourable
William Sharpe, the chief justice, who presided at the trial,
and at several succeeding courts of grand sessions, was honoured with the thanks of the house of assembly, for the
candour and integrity of his conduct.   Hence we may infer
that Mr. Lillington was fairly tried, and legally convicted.
But, on the other hand, it has been asserted, that the
prosecution was malicious*, and that after the heats
and prejudices of party had, in some measure, subsided,
the fine was remitted, and the money ordered to be returned.   Mr. Lillington, however, was forced to submit to the
sentence whether just or unjust.

August.   Meanwhile, the governor having issued writs for calling
a new assembly, the election in several parishes was contested with great warmth and earnestness.   In St. Lucy's
Maycock and Terrill, the late representatives, were guilty
of some acts of illegal violence; they grossly insulted and
obstructed Mr. Gordon, the sheriff, in the execution of
his duty, and encouraged a Mr. Curl to assume and exercise the office of sheriff.   The election, of course, was controverted by Colonel Pickering and Major Lambert, the

---

* Hall's First Settlement of Barb. p. 30. M. S.

other candidates, in whose favour the house of assembly ultimately decided. Maycock and Terril were ordered to be prosecuted by the attorney-general, for high crimes and misdemeanors; and Curl, who had given a false testimony at the bar of the house, was directed to be indicted for perjury. But before the day of trial they were clandestinely taken from the island, by Captain Martin, of the Blackwall frigate.

On the meeting of the assembly, the governor opened the session, in the usual form, with a speech, in which he inveighed, with equal justice and asperity, against the conduct of those members of the former assembly; who, in contempt of the Queen's authority, and in violation of the sacred trust reposed in them, had, pertinaciously, absented themselves from that house; whence the legislature had been prevented from the exercise of its functions, and the administration of government had been suspended. To this cause he ascribed the decline of public credit, and the great hardships sustained by the gunners and matrosses, and other public creditors, whose salaries were unjustly withholden from them. Hence, he said, the seamen on board a brig, in the service of the country, had been provoked to run away with the vessel, as a fair reprizal on those who had employed them without paying their wages. By the unwarrantable secession of some of their members, the assembly, he said, had been prevented from making the provision requisite for the repair of the fortifications,

and for relieving the militia from the toilsome and oppressive duty of guarding the coasts; nor had they been able
to make any inquiry into the expenditure of the public
money. To this omission he attributed the failure of Commodore Walker's attempt on Guadaloupe, the treasurer
having pretended that he had not the means of hiring a
vessel to carry dispatches to General Codrington, on whose
receiving timely notice of the design, the success of the
expedition principally depended; though it was evident,
that had there been no misapplication of it, there would
have been money enough in the treasury for that and other
public exigencies. He next accused the assembly of neglecting to avail themselves of her Majesty's gracious intention of appropriating the four and a half duty to the use
of the fortifications, no application having been made for
the money then due upon that score. He admonished them
to beware of slighting the proffered boon, lest by their
criminal negligence they should lose the golden opportunity
of rendering their country the most essential services. His
excellency concluded with desiring that the house would
continue to sit from day to day, and consult, with unanimity, on the means of promoting the security and prosperity of the country.

The answer of the assembly was modest and respectful.
They admitted the justice of his excellency's animadver-
sions on the misconduct of a part of their house, and condemned, in the strongest terms, the pertinacious opposition

which he had experienced in the legal exercise of his authority. His excellency was represented in this address, as possessing all the virtues which could adorn the character of the most accomplished ruler. His administration was compared to *the dispensations of that Providence which ever designs the happiness of mankind ;* and was asserted to have been *free from spot or blemish, except that with patience and temper he had striven to reclaim a people of a stubborn, obstinate disposition.*

The address having been agreed to, and presented, the house proceeded to the revisal of their rules, when Mr. John Holder suggested, that the irregularity so justly complained of in the proceedings of the late assembly, was occasioned by the rule which required the presence of two-thirds of the representative body to make a house. To obviate this inconvenience, he moved, that thirteen members should, in future, be a quorum sufficient to pass all laws, either of a public or private nature. The motion was vehemently opposed by those members whose turbulent behaviour had been productive of so much confusion, and had deservedly incurred such severe reprehension. But finding all opposition vain, they rose from their seats ; and, in contempt of the speaker's authority, quitted the house, expecting that their retiring would dissolve the meeting ; the other members, however, continued sitting, and agreed to the treasurer's motion.

The attention of the assembly was now directed to another object. The speaker, by his excellency's directions, laid before the house the copy of a memorial which had been presented to the Queen by several factious members of the former assembly, exhibiting a variety of charges against the governor and a majority of that house. The memorialists, after a pompous panegyric on their own loyal and peaceable demeanor, in the faithful discharge of many offices of high trust and responsibility, lament that they should be compelled, by their fidelity to their constituents, to complain of the injurious and oppressive conduct of her Majesty's governor, Sir Bevill Granville. They alledged that the militia had been kept on guard, at the different bays, and accessible parts of the coast, to the manifest injury of her Majesty's subjects, contrary to law, and without even the previous consent of the council; for the ostensible reason of defending the country from invasion, and to prevent evil-disposed persons from running away with boats; but that the real design of this arbitrary and illegal procedure was to compel the representatives of the people to consent to an act for raising two companies of soldiers, for the protection of the towns and adjacent landing places, with a secret view to the governor's private emolument. The annual expense of maintaining this body of men, was estimated at nine thousand pounds; and, as the money was to be entirely at the governor's disposal, they asserted that he would be able to save, for his own use, at least, one-third of the sum.

To their own patriotic opposition to this measure, the memorialists ascribe their removal from offices of trust and profit, which they had enjoyed *without blemish for above thirty years*. They add that, in consequence of the dismissal of many officers of respectability from their military command, the militia had been disorganized and the island exposed defenceless to the terrors of invasion. It was stated that the governor, in direct disobedience to her Majesty's commands, forbidding his accepting any gift or present from the assembly, had, at one time, received from them a present of six hundred pounds; and, at another, of five hundred pounds; besides a present of two hundred pounds from the Jews, who had in consequence many privileges and indulgences granted to them contrary to law: That he had accepted several valuable gifts of plate, horses, and negroes from private persons, especially the natives of North Britain; on whom, notwithstanding their known aversion to the family on the throne, he had bestowed many of the most important civil and military employments. Against these arrangements the memorialists inveighed with great bitterness. They complained that in the room of officers of rank and talent who had been dismissed from the service, persons had been appointed wholly unqualified, inperienced, of mean capacity and low estate. But of none did they speak with more asperity than of the Honourable William Holder, speaker of the assembly, who had been recently appointed chief justice of Saint Michael's precinct, though, to use their own phraseology, *he was never known to be of any christian community, neither had he been baptized.* After several other frivolous accusations, the memorial concluded with praying her Majesty would be graciously pleased to institute an inquiry into the conduct of Sir Bevill Granville, and offering to support the truth of their allegations by the most unquestionable evidence. The memorial was subscribed by John Leslie, Philip Kirton, Thomas Maycock, William Terrill, Christopher Estwick, Enoch Gretton, and Thomas Maxwell, late speaker of the assembly.

The reading of this paper produced the most lively emotions of anger and resentment in both chambers of the legislature. They voted it to be a false, scandalous and seditious libel on the government of the island, and vindicated themselves from the imputations which it contained, in a counter-address to the throne. In this address they expressed the most grateful sense of her Majesty's maternal kindness in the prudent choice of a governor of general Granville's " probity, good conduct, unspotted integrity, and exemplary life; who, by his extraordinary vigilance and prudence, had wrested the government out of the hands of a corrupt faction, whose unwarrantable behaviour would have involved the country in ruin and misery, but for the wisdom and vigour of his administration."

The assembly now thought it necessary to vindicate their rights by punishing the contumacy of those refractory members, whose secession was considered as a contempt of legislative authority. With this view the speaker, by order of the house, issued a summons, commanding their attendance at the next meeting of the legislature. In obedience to this summons the seceders met, at the time and place March 20. appointed, and put into the speaker's hands a written paper, in which they assigned as a reason for their non-attendance, the innovation, which, as they termed it, had been made on the rights of the people, in respect to the number of members required to make a house. They added, that they had submitted the whole affair to her Majesty's consideration, and were in daily expectation of receiving her commands, to which they would most dutifully conform; and, in the interim, they utterly disclaimed the authority and competence of the other members to act as the general assembly of the island. These reasons not appearing satisfactory, the speaker demanded of them severally, whether they would resume their seats and enter upon business conformably to the rules of the house; to which they declined giving any answer and abruptly retired. To discountenance such a dangerous spirit of insubordination, the house unanimously voted for the expulsion of John Leslie, Philip Kirton, Joseph Brown, John Frere, and Christopher Estwick,*

---

* Gretton, who was also one of the seceders, died before the matter was decided. Neither of the expelled members was re-elected until the general election; when Mr. Frere was returned for St. Philip's, and took his seat accordingly.

each of whom was declared incapable of sitting again during the continuance of that assembly; and new writs were immediately issued, by the governor, for the particular election of other members to supply the vacancies occasioned by their expulsion. And to prevent, in future, any factious attempt to impede the public business, by the abrupt, indecorous departure of any member during the session, it became a standing rule of the assembly, that, whenever a sufficient number of members had met to make a house, the door should be locked, and the key given to the speaker, without whose permission no member should be allowed to depart under pain of expulsion.

1705.

It was not long before the governor had the satisfaction of receiving the most unequivocal testimony of her Majesty's approbation of his conduct. In addition to the memorial already mentioned, the four suspended members of council had exhibited a complaint against his excellency, to which was added, a petition from Mr. Richard Downes*, complaining that, notwithstanding he had been honoured with her Majesty's letter of mandamus, appointing him a member of council, he had been prevented by the governor from taking his seat at that board. These complaints were

---

* Mr. Downes had been treasurer of the island, and had presumed, upon his own authority, to pay money to the amount of several thousand pounds, without the usual orders from the governor: this conduct naturally gave offence, and he was removed from the office; and several years elapsed before he settled his accounts, or paid the balance due to the public.

all referred to the consideration of the lords commissioners
of trade and plantations; who, after a due investigation of
the several charges, together with the governor's defence,
made the necessary reports to the Queen in council. And,
upon reading these reports, her Majesty was pleased to
order one of her principal secretaries of state to communicate to Sir Bevill Granville her Majesty's royal approbation
of his proceedings, in the suspension of the four counsellors, who had countenanced and abetted those members
of the assembly, from whose irregular behaviour, and criminal neglect of duty, much inconvenience had arisen.
He was, however, empowered, upon their application and
submission, to admit them, if he should think proper, to
resume their seats at the council board. But with respect
to Downes, her Majesty declared her absolute will and
pleasure, that he should be entirely excluded from the
council chamber.

After expressing her concern and indignation, at the
confusion and disorder that had happened, from the representatives of the people wilfully absenting themselves from
their duty, by which means the administration of government had been greatly embarrassed and obstructed, her
Majesty directed that his excellency should, in her name,
represent to both branches of the legislature, the evils and
inconveniences that must necessarily result from such culpable neglect, and to recommend their making some effectual provision for preventing such abuses in future.

The joy of the assembly, on this occasion, was unbounded. To such of the members of her Majesty's privy
council, as were present on the inquiry, they voted a present of Citron water, in the following proportion : six
dozen bottles to the Duke of Marlborough, five dozen to
the Lord Treasurer, four dozen to the Lord President, and
to the Chancellor of the Exchequer three dozen. They
also voted their agent the sum of one hundred pounds
sterling, to defray the expenses of an entertainment, which
they directed he should give in honour of the Royal
African Company, for their interposition in his excellency's
behalf.

The public mind was again violently agitated by the fear
of invasion. In consequence of some alarming intelligence
April 9. from Antigua, the governor called the legislature together,
and submitted to their consideration the danger to which
the island was exposed by the proximity of a formidable
French force; and recommended their putting the fortifications in the best possible state of defence. In this emergency, the council proposed calling out the militia, and
laying them under martial law for fourteen days. To the
former part of the proposal the assembly readily agreed,
but they refused to sanction the declaration of martial law,
though they were willing to suspend the proceedings of the
courts of justice during the time the militia should remain
embodied; a most extraordinary proposition, for which no
sufficient reason can possibly be assigned. To this plan the

governor objected, that without the restraints of martial law the militia, if called out, would be no better than a tumultuous, undisciplined rabble; where there was no power to punish, no order nor subordination could be expected; and that a suspension of the functions of the courts of justice, under such circumstances, would leave the people without any rule of conduct, without any legal measure of good or evil. After several conferences between the two houses, in which various expedients were suggested to supply the absence of martial law, the bill to enable his excellency to embody the militia, was finally rejected by the assembly.

The commercial intercourse between Great Britain and her colonies had now become an object of great national importance. It was found necessary, for the regulation of the pecuniary transactions between the people of England and her American dependencies, to establish a legal currency among the islands; and to ascertain the true parity of exchange between the different parts of the empire. Sir Isaac Newton, who was then master of the mint, had, by order of the privy council, made an actual assay on most foreign coins, and ascertained the intrinsic value of the bullion contained in each. To obviate the inconveniences arising from the want of an uniform currency in the plantations, the Queen, by proclamation, dated the fourth day of June, in the year one thousand seven hundred and four, fixed the rate at which they should pass in the colonies. By this proclamation, which was afterwards confirmed by act of parliament, 6 Anne, ch. 30, the value of the dollar, which, by assay, had been found to be worth four shillings and sixpence sterling, was established at six shillings colonial currency; and the value of other coins was regulated according to that standard. Hence the true parity of exchange between London and Barbadoes was fixed at one hundred and thirty-three and a third per cent.

Hitherto dollars had passed in the West Indies at eight shillings; and, as the theory of money was, at that time, but imperfectly understood in the colonies, the money-holders highly disapproved of the alteration. Without reflecting that the value of commodities, of which money is but the representative, must be affected in proportion to any depreciation in the nominal value of the coin, they considered the defalcation in the numeral value of the dollar as a real diminution of their wealth. To avert a calamity, merely ideal, the monied men, on the arrival of the proclamation, exported almost the whole of the circulating silver coin of the country. This absurd expedient produced much inconvenience among the mercantile people, which, by a natural communication, was soon felt by the planters; and the want of a circulating medium became a general complaint.

The evil, however, was of a temporary nature; and, had it been left to itself, would soon have found a remedy. A country abounding with valuable productions, can never labour under a permanent scarcity of precious metals. Money will always be brought into exchange for those commodities which the luxury, or necessities of mankind require for their gratification. No considerable nor lasting inconvenience will ever be felt for the want of specie in a country whose balance of trade, if not in its favour, is not greatly against it. Large crops, for exportation, will necessarily furnish the means of paying for those articles which may be required from abroad; and the excess of its exports, should there be any, will afford an unfailing supply of cash. These truths were either unknown or neglected by the legislature of Barbadoes, and they adopted the worst expedient that could have been devised for affording relief suited to the circumstances of the country.

To supply the want of cash, a Mr. Dudley Woodbridge suggested a scheme for the establishment of a bank, proposing himself to be the sole manager. The project was countenanced by the governor, who laid the proposal before the assembly for their consideration. Here it met with a very cold reception; not so much from a dislike to the scheme as from an objection to Mr. Woodbridge's enjoying the whole emoluments of the office, as sole director of the bank. As the plan, however, was pregnant with advantages to those who should be concerned in the management of the business, it was soon revived, with a few trifling alterations, to give it the appearance of originality, and brought forward in the assembly by Mr. John Holder,

CHAP. VI. treasurer of the island, supported by Mr. Sharpe and Mr.
1706.   Alexander Walker, two members of the council.

The influence of this triumvirate was not to be resisted; and, from motives the most corrupt that can actuate the human mind, they procured the passing of a law to supply the deficiency of gold and silver coin by a fictitious currency of paper money. By this law the treasurer was authorized to issue bills to the amount of sixty-five thousand pounds, to be lent to the planters on the security of their lands and negroes, and for transacting the business he was entitled to a commission of five per cent. Holder was not allowed the exclusive enjoyment of this advantage. He was content to share the profits with his friends Sharpe and Walker, as a recompense for their services in promoting the scheme. Walker, not satisfied with his proportion, insisted that his brother William Walker, of the assembly, should be allowed to participate in the gain; and in the event these honest, disinterested guardians of the people quarrelled about dividing the spoil, and the secret was disclosed.

This measure, the offspring of ignorance and corruption, encreased the evil it affected to remove, and diffused the most lively discontent throughout the country. The planters, who had sufficient security to offer, were enabled by the loan of these bills to withhold their crops from market, or to demand the most exorbitant prices for their produce; while the merchant, who could neither remit them to Europe, nor pass them in payment to the American traders for their cargoes, found them of no greater value than so much waste paper, and, of course, refused to receive them in exchange for their commodities. At length, the difficulty of negociating the bills, which might have been easily foreseen from the first, opened the eyes of the people to the deception that had been practised upon them. They complained of the act as a fraud and resented it as a job, intended merely to promote the interest of a few mercenary individuals.

The odium of the measure having drawn on the promoters of the bank the execrations of an injured and incensed people, the assembly, justly dreading the resentment of their constituents, passed a law to prolong their political existence by rendering the election of representatives triennial. While the bill was pending, petitions were presented against it from all parts of the island, except Saint Peter's. The assembly, however, were not to be diverted from their purpose, though, as we shall soon see, their sinister designs were frustrated, and they were denied the impunity which they sought to obtain.

Sir Bevill Granville continued to exercise the right claimed by his predecessor, of appointing his private secretary, and of sharing with him in the emoluments of his office. This produced a second remonstrance from the patentee to the queen, which was referred to the Lords Commissioners of Trade; and, after a lapse of some considerable time, within which Sir Bevill resigned the government,

CHAP. VI.   their lordships reported to her Majesty that the governor
~~~~~   had no right to appoint a private secretary but at his own
1706.   expense, and recommended that Mr. Skeene should be re-
            placed and confirmed in the receipt of all the fees and
            profits belonging to the office.   In consequence of this re-
            presentation Mr. Skeene, by her Majesty's letters manda-
            tory, was restored to the possession of all his rights and
            perquisites both as private and public secretary.*

              The governor finding his situation rendered extremely
            unpleasant by the continual contention of parties, and his
            constitution impaired by the influence of a tropical climate,
September. resigned his authority into the hands of William Sharpe,
            president of the council, with the view of returning to
            England for the benefit of his health; but he lived not to
            accomplish his design.   Death arrested him on his passage,
            and removed him to a state where his virtues and his faults
            will receive their appropriate recompence from the only
            competent Judge.

              Notwithstanding the animosities and disputes which dis-
            tracted the councils at this period, several salutary laws were
            enacted under the authority of general Granville.   Among
            these the most deserving of attention is the act for the en-
            couragement of the clergy.   As this venerable body of men
            have been separated from the busy part of mankind, that

---

* In latter times, however, the commander in chief has been allowed a private
secretary, whose salary, two hundred pounds sterling, is paid by the crown.

they may pursue those studies which would qualify them to instruct others in the great duties of religion, reason and justice demand that their situation should be rendered comfortable and respectable by a competent provision for their maintenance. Hitherto the emoluments of the sacerdotal office consisted in the annual receipt of an assessment of one pound of sugar on every acre of land, and of such fees on marriages, baptisms, and burials as custom had authorized. This was far from being a decent or an adequate maintenance for the clergy. It was therefore enacted, that, in addition to their glebes, most of which are considerable, the rectors of the different parishes should receive a salary of one hundred and fifty pounds, besides fees for the performance of occasional duty. This provision is certainly inadequate to meet the advance which the lapse of a century has made in the habits and expense of living; but it is to be observed, that among the fees of office, to the augmentation of which the people have patiently submitted, those of the clergy have not been neglected; and in most parishes the rector's fees exceed one hundred pounds a year. Besides, in the liberality of the vestry, the incumbent generally finds an ample compensation for the smallness of the legal stipend. The annual presents voted to the rectors are commonly equal to the established salary, and frequently exceed it. Hence the least valuable church living in the island may be moderately rated at four hundred pounds

a year.   In addition to this revenue there is on every glebe
a commodious, nay in most instances an elegant mansion,
built and kept in excellent repair, at the expense of the
parish, for the accommodation of the minister.

*It has lately been doubted whether even this is a suffi-
cient provision for the support of the clergy, of whom many
appear extremely anxious to be made independent of the
bounty of their vestries. Those who are satisfied with
what they receive, need neither wish for more nor for any
alteration in the mode by which it is granted; and the minister who is determined to perform his duty diligently,
and to conduct himself with humility and decorum, need
not fear the resentment of those from whom he expects his
reward.   It were, however, much to be wished, for the sake
of preserving the purity and dignity of the sacred function,
that the rectors of the several parishes were rendered independent of occasional gratuities from their vestries. As
lights of the world they should be placed above the cares
and perplexities of ordinary men. The clergy would then
be no longer under the necessity of temporising, as some
of them too often do, with the principal inhabitants of
their cure. But in providing for the independence of
the clergy, we should not lose sight of the circumstances of

---

* The legislature have just passed a law, augmenting the annual stipend of the
rectors to three hundred pounds.

those by whom they are paid. Vestries should no longer be invested with a power, too frequently abused, of indulging an ostentatious generosity to the injury of their parishioners, whose means of subsistence are often abridged to procure the taxes which are levied on them, for the support of the parochial establishment.

CHAP. VII.

PRESIDENT SHARPE'S ADMINISTRATION—SUCCEEDED BY MIT-
FORD CROWE—DISQUISITION CONCERNING THE CRIMINAL
JUDICATURE—DEATH OF MR. CODRINGTON—MR. LILLINGTON
ADMINISTERS THE GOVERNMENT—MR. LOWTHER APPOINTED
GOVERNOR—HIS TYRANNICAL CONDUCT—MR. SHARPE SUC-
CEEDS TO THE PRESIDENCY—LOWTHER RESTORED—HIS ARBI-
TRARY AND OPPRESSIVE MEASURES—PERSECUTES MR. GORDON
—THE CASE OF BERNARD COOK—THE GOVERNOR RECALLED—
MR. FRERE ASSUMES THE EXECUTIVE AUTHORITY—IS SUPER-
SEDED BY MR. COX—REMARKS ON THE FORTIFICATIONS AND
THE COLONIAL REPRESENTATION.

CHAP. VII. THE Honourable William Sharpe, having succeeded to
~~~~~~
1706. the government, on the departure of Sir Bevill Granville,
commenced his short, but turbulent, administration, by
dissolving that assembly to whose triennial existence he had
lately contributed, by his vote, as a member of council.
The public mind was, at this time, so irritated by political
disputes, and personal animosities, that the elections, in
many parts of the island, were contested with an unusual
degree of warmth and violence; and, in most instances,

terminated in favour of those who were known to be hostile
to the measures of the late executive government. Such
was the general disapprobation of the proceedings of the
late assembly, that only seven of the old members were
re-elected*.

In this violent collision of parties, Mr. W. Holder, speaker
of the late assembly; Colonel J. Holder, treasurer of the
island; his colleague, E. Holder, Mr. W. Walker, and all
who were known to be immediately concerned in the business of the bank, were rejected by their former constituents.
In Saint Joseph's, Colonel Holder endeavoured to prevent
the publication of the election writ, alledging that it had
been illegally issued. Disappointed in his aim, he wreaked
his vengeance on Mr. Fullwood, the rector of the parish,
whom, chancing to meet on the road, in company with his
wife, he assaulted and violently beat. Nor did the lady
escape his brutal violence; for, upon her interposing, he
furiously tore off her head-dress and otherwise unmanfully
abused her. Colonel Cleland not only refused to execute
the office of sheriff at Saint Andrew's, but appeared at the

---

* The new assembly consisted of Mr. Wheeler and G. Peers, for *St. Michael's*; T.
Maxwell and S. Adams, for *Christ Church*; J. Frere and N. Webb, for *St. Philip's*;
H. Peers and T. Neale, for *St. George's*; R. Downes and W. Leslie, for *St. John's*;
W. Cole and W. Carter, for *St. Thomas's*; T. Sandiford and J. Gibbes, for *St. Andrew's*;
R. Sandiford and S. Maynard, for *St. Peters*; T. Maycock and J. Maycock, for *St.
Lucy's*; E. Sutton and R. Yeamans, for *St. James's*; J. Vaughan and W. Grant, for
St. Joseph's: on their first meeting, Mr. Wheeler was chosen speaker.

poll and protested against the election. He, afterwards, in concert with the Holders, Waite and several others, drew up a remonstrance, which they presented to the assembly, denying the president's authority to dissolve the late assembly, declaring the house to be an illegal convention, and protesting against its proceedings. This paper was treated by both branches of the legislature as a factious attempt to excite sedition; and Cleland for his disorderly behaviour was removed from the council board.

Fired with resentment, Cleland presented a memorial to the assembly, offering to make a full disclosure of the corruption and bribery which had been practised by some persons in high responsible situations, for promoting the establishment of a bank; in which, as has been already shewn, the president, and Mr. Walker, of the council, were strongly implicated. The encouragement given to this proposal in the lower house, gave great offence in the council chamber, and the president sent a message to the assembly, disclaiming their authority to proceed on Cleland's information; it being inconsistent, he said, with the dignity of the government, that a member of council should appear before that house to vindicate himself against a criminal charge; and contrary to natural justice to proceed against him unheard. To this the assembly replied, that it was the undoubted right of the representative body of the people to receive information against any member of the other branch of the legislature for oppression, bribery, extortion, or other heinous offences, and to bring the offender to condign punishment.

In the midst of this altercation, Mr. Vaughan brought forward a fresh accusation against the members of the late administration. A contribution, it seems, had been raised among the practitioners in physic and surgery, for the pur-pose of bribing, certain members of both houses to consent to the passing of a law, allowing them to prove their accounts by their own oaths. Doctor Gamble, being examined at the bar of the house, confirmed the information received from Mr. Vaughan; but the charge was so vague and obscure, that it only served to fan the embers of dis-cord, without giving sufficient light to discover the offenders. The council, who were deeply involved in these criminal imputations, warmly resented the proceedings of the assembly, as tending to encourage factious, evil-minded persons to calumniate the most respectable characters in the country. Much time was thus spent in angry contentions, odious recriminations, and mutual revilings, which answered no other end than to expose both houses to general contempt.

In the mean while, the assembly were not negligent in their endeavours to relieve their country from the operation of the Paper Credit Act. Their remonstrances against it were so judicious, that it was repealed by her Majesty's order in council*. Justice, however, required that pro-

October.

---

* Univ. Hist. vol. 41. p. 165. Hall's Settlem. of Barb. p. 30. Laws of Barb. p. 493.

CHAP. VII.
~~~~~~
1706.

vision should be made for the payment of such bills as had been negotiated; the assembly accordingly passed a law for that purpose. At the same time, Holder was compelled to refund the premium which he had received for transacting the business. This, however, was not effected without a struggle. He applied to the Queen to be permitted to retain his ill-gotten gains, but without success.

1707.
June.

Having administered the government for the short space of nine months, Mr. Sharpe was superseded by the arrival of Mitford Crowe, Esquire, whose appointment had been formerly postponed, to make way for Sir Bevill Granville. The governor found the public mind in a considerable state of irritation, occasioned by the disputes concerning the banking business. In pursuance of the royal instructions, his excellency immediately removed from the council-board, and from all offices at his disposal, every person who had promoted or encouraged the late project for supplying the want of cash. Holder had, however, the address to obtain a seat in council; a circumstance which gave great offence to the assembly. They presented an address to the governor, thanking him for the alacrity with which he had obeyed her Majesty's commands; and insisting on the removal of Mr. Holder. To this address, his excellency, after censuring their conduct in presuming, as he said, to meddle with matters not immediately within their jurisdiction, replied, that Mr. Holder had received his mandamus subsequent to the Queen's order for the removal of those counsellors who had been instrumental in promoting the banking scheme; and that he should, therefore, take no notice of their application. Determined on effecting his downfall, they presented a petition, through their agent, to the Queen, in which, besides representing Holder as the original contriver and principal promoter of the bank, they accused him of many other enormities. Her Majesty, ever attentive to the complaints of her subjects, readily complied with their request, and Mr. Holder, by her Majesty's order, was degraded from his recent elevation. This act of justice, far from allaying the popular ferment, served only to increase the spirit of dissension. In the effervescence of party, many complaints were exhibited against Mr. Crowe; and, upon the memorable change of ministry, which was effected in England, at this period, he was removed from his government.

Amidst the rage of faction, and the contention of parties, the legislative councils of the country were occasionally employed in framing and digesting various laws for the government of slaves, the security of property, and the administration of justice; subjects every way deserving the mature attention of an enlightened legislature. But the means provided for the attainment of these noble objects are, in some instances, very inadequate to the end proposed.

The establishment of a supreme court of criminal judicature, is a circumstance of considerable importance, and may reasonably excite an inquiry, whether it is calculated to answer the purposes of its institutions. From the first settlement of the colony, there had been a tribunal for the punishment of offences against the public peace; but how, or by what rules, its proceedings were regulated, does not appear by the statute book. It is probable, that the plan was erroneous or defective, since we find, that very soon after Mr. Crowe's arrival, this important subject attracted the attention of the colonial parliament; and an act was passed, for establishing a court of grand sessions, of oyer and terminer, and general sessions of the peace. By this law it is directed, that a court shall be holden once in every six months, by the governor, as chief justice, assisted by the members of council, the judges of the courts of common pleas, and the justices of the peace. But should his excellency decline the seat, he is authorized to appoint a chief justice, with the consent of his council. From the obvious impropriety of the governor's presiding in this court, the jurisdiction of chief-justice is always delegated to one or other of members of council, or of the judges of the common pleas, who succeed to the chair in regular rotation, without the smallest regard to the legal ability, or forensic skill of the person on whom the appointment devolves. Few of these gentlemen have laid up any stores of knowledge to qualify them for the arduous undertaking; they have never drunk at the fountain of science; but trusting to natural intuition, they assume an awful office, and grasp the avenging sword of justice. Every ordinary justice of the peace, whose vanity prompts him to sit in judgment on the lives and liberties of his fellow creatures, is eligible to a seat on the bench. A court of criminal judicature is thus formed of men unacquainted with the laws which they are bound, by the most solemn obligations, to to administer faithfully. In a court so absurdly constituted, prejudice and partiality may safely exert their deleterious influence, secure within the dark immunities of a crowd *.

In every court, according to an eminent jurisconsult †, there must be at least three constituent parts; the *actor*, *reus*, and *judex*: the *actor*, or plaintiff, who complains of an injury done; the *reus*, or defendant, who is called to make satisfaction for it; and the *judex*, or judicial power, which is to examine the truth, and to determine the law arising upon that fact; and, if any injury be done, to ascertain and apply the proper remedy. Under the two former of these heads the whole bar is included, while the jury is admitted to a participation of the duties of the third. To each, the constitution of the parent state has assigned its peculiar function. It is the province of the

---

* " This court is inconvenient, for the judges are in general unacquainted with the law, and often commit mistakes. Their number is so great, that should they do wrong, there is no getting at them; and as most of the principal men in the colony sit in this court, hardly any thing can come on but some of them are connected with one or other of the parties." *Stokes's Constit. of the Colonies, p. 262.*

† Blackstone's Comment. vol. 3. p. 25.

jury candidly and impartially to inquire into the law and the fact; and, by their verdict, to determine the guilt or the innocence of the accused. The judge, by his superior skill and learning, supplies their deficiencies; he directs their attention to the proper objects; leads them through the labyrinths of legal sophistry and obscurity, and instructs them in the principles of the law by which they are bound to decide.

But very different is the case in Barbadoes. Here we have only the semblance of this noble bulwark of personal security. We have indeed a judge, a bar, and a jury; terms of high significance, but differing widely from their original import. If, in the course of their inquiries, the jury should find themselves involved in difficulties and uncertainty, to whom can they apply for assistance? Reason and common sense point to the bench. But from that quarter no information can be expected to elucidate their doubts. Deprived of this constitutional source of information, they are forced to seek among the venal advocates of the litigants themselves, a solution of the doubts which perplex their minds and render their decision uncertain and irresolute. But what confidence can a conscientious jury place in such partial, interested guides, whose contradictory opinions are calculated to deceive the judgment, when the star, from the bench, whose sober, steady light, should lead them in the way of truth, is eclipsed by the clouds of legal ignorance?

Juries of the present day happily have the advice of an attorney-general*, whose professional talents, luminous understanding, and legal erudition, are his least excellencies. His candour, humanity, and undeviating rectitude of conduct, in the senate and at the bar, justly claim the admiration and esteem of his contemporaries. But it is surely a solecism in criminal jurisprudence to require that the prosecutor for the crown should quit his station at the bar and assume the judicial function of charging and instructing a jury. It is too much to expect, that after the faithful performance of his duty to his client, in the support of a criminal charge, he should turn about and gravely assure the jury that the prisoner is less criminal than he had been labouring to make him appear; or that he should instruct them, with candour, in the nature of the verdict which they are bound, by their oaths, to return.

Besides, the human mind is by nature susceptible of wrong impressions; and, perhaps, the judgment of no man is more liable to perversion than that of a public advocate, or pleader. Whether he is the prosecutor of guilt or the vindicator of innocence, he views but one side of the question. Studious only of serving his client he twists and perverts the law to answer that sole purpose; and, while he seeks for ingenious arguments to maintain the point which he wishes to establish, his own understanding yields to the im-

---

* The Honourable John Beckles.

position of a plausible fallacy, contrived to influence the opinion of others. Such a man can never be a proper expounder of the law to an unenlightened jury. But, however the present attorney-general may reconcile these inconsistencies, and honourably exercise functions so incompatible, all men are mortal, and we must look forward, with painful apprehension to the day which shall deprive us of the services of this able and upright Crown-lawyer. Some mercenary tool of despotism may then be placed at the head of the bar, in whose hands this absurd custom may degenerate into the most arbitrary injustice and tyrannical oppression.

The remedy is obvious, Great Britain presents an example, which it would be true wisdom to emulate. Her bar is the school whence her seats of justice are supplied with those sages of the law, whose learning and virtue are their country's boast, and the admiration of surrounding nations. And why should a system, which has been beneficially adopted by the mother country for a long succession of ages be rejected and despised by her colonies? Instead of a bench, composed of an indefinite number of unlearned magistrates, let there be a chief justice appointed, who has been bred to the bar, and whose knowledge has been matured by experience; with him may be joined three puisne judges, selected from among gentlemen of rank, the most eminent for their talents and integrity. I should prefer, says an eminent philosopher, an even to an odd number of judges, and four to any other number: for in this number, besides that it sufficiently consults the idea of separate responsibility, nothing can be decided but by a majority of three to one. If the court be equally divided, nothing can be done; things remain as they were, with some inconvenience to the parties, but without any danger to the public of a hasty precedent*.

To render the judges independant of the governor, they should be appointed for life, with competent salaries to support the dignity of the office. The warmest acknowledgments of the people are due to his Majesty for the appointment of an eminent civilian to preside in the court of Vice-admiralty of this island: and happy would it be hereafter for the inhabitants in general, were this appointment followed by others of gentlemen equally eminent for legal ability, firmness, and integrity, to preside in the principal courts of judicature. Under the direction of great professional talents, the dignity of the public tribunals would be preserved, and the people would enjoy the blessings of liberty and property, certain of a steady, uniform, and impartial administration of justice. Nor let the frugal statesman startle at the proposal, " for that economy must be bad, which sacrifices the public welfare to the sordid considerations of an illiberal parsimony, and would parcel out

---

* Paley's Philos. vol. 2. p. 237.

the different offices of state, as it would arrange the establishment of a private family."

This year is rendered memorable by the death of Christopher Codrington, son of Sir Timothy Thornhill's brave companion in arms. Gratitude, for the memory of this illustrious benefactor of his country, may probably render a few biographical sketches of his life acceptable to the Barbadian reader. He was born in Barbadoes in the year 1668, and educated at Oxford. Equally distinguished for his learning and benevolence, he entered into the army, where his courage soon recommended him to the favour of King William, by whom he was made a captain in the first regiment of foot-guards. He was at the siege of Namur in 1695; and, upon the conclusion of the peace, was appointed captain-general and governor of the Leeward Islands. In 1701, several articles were exhibited against him in the House of Commons in England; to which he published a distinct and particular answer, and was honourably acquitted of all imputations. He shewed great bravery at the attack of Guadaloupe in 1703; but at last he resigned his government and lived a studious retired life, applying himself chiefly to church-history and metaphysics. He died at Barbadoes on the seventh of April, and was buried at Bridge-town the following day; his body was afterwards carried to England, and interred in the chapel of All Soul's College, Oxford, of which he had been a fellow. To this college he left a noble legacy, consisting of his library, valued at six thousand pounds; and ten thousand pounds in cash, to be laid out in building a library, and furnishing it with books*.   By his last will he bequeathed two valuable plantations in Barbadoes to the Society for propagating the Christian Religion in Foreign Parts.   He directed that these plantations should be kept entire, with at least three hundred negroes upon them.   The produce of these estates was allotted to maintain a convenient number of professors and scholars, under the vows of poverty, chastity and obedience; who were required to " study and practise physic and chirurgery, as well as divinity, that they may endear themselves to the people, and have the better opportunities of doing good to men's souls, whilst they are taking care of their bodies †."

The public have not hitherto derived those advantages from this princely benefaction, which might have been expected from it.   A college was built on one of the plantations, in a healthy part of the parish of Saint John, and endowed for the education of youth.   And proper masters were employed, with suitable salaries, for their instruction, furnished with every thing necessary for their support, at the expense of the foundation.   But the calamities incident to West Indian property, the failure of crops, the mismanagement of faithless and negligent stewards, and the misapplication of the revenue, soon occasioned the de-

---

* Encyclo. Brit. vol. 5. p. 120.   † Mem. Barb. Appen. p. 2.

cline of this beneficial institution. At length the estates were farmed by Mr. John Brathwaite, under whose judicious and skilful direction they attained a more prosperous condition; and, at the expiration of the lease, he gave them up to the trustees, free from all incumbrances, with a considerable surplus, which he was entitled to retain for his risk and trouble; but which he generously relinquished, for the benefit of the establishment. Hence this admirable man may, with propriety, be considered as the second founder of this noble institution. These plantations are now under an excellent system of management, and the direction of persons disposed to a faithful performance of the trust reposed in them. The college is under the presidency of the Rev. Mark Nicholson, A. M. an accomplished scholar, and a pious divine, peculiarly qualified, by his learning and virtue, to be the preceptor of youth.

May 10: On the departure of Mr. Crowe the executive authority devolved on George Lillington, president of the council. A new excise bill now furnished the factious and turbulent with a fresh subject of contention. The house of assembly had hitherto exercised the exclusive right of nominating the treasurer and comptroller of the excise. This was certainly an unconstitutional assumption of power, but, as the right had been once admitted, the propriety of its being now disputed is, at least, doubtful. When men's minds are heated they seldom reason rightly; and the council thought this a favourable opportunity of resenting the indignities which they had received from the assembly, by opposing their encroachments on the royal prerogative, and, therefore, rejected the bill; insisting that they had an equal right with the assembly to nominate the treasurer and comptroller. This added fresh fuel to the flame, and produced an intemperate altercation between the two branches of the legislature. Both parties continuing obstinate, the point in dispute was, at length, submitted to the Queen's determination; and, her Majesty, more anxious to restore tranquillity to a distracted country than to preserve her prerogative in a matter so trifling and unimportant, declared it to be her royal will and pleasure, that the president and council should consent to the excise bill, without insisting on a right to disapprove of the person proposed to be treasurer*. This order, in effect, transferred to the representatives of the people a branch of the executive power, which they have ever since continued to exercise, and, in many instances, they have gradually extended their authority, by appointing to offices not then within the contemplation of either party.

Sept. 27

Mr. Lillington lived just long enough to resign the reins of government into the hands of Robert Lowther, Esq. who having been appointed, in an evil hour, commander in chief, arrived in Carlisle-bay, on the twenty-third day of June. The overbearing pride and arrogance of this gentle-

1711.
June 23.

---

* Hall's First Settlem. p. 30. MS. Mem. of Barb. p. 52.

man soon created him many enemies, among a loyal and high-spirited people, who could not easily be brought to submit to the imperious sway of a despotic ruler. Aggravated by opposition, the impetuosity of his temper hurried him into many acts of injustice and oppression. Among these was the suspension of Mr. Sharpe, Mr. Walker, and Mr. Berisford, who had the firmness to oppose his measures in council. These gentlemen were not indolent in seeking redress. They carried their complaints to the foot of the throne, and were honoured with her Majesty's order for their restoration. Lowther, however, ventured to disobey the commands of his Sovereign, and, for several months, refused to admit the suspended members to resume their seats. Such an audacious contempt of authority necessarily interrupted the progress of public business, and excited the most lively discontent throughout the island. In a council, composed of twelve members, appointed by letters of mandamus, forming an essential part of the legislative and judicial establishments of the country, it was maintained with great strength of reasoning, that, while the three excluded members were thus arbitrarily hindered from sitting and voting, there could be no legitimate government existing in the island. The governor's right of suspension was not disputed; but, as the suspension, in this case, had been annulled by a superior authority, it was insisted that no council, court of error or of equity, could be properly holden without the presence, or concurrence, of every member,

whose attendance was not prevented by legal disability;
and, consequently, that all acts performed by the sitting
members, either as a branch of the legislature, or as a
court of chancery, were absolutely null and void.

Mr. Lowther's insolence and disobedience, soon drew on
him the indignation of insulted Majesty. He was recalled
from his government; but, unwilling to relinquish his
power, he delayed his departure so long, that some of the
principal men of the island disclaimed his authority; upon
which he threatened Mr. Cox and Mr. Salter, two members
of council, with a criminal prosecution, for treasonable
designs.* At length, finding all tergiversation fruitless, he
reluctantly submitted to her Majesty's commands, and
returned to England.

On this joyful event, the Honourable William Sharpe   May.
again succeeded to the presidency. The mild and conciliatory temper of the president, had a considerable share
in tranquillizing the public mind. His short administration
was so perfectly unexceptionable, that he had the honour
of receiving the thanks of the British ministry, for his meritorious conduct. But unhappily for the peace of the
colony, on the accession of George I. Mr. Lowther was   1715.
re-appointed governor of Barbadoes. No appointment
could have been more unpropitious and displeasing to the
Barbadians than this. Absence had not softened the   May 12.

---

* Univ. His. vol. 41, p. 165.

haughty and vindictive spirit of the man. He returned to the island, with all his former prejudices and inveterate animosities rankling in his breast, and eagerly embraced the opportunity which his restoration to power afforded him, of wrecking his vengeance on those who had opposed his former administration.

The first victim of his malice was the Reverend Mr. Gordon, the Bishop of London's commissary, and rector of the parish of Saint Michael. This gentleman, having incurred the governor's displeasure, was deemed to suffer a tedious and rigorous persecution. In consequence of the most scandalous misrepresentations of his character and conduct, which his excellency had transmitted to England, with the assistance of the colonial agents, Mr. Gordon was exposed to the censure of his diocesan, and experienced some unmerited severity from the Board of Trade. Consci-

ous of his innocence, Gordon resorted to the fountain head for redress. He presented a memorial to the King, complaining not only of the governor's malicious misrepresentation of his conduct to the Bishop of London, but of the agents' petition to the Board of Trade, and of their lordship's report upon it. The matter being referred to a committee of the Privy Council, Gordon obtained a commission for the examination of witnesses on the island; but the governor, pretending to doubt the authenticity of the order, committed Gordon to prison, and had him indicted at the ensuing court of grand sessions, where his excellency presumed to preside in person, thus uniting the incongruous characters of prosecutor and judge. This step, the most unprecedented in the annals of criminal judicature, was strictly conformable to the ridiculous law of the island, by which a palpable inconsistency is authorized. Common decency should have restrained the governor from deviating in this particular from the established usage of his predecessors, who had invariably delegated their authority in this court to some other person; but, yielding to the dictates of passion, he pursued his vindictive purpose, unawed by religion or morality. His criminal designs, however, were frustrated. Gordon's defence was ably and successfully conducted by Mr. Hope, a respectable attorney, and Jonathan Blenman, an eminent barrister; who, undismayed by the frowns of power, stood forth the assertors of injured innocence.

This spirited conduct necessarily involved these gentlemen in the resentment of the tyrant. Blenman was immediately committed to the common gaol, whence he was released, on giving bail, in the sum of one thousand pounds, to appear at the next court of grand sessions. This recognizance was, in the end, forfeited; for Blenman, accompanied by his client and their faithful solicitor, hastened to England, and implored redress at the foot of the throne. In short, the lords justices, the King being then absent on a visit to his electoral dominions, pronounced the charge against Gordon to be groundless and malicious; it was, therefore, dismissed. Blenman, in his turn, enjoyed the most complete triumph over his rancorous adversary. The lords justices, after declaring the whole of the governor's conduct to have been arbitrary and illegal, ordered that Mr. Blenman's recognizance, and all the proceedings thereon, should be vacated; and that, if any levy had been made for the forfeiture, the full sum should be returned and paid to him without delay*.

His presiding at the court of grand sessions, was not the only instance in which Mr. Lowther arrogated to himself extraordinary judicial powers. Under colour of the law, authorizing the governor and council to hear and determine petitions in equity, and writs of error on matters cognizable in the courts of law, he constituted himself and his creatures at the council board, into a court of grievance, in which they exceeded the bounds of their legal jurisdiction. The arbitrary proceedings of this court, occasioned many complaints against the governor; the result of which was, an order from the lords justices, abolishing the court of grievance; observing, that the only proper jurisdiction of the governor and council, as a court of error or equity, is to correct the errors and grievances arising in the proceedings of the inferior courts; but not to proceed originally in causes, except upon petitions in matters of equity.

The case of Bernard Cook, a native of Hanover, is

---

* Caribbeana, vol. 1. p. 269.

strongly characteristic of the genius and temper of Lowther's administration. Mr. Cook had been endeavouring to establish a right to an estate, which he alleged was unjustly withheld from him by Mr. Frere, a gentleman nearly related to the governor. This claim was sufficient to inspire his excellency with resentment against the unfortunate Hanoverian. When a man is once marked for destruction, the means of accomplishing his ruin are easily found. Cook was reported to have reflected, in careless conversation, on the chastity of two ladies : one, the wife of Robert Warren, an artful attorney; the other, the wife of Samuel Adams, a gentleman of some distinction. So favourable an opportunity of gratifying their patron's spleen, as well as their own resentment, was not to be neglected. The angry husbands, therefore, determined on a most vigorous prosecution. A court of quarter sessions was immediately called, composed of Guy Ball and F. Bond, members of council, with T. Maycock, R. Bishop, G. Barry, J. Fereharson, S. Thomas, and W. Kirkman, justices of the peace, selected from different parishes. Before this tribunal, Cook was arraigned on two separate indictments for defamation. Sensible that he could expect neither justice nor mercy from such prejudiced judges, he objected to the jurisdiction of the court, and claimed the privilege of a trial by a jury of his peers. Malice, however, was not to be deprived of its victim. Cook was found guilty of both charges, and condemned to receive

thirty-nine lashes for each offence. The sentence was carried into immediate execution, by the common whipper of
slaves, in the presence of the justices, who stood by, like
demons, enjoying the agonies of the degraded sufferer.

The injured Hanoverian flew to his sovereign for redress.
His complaints were referred to the Lords of the Committee
for hearing Appeals; and, before their lordship's came to
any determination on the subject, they issued a commission
for instituting an inquiry, in Barbadoes, into the particulars of the affair; directing the necessary proofs to be sent
to England, under the seal of the island. Having at length
collected sufficient evidence to form a correct judgment,
their lordships reported to his Majesty, that the complaint
against the governor had not been substantiated; but that
the charge against the justices had been fully proved; that
they had proceeded against the prisoner without any crime
alleged against him; for that scandalous words, spoken of
private persons, are no ground of criminal prosecution.
Upon the whole, their lordships were of opinion, that the
justices, who had sat on the trial, had acted illegally, for
that they had not proper cognizance of the matter before
them, but had taken upon them to examine witnesses, and
to determine matters of fact without a jury, and had finally
given two sentences, which were arbitrary and unjust. In
consequence of this representation, his Majesty was graciously pleased to order, that the names of the justices,
who presided on the trial, should be struck out of the

commission of the peace; and that Mr. Ball, and Mr. Bond, should be removed from the council board*.

A Mr. Brenan, who had been guilty of a much greater offence than that imputed to Cook, experienced, at the same time, much milder treatment. Having killed a gentleman in a duel, he applied to the governor for protection; and, although he had never been brought to a trial for the crime, he found no difficulty in obtaining his excellency's pardon. But, justly apprehensive that so ridiculous and unconstitutional an interposition in his favour could afford him no efficient security in the event of a prosecution, Brenan went to England, and was indebted for security to the clemency of his Prince †.

Nor were these the only instances of tyranny and injustice of which Mr. Lowther was guilty. With a view to his own private emoluments, he permitted a few favoured persons to carry on an illicit and lucrative traffic with the Spaniards, and even admitted a Spanish vessel to frequent the port of Bridge-Town; while, from the same corrupt motives, he caused a ship belonging to Mr. Lansa, a merchant of that place, to be seized and condemned. In fine he had the address to procure a handsome settlement, by which he amassed the sum of twenty-eight thousand pounds: thus plundering a loyal and oppressed people, whom he re-

---

* Caribbeana, vol. 1. p. 342.   † Short Hist. of Barb. p. 101.

presented to the British ministry as French smugglers, disaffected to government. To this cause, perhaps, it was
owing that he was removed, since the money was received
in open violation of the Royal instructions, by which he
was expressly forbidden to take any salary or present from
the assembly.

Lowther's tyranny had now grown so grievous and intolerable, that many of the most respectable inhabitants of
the colony concurred in a petition to the king, stating the
various acts of delinquency which he had committed in the
course of his long and oppressive administration, and humbly beseeching his Majesty to remove him from the government. To oppose this application, the governor procured
addresses from the sycophants by whom he was surrounded,
commending the mildness, wisdom, and equity of his administration. But all was in vain. The application for
the governor's dismissal was supported by Sir Robert Davers,
Mr. Walter, and Mr. Alleyne, men of considerable property in the island, of whom the two former were members
of the English House of Commons.

The governor was at length called home to answer the
charges exhibited against him. To avert the storm which
seemed ready to burst on his head, he took every precaution
which an artful insidious policy could dictate, and the last
moments of his expiring power were occupied in annoying
his enemies and in providing for the security of himself and
his adherents. All the public employments were filled by

his friends, who possessed a decided majority in both houses of the colonial parliament. Suspecting that should they be removed by his successor, his own misdemeanors would be detected with greater facility, he procured a law to be passed, the professed object of which was to preserve the peace and tranquillity of the community; but its real design was to keep the creatures of the governor in power, by restraining the president from making any changes in the official departments. The plan was yet incomplete. To guard every avenue it was necessary to place his nephew, Mr. John Frere, at the head of the government. There was one obstacle, however, to be removed; Mr. Cox, as senior member of the council was entitled to the succession. But this difficulty was quickly obviated; Mr. Cox and Mr. Salter were both suspended to make room for his relative. After completing these arrangements Lowther took his last farewell of Barbadoes; and Mr. Frere immediately assumed, or rather usurped, the direction of affairs.

June

Mr. Lowther on his arrival in England was summoned to appear before the lords justices, his Majesty being absent on an excursion to the continent, to answer the various complaints which had been preferred against him. After a long and patient investigation of the several allegations contained in the petition of the Barbadians, their lordships determined that the charges were amply and clearly established; they therefore directed him to be taken into custody, and ordered that he should be prosecuted for high crimes and misdemeanors. But the prosecution was most unaccountably protracted until the accession of George II. when an act of grace rescued the culprit from the hands of justice, and saved him from condign punishment.

Meanwhile Sir Charles Cox presented a memorial to the lords justices, complaining of the arbitrary suspension of his brother, and of his having been superseded in the presidency by a younger member of council. This application produced an order from their lordships for the restoration of Cox and Salter, and commanding Frere to resign the government. But, pleased with his surreptitious authority, he hesitated to comply, until upon a fresh representation of his refractory conduct, he was cited to appear before the king and privy council, to account for his disobedience. Being thus compelled to submit, he went to England, where he died, soon after his arrival, of the small pox.*

Cox having at length succeeded to the presidency, an extraordinary scene of anarchy and confusion ensued. All offices of trust and profit were in the hands of the late governor's friends, who made a point of thwarting and opposing all the measures of the president. Not being of a temper to submit patiently to such pertinacious opposition, Cox had re-

---

* Tenderness for the memory of his grandfather has induced the author of the short history of Barbadoes to gloss over this transaction; but have divested it of its false colouring, on the authority of the Caribbeanna, vol. i. p. 342. and the Univ. History, vol. xli. p. 166.

course to a harsh expedient. Disregarding the tranquillity act, as it was termed, by which all public officers had been confirmed in their places, but which had not yet received the royal assent, he suspended six members of council at once;* he displaced Mr. Sutton, chief judge of one of the courts of common pleas, and removed Mr. Gibbes, chief baron of the court of exchequer. He dismissed several military officers from their commands; and, to strengthen his administration, filled their places with persons more readily pliant to his views. This violence served only to fan the flame of discord. The assembly petitioned the king, complaining of the arbitrary proceedings of the president; and the suspended members of council, on an application to the throne, were restored to their functions. This circumstance afforded matter of such exultation to the opposition, that they determined to preserve no terms with the president; and, in the blindness of their intemperate resentment, the interests of the country were sacrificed to the indulgence of personal animosity.

It has been mentioned by some of our colonial historians, as an instance of Mr. Cox's want of moderation, that he removed from the bench of magistrates several gentlemen of fortune and respectability, and encouraged vexatious pro-

---

* These were T. Maxwell, T. Maycock, J. L. Blackman, W. Carter, G. Ball, and F. Bond: the two last were suspended in pursuance of the King's order, for being concerned in the illegal proceedings against Bernard Cook.

secutions against them. But this was, in fact, an indispensable part of his duty, in obedience to the commands of his sovereign. For although the order for the degradation of those persons who had been concerned in the arbitrary and illegal prosecution of Bernard Cook, was issued previous to Mr. Lowther's recal, it did not reach Barbadoes till after Mr. Cox had been placed in the president's chair. With regard to the vexatious prosecution which he is charged with having countenanced, if conjecture may be allowed to supply the place of positive certainty, it might not be thought improbable that these suits were commenced by Cook, to recover, from his unjust judges, a pecuniary compensation for the injury which he had sustained by their illegal sentence. The conduct of the president in executing the royal order, added only to the number and the virulence of his enemies; for such are the selfishness and perverseness of mankind, that a commander in chief, who holds the reins of government with a steady equal hand, will often give offence to the petty despots, whose tyranny and licentiousness he punishes or restrains.

Among the various disputes in which Mr. Cox was involved, there is one which deserves to be remembered, for the independent spirit displayed on the occasion by a gentleman who then held the highest law office in the country. The president was engaged in a correspondence, on some political subject, with Mr. Sutton, a member of the general assembly, whose letters happening to be written with a freedom and a poignancy, which his honour thought inconsistent with the respect due to his exalted station, he laid them before the council. Concurring in the resentment of the president, the obsequious board voted that the writer should be prosecuted for a libel. Mr. Richard Carter, the attorney-general of that day, was accordingly ordered to proceed against Mr. Sutton for his supposed offence. Disdaining the servile office of avenging Mr. Cox's personal quarrels, this upright crown lawyer declined the invidious task. In a memorial addressed to the president, he stated that Sutton's letters contained nothing sufficiently libellous, scandalous, and defamatory to make up the necessary ingredients in an indictment for a misdemeanor by writing. The learned gentleman added, "That by the laws of all civilized nations, if even a prince require something to be done which the person who is to do it takes to be unlawful, it is his duty to refuse the performance of so illegal a command, and I fear, that should I carry on any prosecution, by indictment or information, against any of the king's subjects, which should hereafter be judged unlawful, it will be no justification for me to say that I had your honour's order, grounded upon the opinions of five members of council, for so doing." *

About this time the duke of Portland, accompanied by his accomplished lady, arrived in Carlisle-bay, on his pas-

---

* Caribbeanna, vol. i. p. 401.

sage to Jamaica, of which island his grace had been appointed governor. This event seemed, for awhile, to abate
the rage of party. The opposite factions suspended their
mutual animosity, and all ranks of people appeared emulous of recommending themselves to their noble visitants by
courteous display of a munificent hospitality. The august
pair were highly gratified with their reception, and left
Barbadoes impressed with a favourable opinion of the taste
and politeness of the inhabitants.

As the president was allowed no salary from the country,
the expenses of the entertainments which he gave in honour of the duke and duchess of Portland, amounting to
eight hundred and ten pounds, were defrayed, with the
consent of the legislature, by an order on the treasury for
that sum. This circumstance, as will be seen in the sequel,
was productive of much illiberal altercation.

Such was the factious temper of the times and the little
decorum with which even the first magistrate was treated,
that Mr. Cox, while presiding in the court of chancery, was
grossly insulted by Gelasius Mac Mahon, a turbulent factious lawyer; who, among other insulting expressions, charged the president with countenancing and supporting perjury. For this offence Mac Mahon was prosecuted at the
ensuing court of grand sessions; where he was sentenced
to pay a fine of one hundred pounds; and to make a public
apology, in a particular form of words, prescribed by the
court, to Mr. Cox, at his next sitting in council; or, to

be suspended from practising as a barrister in any court of law or equity, until he should comply with this part of the sentence. Mac Mahon objected to the legality of this judgment, and the point was referred to the determination of the attorney-general, who gave a very evasive and uncandid opinion. The case was then transmitted to England and laid before serjeant Pengelly, who pronounced the judgment of the court to be erroneous and illegal, and ought to be reversed. The reasons assigned by the learned serjeant were these: that it imposed a submission and a confession of the offence in a prescribed form of words; that it was not, as it ought to have been, absolute and unconditional; and that the court of grand sessions had no authority to restrain the defendant from practising in either of the other courts. This erroneous proceeding probably would not have happened had the chief justice been a lawyer.

It is not to be doubted that the divisions and the dissentions which, at this period, distracted the country, were not more disgraceful to its character than prejudicial to its interests. Perplexed with the acrimonious and contradictory complaints, alternately transmitted by either faction, the British ministry resolved to send out a commander in chief with full power to enquire into, and, if possible, to adjust all differences subsisting in the colony, and to punish all disturbers of the public peace. Lord Belhaven, a Scotch nobleman, high in favour with the Prince of Wales, was first appointed to the important office; but his Lordship, unfortunately perished at sea. The appointment was next conferred on Lord Irwin, but he too had the misfortune to die on his passage. At length, the government was bestowed on colonel Henry Worsley, a gentleman of a steady inflexible temper.

Disgusted with the tedious detail of factious disputes, the mind turns with complacency to the contemplation of more tranquil scenes, and seeks a temporary relief in reviewing the means which have been adopted, in the progress of legislation, for the public security and happiness. These important objects, notwithstanding the anarchy and confusion which then prevailed, were not entirely neglected. Many laws were framed during this turbulent period; and, though some of them are extremely erroneous and defective in many material points, others are judiciously adapted to the circumstances of the people and the advancement of their welfare. It is not proposed to take a general review of the legislative acts of this period; a few will suffice for present observation.

To governor Lowther's quarrel with Mr. Gordon it is probably owing, that the bounty of the parochial vestries to their rectors was limited by law to a sum not exceeding seventy pounds, unless a donative to a larger amount should be confirmed by the governor and council. This law is now wholly disregarded, and the vestries are left to pursue their own inclinations, certain that their largesses will be sanctioned by a higher authority.

To the same improper cause may be ascribed the law for preventing the establishment of a spiritual court in this island. As the colonies had never been formed into dioceses, nor annexed to any particular bishopric, the bishop of London proposed to the King that they should be subjected to his spiritual jurisdiction. His Majesty, having previously advised with the crown lawyers, granted the bishop a commission, giving him full power and authority by himself, or by his commissaries, to exercise an ecclesiastical jurisdiction in the several colonies, according to the laws and canons of the church of England; reserving to the governor the right of collating to all benefices, granting licences for marriages, and probates of wills

By this commission his lordship was authorized to inquire into the manners and conduct of all rectors, ministers, curates, and incumbents of the several churches, and of all parish clerks; and to correct and punish them, according to their demerits, by amoval, deprivation, suspension, excommunication, or other ecclesiastical censure. He was also empowered to inquire concerning the reparation of the parish churches and houses belonging to the rectors; to compel those whose province it was to keep them in suitable repair; and to punish all who should be found delinquent and contumacious. This seems to have been a proper jurisdiction to correct any irregularities in the conduct of our spiritual pastors, and to decide in all differences between them and their flock. But after his dispute with Mr.

CHAP. VII. Gordon, his lordship's commissary, the governor obtained
1722.   the passing of a law " to quiet the minds of the people
against the terrors of a spiritual court."   The preamble of
this law states, that such a court would clash with the municipal laws of the place, embarrass the government, vex
and torment the gentry, *depauperate* the substantial freeholders, and ruin the common people.   It is difficult to
conceive how these effects could result from the cause to
which they are assigned; but to obviate these mischiefs,
real or imaginary, it was enacted, " that no ecclesiastical
law or jurisdiction shall have power to enforce, confirm, or
establish any mulct or punishment, in any case whatsoever,
within this island."

From the number of bays and landing places with which
the whole western coast of the island is indented, the Barbadians early saw the necessity of guarding, with care and
vigilance, against the incursion of a marine foe.   They
were more solicitous of securing their property from the attacks of hostile freebooters, than of accumulating wealth,
uncertain of its enjoyment.   A chain of fortifications was
erected from Maycock's-bay to Oistin's-town; in which
were enumerated forty-eight castles, forts, and batteries,
mounted with four hundred and sixty-three pieces of ordnance.   The laws which provided for the support of this
establishment were at first temporary and occasional, but
under Mr. Lowther's second administration, a more permanent and efficient plan was adopted.   The island was sepa-

rated into five divisions, and the war establishment consisted of seven chief gunners, twenty under gunners, and one hundred and fifty-nine matrosses, besides five clerks, and five supervisors. The under gunners and matrosses are required to be on constant duty, and to be instructed by the chief gunners in the art of gunnery, and the use of small arms.

If the plan be examined with an eye of candour, abstracted from the abuses which have crept into its execution, it certainly is entitled to approbation. A line of defence is judiciously extended the whole length of the accessible part of the coast; and an effective body of men are kept in continual readiness to repel the desultory irruptions of maritime marauders, or to sustain a more serious attack until they can be sustained by the militia. But the wisest of human institutions is liable to perversion, and the best concerted plans must fail, when those to whom the execution of them is entrusted, are negligent or incapable.

This expensive establishment, whatever might have been its original design, has degenerated into a grievous and intolerable burthen. The pay of the officers and men, independent of the supervisor's salaries, which, being contingent, are not easily ascertained, amount to five thousand and twenty pounds annually; to which must be added fifteen hundred pounds a year, part of the tonnage duty, appropriated to the purchase of gun-powder. Nor does the evil end here. Besides an immense expenditure of stores, in which prodigality wantons without controul, great abuses are committed by the boards of commissioners *. To answer some sinister purpose ; to promote the interest of a favourite supervisor, or to gratify the capricious vanity of an hospitable captain gunner, considerable sums of the public money are squandered in repairing or erecting commodious houses and elegant apartments for his accommodation. Hence the annual expense of the fortifications may be fairly computed to exceed eight thousand pounds. Notwithstanding this profuse and wanton waste of the public treasure, many of the forts, particularly those which command the harbour of the second town in the island, are literally mouldering in ruins ; they contain scarcely a single piece of serviceable ordnance, and are so completely destitute of ammunition as to be frequently incapable of exciting or propagating an alarm.

The accessible nature of the whole western coast lays the country so open to the predatory incursions of a daring or rapacious foe, that nothing can be more evident than the imperative necessity of putting some of our forts and batteries in a proper posture of defence. The impracticability of constructing regular fortifications capable of with-

---

* In 1776, Mr. Duke asserted, in the house of assembly, that the disbursements for the use of the fortifications were annually estimated at three thousand pounds, exclusive of gunpowder. This estimate was made in time of peace.

standing the approaches of a hostile squadron, or a besieging army, is admitted, yet the reparation of our principal forts, and the supplying them with cannon and ordnance stores, are measures which common prudence enjoins, if they be considered merely as the means of protecting our peaceful citizens from the casual irruptions and ruinous depredations of privateers.

Were the fortifications kept in suitable repair, no man, capable of thinking justly, could suppose, for a moment, that the gunners and matrosses are an useless body of men. But in their present ruined and dismantled condition, it cannot be dissembled, that the expenditure of the enormous sum annually thrown away upon them is unjust and oppressive. To provide for the support of government, and the maintenance of the public security, are duties incumbent on every good subject; but the power which wrests from him a single shilling unnecessarily must be tyrannical. To reconcile the people to the burthens imposed on them for the support of this establishment, some show of decency should be preserved. They should, at least, be amused with the idea of security. But the money drawn from their pockets is squandered in thoughtless profusion, without the most flimsy pretext of necessity or expediency. The voice of justice calls loudly for the redress of this grievance. It is the duty of the representatives of the people to apply the proper remedy. No objection is made to the quantum of the sum annually expended on the fortifications; the misapplication of it is the only ground of rational complaint. Were they repaired and rendered capable of protecting our defenceless towns, the money required for their maintenance would be paid without a murmur. No people in the world, who contribute at all to the support of government, are more moderately taxed than the Barbadians ; nor would they be dissatisfied at any augmentation of their burthens, were the produce of their taxes faithfully employed in providing for their safety.

It has been proposed to abandon our forts, or to sell them to the crown, rather than be at the expense of repairing them. Pitiful economy! Is there a man so lost to every sense of public virtue, as not to contemn the insidious proposal? So blind as not to see its folly and danger? Or so ignorant as not to be sensible of the necessity of keeping in repair the batteries within the vicinity of the towns, for the protection of the adjacent harbours? Far from my intention be the idea of recommending the rebuilding of our fallen forts, on the extensive scale on which they were originally planned, or of supplying them with the same number of superfluous cannon. It will be sufficient if our principal bays are enfiladed with strong batteries, mounting from two to six pieces of heavy ordnance*, with

---

* Professional men say, that a battery of four guns, well posted, is a match for a first-rate man of war. *Pocket Gunner, p. 50.* Iron ordnance, exclusive of the carriage, costs twenty pounds sterling a ton. Eighteen pounders weigh two tons, and

guard-houses for the matrosses, and barracks for the militia on alarms. The expenses of this undertaking seem to be greatly over-rated. In most places, the materials are already on the spot, and will be sufficient for the construction of batteries, on the reduced scale proposed, after every allowance is made for waste.

In the interim, the gunners and matrosses, who, at present, are incapable of being usefully employed, may be dismissed from the service. The saving of stores, gunpowder, and salaries, which may be thus obtained in one year, may be estimated at eight thousand pounds. This would be a sufficient fund for the purchase of fifty iron eighteen pounders, and twelve brass six pounders, with limbers, harness, and ammunition carts, complete. When cannon are procured, and the batteries rebuilt, the full complement of gunners and matrosses, might be restored with propriety; and provision should be made for the punctual payment of their salaries. At present, they are annually paid half the salary due to them; hence they are often obliged to sell their orders at a discount of more than one-fourth of their value. This is a great discouragement to the service. It prevents that strict attendance to their

---

twelve pounders a ton and a half. *Ibid. p.* 155 *and* 209. A light brass six pounder, with limbers and harness, complete, will cost 215l. sterling; and every two guns will require an ammunition cart, which will cost 20l. more. Hence, an estimate may be made of the moderate expense at which the accessible points may be guarded.

duty, which, were they more regularly paid, ought to be enforced; and which, under a better regulation, their officers would have a right to demand. They should be formed into brigades of artillery, and, while on duty, should be subject to the articles of war, and disciplined with the same regularity as is usually practised in the King's garrisons. Thus would they be rendered an useful body of men; the country would enjoy, at a moderate expense, the advantage of a permanent defence against the predatory attacks of privateers; and possess a formidable corps of artillery, ready, in case of invasion, to join in the more important duties of the field.

From this review of the act, respecting the fortifications, we shall proceed to that which was passed by president Cox, for preserving the freedom of elections. By this law, every free and natural born subject, except the descendants of negroes, of the age of twenty-one years, professing the Christian religion, who is actually and rightfully seized, and possessed of ten acres of land, or of a house, in either of the towns, of the yearly value of ten pounds, in fee simple or fee tail, in right of marriage, or of dower, by the courtesy of England, in right of the church as rector; or by five years quiet and lawful possession, is declared to be a freeholder capable of electing, or being elected, an assembly man. The first thing observable in this law is, that it makes no difference between the qualifications of the candidates and the electors. In England, every knight of the shire must have a clear estate, to the value of six hundred pounds per annum; and every burgess, to the value of three hundred pounds; nor is it required that these estates should lie in the borough or county for which the members are chosen. But, in Barbadoes, every illiterate possessor of ten acres is born a legislator, or is at least eligible to a seat in the general assembly, as a representative of the parish in which his freehold lies. The second point, deserving of notice, is the qualification of the electors. And here, without adopting the wild theories and maxims of the parliamentary reformers, it may be fairly assumed, as a just objection to the colonial election law, that the electoral franchise is too limited. The principal qualification required of a voter for members of the British parliament, is that he should have a freehold of the value of forty shillings a year. Why the privilege of voting for representatives was not made equally extensive in Barbadoes, is a question not easily solved, unless we conclude that the law was intended to enable those, by whom is was framed, the more readily to exercise a corrupt and an undue influence at elections.

One of the most invaluable privileges of a British subject, is that of appointing representatives to consent to the making of such laws as may be necessary or convenient. To preserve this fundamental right pure and inviolate, should be our primary care, our noblest ambition. The freedom essential to the due exercise of this privilege, can be maintained only by an extension of its benefits. All the inhabitants of every district, says Montesquieu, ought to have a right of voting at the election of a representative, except such as are in so mean a condition, as to be deemed to have no will of their own. The paucity of those, who, in most precincts, are entitled to vote, facilitates the sinister designs of the opulent and powerful; and often contributes to raise very unworthy candidates to seats in the legislature, while it degrades some of our parishes to the contemptible level of venal boroughs. Though no advocate for universal representation, I conceive that the electoral franchise is justly due to every Christian freeman, possessed of the smallest real estate. The humble possessor of a single acre is not less personally affected by the laws of his country, than the opulent proprietor of a thousand acres.

In some districts it often happens, that the freeholders are deprived of the power of making a discreet choice, by the difficulty of prevailing on gentlemen of respectability to accept the representation of their parishes. This inconvenience might, perhaps, be remedied, by imitating the policy of the mother country, and making it no longer necessary that the property of the person elected should be situated in the parish which he represents. In a country, circumscribed within such narrow boundaries, no danger need be apprehended from a dissimilarity of interests, or a want of local attachment; nor are genius and knowledge confined to any particular spot. An inhabitant of Christ

Church may be as well qualified to represent the parish of Saint Lucy, as though he had been born and bred in the vicinity of Pye-Corner. Thus the deficiencies of one parish may be supplied by the talents of another; and the abilities, which, for the want of an opportunity to display themselves, remain inert and undistinguished, may be placed in a sphere of action, in which they may be beneficially exerted for the general welfare.

CHAP. VIII.

GOVERNOR WORSLEY'S ADMINISTRATION—MR. COX DISGRACED—
VIOLENT DISSENTIONS IN THE COUNTRY—THE PEOPLE REFUSE
TO PAY THEIR TAXES—MR. WORSLEY RETURNS TO ENGLAND—
THE GOVERNMENT DEVOLVES ON MR. BARWICK—DISORDERLY
CONDUCT OF THE ASSEMBLY—CASE OF MR. BENNETT—MR. BAR-
WICK DIES, AND IS SUCCEEDED BY PRESIDENT DOTIN.

CHAP. VIII.

1722.

HENRY Worsley, Esquire, having received his Majesty's commission, appointing him governor of Barbadoes, arrived in Carlisle Bay, on the twenty-second day of January, one thousand seven hundred and twenty-two. He brought with him the most inveterate prejudices against the president and his party ; but, like a consummate politician, carefully concealed his sentiments, till he had concluded an advantageous bargain for himself with those who held the strings of the public purse. Having received his Majesty's permission to accept a settlement from the legislature*, he

---

* Willing to provide for the support of the colonial government, his Majesty, by his instructions to Mr. Worsley, directed, in case of the governor's absence from the island, that one full moiety of the salary allowed by the crown, and of all perquisites,

refused to set his foot on shore, till the leading members of both houses had agreed on the revenue to be raised for his support. The ambitious views of the opposite parties, proved highly beneficial to the governor. Each seemed anxious to purchase his favour; and, during the time which intervened, between his arrival and the meeting of the assembly, the competition was conducted with a spirit extremely disastrous to the people*. It was finally determined to settle on his excellency a salary of six thousand pounds, sterling, a year. A sum, at the stipulated rate of exchange, equal to seven thousand eight hundred pounds currency. Thus, in the ridiculous attempt to propitiate the kindness of a venal chief, the assembly sacrificed the permanent interests of their constituents, to their own silly vanity and puerile ambition. To provide for the payment of this enormous salary, a capitation tax of two shillings and sixpence was laid on all slaves, besides an assessment on the inhabitants of the several towns, in proportion to their population and opulence; and a tax on lawyers, patentees, and other public officers.

His excellency accepted the settlement, with evident marks of satisfaction; and, besides promising a redress of

---

and emoluments whatsoever, which should become due to him, should, during the m? of his absence, be paid to the president, for the time being, for his maintenance tand the support of the dignity of the government.

* Mem. of Barb. p. 53. Univ. Hist. vol. 41. p. 171. Hall's Settle. of Barb. p. 31.

grievances, pledged his word that he would make no farther demands on the public generosity; promises which
seem to have been wholly disregarded. Having thus succeeded to the full extent of his most sanguine wishes, Mr.
Worsley entered upon the duties of his high office, by
instituting an inquiry into the causes of the late disturbances In consequence of the many complaints exhibited
against Mr. Cox, he was summoned to appear before the
governor, where his conduct underwent a rigid scrutiny,
that lasted several days. The crimes imputed to Cox were,
in the first place, that he had greatly harassed the members
of his Majesty's council, by requiring their frequent attendance without sufficient cause; secondly, that he had
grossly insulted them by using insolent and unbecoming
language in council; thirdly, that he had, in the most arbitrary manner, removed many officers of distinction from
their civil and military employments; and, lastly, that he
had, illegally, committed Gelasius Mac Mahon, a member
of the general assembly, to prison. To these charges, Mr.
Cox pleaded, that the frequent calls of council were owing
to the factious conduct of those members, who obstinately
absented themselves, when their presence was required for
the dispatch of public business; that any intemperance of
expression, into which he might have been betrayed, had
been provoked by the disrespectful and contumelious behaviour of those to whom it was applied; that those public
officers, who had been dismissed from the service, had for-

feited their employments by their turbulent, factious disposition; that Mac Mahon had deservedly incurred the commitment complained of, by his disorderly contemptuous deportment before him, in the court of error, of which offence he had been legally convicted by a jury*.

The able and judicious defence made by Mr. Cox, availed him nothing. Upon these frivolous and malicious charges, unsupported by any evidence of criminality, he was condemned for having acted arbitrarily, corruptly, and illegally; his excellency, therefore, removed him from his Majesty's council, and declared him unworthy of being reappointed to a seat at that board; adding, that he ought to be prosecuted in the courts of law, agreeably to the nature of the crimes proved against him. The sentence was communicated to Mr. Cox, in a letter from his excellency's secretary, Mr. Hammond, who received two hundred and fifty pounds from the treasurer, for attending the trial, and making out a copy of the proceedings, to be transmitted to the Board of Trade †.

The judgment against Mr. Cox was not only resented by his particular friends, but was condemned, according to a contemporary writer ‡, by the candid and impartial part of the community, for its extreme severity and injustice. Having been denied the benefit of an appeal, Cox went into a voluntary exile on the continent of North America,

---

* Vide Ante. p. 196.   † Univ. Hist. vol. 41. p. 172.   ‡ Caribbeanna, vol. 1. p. 342.

where his death, soon afterwards, expiated all his political sins, and removed his cause to that unerring tribunal, where he will find more justice and mercy than he experienced before an earthly jurisdiction.

By the rigour of this procedure, the governor stirred up the unextinguished embers of party, and laid the ground-work of an opposition, which, by the operation of other causes, continued to gain strength, during the whole of his subsequent administration. The inflammable tempers of Cox's friends instantly took fire at the injury done to their patron ; nor were materials wanted for spreading the flame among a people so well prepared for the ignition as the Barbadians were at that time.

The enormous settlement made on the governor was soon found to be a burthen totally disproportioned to the strength of those by whom it was to be borne ; and was rendered the more insupportable by the impoverished state of the country, occasioned by the heavy imposts on the merchantable products of the soil, and the restraints with which the commerce of the colonies was fettered. The policy by which Great Britain regulated the trade of her West Indian settlements, though it might have promoted the national prosperity, was little calculated to afford satisfaction to the colonists, or to contribute to their individual welfare. The monopoly of the sugar trade, claimed by Great Britain, by requiring that all colonial produce, intended for European consumption, should pass through the English market, subject to a duty, on importation, besides other charges incident to a double voyage, afforded the French and Dutch adventurers, who were free from similar restrictions, a decided advantage over the British merchants in the sale of West Indian produce on the continent.

The assembly had not only deceived themselves, but their constituents too, with a hope that their liberality to Mr. Worsley would have attached him to their interest, and that by his mediation, the restraints on their agriculture and commerce would be removed; while, by his firmness and impartiality, tranquillity would be restored to their distracted country. Far from obtaining these advantages, the people found their complaints disregarded, and their calamities encreased by their own culpable profusion to the governor. Disappointed in the expectations which they had fondly cherished, and smarting under the effects of their own indiscretion, they turned the edge of their resentment against his excellency, as if he had been the sole author of all their grievances and misfortunes. Nor was Mr. Worsley's proud and supercilious carriage calculated to soften the popular resentment, nor to reconcile the people to the weight of the oppressive burthens imposed on them for his support.

The deplorable condition of the country, and the state of the public mind at this period, may be best collected from the representations transmitted to the lords commissioners of trade. In a memorial presented to that board,

CHAP.VIII. the assembly did not affect to conceal the views by which
1727.   they were actuated in fixing the amount of the governor's
salary.   Expecting to silence the contention of parties, and
to obtain a redress of other grievances, they acknowledged
that they had been prevailed upon to consent to a settlement
which the country was unable to bear. Yet, far from deriving these benefits from their indiscreet generosity, no measures, they observed, had been taken to relieve them from
the oppression under which they were struggling; the public welfare had been entirely disregarded; the militia was
neglected and undisciplined; the forts and batteries had
gone to decay, and the stores were wasted or embezzled;
while his excellency, and all persons in office under him,
were solicitous only of enriching themselves by the spoils
of the people.

Against these representations Mr. Worsely defended himself, by his agents in London, with great spirit and ability.
He repelled every charge, and finally triumphed over his
accusers. His success was principally owing to the enco-
miums bestowed on him by the council and the grand jury,
who at the preceding sessions had presented his excellency
with a very flattering address, praising the mildness and
prudence of his administration, and, at the same time, condemning the proceedings of the opposition. Hence let
grand juries learn more caution in the composition of their
addresses, since they see how easily their unmeaning panegyrics may be turned to their own injury.

Historians are seldom free from the prejudices and partialities of other men. Influenced by the spirit of party, they too often distort and pervert the facts which they relate. Hence it is difficult, after any considerable lapse of time, to reconcile the contradictory accounts transmitted to us of the transactions of former ages. Nor is it an easy task to ascertain the truth of the imputations against Mr. Worsley. On the one hand it is asserted, that besides the general complaints contained in the memorial to the board of trade, his excellency had been guilty of many particular acts of injustice and oppression on the merchants of Bridge-town; who, from the servility of the council, were precluded from the means of redress*. Opposed to this is the testimony of a contemporary author, to this effect: although Mr. Worsley's pride and reserve had rendered him extremely unpopular, he carefully refrained from all oppressive measures, and was not liable to be removed on any other principle than that of easing the inhabitants of the burthensome settlement which he had obtained †. Upon the whole, his excellency's conduct does not appear to have been altogether unexceptionable. Notwithstanding his promise to the assembly, on accepting the salary which they had settled on him, he occasionally received several large sums; besides being paid upwards of *two thousand pounds* for the repairs of the house and gardens at Pilgrim; that very

---

* Univ. Hist. vol, 41. p. 174. † Memoirs of Barb. p. 54.

house, which only seven years afterwards was purchased by the legislature, with twenty acres of land, for *thirteen hundred and fifty pounds**.

The people of Barbadoes were in the highest degree dissatisfied with the payment of Mr. Worsley's salary, when the death of George I. afforded them a favourable pretext, as they erroneously thought, of disengaging their necks from the galling yoke. A time of popular discontent and confusion is generally the season in which men of depraved hearts and wicked designs, under the mask of patriotism, distinguish themselves most by their flagitious enormities. Gelasius Mac Mahon, a turbulent lawyer, of infamous celebrity, and Robert Warren, register in chancery, and clerk of the general assembly, now appeared the professed champions of their oppressed countrymen; whom, with a view to their private emolument, they sought to embroil more deeply with the governor.

As all commissions and patents were known to determine with the death of the King, by whom they were granted, unless continued or renewed by his successor, these artful incendiaries pretended that Mr. Worsley, having received no new commission from his present Majesty, was no longer the lawful governor of the island; and that consequently the act of settlement had expired. The bulk of the people, blinded by their wishes to be relieved from their

---

* Hall's First Settle. of Baib. p. 31, M. S.

burthens, readily assented to this doctrine; the fallacy of which they were incapable of perceiving, and peremptorily refused to pay their taxes, or even to give in returns of their slaves. And such was the inefficiency of the executive government, and the illegal combination among men in power to resist the administration of the laws, that no effectual measures were, nor could be, taken to enforce the penalty against defaulters.

The agitation of the public mind was encreased to a considerable degree by a disagreement between the council and assembly concerning the excise bill. In this dispute, as in most domestic quarrels, there seem to have been faults on both sides. The council had made some amendments to the bill which, abstractedly considered, were highly proper. They proposed, that all seizures to be made by virtue of the act should be prosecuted by the attorney-general instead of the treasurer, in the name of the treasurer or such other officer as should make the seizure. This they contended was absolutely necessary, as seizures might sometimes be made by the excise waiters, and the crown lawyers must, of course, be consulted on such occasions. By the bill the treasurer and all inferior officers were prohibited from receiving any fees on the entering or clearing of vessels under a forfeiture of five pounds, *recoverable before any justice of the peace.* To this summary mode of proceeding the council objected; and proposed, that the penalty should be recovered by action of debt in any court of record. They remarked, that on a recent occasion, a similar mode of proceeding had been condemned by the board of trade, and disapproved by his Majesty, as taking from the subject his most inestimable privilege, the trial by jury. But the principal ground of contention was the proposal made by the council to omit that clause of the bill by which the lower house had prohibited the treasurer from paying any money by virtue of orders issued by the governor and council, otherwise than on the address of the assembly, for payment of accounts previously submitted to their inspection and approbation. To this clause, their honours said they could never consent without a forfeiture of their seats, as it was in direct violation of the King's instruction to his representative. The manner of providing for the payment of the agent's salary was next objected to, as affording the assembly, from its latitude of expression, an opportunity of disposing of immense sums of the public money, under that pretence, to persons whom the council did not approve*.

The attempt of the council to alter a money-bill was evidently an infringement of one of the fundamental principles of the constitution, by which the right of granting supplies is vested exclusively in the representatives of the people. And the commons of England, justly tenacious of such an invaluable privilege, have uniformly resisted any encroach-

---

* The council's reasons, in support of their amendments, were ingeniously drawn up and published. They are preserved in the Appendix to the Caribbeanna.

ment on their right, by invariably refusing any amendment to a bill for raising money on the subject by the house of peers.

The amendments having, of course, proved fatal to the bill, the assembly prepared a new draught, in which they stipulated, that no orders on the treasury should be issued by the governor and council on any occasion, not otherwise provided for by law, but upon an address from their body. This was considered by the upper house as an infringement of their rights, and the prerogative of the chief magistrate. They, therefore, rejected the bill, grounding their dissent on the royal instruction first given to Mr. Grey, and since continued to every succeeding governor, " not to suffer any public money to be disposed of otherwise than by warrant under his hand, by, and with the advice of his council ; permitting the assembly, nevertheless, from time to time, to examine the accounts of money to be disposed of by laws made by them*."

Contrary to the letter and the spirit of this instruction, the assembly insisted on their right to scrutinize all accounts previous to the emission of orders for payment. A posterior examination, they contended, would avail nothing ; as, in case of abuses in the public expenditure, it would be much too late to find fault after the money was gone. The council disputed this claim ; contending for the com-

* Mem. Barb. p. 55.

petence of their board to investigate all demands of a public nature, and to sanction the issuing of orders for whatever sums they should think proper, without any previous
reference to the popular branch of the legislature; and in
this they maintained, that they were warranted by the constant practice of parliament.

Both parties continuing obstinate, a copy of the bill was
sent to England by the governor, and, by his Majesty's
order referred to the lords of the committee of privy council. Their lordships, after due consideration, reported to
the King, " that by some clauses of the bill, the assembly
would deprive the governor of the power, given him by his
Majesty, to sign warrants for the issuing of money, without
their approbation previously obtained, which was contrary,
they observed, to the established usage of all his Majesty's
colonies, and derogatory from his royal prerogative. To
discourage such attempts in future, their lordships humbly
advised his Majesty to signify his disapprobation of the
draught*. The bill was accordingly rejected, and the assembly passed a new one, in which they omitted the exceptionable clauses; refusing, however, to provide for the
payment of those public creditors, whose demands, sanctioned by the council, had originally given rise to the dispute. But, after a lapse of several years, a subsequent

---

* Caribbeanna, vol. 2, p. 318. Mem. of Barb. p. 57.

assembly, having examined the accounts, consented to their being paid.

Meanwhile, a general coalition was formed among persons of all parties to oppose the levying of taxes for paying the salary of the governor. The vestry of Saint Michael's, doubting their authority to assess the inhabitants of Bridgetown, conformably to the act for the support of government, consulted Mr. Blenman, his Majesty's attorney-general; who, with his usual candour and integrity, pronounced that the act had not expired. This opinion was far from proving satisfactory. Upon cases partially and imperfectly stated, Warren and Mac Mahon had obtained the opinion of two eminent English lawyers, much more agreeable to the views of the malcontents*.

---

* I have here subjoined Mr. Blenman's opinion, as it will serve to elucidate the text, and as it does honour to the memory of a man whose virtues and talents rendered him one of the brightest ornaments of his country. It has been generally held at common law that all patents determined by the death of the king, by whom they were granted. However by the statute 7 and 8 Will. III. explained by 1 Anne ch. 8. all commissions or patents are made to continue for six months after the demise of the king, unless superseded in the mean time by his successor. Now the governor holding his place by virtue of a commission from the late king, and that not having been renewed by his present Majesty, till after the six months were elapsed, it would seem reasonable enough, taking it in that light, to infer that his excellency had ceased to be governor at the expiration of six months; and consequently that the act was no longer in force, it being limited to the time that Mr. Worsley should continue to be his Majesty's captain-general and governor in chief; and in that quality personally to reside on the island. But this case rests on the construction of the act referred to.

Mr. Worsley finding there was no chance of obtaining justice by any ordinary means, presented a memorial to the lords commissioners for trade and plantations, fairly stating the particulars of the affair, with the doubts that had arisen on the subject; and requesting that his complaints might be laid before the king, and imploring his Majesty's interposition. The memorial was, by order of his Majesty, referred to the consideration of the attorney and solicitor general of Great Britain. The report of these crown lawyers, which may be seen at length in the Caribbeanna, decided the point in favour of the governor, and corresponded in every particular with that delivered by Blenman.

This decision, it was thought, would have removed every doubt: but although these opinions were immediatly made known, the popular delusion was still kept up by the agency of evil minded persons; and people of the first rank and distinction determined to oppose the execution of that law, to which, in their legislative capacities, they had given

---

The intention of the law was to make a suitable provision for his excellency as long as he should continue in his government; and, since the king, in a legal understanding never dies, it seems clear that these words do not confine the provision for the governor to that reign only; but that they take in the whole time of his residence here as chief magistrate. Now as Mr. Worsley has continued to reside in the island, ever since his first arrival, in quality of commander in chief, it follows that the act for supporting the honour and dignity of government is not determined."—*Vide Caribbeanna. vol.* 1. *p.* 40.

their sanction. Many had refused to give in the number of negroes on whom the tax was to be paid, and as many changes of property had been effected, it was deemed impracticable to recover the arrears by any legal process. At length tired with a tedious contention, to which there seemed no prospect of an amicable or successful termination, Mr. Worsley resigned the government and returned to England.

Sept. 21.

Upon Mr. Worsley's departure the government devolved on Samuel Barwick, president of the council. The accession of this gentleman produced no change in the temper of his countrymen. The gloom of discontent still loured over the political horizon. Mr. Barwick had, indeed, rendered himself obnoxious to the demagogues of the popular party by the prudent submission to the law, respecting the salary of the governor, which he both practised and recommended.

On the first meeting of the legislature, the president took the occasion of addressing them collectively to remark, that, as they had the happiness of enjoying the protection of one of the best of princes, who, among his other royal virtues, was particularly attentive to the welfare of his colonies, it was their bounden duty to shew themselves worthy of his paternal care, by an implicit obedience to his commands. The annual excise bill having expired, his honour suggested to the assembly the necessity of preparing a new one without loss of time; and to obviate as much as possible any alteration, he recommended that they would frame the bill

November 7.

on true constitutional principles, and make the money applicable only to the support of government. He next adverted to the ruined state of the fortifications, submitting
to the representatives of the people the propriety of making
some effectual provision for their repair. They ought not,
he said, to suffer the hardships of which they complained to
impede this necessary business, as they were not then subject to any other impositions on their produce than such as
they had borne nearly seventy years. He concluded with
assuring both houses of his readiness to concur in any measure that should be proposed for the real honour and interest of the country, consistent with the royal instructions.
And, as it was impossible to succeed in any useful undertaking, without a perfect union among themselves, he indulged the pleasing hope of finding the most cordial unanimity in the public councils. As they were all equally interested in the welfare of the country, it was not likely, he
said, that they should disagree as to the means of promoting it, if all were actuated by the same generous and patriotic
spirited principles.

The council presented a polite and respectful address to
the president, which, as usual, was little more than an echo
of the speech. But his honour's loyal and exalted sentiments made no impression on the members of the assembly.
Such was the ill humour which prevailed in that house, that
they would not even observe the common civility of addressing the chair, nor would they consent to make any

provision for Mr. Barwick's support during his administration.

The house of assembly, at this period, appear to have been entirely resigned to the will of their speaker, the honourable Henry Peers; a man, ambitious, bold, intriguing and vindictive. Under the influence of this leader, the proceedings of the assembly assumed a character distinguished by an inordinate thirst of power, continually manifesting itself by encroachments on the prerogative of the crown, a contempt of the authority of the king's representative, and in attempts to invade the privileges of the council. Notwithstanding his Majesty's disapprobation of the late excise bill, the assembly again claimed the same unconstitutional controul over the public disbursements which had been peremptorily denied them three years before. Influenced by the same sentiments which had operated with them on the former occasion, the council rejected the bill, which was now sent up for their concurrence. The dispute, however, was not, at this time, confined to the privileges of either branch of the legislature. An additional topic, of a different complexion, was now started by the president.

It will doubtless be remembered, that when the Duke of Portland visited Barbadoes, president Cox had incurred a considerable expense by entertaining his noble guest and his suite; for which he had been reimbursed by two orders on the treasury for eight hundred and ten pounds. The exhausted state of the public coffers rendering the payment of the money somewhat uncertain, Mr. Cox, for the accommodation of Sandford, the treasurer, transferred the orders to him, and took his personal security for the amount. These orders were regularly charged by the treasurer, as if the money had been paid, and were settled by the committee of public accounts. He had, nevertheless, omitted to pay Cox; who, as we have already seen, had gone to America, where he died, leaving Mr. Peers, the speaker of the assembly, to whom he owed a considerable sum, his executor. Sandford, having proved insolvent, was imprisoned by his creditors; and as there was no chance of collecting the money due from him to Cox's estate, Peers and Bignall, his two securities, anxious to provide for their own safety, prevailed on the obsequious assembly to assert a clause in the excise-bill, directing the payment of these very orders to Cox's representatives, which had been discounted nine years before with the late treasurer. Happily the president discovered the imposition, and explained it to the council, in time to frustrate the fraudulent design.

Though Mr. Barwick, in this instance, acted as became a faithful guardian of the people, his upright conduct irritated the minds of those whose malversation he had detected, and provoked a torrent of illiberal invective from Mr. Bignall, in the house of assembly, on a speech replete with the most acrimonious expressions. A committee of council was appointed to make a minute enquiry into the circumstances of this transaction, and had drawn up their report on the subject, but the arrival of Lord Howe, in the interval, opening a new scene of politics to both parties, the affair was compromised, and all pretensions to the money in question given up*.

The assembly, for the dispatch of public business, had been permitted to adjourn themselves *de die in diem*; but, as they persisted in refusing to pass an excise-bill, free from the objections to which the last was liable, the president, hearing that they were proceeding to other business, sent the provost marshal to adjourn the house to a future day, intending, in the mean time, to dissolve it by proclamation. The marshal, instead of waiting till the house had sat, communicated his errand to Warren, the clerk, who immediately flew to the different members with the intelligence. Determined not to relinquish their scheme, they privately assembled at the store of Othniel Haggat, member of council, where they proceeded on the business in hand, and continued their illegal sittings, without any regard to the authority of the chief magistrate, until their place of rendezvous being, at length, discovered, they were adjourned by the president's order. His honour soon after dissolved the house, and issued writs for a new election.

Nor were these the only disorders and irregularities which the annals of this period afford. A few bold, turbulent,

---

* Caribbeanna, vol. 2. p. 355.

licentious men, assumed a domineering influence over every department of the state; and, with democratic insolence, obstructed the legal exercise of the executive authority.

Mr. Bennett, a gentleman of respectability, had commenced an action against Doctor Warren, for the recovery of a plantation; and the defendant, to impede his adversary's proceedings, had removed the cause, by a bill of injunction, into the court of chancery. In the progress of the suit, an attachment had been issued against Bennett, for an imputed contempt of the court; but, as it was then likely that the affair would be compromised, the writ was never executed. After an interval of nine months, when all prospect of an amicable adjustment of the cause of litigation had disappeared, Mac Mahon, the advocate in this suit, without any order from the court of chancery, which was not then sitting, obtained from Warren's brother, the register of the court, a second attachment, directing the serjeant at arms to take Mr. Bennett into custody. The order was instantly obeyed, and the man conveyed to prison, though he offered sufficient bail for his appearance, whenever it should be required. Unfortunately for the prisoner, the court of chancery was prevented from sitting on the day in course; and as its adjournments were monthly, it seemed probable that his incarceration would be protracted to an unreasonable length. He therefore petitioned Mr. Barwick to interpose his authority, as chancellor, and to order his enlargement. The attorney-general, on being consulted, pronounced the whole transaction to be irregular and illegal; and, as Bennett was not committed by order of the court, the learned gentleman recommended the president to direct a supersedeas to be issued for his liberation.

The necessary orders were accordingly given, but the register, who had not hesitated on the authorized application of his brother's counsel, to issue a writ for confining Bennett, suddenly became so tenacious of his duty, that he peremptorily refused to obey the president's order for his release, alleging that the chancellor had no authority out of court to direct a supersedeas. As Bennett had not been committed for actual contempt, but merely to answer the imputation, his counsel contended that he was entitled to bail, but the serjeant at arms pertinaciously refused to take security for his appearance in court.

At the end of three weeks, during which he had lain in the common gaol, Bennett petitioned the Honourable Francis Vaughan, chief judge of a court of common pleas, for a writ of *habeas corpus*. The judge prudently consulted the attorney-general, who, with characteristic candour and ingenuity, gave his opinion at length. If the prisoner had been taken up, by an order of the court of chancery, he admitted, that the judge would have no power to interfere. On the other hand, if the court did not direct the process upon which he had been arrested,

CHAP.VIII. the learned barrister insisted, he might be legally discharged.
1723. And, as, upon a review of the whole proceedings, it did
not appear that the court of chancery was at all concerned
in the commitment, Mr. Blenman thought the judge would
not interfere with the jurisdiction of that tribunal, by discharging the prisoner.   In pursuance of this advice, Bennett was liberated, by virtue of a writ of *habeas corpus.*
Provoked at having the victim thus rescued from their
fangs, Warren's party not only abused Bennett and his
counsel, in the most outrageous manner, but Mac Mahon,
more violent than the rest, insulted and even challenged the chief justice.   For this flagrant outrage he
was indicted at the next court of grand sessions, and was
convicted of the offence; but, from the faulty constitution
of our criminal judicature, and his influence over the
bench, he escaped with impunity*; or, at most, with a
moderate fine.

These abuses and disorders, in the administration of
government, were not the only evils under which the Barbadians laboured.   The decay of commerce, and the decline of agriculture, were ills most sensibly felt and loudly
complained of. The onerous imposts on their staple products
were rendered more oppressive by the extreme rigour with

---

* Caribbeanna, vol. 1. p. 259 and 302.   This flagitious character was a person of
considerable property, owner of Locust Hall plantation; a lawyer by profession, and
a member of the general assembly.

which they were exacted; particularly the duty on sugar, which was actually paid on the wood of which the casks were made. But the injury of which the Barbadians complained most, was occasioned by the permission given by Great Britain to Ireland, and her North American colonies, of importing sugar, rum, and molasses, from the French and Dutch settlements. The adventurers of those places, free from the heavy duties on exportation, to which the merchants of Barbadoes were liable, had not only obtained a decided advantage over the British on the continent of Europe; they were enabled to undersell them in their own markets, in the American provinces; whence they received, in exchange, every article required for the support and improvement of their plantations. The French, unacquainted with the principles of distillation, furnished the Americans with considerable quantities of molasses, for the support of their distilleries, which, but for that intercourse, must have been thrown away. Hence the consumption of West Indian spirits was materially lessened on the American continent, to the manifest injury of the planters of Barbadoes, with whom rum was an important staple.

Under circumstances so depressing to the commercial and agricultural interests of the country, the Barbadians concurred in an humble petition to the throne, in which, after a pathetic enumeration of the grievances and oppression to which they had long patiently submitted, they prayed that the importation of foreign rum, sugar, and molasses, into Ireland, or the Anglo-American provinces, should be prohibited, unless they had been previously landed in England, or made liable to such duties as should put them on a level with the productions of the British colonies. The truth of these complaints, and the equity of the demands which accompanied them, seem to have awakened the attention of the British ministry, though nothing was immediately done for the relief of the petitioners.

December.

Meanwhile, on the day appointed for the meeting of the new assembly, the president, being prevented by ill health from going to Bridge-Town, was under the necessity of receiving the other branches of the legislature at Lancaster plantation. His honour opened the session with a speech, in which, after descanting on the usual topics, he declared, that in dissolving the last assembly, he had been influenced by no other consideration than that of affording the house an opportunity of passing an excise bill with consistency; which, he observed, the public service required should be done without delay. He concluded with an assurance, that as long as he lived, which, in all probability, could not be long, the prosperity of his country would be the first wish of his heart. These words seem to have been uttered with a prophetic spirit. He survived the patriotic declaration little more than a week; he died on the first

day of the new year, and was buried in a private manner,
at St. James's church, the next day *.

Whatever faults the violence of party, or the malevo-
lence of his political opponents, may have imputed to Mr.
Barwick, his public conduct, if we may rely on the testimony of an author of his own times, was free from any
vicious stain. His administration was distinguished by prudence, equity, and moderation. Unwilling to rely, entirely, on the soundness of his own judgment, he commonly
endeavoured to render his good intentions more efficacious,
by the advice of others; and was implicitly guided by the
counsel of those in whose integrity and superior understanding he knew that he could place the utmost confidence.
It was his felicity to perform the duties of his high station, without blame, to the satisfaction of the candid and
impartial, and to the utter disappointment of his enemies.
In all cases of difficulty, he resorted to the attorney-general,
Blenman, for assistance; happy in having a friend of such
probity and talents to solve his doubts and confirm his
honest purposes; and yet more happy in the sagacity and
humility with which he availed himself of an advantage
so inestimable.

The death of Mr. Barwick placed the reins of government in the hands of the Honourable James Dotin. This
gentleman seems to have possessed a much greater portion

---

* Caribbeanna, vol. 1. p. 102.

CHAP.VIII.
1733.

of the esteem of the assembly than had fallen to the lot of his predecessor. They voted the sum of one hundred pounds to prepare for his reception at Pilgrim, and a present of five hundred pounds to provide for his accommodation during his residence there. Whatever might have been the talents or virtues which procured him these marks of distinction, he had very little opportunity to display them. He was quickly superseded by the arrival of Lord Viscount Howe, who had been appointed to the government of Barbadoes.

CHAP. IX.

LORD HOWE'S POPULAR ADMINISTRATION—PAYMENT OF MR.
WORSLEY'S SALARY ENFORCED—ESTABLISHMENT OF A PRESS—
MURDER COMMITTED BY MAC MAHON—DEATH OF LORD HOWE
—PRESIDENCY OF MR. DOTIN—MACK MAHON'S TRIAL—AR-
RIVAL OF GOVERNOR BYNG—DISPUTES BETWEEN THE GOVERNOR
AND THE ASSEMBLY—DEATH OF MR. BYNG—LEGISLATIVE PRO-
CEEDINGS.

ON the first meeting of the legislature, Lord Howe addressed the council and assembly in a plain respectful speech.
He regretted that the arrangement of his private concerns
had detained him much longer in England, after being
honoured with his Majesty's commands to take upon him
the government of the island, than he expected. But he
assured them, that he had endeavoured to make his absence
useful to the colony, by employing himself, during that
interval, in representing to the ministry the many hardships and disadvantages under which the trade laboured;
and in soliciting a redress of their grievances; and he
was happy in bringing with him the glad tidings of a
speedy and effectual relief intended for them by the King

CHAP. IX.
1733.
April 17.

and his parliament.　Turning to the assembly, he observed, that although it had been usual with former governors to issue writs, on their arrival, for a new election, the confidence which he had in their wisdom and zeal for the public welfare, together with his desire of giving every possible dispatch to business, had induced him to depart from this custom; and, with a view to their personal ease, he had preferred their meeting on the day to which they stood adjourned.　He informed them, that he had received orders from his Majesty to lay before them several instructions, tending to the honour, security, and advantage of the island; which, at proper times, should be communicated to them.　There was one, however, which, as it concerned himself, he should immediately submit to their consideration, without any comment of his own.　Professing to have nothing nearer to his heart than the prosperity of the country, he declared, that inclination, as well as obedience to his sovereign's commands, would impel him to use his best endeavours to restore the trade of the island to its former flourishing condition.　To render effectual his Majesty's gracious intention towards them, he urged unanimity and concord among themselves; a constant attendance on the duties of their several stations; and a perfect union in the pursuit of such objects as were connected with the general welfare; promising, on his part, that he would contribute every thing in his power to effectuate a propitious change in their affairs. He concluded with declaring his readiness to comply with any request, or to acquiesce in any proposal for the advantage and benefit of the inhabitants of the island.

This speech made a powerful impression on the public mind. The people of Barbadoes, ever credulous, and easily deceived by those who find it convenient to flatter their vanity, or sooth their expectations with specious professions, listened with admiration and complacency to his lordship's patriotic sentiments and polite expressions of regard. That they might not, by any unreasonable parsimony, obstruct the tide of prosperity which now seemed ready to flow into their bosoms, the assembly generously settled the sum of four thousand pounds sterling annually on his lordship, to support the dignity of his government: no trifling sum, if we take into consideration the circumstances of the country at that period, when sugar sold for only ten or twelve shillings sterling the hundred weight. Nor had the Barbadians the smallest cause to regret their liberality on this occasion. Lord Howe was generous to profusion, and by his munificence replenished the streams which supported the vigour of his establishment. Through the whole of his administration, he invariably acted upon the purest principles of moral and political rectitude: a conduct, which rendered his government as honourable to himself as it was happy to the people over whom he presided.

The general satisfaction which this amiable nobleman's

accession had diffused throughout the community, soon experienced a temporary interruption by the revival of the disputes concerning the payment of the large balance due to the late governor Worsley. That gentleman, on his return to England, had not been forgetful of the injustice with which he had been treated in Barbadoes. He presented a memorial to the King, stating the particulars of his demand, with the grounds on which the payment of his salary had been refused; and praying that his Majesty would be pleased to direct such measures to be pursued for his relief as the nature of the case might require and admit. This request was so reasonable, that the King, in council, on the twenty-second day of September, one thousand seven hundred and thirty-two, issued an order, directing the colonial attorney-general, in case the taxes were not paid by the first day of July in the following year, to take the most effectual measures, by due course of law, for the recovery of the arrears from the persons liable to pay them.

Though Blenman gave notice of this order, and of his determination to obey the commands of his Sovereign, the populace were still influenced by the conduct of persons of superior rank and superior means of information, who yet pertinaciously refused to pay their taxes, expecting that their personal influence would induce the governor to interfere and protect them in violating the law. But Lord Howe was too noble minded to aim at short-lived popula-

rity, or to endeavour to strengthen his interest by obstructing the course of justice.   Nor was Blenman of a temper
to be intimidated by the frown of despotism, or seduced
from his duty by the smile of power.   He was heedless of
pleasing the gilded knave, and still less inclined to oppress
the poor.   Determined to strike at the root of the evil, he,
on the appointed day, commenced suits in the court of exchequer against President Dotin, Othniel Haggatt, member
of council, General Peers, speaker of the assembly, Thomas Maycock, chief justice of a court of common pleas,
John Maycock, member of the assembly, and Robert
Warren, clerk of that house, for the recovery of the sums
respectively due from them.   At the same time Mr. Hothersal, the late treasurer, being about to leave the island,
without giving the necessary information respecting the
names of the defaulters, and the amount of their arrears,
was detained by a writ of *ne exeat insula*; and compelled
to enter into bonds not to leave the island without his excellency's permission.

Such spirited proceedings, so judiciously directed, produced the desired effect.   Finding that neither rank nor
fortune afforded any security in cases of public delinquency, the commonalty voluntarily came forward and
paid their arrears.   Thus, in the short space of five weeks,
the hydra was subdued, and upwards of seventeen thousand pounds were collected, and paid to Mr. Worsley's
agents.

Soon after Lord Howe's arrival, a curious and interesting question arose between his lordship and the president. During Mr. Dotin's administration, though several months after his excellency had received his appointment, a sloop and cargo, valued at eleven hundred pounds, were seized by the officers of the customs at Bridge Town, and condemned in the court of vice-admiralty. The law, in such cases, expressly directs that all forfeitures incurred by the violation of the acts of trade shall be to his Majesty, the *governor* of the plantation where the offence is committed, and the officer by whom it is prosecuted. But, as his Majesty had been pleased to order that one half the salary, perquisites and emoluments, which the governor was entitled to receive, should be paid to the person exercising the supreme authority during the governor's absence, his lordship claimed only one moiety of the third to which he thought himself entitled. Mr. Dotin not being disposed to admit the propriety of this demand, an action was filed against him at the governor's suit for the recovery of the money. The case was perfectly new, and the court, after a hearing of the matter, upon a motion made for that purpose, agreed to a reference to the attorney and solicitor-general of Great Britain; by whose concurrent opinion the question was finally decided in favour of the claimant *.

---

* The opinion of Mr. Attorney General Willis was thus expressed: " Notwithstanding the eldest counsellor is directed to take upon him the administration of go-

This determination gave rise to a second demand on the part of Lord Howe. On the president's accession the assembly had voted him a donative of five hundred pounds, for the purpose of defraying the expenses incident to his residence at Pilgrim. His excellency insisted that this was an emolument of office within the meaning of the instruction already alluded to; but Mr. Dotin was as little inclined to yield to this new demand as to the former. The question therefore was referred to Mr. Blenman, the colonial attorney-general, who pronounced that, whatever might have been the motives by which the assembly were actuated in the provision made for the president, as it was granted after the date of his lordship's commission, he had, by virtue of the instruction, an indisputable right to one moiety of the sum, as a perquisite of office.

Lord Howe was eminently endowed with all the virtues of a noble and generous mind: courteous, affable, hospit-

---

vernment during the absence of the governor, yet the governor himself, though absent, is to be considered as governor within the meaning of the acts of parliament, and is the person entitled to one-third of the forfeitures. But as the governor is bound by his instructions, as well as by his commission, his acceptance of the government under them, amounts to an agreement on his part, that the eldest counsellor, in his absence, shall have one moiety of his salary, and of all the perquisites belonging to his office. I am therefore of opinion, that one-third of the forfeiture in question is, by law, vested in Lord Howe, as the same accrued after the date of his commission; yet that, by reason of his instructions, he can claim only one moiety thereof, as it happened before his arrival in Barbadoes."---*Vide Mr. Eversley's Manuscript, mentioned in the Preface.*

CHAP. IX. able, and condescending, he engaged the esteem of all

1733. with whom he conversed. Temperate but firm, candid and impartial, he acquired a greater degree of popularity than has ever been enjoyed by any other governor of Barbadoes. By a familiar and unreserved intercourse with the people, he was enabled to calm the animosities of party, and contributed to unite the warmest political opponents in social amusements and festive entertainments. All angry contention was silenced by his firmness and impartiality; and concord once more resumed her pacific reign.

In effecting this happy change, his lordship's endeavours were greatly facilitated, according to a judicious historian *, by the circulating of a weekly paper, published by one Keimer, under the title of the Barbadoes' Gazette †. Some of the most enlightened members of the community availed themselves of the advantage of a free press, and devoted their pens to the instruction of their countrymen. By the publication of many spirited and ingenious letters and essays on political and commercial subjects, the mischievous designs, sinister views and corrupt motives of those incendiaries, who, under the specious garb of patriotism, had plundered the public and disturbed the peace of society, were developed, scrutinized and frustrated. Relieved from the illusion which had long imposed on their senses, the Barbadians now began to see and understand their true

---

* Vide Univ. Hist. vol. 41, p. 176.   † Keimer's press was established in 1731.

interests. Nor let it be thought that the cause was disproportioned to the effect. There is no stronger principle in
human nature than the fear of shame. The freedom of the
press derives its utility from its influence over this powerful
spring of action; and furnishes the only weapon which can
be safely and effectually employed against folly and corruption acting with authority. The man in office who
fears not to offend against the laws of his country and his
God, when he can do so with the *prospect* of legal impunity,
is often restrained from the commission of injustice and
oppression by the dread of having his crimes revealed, and
of being held up to the scorn and execration of mankind
by means of an open press. Hence the arbitrary ruler,
the corrupt magistrate and the profligate legislator, of all
countries, have ever been inimical to the liberty of the
press, and anxious to deprive the subject of the privilege
of canvassing the measures of government, and scrutiniz-
ing the conduct of those who are placed in authority over
us. Happily, by the principles of the British constitution,
the people are themselves the guardians of this inestimable
privilege; and it is hoped that, in the hands of a jury of
Barbadians, it will never be impaired, nor surrendered to
the rude gripe of despotism.

The inhabitants of Barbadoes had not long enjoyed this
advantage, when an attempt was made to restrain the exercise of it. Mr. Adams, one of the council, had published
some remarks on the sugar trade of the colonies, which

produced an answer, in which the honourable author's literary talents were treated with less ceremony and respect
than some of his friends thought due to his rank. At the
instigation of some persons, smarting under the censorial
rod, the grand jury presented Keimir for publishing a malicious, scandalous and seditious paper, and particularly
for printing a false and defamatory libel on Mr. Adams.
When the presentment was brought before the court, the
attorney-general declared that there was nothing in the
publication complained of which could possibly warrant
a criminal prosecution ; but the printer was nevertheless
bound to keep the peace for six months.

The system of peculation and extortion on which the
lawyers and deputy patentee officers had long subsisted,
had at length become so injurious and oppressive to the
bulk of the people, that it was found necessary to restrain
them within more moderate bounds. With this view, a
committee of the assembly was appointed to prepare a bill
for regulating the fees of public offices and courts of justice. But Warren, their clerk, who was himself a deputy
patentee, contrived to impede their progress, under a pretence that it was a matter of too much importance to be
hurried over lightly. At length the commendable diligence
of the committee surmounted all the obstacles thrown in
their way. The bill passed both branches of the legislature without a dissenting voice, and finally received the governor's assent. But as the royal approbation was also

necessary, Warren, assisted by Mac Mahon, resolved on trying another effort to prevent its success. Carefully concealing their design, they prepared a petition, accompanied by several affidavits, to prove that the interests of the patentees would be materially affected by the operation of this law. Warren, after stating his long practice as a lawyer, and perfect knowledge of the subject, deposed that the prothonotary alone, in the event of the acts receiving the royal sanction, would lose from three to four hundred pounds annually *. These depositions were concealed from Lord Howe till the evening before the packet sailed, when they were presented to his lordship to be authenticated under the great seal of the island. It was then too late to take steps to counteract the effect of this artful, uncandid representation; which, being supported by the patentees on the other side of the Atlantic, succeeded to their utmost expectation. This was the last legislative attempt to correct these abuses.

An event now occurred, which, by removing that turbulent incendiary Mac Mahon from the country, contributed more, perhaps, than any other circumstance, towards preserving its tranquillity. Keeling, a deputy in the powder office, having furnished his employer's son-in-law with

---

* The prothonotary's office was farmed at three hundred and fifty pounds a year. Consequently, if Warren swore true, the patentee would have lost the whole emoluments of his office; which was impossible, unless the payment of all fees had been forbidden.

money, contrary to his positive orders, alleged, by way of excuse, that he had been persuaded to do so by Mac Mahon. This was communicated to Mac Mahon, who meeting Keeling afterwards at a tavern beat him violently, and thrust him out of the house. Keeling, the same evening, wrote to him, desiring to be paid for some shingles which he had sold him, and requested an interview for the purpose of passing receipts. Mac Mahon readily construed this note into a challenge; and swore most vehemently that he would go and beat the rascal. Accordingly, accompanied by Perry, Lawrance and Morris, who lent him a sword, he proceeded to Keeling's lodgings, whom they found at the door preparing to go out, his horse being in the street ready saddled. Perry, without hesitation, secured the pistols which were in the holsters, and Keeling, finding that some violence was intended, drew his sword, but made no attempt to use it until Mac Mahon drew, when they both advanced and engaged. Keeling was soon disarmed, it was said by Morris, and retreating called out he had lost his sword; but finding himself hard pressed by his dishonourable adversary, he ran into a neighbouring store, and endeavoured to conceal himself under the stairs. The infuriate Mac Mahon, having obtained a light, renewed the attack; and Keeling, incapable of resistance, cried out murder; and, in the most supplicating terms, begged for mercy. Perry and Lawrance, holding his weapons, were calm spectators of the bloody

scene; while Morris guarded the door to prevent the interference of the crowd which had gathered in the street, till
Mac Mahon, having perpetrated his savage design, withdrew. The hapless victim of his cruelty was then taken
up and placed in a chair, whence he immediately fell, exclaiming, " the villain has murdered me as I lay on the
ground," and instantly expired. Miller, a surgeon's ap-
prentice, who had been a witness of the whole transaction,
was clandestinely conveyed from the island; but as, upon
enquiry, there still appeared to be sufficient evidence to
convict the inhuman monster, he thought proper to consult
his safety by a precipitate flight beyond sea. Perry, Morris, and Lawrance, were afterwards successively apprehended, and tried for the murder as accessaries, but they
were all acquitted.

The time seemed now to have arrived when the Barbadians were to enjoy the benefits of the long expected relief
promised them on the arrival of Lord Howe. Upon an
address to his Majesty from the House of Peers, the complaints of the colonies were referred to the consideration
of the lords commissioners for trade and plantations;
and their lordships, in obedience to his Majesty's
order, made an ample report concerning the commerce, strength, and fortifications of the West-Indian settlements; suggesting the steps which were proper to be
taken for the encouragement of the trade and the security
of the islands in general.

In consequence of this representation, the importation of foreign rum, sugar and molasses, into Ireland, was prohibited by act of parliament, and the same commodities, on being imported into any of the American provinces, were made subject to heavy duties. The exportation of sugar from the English colonies directly to foreign parts was permitted in ships built and navigated according to law; but this indulgence was clogged with such difficulties and restrictions, that the West Indians received no advantage from it. These marks of favour on the part of Great Britain were accompanied by a donative of cannon and ordnance stores. And, on the representation of Mr. Dunbar, the inspector-general, the original method of collecting the duty on sugar was revived, with an ample allowance for tare and tret. The people were impressed with the most lively sentiments of gratitude for these favours; and the

grand jury transmitted to England a most dutiful and loyal address to the King, replete with the warmest acknowledgments of his paternal goodness.

The joy to which these concessions gave rise was soon damped by the death of Lord Howe: an event which occasioned a general consternation, and a mourning as sincere as it was universal. His lordship had been attacked by a fever, supposed to have been produced by excessive fatigue in reviewing the different regiments of militia. From the moment he was taken ill he entertained a presentiment of the fatal termination of the disease; and seemed per-

fectly resigned to his fate. When he was dying, he inquired
if there were any gentlemen in the house, and, being answered in the affirmative, he desired one of his attendants
to go down and remember him to them most affectionately;
and to tell them that he heartily wished them all well, as
he did the inhabitants in general; adding, " they might
have a governor more capable of serving them, and he sincerely hoped they would, but that none could endeavour
for it more zealously than he had done."* His lordship died
on the twenty-seventh day of March, leaving issue by his
amiable consort four daughters, who were with their dis-
consolate mother in Barbadoes, and three sons, then in
England, whose gallant exploits will be remembered with
admiration as long as bravery and patriotism continue to
be esteemed virtues among mankind. His lordship's remains were interred in General Codrington's vault, whence
they were afterwards removed to England †.

All our colonial historians concur in representing Lord
Howe's administration as the happiest era in the history of
Barbadoes. Yet, in reviewing the transactions of this period, we are unable to discover any particular acts of his
lordship's government which could justly entitle him to the
extraordinary celebrity which he attained. We must therefore ascribe the popularity, which he most deservedly ac-

---

* Caribbeanna, vol. 2. p. 62 and 110.   † Ibid. vol. 2. p. 54.

quired, and the esteem attached to his memory, to the amiable domestic virtues which he practised; to his unbounded generosity; his exalted charity, and the engaging suavity of manners, by which he conciliated the esteem of all who knew him. Though the profound policy and noble institutions of statesmen, the brilliant actions and hazardous achievements of conquerors, may dazzle us with their splendour; it is the milder virtues of humanity which cheer and delight us with their pure and steady ray. Affability, courtesy and condescension, will gain the tough, impracticable heart, which disdains the pride and pomp of imaginary greatness, and spurns the insolence of him whose power and superiority are manifested only by arrogance, injustice and oppression. It has been objected to this nobleman's administration, that, had he lived longer, he would have ruined Barbadoes by the introduction of luxury. But luxury can never be prejudicial to a community in which there exists an inequality of conditions. It is the only remedy for the partial distribution of property, by diffusing among the industrious poor and middling classes of people, the superfluous wealth of the opulent.

The council and assembly demonstrated their gratitude for the blessings which they had enjoyed under the mild, equitable and prudent administration of their beloved governor, by a liberal donative of twenty-five hundred pounds to his noble and accomplished relict. As a reciprocal mark of respect, her ladyship presented them with a portrait of her deceased lord; which was placed in the most conspicuous part of the town hall.

The much lamented death of lord Howe placed Mr. Dotin a second time on the seat of government. No fixed salary was allowed the president on his succeeding to the chair; but to compensate for this omission, the assembly voted him a present of seven hundred pounds; and, the next year, settled on him the sum of six hundred pounds a year, to support the dignity of his station.

Mr. Dotin's administration has been generally commended for its mildness and inoffensiveness; but there is great reason to suspect that justice was not distributed with an even, steady hand. Two French prisoners having been convicted of wilful murder, were respited by the president and successfully recommended to the clemency of the crown. This was but the prelude to a more disgraceful and flagrant violation of the laws of society. The melancholy event which had deprived the country of the services of its late faithful and inflexible chief magistrate, by opening a prospect of impunity to offenders of a certain description, was considered as a signal for the return of Mac Mahon. His arrival at Barbadoes was more like the triumphal entry of a victorious general returning from extending the dominion of his sovereign than the return of an unconvicted felon, awaiting the punishment due to his crimes. Instead of being conveyed to prison by the constables of Bridge

Town, he was conducted from the wharf by a party of his friends, in the elegant chariot of General Peers to the house of the provost marshal. Here he remained under a nominal confinement until he was bailed by four gentlemen of the first rank and fortune in the country.

The whole of the subsequent proceedings was of a piece with this illegal and indecorous beginning. On the eleventh day of December he was brought to the bar of the court of grand sessions and arraigned for the murder of Thomas Keeling. One of the most material witnesses being dead, his written deposition taken in due form before a justice of the peace, was produced by the attorney-general, who supported the prosecution with great firmness and ability; but the prisoner's counsel objecting to the reading of this evidence, the court, contrary to every principle of justice, rejected it. The prisoner rested his defence principally on the testimony of Perry, who had been indicted for the same offence and acquitted. His evidence tended to prove that the deceased had received the fatal wound while fighting with Mac Mahon; and not while he was under the staircase. Perry's testimony, at best, was entitled to little credibility; and though his assertion was contradicted by several unexceptionable witnesses, particularly by four surgeons who examined the wounds, which were all on the left side, and could not therefore have been received while Keeling was in a posture of defence, the jury, nevertheless, returned a verdict of manslaughter. Mac Mahon immediately claimed the benefit of clergy and petitioned the president for a pardon; which was granted without the smallest hesitation, extending as well to the remission of the punishment of branding as to the forfeiture of goods and chattels. Every art had been practised to influence the minds of the court and jury; and to prepare the public for this misplaced act of clemency. The usual assize sermon and the chief justices' charge on opening the sessions were both calculated to impress the audience with an idea of the excellence of that celestial attribute, mercy.* But mercy to such atrocious offenders is injustice to the community.

To Mr. Dotin's administration has been ascribed the credit of correcting and establishing the fees of the public offices†; an act which would have consecrated his memory. But it is a degree of merit to which, unfortunately, he was not entitled. The laws which were passed during his presidency are in no respect more remarkable than for a spirit of restraint, which, with a view of guarding against the dangers of monopoly, tends to repress the freedom of commerce. A permanent and arbitrary valuation was set on every species of butcher's meat; the exportation of cattle and other live stock, together with all kinds of grain and provisions of native produce was prohibited; and, lest the

---

* Caribbeanna, vol. ii. p. 103.   † Univ. Hist. vol. xli. p. 177.

soil should be removed, an act was passed to prevent the exportation of clay.* In the same spirit another law was enacted, under the specious pretext of preventing and punishing forestalling and regrating. A maximum was established for various articles of salted provisions, and grain of every denomination; beyond which no person was allowed to purchase those articles even from the original importer, for the purpose of revendition or exportation.

The impolicy and injustice of the statutes against forestallers and monopolizers are so palpable, that they are suffered by a kind of common consent to slumber in obscurity. This is not enough, they should be repealed. The exportation of articles of the first necessity, during a general scarcity in our own country, is a practice which prudence and humanity must condemn. And, although I am not in the habit of placing much confidence in governors, it were

---

* " These laws," said the ingenious Mr. Joshua Steele, " are unwittingly levelled against the two rural branches of agriculture and pasturage. Could it have been expected that planters would have employed their labour and land otherways than under the allurement of a lucrative return in the sale of their produce ? And unless the planter could have had the liberty of exporting his horses, or asses, his oxen and live stock, with his corn and other provisions, to whatever market would have afforded him the best price, it would have happened, *and it has happened*, that he would desist from raising any more horses, asses, cattle, corn, or other provisions than would barely serve for his own plantation use; and, of some of them, he would, perhaps, raise none at all ; but would convert his land and labour to the cultivation of canes, or of some other species, not under the frowns of those impolitic statutes." Thus a real scarcity of those articles has been produced by the means which were expected to occasion plenty.

better, perhaps, to lodge a discretionary power in the hands of the commander in chief, to interpose his authority occasionally, than to cramp the genius of commerce by any permanent legal restrictions. By leaving the exporter to pursue the bent of his own inclinations, or the dictates of his judgment, our imports will undoubtedly be increased, and a scarcity more effectually guarded against than by arbitrary prohibitions.* For though it may sometimes happen that the neighbouring colonies may drain this country of many articles required for internal consumption, upon a general view, we may safely conclude that the liberty of resorting to another market, when our own ceases to have the preference, will operate as a strong incentive to the enterprising trader to import more abundantly than he would otherwise have done. The advantage of this double species of traffic is evident. The merchant will profit by enlarging his concerns; the planter too will benefit by the augmentation of our imports, some of which in passing through the market will, in case of demand, circulate for the consumer's convenience; the number of our shipping will be increased; the demand for produce will be affected in a relative degree; and, finally the general welfare will be promoted by

---

* "It is generally true," said a great master of political knowledge, "that commerce flourishes most when left to itself. Interest, the great guide of commerce, is not a blind one. It is very able to find its own way; and its necessities are its best laws." *Vide Burke's Speech on Economical Reform.*

the circulation of that wealth which will be thus drawn from
foreign sources.

In a country circumscribed within such narrow limits, and crowded with such an immense population as Barbadoes, the soil is incapable of furnishing the means of subsistence for the numerous sons and daughters of industry by whom it is inhabited. Under these circumstances, commerce enlarges the sphere of human activity; extends, as it were, the boundaries of nature, and overleaping the insular barriers which separate us from the other parts of the globe, furnishes employment and support to the industrious and enterprising. Instead, therefore, of repressing the beneficial spirit of commercial speculation, a wise and prudent legislator should encourage those laudable exertions, which, in the pursuit of private interest and personal aggrandizement, open new sources of national prosperity.

Mr. Dotin had the good fortune to preside as commander in chief longer than any other president before or since his his time. For this advantage he was principally indebted
1739. to accident. A Mr. Walter Chetwynd had been appointed to succeed Lord Howe; but his death, which happened soon afterwards, left the executive power in the hands of Mr. Dotin until the fifteenth day of December, when the Honourable Robert Byng, elder brother to the unfortunate admiral of that name, arrived in Barbadoes; and, by virtue of his Majesty's commission, assumed the government.

On the arrival of Governor Byng, faction again reared
her head. General Peers, having been disappointed in his
hope of succeeding to the chief magistracy, could not
help regarding his more successful competitor with an
envious eye. The house of assembly, as has been already
hinted, were entirely under the influence of their turbulent and ambitious speaker; who had accordingly no difficulty, in persuading the members of that body to limit the
settlement of his excellency to only one half the sum allowed
his predecessor. Mr. Byng could not conceal his chagrin
at a salary so inadequate to his expectations, and to the
dignity of his station. He remarked to the assembly, that
the country was now in a more prosperous situation than at
the time of Lord Howe's arrival; that he was conscious of
bringing with him as good intentions as any former governor
had ever done; and, if he was treated with less consideration than his immediate predecessor, he should think it was
an ignominious distinction, which he could not cheerfully
endure. The assembly, however, were inflexible; they
could not be prevailed upon to depart from their first
determination, though they at last consented to vote his
excellency a present of twenty-five hundred pounds, to
repair the loss of his furniture and equipage, which had
been captured by the Spaniards.

Notwithstanding the just cause of dissatisfaction and
complaint, which the parsimony of the assembly had given
Mr. Byng, he applied himself with diligence and fidelity

to the performance of his duty as a watchful, conscientious guardian of the public weal. Nor did he suffer his private resentment to influence his public conduct, except in a single instance relating to Mr. Peers. This gentleman, besides being speaker of the assembly, held a high military rank in the country; he was lieutenant-general of the militia, colonel of the royal regiment of foot, master-general of the ordnance, president of the council of war, and a justice of the peace*. From his known influence over the assembly, Peers was justly considered the leader of the opposition against the governor; his excellency, therefore, marked him out as the proper object of vengeance, and dismissed him from all his military employments.

July 8.
This harsh exercise of prerogative, gave great offence to the friends of Mr. Peers. The assembly, warmly espousing their speaker's quarrel, entered into two resolutions at their next meeting: First, that the displacing of any able, experienced, military officer, without sufficient reason, directly tends to render the militia unserviceable, and to

---

* The enumeration of the different offices and employments, enjoyed by Mr. Peers, calls to our recollection the remark of the celebrated Earl of Guildford, on John Hely Hutchinson, who, being at one and the same time, a privy counsellor, reversionary secretary of state, major of the 4th regiment of horse, provost of Trinity College, Dublin, and searcher, packer, and guager, of the Port of Strangford, his lordship said, " If England and Ireland were given to this man, he would solicit the Isle of Man for a potatoe garden."

cause the resignation of other officers. Secondly, that the
Honourable Henry Peers had faithfully and diligently discharged his military offices, for which he deserved thanks,
as well of the house as of every inhabitant of the island.

The house also agreed to an address to his excellency,
in which they reproached him with interrupting the harmony which was subsisting at the time of his arrival; and
complained that their liberality towards him, manifested
by a voluntary settlement for his support, followed by a
large gratuity, had failed in his mind to produce those
sentiments of gratitude, which would have rendered his
government agreeable. After several insinuations respecting his excellency's unfriendly disposition towards the people, contrasting his conduct with that of their *late good and
candid governor*, they concluded with these words, " When
the officers of the militia are persons who deserve the love
and esteem of their country, the defects in the establishment of that useful body of men, are seldom attended with
any great inconveniences. But the late use your excellency has made of your authority, shews how highly imprudent it would be in us to trust a greater power in your
hands. You have thought fit to displace the ablest and
most experienced officer of which we can boast; to dismiss
him at so critical a juncture, is a circumstance that little
manifests your concern for our welfare. The condition to
which you have reduced the royal regiment by this step,
cannot be retrieved under a considerable term; nor will

proper officers easily be obtained, if an implicit concurrence, in all your measures, should become the only tenure of their commissions."

This address was presented by Mr. Waterman and Mr. Gibbes: and though his excellency had every reason to suspect that the contents were not of the most pleasing kind, he received it with great complacency, put it into his pocket unopened, and, without making any reply, treated the two gentlemen with the utmost politeness and condescension. And Mr. Gibbes, who was one of the governor's warmest political opponents, was the very next day appointed chief judge of a court of common pleas. This was a noble instance of generosity and moderation. Were it admitted that his excellency's treatment of Mr. Peers was arbitrary and unjustifiable, it should be remembered, that no rank nor station has ever been found to exempt men from the passions and infirmities common to human nature. We may lament, that the political opinions of persons in high responsible situations, or the imperious calls of public duty, should render them obnoxious to the displeasure of the supreme authority, yet it should never be forgotten, that governors and the rulers of nations are not less susceptible of anger and resentment than those whom they govern. How unreasonable is it then to expect that forbearance in them, which we find ourselves unable to practise in the most ordinary concerns of life ?

Mr. Peers survived his fall from power but a short time.

He died on the fourth day of September, not quite two months after his dismissal. This gentleman's character has been transmitted to posterity in very opposite colours, by different writers. By one it is said, that his ambition had plunged him early into factious designs, in the pursuit of which he acquired a peculiar dexterity in the management of a party. His passions were violent and ungovernable, in friendship warm, in resentment implacable; he was the enemy of every man who opposed his measures*. On the other hand, he is represented as a man of integrity, lenient in his disposition, perfectly disinterested in his views, indefatigable in his endeavours to serve his friends, and disdaining to exert his power to the injury of those from whom he differed in politics†. We presume not to reconcile opinions so contradictory.

The death of a man, whose turbulent disposition, and ambitious, intriguing spirit, had frequently disturbed the repose of the country, contributed in no small degree to the restoration of peace and harmony. And the Barbadians were just beginning to enjoy the benefits of Mr. Byng's prudence and zeal for the public service, when he was unfortunately seized by a malignant fever, which, in a few days, put a period to his existence. Mr. Byng's short administration was characterised by his firmness as a man, and his

October 8.

---

* Short Hist. of Barb. p. 69.   † Mem. of Barb. Appen. p. 4.

integrity and activity as a magistrate; by an unwearied application to the duties of his office, a strict attention to the organization of the militia, and the repair of the fortifications. And, to their honour be it added, the assembly, notwithstanding their disputes with the governor, cheerfully and liberally contributed to his patriotic designs, wisely considering that no party contention ought to divert them from providing the means of defending their country against the common enemy.

On the demise of Mr. Byng, the executive authority once more devolved on the Honourable James Dotin. Two days after this event, the assembly met; and, considering the mischiefs and inconveniences which had resulted from their liberality to their governors, unanimously resolved, on the motion of Judge Bruce, to make no settlement whatever upon any succeeding commander in chief. This was certainly a most extraordinary determination, evidently calculated to produce effects the most opposite to those which were expected from it. Nothing could be more preposterous than to suppose that any gentleman would forego the pleasures and enjoyments of his native country, and encounter the inconveniences and perils of a voyage across the Atlantic, to become the governor of a West Indian province, in a climate unfavourable to European constitutions, without a prospect of deriving some more solid advantages from the appointment than the honour of the station, or the trifling salary allowed by the crown.

Effectually to obviate all possibility of future altercation between themselves and their governor, on this point, the assembly would have acted with much more prudence and foresight, had they at once established a permanent revenue, sufficient, without any ulterior augmentation, to support the dignity of the chief magistracy. Had this been done, every candidate for the government would know before he left England, the full extent of his reward. No disappointment could blast his hopes, nor sour his temper; and a fruitful source of strife and discontent, equally disgraceful and injurious, would have been removed. Instead of resolving to allow no salary to the representative of the crown, a just regard to the honour and interest of their constituents should have induced the assembly to proportion the settlement to the full extent of the public ability. A liberal provision would reflect lustre on the character of the government, and render it worthy the acceptance of gentlemen, whose valuable qualities and respectable connexions might enable them to be useful; while, on the other hand, a mean, scanty allowance can be acceptable only to needy adventurers without talents or principle.

It is a favourite maxim with some colonial politicians, that the governor's reward should be proportioned to his merit. But this, however specious, is improper and impracticable. The settlement on the governor must, in conformity to the royal instructions, be made at the first meeting of the assembly after his arrival, when a disappointment often occasions disagreeable dissensions. Nor can it be said that any subsequent encrease of salary has ever been productive of benefit to the country. On the contrary, it has sometimes happened, that the measures of the court have assumed a very different aspect as soon as his excellency found that he had nothing farther to expect from the generosity of the people. Besides, this doctrine betrays too much of that democratic spirit, which has been long labouring to transfer to the popular branch of the government the sole legislative and executive authority of the state. It betrays a wish to acquire and exercise an undue influence over the executive power: a wish in which no true patriot should ever concur. The perfection of our constitution consists in the exact equilibrium of the three branches of the legislature and the harmonious union of all its parts. Whenever this balance is destroyed, whether it be by the preponderance of the monarchic, aristocratic, or democratic part of the constitution, there is equally an end of civil or political liberty.

The next year the assembly confirmed their resolution concerning the governor's salary; and, on the motion of Mr. Tobias Frere, unanimously entered into several other resolutions, for supporting the privileges of the people, without infringing, as they professed, the prerogative of the crown; and for regulating the proceedings of the assembly, according to the usage of the house of commons. They insisted that the representatives of the people possessed the sole, inherent right of imposing taxes, and appropriating the public money to the uses for which it was raised ; and resolved to exclude the council from all but a negative participation in the business of raising supplies. Had they stopped here, all would have been well. But in their excessive zeal for the maintenance of their own privileges, they resolved, in direct opposition to the royal instructions, to provide for the payment of no account which had not been previously examined, and approved by the house. Thus they industriously sowed the seeds of discord, between themselves and the other branches of the legislature ; and revived a cause of litigation, which had been already peremptorily decided against them.

CHAP. X.

ADMINISTRATION OF SIR THOMAS ROBINSON—DISPUTES BE-
TWEEN THE GOVERNOR AND THE ASSEMBLY—COMMODORE
KNOWLES—AN INQUIRY INTO THE STATE OF CHARLES FORT
—SIR THOMAS IS SUPERSEDED BY MR. GRENVILLE—THE
GOVERNMENT DEVOLVES ON MR. WEEKES—SUCCEEDED BY
DOCTOR PINFOLD—LOYAL AND SPIRITED CONDUCT OF THE
BARBADIANS—MR. ADAMS EXPELLED THE ASSEMBLY—THE
GOVERNOR'S RESIGNATION.

CHAP. X.
1742.

THE progress of the work now brings us to the administration of Sir Thomas Robinson, a period which is represented to have been of some importance in our colonial history. Yet, from the scantiness of the few annals which I
have been able to collect, I am apprehensive that my relation of it must be extremely defective. Every deficiency
of this sort might have been supplied, could I have obtained
access to the journals of the assembly; but this advantage,
as I have elsewhere observed, was refused, with more
than Spanish jealousy.

Sir Thomas Robinson arrived on the eighth day of August, and, after going through the usual forms and cere-

monies of attending divine service, and taking the state oaths, received the reins of government from the president. The assembly at first seemed firm in their resolution of giving the governor no salary; their constancy, however, soon yielded to the impulse of justice and generosity; and after some opposition, the house agreed to settle on his excellency, the sum of six and twenty hundred pounds a year, during his possession of the government. A few months afterwards, an addition of four hundred pounds per annum was made to the salary, by a majority of two voices only.

Though one cause of contention was thus removed, at some expense of consistency, others were perpetually springing up. It is probable, that Sir Thomas Robinson, in many instances, acted without a due regard to the constitutional privileges of the people, and failed in treating the popular branch of the legislature with that respectful attention to which it was entitled. Either for his personal convenience, or to gratify his taste in architecture, he precipitately pulled down one of the best and largest apartments at Pilgrim, and made several expensive alterations and repairs without consulting the assembly. They very properly objected to this mode of proceeding, and refused to provide for the payment of a debt which had been so irregularly incurred, without their consent; but, on his excellency's making a suitable apology, the affair was compromised.

The ill humour of the assembly had scarcely subsided, before his excellency very incautiously furnished them with a fresh subject of discontent. There happened to be, at that time, no convenient armory in the island. The utility of such a building was unquestionable; the governor, therefore, determined, of his own authority, to erect one, with a small magazine adjoining, in which a sufficient number of small arms, and a due proportion of ammunition, might be carefully deposited for the use of the militia, in case of their being called into actual service. When the work was completed, his excellency laid the accounts, accompanied by the proper vouchers, before the assembly, requiring them to raise the necessary supplies to enable him to liquidate the debt which he had contracted. The assembly acknowledged the utility of the undertaking; but peremptorily refused to comply with his excellency's demand; alleging, that he had acted unconstitutionally, and in open violation of the rights of the people. As the delegated guardians of the public purse, they insisted that they ought to have been consulted on an undertaking, the expense of which was to be paid by their constituents; that, as his excellency had presumed to erect the armory without deigning to advise with the representatives of the people, they could not vote for his reimbursement without committing a breach of the sacred trust reposed in them, and establishing a precedent not less dangerous to the interests and privileges of the people than injurious to the honour and independence of their own body*.

This reasoning was invincible. But as legislative assemblies are not bound, like courts of justice, to strict observance of former decisions, there would have been less immorality in establishing a precedent, which, at the worst, could only have been quoted on any similar occasion, than in violating the laws of justice, which being immutable and eternal, ought never to be transgressed on any plea of policy or expediency.

A clandestine attempt was made by the commissioners of the fortifications to secure a part of the money for his excellency; they certified, that the lumber and materials used about the armoury had been applied to the use of the fortifications; and an order was regularly passed at the council-board for the amount. The treasurer, from a previous knowledge of the circumstances, doubted the legality of both the certificate and the order; and consulted the attorney-general; who thought, that though the commissioners had exceded the bounds of their authority, as the order had passed the council-board in the usual manner, the treasurer was bound to pay it. But the assembly not concurring in this opinion, withheld the supplies, and Sir Thomas was left to sustain the undiminished expense of the

* Short Hist. of Barb. p. 74. Remarks on the Short Hist. p. 22. First Sett. of Barb. p. 32.

CHAP. X. building, amounting nearly to two-and-forty hundred

1745. pounds. In the course of the disputes, to which this transaction gave rise, Colonel Gibbons (afterwards Sir William)
who had been recently elevated to the speaker's chair, and
had been appointed to the command of Speight's division by
Sir Thomas himself, thought proper to resign his commission, either to render himself independent of the governor's
favour, or to anticipate his dismissal.

Notwithstanding these domestic feuds, and the animosity which prevailed against the governor, it is a circumstance much to the honour of the assembly, that the public
safety was neither neglected nor sacrificed to an idle opposition to the measures of government. Two sloops were
fitted out to guard the coasts against the depredations of
privateers ; and the sum of seven hundred pounds sterling
was voted for the purchase of paterraroes for the use of the
forts ; a good intention, miserably perverted. At the same
time, a suspicion being entertained that there were some
persons in the country base enough to hold a traiterous correspondence with the French at Martinico, an act was passed, empowering the governor to cause any person whom he
should have reason to suspect of disaffection, or of corresponding with the enemy, to be apprehended, by warrant
from any justice of the peace, and committed to the common gaol, till he should be released by an order of council.
This was, in fact, an absolute suspension of the habeas corpus act. A formidable power was thus lodged in his excel-

lency's hands, which an arbitrary and vindictive ruler might have employed in oppressing his Majesty's subjects; especially such, as by thwarting his measures, might have provoked his resentment. But Sir Thomas exercised this alarming authority with becoming moderation. Three men of low rank only were arrested; and they were discharged in a few days, on giving security, not to engage in any treasonable correspondence during the continuance of the act, which was limited to three months.

A circumstance happened at this time, which, though it may be deemed beneath the dignity of history to record, ought not to be omitted in a narrative of domestic occurrences. Mr. Bedford, a merchant of Bridge-town, having a sloop arrived from Essequebo, laden with timber, sold the cargo to Commodore Knowles, who hired the vessel to carry it to Antigua, after she had been duly entered at the proper offices. Bedford was sensible that the sloop ought to be entered outwards, before she could be allowed to proceed on her voyage, and accordingly mentioned the matter to the commodore, who most unaccountably forbad it; giving him a certificate of her having been hired into the King's service, adding, that he would hoist a pendant, and protect the sloop and the owner from all damages. At length, Captain Pare, the chief gunner at Needham's, being informed that the sloop was to sail without clearing at the offices, as the law directs, consulted Colonel Charnock, who advised him not to let her go without the usual order from the governor. In the mean time the sloop, accompanied by Commodore Knowles's flag-ship, was got under weigh ; and Captain Pare, finding she was out of shot of Needham's, hastened to James Fort, and ordered two guns to be successively fired at her. The Woolwich, which was then in a very different direction from the sloop, immediately fired a shot over the fort, which penetrated a storehouse in the town. Pare, not to be intimidated from his duty, fired a third shot at the sloop ; but finding she had got beyond the range of his cannon, the firing was discontinued. Commodore Knowles was violently exasperated, and wrote a passionate letter, directed to the governor *in council*, complaining of the unparalleled insult, as he termed it, on his Majesty's flag ; asserting, contrary to the fact, that two of the shot were very near striking the Woolwich, and declaring, that had the ship been struck, he would certainly have beaten down the fort ; and concluded with insisting, that the person, by whose orders the guns were fired, should be exemplarily punished.

The matter, by order of the governor and council, was referred to the consideration of the attorney-general, Blenman ; who, after an elaborate review of the whole affair, reported, that notwithstanding the cargo had been purchased by Commodore Knowles, the vessel ought to have cleared as the law directs, and that the captain-gunner had done extremely right in endeavouring to stop her. But he thought that Pare ought to have informed the commodore of the necessity of the vessel's clearing out before he could allow her to pass the fort; and that then, though he might have fired a single shot, to signify that the vessel had not complied with the law, it would have been prudent to have gone no farther. But as to punishing the officers of the fort, Mr. Blenman averred there was no foundation for such a proceeding by any legal course, whatever might be the measure of naval discipline. In remarking on the threat of beating down the fort, the spirited Crown lawyer congratulated the commodore on the shot from the Woolwich having produced no worse consequences, " since, if it had, he might possibly have found, on his return to Barbadoes, that we are neither without good laws for our protection, nor a suitable spirit to put them in execution."

Upon the meeting of the general assembly, Mr. Fairchild, after some prefatory remarks on the defenceless state of Charles-fort, and the allusion to some disorders which had recently happened in that garrison, moved, that a committee be appointed to inquire into the condition of Charles-fort at the time of the three preceding alarms, the causes of the deficiency of stores, and of the disorders reported to have happened there; and that the committee be empowered to send for papers and records, and to examine witnesses. The motion being agreed to, a committee was appointed to prosecute the proposed inquiry.

The proceeding gave great offence to his excellency, by whom it was considered as an infringement on the rights of the executive power.   He called the committee before him, and endeavoured to intimidate them from pursuing their design.   But finding his menaces ineffectual, he consulted the attorney-general, and demanded a categorical answer to the following queries—1. Whether, by the laws and constitution of Barbadoes, the assembly have a power of inquiring into any deficiency of stores, or into any disorders that may happen in either of the forts, without any previous address or application to the governor ? 2. Whether the assembly have a right to send for persons, papers, and records, and to examine witnesses upon oath, or to direct a justice of the peace to take depositions for their satisfaction ? Whether the assembly have power to compel witnesses to appear before them, and to oblige persons to produce papers and records ; and what methods of compulsion may they use for these purposes ?

Mr. Blenman's report, in answer to these interrogatories, was in substance as follows : it is the indisputable prerogative of the commander in chief to inquire into all grievances of a public nature, and to redress them by the removal of those officers whose negligence or incapacity are the causes of the abuses complained of.   But, as various circumstances may concur to prevent his excellency's coming to the knowledge of many existing evils, it is equally the privilege of the assembly to inquire into, and represent them to the governor, that they may be corrected, and the offenders punished by his authority.   Nor did the honourable gentleman conceive that the present inquiry had any tendency to encroach on the prerogative of the Crown. He thought that a previous address to the governor, on the subject, would have been a more regular and useful mode of proceeding; but, as the assembly had preferred another, which appeared to them more effectual, he knew of no law which could restrain them in the exercise of their inherent privilege; nor could they be controlled otherwise than by his excellency's undoubted power of dissolving the house. But he earnestly recommended to his excellency to take no step to retard the progress of an inquiry, of so much importance to the community, and which was universally expected at that perilous juncture. Having already said, that the assembly had an unquestionable right to examine into all public grievances, the learned counsellor thought they must have power to send for persons and papers, and to examine witnesses; but not upon oath*. And, although he would not presume to determine precisely the power of the assembly, or their committee, in cases of this nature; yet, if they thought it essential to the public interest or safety to ascertain the truth of any particular fact, relating to any affair depending in their house, by deposition taken by a justice of the peace, he apprehended it

---

* Mr. Christian, in his notes upon Blacks. Comm. vol. 1. p. 181, says, " the committee (appointed to determine controverted elections) may send for witnesses and examine them upon oath: a power which the house of commons does not possess."

would be highly injurious to dispute their right to pursue that method. As the third query concerned the conduct of the assembly and their committee in their proceedings, Mr. Blenman declined giving an explicit answer, as their privileges were no where expressly defined.

Meanwhile the committee, having finished their inquiries, made their report to the house; upon which they presented an address to his excellency, insisting upon the removal of the chief gunner of Charles-fort. The attorney-general was again consulted; and, in a report written with manly sense, candour, prudence, and moderation, he advised a compliance with the wishes of the assembly, as the only means of restoring harmony to the public councils. But the seeds of discord were too deeply sown, and too industriously cultivated, not to produce the most deleterious fruits. The governor, encouraged by the indiscreet interference of the council, disregarded the sober admonitions of his sage monitor. There was, perhaps, a stronger influence yet behind the curtain. Sir Thomas had married Mrs. Salmon, a widow lady, whose daughter, by her former husband, was married to Captain Pare, chief gunner of Charles-fort.

The dissensions between his excellency and the assembly were encreased by mutual opposition, until the resentment of the house could no longer be restrained within the bounds of moderation. They presented a petition to the throne, containing several allegations against the governor, for an abuse of the prerogative, and a violation of the privileges of the commons of Barbadoes. His excellency was represented as having, in numberless instances, shewn himself destitute of every talent for government; as having abused and disgraced the sacred trust reposed in him; and rendered himself contemptible in the eyes of all his Majesty's subjects. In consequence of these complaints, Sir Thomas Robinson, on a change of ministry, was recalled from his government, and the Honourable Henry Grenville, brother-in-law to Lord Temple, appointed to succeed him. Sir Thomas, nevertheless, continued to exercise the supreme authority, until the arrival of his successor, to whom he resigned the administration, and remained some time on the island as a private gentleman.

The assembly now seemed sensible of the impropriety of their former determination respecting the governor's salary, and felt no difficulty in departing from a resolution equally impolitic and unjust. On their first session, after Mr. Grenville's arrival, they settled on him the sum of three thousand pounds a year, with a resolution not to increase that allowance on any pretence whatsoever*. The mild and pacific administration of Mr. Grenville affords few occurrences worthy of attention, except the dispute in which he

---

* One of the first acts of Mr. Grenville's administration, was to restore Sir William Gibbons to his military rank and authority.

was involved with M. de Caylus, concerning the island of Tobago.

That island had always been considered as a dependency on the government of Barbadoes ; but by the peace of Aix-la-Chapelle it was stipulated to be neutral, and to be in common to such of the subjects of England and France as might occasionally resort thither for refreshment. Within two short months after signing the definitive treaty, the French court privately ordered a settlement to be made on the island, under the protection of de Caylus, governor of Martinico. The design was no sooner known in Barbadoes, than Mr. Grenville dispatched a frigate to Tobago, with a proclamation, requiring the French settlers to evacuate the island within thirty days, under peril of military execution. De Caylus immediately published an ordinance, in which, after treating Mr. Grenville's proclamation as a forgery, he claimed the sovereignty of the island for his most Christian Majesty; promising protection and support to such French subjects as should settle there, and prohibiting all intercourse with the adjacent English, Dutch and Danish colonies. To shew that he was in earnest, the French General stationed two stout frigates at Courland-bay, and erected two strong batteries on shore. In the interim, the Boston frigate having touched at Tobago for wood and water, Capt. Wheeler was not allowed to land, but was told, that if he should be seen there again he would be expelled by force.

A detail of these particulars was transmitted by Mr. Grenville to England, where they excited a considerable degree of popular indignation at the perfidy of the French, and the supineness of the English ministry. Lord Albemarle, the British ambassador at Paris, was, at length, instructed to remonstrate against such a palpable breach of friendship and good faith. The French minister, in reply, accused Mr. Grenville of precipitancy and exaggeration; he, however, unequivocally disavowed the proceedings of De Caylus, and promised that care should be taken to prevent similar complaints in future. Orders were accordingly issued by the court of Versailles for the immediate evacuation of Tobago and the other neutral islands. These orders were sent to Mr. Grenville to be forwarded to De Caylus, who refused to obey them, saying that he had received no instructions from the king, his master, on the subject. For the sake of procrastination, he entered into a discussion with Mr. Grenville on the rights of the two crowns, which was interrupted by his death, and the point was ultimately decided by an appeal to the sword.*

Meanwhile the government of Barbadoes was conducted by Mr. Grenville with becoming dignity and firmness. The world, which seldom looks beyond the surface of things, is ever caught by appearances, and governed by opinion.

---

* Univ. Hist. vol. xli. p. 179.   Entick's Hist. of the late war (1765) vol. i. p. 22, &c.

During the long contests between the people and the representative of the crown, the chief magistracy had gradually sunk into a state not far removed from contempt; but Mr. Grenville soon restored the dignity of government by the splendour and magnificence with which he supported his rank; and yet more by his dignified deportment and patriotic conduct. His candour, integrity, and impartiality removed all cause of party disputes, and silenced the clamours of faction. His stern political rectitude disdained the base arts by which ignoble minds court an evanescent popularity, and sought only to establish his fame on the durable basis of a conscientious discharge of his duty. With no other object in view than the public good, he aimed to acquire no undue influence over the legislative councils by gratifying the selfish or ambitious desires of men in power; but bestowed such employments as were at his disposal on the most deserving, regardless of personal connexions, or the solicitations of private friendship. He had thus the felicity, known to few in his exalted sphere, of drawing talents from obscurity and rewarding merit in a stranger.

Having administered the government for six years and one month, Mr. Grenville indulged a wish most natural to an ingenuous mind; he languished for his native home; and, having obtained his royal master's permission, resigned his authority, with the design of returning to England. Previous to his departure, the house of assembly, as a testimony of their grateful sense of the blessings which the people had enjoyed under his auspicious administration, voted a liberal donative to defray the expenses of his voyage. But his excellency generously refused to increase the burthens of a people, whom he could no longer aid with his counsels nor benefit by his exertions. Impressed with becoming admiration of such an extraordinary instance of disinterestedness, the assembly resolved to perpetuate the memory of his exalted merit, by erecting a marble statue, representing his excellency at full length, in the most conspicuous part of the town hall.*

On Mr. Grenville's departure, the government devolved on the Honourable Ralph Weekes, president of the council. Though this gentleman retained the executive authority for more than three years, the colonial records furnish no memorial of his talents for government, nor of his genius for legislation, except an act prohibiting the firing of squibs, serpents, and other fire-works, the usual demonstrations of popular attachment to church and state, on the anniversary of the papists' conspiracy, This law is annually trampled upon with impunity by vulgar loyalty and tumultuous piety. Mr. Weekes was rewarded with a salary of twelve hundred pounds a year. His uninteresting admi-

* Hall's first settlement of Barb. p. 33. This statue, together with Lord Howe's portrait, was destroyed by the great hurricane in 1780.

nistration was at length terminated by the arrival of Charles Pinfold, LL.D. who had been honoured with his Majesty's commission as governor of Barbadoes. The revenue allotted for the support of Mr. Pinfold was the same as that which had been allowed to the two last governors.

Whenever Great Britain is engaged in actual hostilities with any other maritime power, the effects of the contest are quickly felt in the remotest parts of the habitable globe. The war which was now kindled in Europe soon extended itself to the West Indies, and presented the Barbadians with an opportunity of proving their zeal and fidelity, by the readiness with which they contributed their feeble aid to promote the enterprises of the British government in the western hemisphere. Towards the end of this year, the cabinet of Saint James's formed the design of reducing the power of France in the Caribbean sea. For this purpose, a fleet of six sail of the line, with a body of five thousand troops, were ordered from Saint Helens to join

Commodore Moore in Carlisle Bay. The junction was effected on the third day of the new year. The governor immediately convoked the legislature, for the purpose of affording such assistance as might be in their power to facilitate the expedition. With a spirit and promptitude highly creditable, they granted a number of negroes for the removal of artillery and other laborious services, and furnished the seamen and soldiers with every species of refreshment and accommodation which were deemed necessary or acceptable.*

The British armament left Carlisle Bay on the thirteenth day of January, and entered the harbour of Fort Royal, at Martinico two days afterwards, when the troops were disembarked at Point des Negroes. But in consequence of some difference in opinion between general Hopson and Commodore Moore, they were re-embarked within twenty-four hours after their landing, at the very moment when the principal inhabitants were employed in arranging a plan for the surrender of the island. The British fleet then proceeded to Basseterre at Guadaloupe, where, though they experienced a vigorous resistance, they were ultimately successful.†

During the progress of the siege, the commodore, having received intelligence of the arrival of M. de Bompart, with nine sail of the line at Martinico, left the troops to protect themselves, and retired to Dominica with his squadron, consisting of ten line of battle ships. With this superior force Moore ingloriously lay at anchor in Prince Rupert's

---

* Smollet's Cont. vol. v. p. 5. Hall's laws, p. 525. The compiler of the Universal Hist. vol. xli. p. 181, erroneously assert that Barbadoes, on this occasion, furnished a large body of volunteers, raised and disciplined at the expense of the country. This error has been implicitly adopted by Mr. Frere in his Short History, though his means of information ought to have shewn him that the Barbadian volunteers were not raised till nearly three years afterwards.

† Entick's Hist. of the War (1765) vol. iv. p. 144.

bay, above eleven weeks, in which time upwards of ninety sail of English merchantmen were captured and carried into Martinico. The inactivity of the commodore excited considerable murmurings in Barbadoes; where he was burnt in effigy; his person treated with indignity, and his name held in absolute detestation. This occasioned some ill-blood between the inhabitants and the officers of the navy; and the character of the country was afterwards grossly calumniated, in a pamphlet, published by Captain Gardner; which produced a spirited reply from the classical pen of Sir John Gay Alleyne, who, for his judicious defence, was honoured with the public thanks of the generaly assembly.

1761.
The design of annihilating the power of France in the American archipelago, was revived by Mr. Pitt, though the execution of it was destined to bestow a splendour, little deserved, on the ministry of his unpopular successor. Governor Pinfold lost no time in communicating to the council and assembly of Barbadoes, the intentions of the British cabinet; and called upon them to second his efforts to promote the public service. Nor was the application made in vain. A regiment of five hundred and eighty-eight men was raised, for the use of government, under the command of Sir John Yeamans, armed and accoutred at the expense of the country; to which was added a body of five hundred and eighty-three negro men to serve as pioneers. The expense of raising and equipping this corps amounted to twenty-four thousand pounds; no inconsiderable sum to be paid

by a small colony, which had never been distinguished by
the kindness nor the partiality of its parent state.*

The naval force allotted for the reduction of Martinico, under the command of Sir George Bridges Rodney, arrived in Carlisle-bay in November; but it was not till the day before Christmas that general Monckton was able to collect the whole of the troops placed under his direction. From that moment, however, no unnecessary delay retarded the sailing of the fleet, which reached Saint Anne's bay, at Martinico, on the seventh day of January. General Monckton soon found it necessary to occupy the almost inaccessible heights of Morne Tortenson and Morne Garnier, whose natural strength had been improved with great skill and judgment. Proper arrangements having been made for the attack of Morne Tortenson, the troops advanced by break of day. The engagement commenced with the grenadiers,
led on by Major Grant; while another brigade, assisted by a thousand seamen in flat-bottomed boats, fell upon their redoubts along the shore. A third division, supported by the light infantry, after attacking a plantation which lay in their way, marched round in the rear of the enemy. The

---

* The House of Commons on the 7th May 1765, voted the sum of ten thousand pounds, " to enable his Majesty to make a proper compensation to the government of Barbadoes, for the assistance which it gave his Majesty's forces under Major General Monckton, in the expedition against Martinico." *Annual Register, vol.* 8. *p.* 240.

attack was made with so much impetuosity, that by the ninth hour of the day the assailants were completely in possession of the enemy's works on Morne Tortenson. As their batteries on Morne Garnier were capable of greatly annoying the British troops, General Monckton ordered several batteries to be erected, for the purpose of covering his operations against Fort Royal. On the other hand, the enemy formed the resolution of attacking the British troops. The attack was sustained with great firmness; the assailants were soon repulsed; and, such was the ardour of the English, that they pursued the flying enemy across a deep ravine into their own batteries, and established themselves on the redoubts of their adversaries. Morne Garnier was thus, in a few hours, transferred to the occupancy of the British.

The possession of these important posts enabled Monckton to direct his views against Fort Royal. Batteries were immediately erected, and were nearly ready to begin the work of destruction, when the inhabitants proposed to capitulate. The terms were easily adjusted, and the garrison was delivered up to the British troops. The conquest of Martinico was yet incomplete. La Touche, the governor general, had retired to Saint Pierre's, with a determination of maintaining the rights of his sovereign. But the inefficacy of any opposition in his power, to make to the preparations which he saw going forward for the siege of that fortress, induced him to submit to the conquerors. The

Feb. 4.

terms of capitulation were liberal and characteristic of
British generosity; and Martinico was finally surrendered
to General Monckton on the fourteenth day of February.

The distinguished part borne by the Barbadians in the
campaign in the West Indies, reflected great lustre on their
character, and procured them the most flattering testimonials of their sovereign's approbation.   On the meeting of
the general assembly, the governor opened the session with
a gracious speech; in which, after congratulating the council and assembly on the conquest of Martinico, his excellency was pleased to add to his own commendation of their
conduct, the most gratifying information of his Majesty's
sentiments of their meritorious exertions to aid his arms in
this distant part of the empire.   " Upon receipt of his
Majesty's commands," said Mr. Pinfold, " zeal and unanimity appeared in every branch of the legislature.   With
the greatest dispatch, ample provision was made for the
assistance of the king's forces ; and the hands of government
were strengthened with great and extensive powers.   By
your influence and example, a vigorous spirit was diffused
and communicated among all ranks of men.   Each in his
proper sphere, with a laudable contest, aimed to be the
most active in promoting the public service.   The concurrence of these circumstances enabled me to raise the most
complete, best accoutred, and best trained corps that ever
was sent from the island, whose behaviour has exceeded the
most sanguine expectations, and merited the approbation

of their commander in chief. Happy am I to have it in particular command from his Majesty, to convey to you his gracious sense of the cheerfulness and unanimity with which you enabled me to execute his commands; and his firm reliance, that his faithful and loyal subjects of Barbadoes will not cease to manifest the same laudable spirit in any future operations that may be undertaken, for annoying and distressing his enemies in the West Indies!"

From the proud contemplation of the national successes abroad, the attention of the general assembly was turned to less pleasing objects of consideration at home. John Adams, member for Christ Church, had, with a body of armed slaves, opposed the provost marshal in the execution of his office. For this violent outrage he had been indicted at the court of grand sessions, fined and imprisoned. Not satisfied with this punishment, the assembly expelled Mr. Adams from their house; and, upon their application to the governor, a new writ was issued for the election of another member. Adams's friends thought that the misdemeanor, for which he had been expelled, was cognizable only in the courts of law, to which he had submitted and received sentence: a sentence which, it was contended, could by no legitimate construction whatever be deemed to affect his seat in the legislature; the freeholders therefore re-elected him without hesitation or opposition. The assembly, persuaded that the power of expulsion would avail but little, if the obnoxious member could thus be

retorted upon them, expelled him a second time. This procedure was warmly resented by the electors of Christ Church.
They considered it as an arbitrary encroachment on the
liberty of the subject, completely subversive of the elective franchise. It was insisted that the assembly did not
possess an inherent, original authority, but a delegated
power; for which, whoever receives it, is accountable to
those who gave it; since it is obvious that those, who
bestow authority by commission, always retain more than
they grant.

Whatever weight this reasoning may be thought to possess, the right of the assembly to expel any of its members,
guilty of flagrant offences, is clear and incontestible. According to an eminent law authority, if any person is made
a peer by the king, or elected, to serve in the House of
Commons, by the people, yet may the respective houses
upon complaint of any crime, and proof thereof, adjudge
him disabled and incapable to sit as a member*. In support of this doctrine, the learned commentator on the laws
of England, refers to many respectable authorities; and
the journals of parliament furnish many precedents to justify the right of expulsion, claimed by both houses. No
doubt then can exist that the assembly of Barbadoes, whose
functions and privileges are in all respects analagous to

---

* Blackstone's Commentaries, vol. i. p. 163.

those of the Commons of Great Britain, have the same paramount jurisdiction over the conduct of its members.

Finding that the freeholders were determined to persist in asserting their right to re-elect Mr. Adams, the assembly suffered their resentment to hurry them too far, and they passed a law, to disqualify him from being elected a member of the assembly, or from bearing any office, civil or military, in the government of the island. Adams was not of a temper to submit to such an ignominious disfranchisement. He appealed to the justice and moderation of his Sovereign; and, after a due investigation of the circumstances, the act was repealed by his Majesty's order, grounded on the opinion of Sir Matthew Lamb, counsel to the Board of Trade, by whom it was represented as arbitrary, and contrary to the spirit of the British constitution, tending to establish a dangerous precedent, and to deprive his Majesty of the services of a subject. *   It is to

---

* It is a little singular that, within eighteen months after this affair, the public mind was agitated by a similar transaction in England. The circumstances of this occurrence are briefly these. John Wilkes, on the 19th of January, 1764, was expelled the House of Commons for a seditious publication. At the next election he was returned for the county of Middlesex, upon which it was again resolved, that John Wilkes, Esq., for having published several libels, be expelled this House; and a new writ being issued, Mr. Wilkes was re elected without opposition. On the 17th of February, 1769, the House resolved, " that John Wilkes, Esq. having been in this session of parliament expelled the House, was, and is, incapable of being elected to serve in this present parliament;" the election was therefore declared void, and a new writ ordered. Mr. Luttrel now offered himself a candidate, in opposition to Mr.

be observed, that the right of expulsion was not affected by this declaration; it was the act of disqualification to which the King objected.

The unexampled success of the British arms in every quarter of the globe, was soon followed by a general pacification. The Barbadians saw with regret the most important conquests in the West Indies restored to their national enemy; for, although some politicians pretended to discover, in the acquisition of the French colonies, much future injury to the commerce of Barbadoes, by depreciating the value of its staple productions, men of more enlarged views, justly considered the possession of Martinico and Gaudaloupe in the highest degree essential to the safety of the English settlements in their vicinity, and to the security of their trade and navigation. Nor was this the only source of uneasiness to the Barbadians.

Wilkes. On the election Wilkes, having a vast majority in his favour, was returned by the sheriff as duly elected. The House of Commons, nevertheless, resolved that Mr. Luttrel ought to have been returned, and ordered the return to be amended. The freeholders of Middlesex presented a petition to the House, complaining of this invasion of their rights; but the House, on the 8th of May, again resolved that Mr. Luttrel was duly elected. In this state the matter remained nearly 14 years, when, upon the memorable change of ministry in 1783, it was resolved by the House of Commons, that the resolution of the 17th February, 1769, and all other declarations, orders and resolutions, respecting the election of J. Wilkes, should be expunged, as being subversive of the rights of the whole body of electors. Thus was it established that, although the Commons have a right to expel their members, expulsion does not create a disqualification from re-election.

CHAP. X.
1765.

The expense incurred in the prosecution of the late war had been most severely felt by the people of England ; and to remove in some measure the exclusive burthen from their shoulders, it was thought to be but fair and equitable that the North American colonies, for whose defence the war had been originally undertaken, should contribute a due proportion towards defraying the expense incurred for their protection. To this end, it was proposed by Mr. Grenville, among other financial expedients, to impose on them the payment of certain stamp duties. Parliament readily concurred in the arbitrary and unconstitutional scheme, and passed the celebrated stamp act. The effects produced by this fatal measure, are too well known to require repetition in this place. The universal discontent which it excited on the continent of North America, soon communicated itself to the neighbouring islands. Conscious of their weakness, the West Indians only remonstrated against the oppression, except the inhabitants of Nevis and Saint Christopher's. In the latter, the populace proceeded to as great lengths of tumultuous opposition, as the people of New England; and, having burned the stamped paper of their own island, went over in a body to assist their neighbours of Nevis in the same patriotic work.* The Barbadians, more moderate, wisely refrained from a fruitless opposition; and, having tried the mild and legal

---

* Annual Register, vol. 8. p. 56.

mode of remonstrating against a measure so evidently pernicious and subversive of their chartered rights, calmly
submitted to the injustice which they could not resist. It
was not long, however, before the ministry, to preserve the
peace of the empire, were compelled to abandon their project, but for the short time during which the stamp act
was enforced, the sum of twenty-five hundred pounds was
exacted from the people of Barbadoes, and remitted to
England.*

Governor Pinfold having exercised the executive authority for nine years and nine months, with a propriety
which added lustre to his reputation, and afforded satisfaction to the community over which he presided, resigned his
government and returned to his native country.† Although
Mr. Pinfold has been invidiously represented as " a quiet,
easy governor, whose qualities were wholly negative,"‡
there seems to have been no just cause of complaint against
him ; for, though we cannot agree with the author referred
to below, that *a quiet, easy governor best suits a colony,* it
does not appear that the qualities, here sneeringly imputed
to him, ever obstructed the performance of his public du-

---

* Short Hist. Barb. p. 79.

† Mr. Pinfold, died on the 4th of November, 1789, in the eightieth year of his
age.

Short History, p. 77.

ties.* Some men may probably prefer a governor of that character, because the indolence of his disposition may afford them opportunities of accomplishing their own ambitious projects, and of oppressing the people. To the authority of such *easy, quiet* rulers may the inhabitants of Barbadoes never be subject. Better is the tyranny of a single person, however oppressive, than the despotism and misrule of a corrupt and arbitrary oligarchy.

The abuses committed by the deputy provost marshal, in the execution of his office, were so generally and loudly complained of, that the legislature determined to take the direction of the office into their own hands. To this end a law was enacted, under the administration of Mr. Pinfold, authorizing the colonial agent to farm the office from the patentee for the public benefit. Great advantages were reasonably expected from a measure by which the legislature obtained the exclusive right of nominating the deputy

---

* Nor was the governor deficient in spirit upon proper occasions. Sir William Gibbons, a man of the most considerable influence in the country, having resigned his seat in the assembly, of which he had been speaker many years, on account of his advanced age and ill health, yet wished to retain his commission as colonel of Speight's division. But his excellency thought that, if age and infirmities rendered him incapable of attending the house of assembly, they disqualified him for the more active duties of a military command; he therefore, on the 28th of March, 1760, dismissed him from all his military employments. Sir William survived his loss of power only fourteen days, and died suddenly during the firing of a salute on his successor's taking possession of the division. He was succeeded by the Honourable Henry Thornhill.

provost marshal, whose continuance in office would necessarily depend upon the honest performance of his duty. But within less than two years after the passing of this law, notwithstanding some pecuniary profit had been derived from it, the assembly came to a resolution to relinquish the contract. It was alleged that the agreement entered into by the agent with the patentee was illegal, and could not be carried into effect without the violation of an act of parliament; and that it would be highly improper for the legislature to take an assignment of the contract, as it could not be made without an act of the island, which would render the transaction too conspicuous to escape the censure of the lords of trade, before whom it must appear for confirmation. This reasoning was founded on the statute of Great Britain, against buying and selling of offices; but this point had been already so clearly decided, as to remove every doubt of the legality of the covenant. Blanchard, the provost marshal of Jamaica, had granted a deputation of his office to Galdy, of that place, who had given a bond for the performance of the agreement, upon which an action had been brought to enforce the payment. The defendant pleaded that, by the statute against buying and selling of offices, both the bond and the articles of agreement were void; and that Jamaica having become a part of the territories of Great Britain was subject to the laws of the realm. But it was ruled by the court, that neither Jamaica, nor any other of the colonies, was bound by the laws of England, unless particularly mentioned, but that they were to be governed by their own laws and customs; and judgment was therefore given for the plaintiff.* This case was in point; but perhaps it was not within the contemplation of the legislature, and they relinquished the obvious advantage of possessing a paramount control over the offices.

Among the laws enacted under Mr. Pinfold's administration, there is one which ought not to be passed over in silence. This is an act to regulate sales at outcry, by which, to avoid all doubt or ambiguity on the subject, it is expressly declared that slaves shall be included in the legal construction of the words *goods, chattels and effects,* and as such may be taken and sold in execution for debt. This indeed had been the practice for more than a century. In the time of president Walrond a law had been passed, allowing the creditor to attach the slaves of his unfortunate debtor, and to have them sold as mere chattels. This law was calculated to serve the sinister purposes of itinerant adventurers; who, after making a fortune in the colony, were anxious to return and enjoy it at home. They had no permanent interest in the country, and were heedless of the remote consequences of those laws which answered

---

* Vide Modern Reports, Blanchard v. Galdy. Vide etiam Godolphin v. Tudor. Salk. 468, and Culliford v. De Cardonell, Salk. 466. In what cases a *deputation is legal.*

their present convenience, by facilitating the collection of debts. But now, in a more enlightened state of society, when the colony was firmly established, and its population consisted of a race of free-born sons, fondly attached to their native soil, and deeply interested in its prosperity, it must be a subject of no small surprise, that the legislature should recognize and confirm a principle so impolitic, inhuman and unjust.

There is scarcely a law in existence, from whose operation the island has suffered greater injury than this. By the authority given to a rapacious creditor to seize the slaves of his debtor, and to sell them to the highest bidder, the population of the country has been lessened; its agricultural improvements have been impeded; many respectable families have been reduced to indigence, and many driven into exile. When the labourers are swept away from the plantations, the lands cease to be valuable; the buildings are left to moulder into ruins by a gradual decay; and the fields, whose fertility added to the national wealth, become a barren waste over-run with noxious weeds. Of the slaves thus sold the rich only can become the purchasers, to the utter extinction of those small estates, which, in reality, constitute the real wealth and opulence of the country. It is a gross, though a popular error, to suppose that this transfer of property is attended with no detriment to the state, because the negroes, who are removed from one plantation are employed on another. The argument might assume a plausible tone, if the real and personal estate went together; the aggregate wealth of the country might then be the same; though it is obvious that the general prosperity would be diminished by limiting the diffusion of the means of subsistence. Wealth might accumulate in the hands of the rich, but the inferior orders of society, deprived of the means of cultivating their little farms, would be driven from the island to seek security under the shelter of a wiser policy.

It will probably be objected, that these evils do not now exist in their full extent; that there are few attachments made under this law; and that, in the present prosperous condition of the country, no man is without a home, or negroes to cultivate his land. But we should not suffer our judgment to be blinded by prosperity. It is now only thirty years since we witnessed the melancholy verification of the arguments against this law. In the vicissitudes of human affairs, similar misfortunes may be approaching to overwhelm us. During the American war, when, added to the evils incident to a state of hostility, the hopes of the industrious planter were frequently frustrated by a series of natural calamities, the fairest portions of the island were desolated and sacrificed to an unwise and iniquitous policy. Afflicted by continued drought, and visited by tribes of vermin, more destructive than the locusts and caterpillars of old, Barbadoes was then reduced to a state of comparative poverty; her soil and her negroes had sunk fifty per cent. below their original value. A total failure of crops, instead of exciting commiseration, sharpened the avidity of the rapacious; and the wretched slaves of the unfortunate debtor were dragged in crowds to the market, and thence transported to cultivate and enrich by their labour those colonies which, at the conclusion of the war, passed into the hands of our enemies. At that season of calamity, the pernicious tendency of the law was made visible as the sun at noon day. The slaves were sold for less than half their value; the soil remained uncultivated; the original proprietors were ruined, and the junior creditors were defrauded of their just due, by the accumulation of expense, and the rapacity of the provost marshal. The evil of that day is happily passed. How soon we may be reduced to the same deplorable condition, is known only to that omnipotent Being, by whose providence all things are ordered. It may be prudent to guard against the adverse change; and, in this our better hour, repeal a law, which experience has shewn to be so pernicious.

The most enlightened writers on the subject of West Indian concerns,* have uniformly condemned this impolitic

---

* Vide Long's Hist. of Jamaica, vol. i. p. 392. Edwards's West Indies, vol. ii. p. 153. Raynal's History of the East and West Indies, vol. vi. p. 228; and an excel-

and inhuman law. In the whole system of colonial slavery, so universally, and often unjustly, censured in Europe, there is none more injurious and oppressive to the negroes than the legal usage of levying upon them; and selling them at auction. It is by far the highest degree of cruelty annexed to their condition. One of the strongest principles of human nature is, that local attachment, which man feels for the place of his nativity. The untutored African shares this universal sentiment in common with the civilized European; and the sable creole is no less tenderly attached to the spot on which the careless days of infancy were spent; to the humble tenement which he has cultivated; to the friendly tree, under whose verdant shade he has passed the noon-tide-hour; to the peaceful cot, beneath whose lowly roof he has participated with his wife and his children the few domestic comforts which have fallen to his lot. By a barbarous, erroneous policy, the wretched slave is dragged from this scene of all his enjoyments; torn from the hallowed spot which contains the remains of the mother whom he revered, the wife that he loved, or the child who was dear to his heart; dispossessed of the little property which bestowed on him an ideal importance in the eyes of his fellow-labourers; and sold into a new bondage, into a

---

lent Memoir, written by the late Hon. Joshua Steele, and presented to the Society of Arts in Barbadoes, 1783.

distant part of the country, under the dominion of an un- CHAP. X.
known master.   Separated from   the   only consolations   766.
which can beguile the rigour of servitude, these wretched
victims of avarice and folly often sink into a premature
grave.

CHAP. XI.

CHAP. XI.
1766.
May 26.

THE chief magistracy, on the departure of Mr. Pinfold, devolved on the Honourable Samuel Rous, senior member of council. The first care of the legislature was to make a suitable provision, to support the dignity of government; they accordingly settled on the president the yearly sum of fifteen hundred pounds, during his residence at Pilgrim, in quality of commander in chief.

The commencement of Mr. Rous's administration was marked by the assembly's first claim to parliamentary privileges. Mr. John Gay Alleyne, having been called to the speaker's chair, on the death of Mr. Lyte, determined to remedy the omission of which his predecessors had been guilty. Mr. Alleyne possessed great talents and extensive erudition. He was thoroughly acquainted with the principles of the English constitution, and with the forms and practice of the house of commons. With an incorruptible integrity, he had understanding to discover, and spirit to assert, the rights of the people. His chief fault, if it be one, was that of a great mind, an insatiable thirst of praise; and, though he pursued the phantom popularity, with unceasing ardour, he assiduously strove to attain it by the noblest means, the welfare of his country. His appointment having been confirmed by the president, the speaker, in an appropriate speech, demanded of his honour the privileges to which the assembly were entitled. First, security to their persons and servants from all arrests and other disturbances, that may obstruct their regular attendance on the house: secondly, freedom of speech in their proceedings; and, lastly, free access, at all times, to the commander in chief. The president was a little startled at the novelty of the demand, and excused himself from giving an immediate answer. The house sat again the next day, when, receiving no answer to the speaker's demand, they resolved to enter on no business till they had obtained satisfaction on this important point. On the next meeting of council, the president commanded the attendance of the assembly, in the council chamber; and, after an apology for the delay, " granted them, as far as was consistent with the royal prerogative, and the laws and constitution of the island, every privilege which had been enjoyed by any former assembly."

June 3.

July 7.

These privileges are inherent in all legislative bodies, since, without them, their power must evidently be more nominal than real. It is declared, by statute of England, that the freedom of speech and debates, and proceedings in parliament ought not to be impeached nor questioned in any court nor place out of parliament. And this freedom of speech, with the other privileges of security of persons, servants, lands, and goods, is particularly demanded of the King, in person, by the speaker of the house of commons, at the opening of every new parliament *.

A colonial historian † treats the speaker's demand of privileges with a levity, that betrays an ignorance of the constitution of his country, and an indifference to the rights of the people; and represents it as a precedent pregnant with
fatal consequences to the credit of the colony. Under the protection of servants, he conceives, the power may be given of screening from debt, and of conveying from the island a number of slaves. But it is obvious, that the security from arrests, and other disturbances, here claimed, is confined to the person of the member, and to such do-

---

* Black. Comm. vol. 1. p. 164.

† Mr. H. Frere, vide Short Hist. of Barb. p. 83. These strictures provoked Sir John to publish a criticism on the work which contained them, as just as it was pregnant. This produced a duel between the two gentlemen; and, though it ended without bloodshed, the dispute laid the foundation of an enmity which had a visible influence on the politics of the literary antagonists during their lives.

mestics only whose services he may require, during his attendance on the legislature, at its stated times of meeting, which are usually monthly. The course of justice cannot be obstructed by a privilege, which affords protection for the short space of no more than one day in every four weeks. At all other times, the person and property of the privileged debtor, is subject to the ordinary modes of judicial proceeding. Neither does the privilege of parliament sanction nor facilitate the transportation of slaves, belonging to those debtors who may happen to occupy a seat in the house. The danger is effectually guarded against, by the legal formalities which must be complied with, before any slave can be sent from the island.

Personal security is absolutely essential to the exercise of legislative functions. The strong arm of power might otherwise be occasionally extended, to prevent the attendance of those members from whom opposition may be expected. A sycophantic creditor may become the willing tool of despotism; and, by detaining his debtor, obstruct the progress of public business, whenever the casual impediment may suit his sinister views, or enable a corrupt faction to accomplish their designs, by hurrying their pernicious measures through a house thinly attended*.

---

* This point seems to have been placed beyond all dispute by the royal authority. A merchant of Spanish Town, in Jamaica, in 1764, caused a writ of *venditioni exponas*, to be executed upon the coach horses of a member of the assembly of that Island.

CHAP. XI.   A few days previous to the departure of the governor,

1767.   the inhabitants of Bridge-town had experienced a most
dreadful calamity ; a considerable part of that metropolis

The assembly considered this a breach of privilege, and the officers who had executed the writ were immediately taken into custody, by order of the house. The prisoners were quickly released by *habeas corpus*, granted by his excellency, Mr. Lyttleton, as chancellor. The assembly resented this act of power, as an invasion of their privileges, and again ordered the provost marshal and his assistant to be taken into the custody of their messenger. A petition was again presented to the governor, by the prisoners, for a writ of *habeas corpus*, which was granted, and they were once more set at liberty by a decree of the court of chancery. This order produced a violent ferment in the assembly. They resolved that the governor had acted in an unjustifiable manner, and was guilty of a flagrant breach and contempt of the rights and privileges of their house, And that a remonstrance against his conduct should be drawn up and laid at his Majesty's feet. The governor immediately dissolved the assembly and issued writs for a new election. No advantage, however, was derived from this expedient. Upon their meeting, the speaker omitted to apply to the governor in the usual manner for the privileges of the house. His excellency therefore again dissolved the assembly, alleging that it was his duty to see that their usual privileges were maintained, as well as that of the King's prerogative suffered no violation. *Annual Register, vol. 8. p.* 179. Five different assemblies were successively called and abruptly dissolved, because they refused to raise the supplies, unless satisfaction was given them in this business. At length, on a change of ministers in England, the governor was recalled, and the lieutenant governor, Roger Hope Elletson, was directed to gratify the wishes of the assembly ; and the whole of the preceedings in chancery were solemnly annulled and vacated. *Edwards's West Indies, vol. 2. p.* 354. The privileges of domestics, lands, or goods have been since taken away in England, by Stat. 10 Geo. III. c. 50. which enacts that any suit may at any time be brought against any peer or member of parliament, or their servants, which shall not be impeached or delayed on pretence of any privilege of parliament ; except that the person of a member of the house of commons shall not thereby be subjected to any arrest of imprisonment. *Blackstone's Comm. vol. 1. p.* 165.

was consumed by fire*. The frequency of the misfortune awakened the attention of the assembly, and they passed an act for rebuilding the town on a more safe and commodious plan; but unfortunately this prudent precaution was disapproved of in the council chamber. Seven months had scarcely elapsed, when the capital was again reduced in ashes, by a conflagration still more dreadful than the former†. This was the fourth time, in little more than ten years, Bridge-town had suffered a similar disaster.

The necessity of rebuilding the town, with greater order and regularity, was now admitted by those who had before doubted the propriety of legislative interference; and a law was enacted for that purpose. At the same time, the assembly adopted a scheme for deepening and cleansing the mole-head, and building convenient quays and wharfs for mercantile accommodation. But, sensible of the inability of their constituents to prosecute such an expensive undertaking, they determined to apply to the house of commons for pecuniary assistance. Such was their impatience,

---

* May 14th, 1766.

† December 27th, 1766. On this occasion, the legislature of South Carolina voted the sum of seven hundred and eighty-five pounds sterling, for the relief of the sufferers. The money was paid into the treasury of Barbadoes, where it was allowed to remain, unless the treasurer used it, till the 29th of April, 1773, when an act was passed to enable the commissioners for cleansing the mole-head to borrow it, and apply it to that undertaking. Whether it was ever repaid, and applied agreeably to the intentions of the benevolent donors, would now be an unnecessary inquiry.

CHAP. XI. on this occasion, that the petition was dispatched to the
1767. colonial agent, in London, with directions to present it,
without the concurrence, or even the knowledge, of the
other branches of the legislature. By the same conveyance
they transmitted a memorial to the King, complaining of
the great obstruction to public business, occasioned by the
absence of many members of council, who, regardless of
the welfare of their country, were dissipating their time
and fortune, amidst the pleasures and gaieties of the British
capital.

1768.   The application to parliament was countenanced by the
ministry, and a donative was proposed by Mr. Grenville,
to enable the legislature of Barbadoes to commence the
work in contemplation ; but it was thought advisable, to
ascertain, previously, what they would do of themselves,
towards accomplishing the design. This was fair; the
question, however, was retorted on the house of commons,
and four years had nearly elapsed before any assistance
could be obtained. At length, parliament, tired with continued importunity, granted the trifling sum of five thousand pounds for the projected improvements*.

Feb. 11.   Meanwhile, William Spry, LL.D. having been honoured
with his Majesty's commission, as governor of Barbadoes,

---

* In 1775, Mr. Walker, the colonial agent, obtained from parliament another grant
of five thousand pounds, for which service he was honoured with the unanimous thanks
of the assembly, presented in a gold box.

arrived in Carlisle Bay, accompanied by his lady, and assumed the government of the island. To enable Mr. Spry
to support the dignity of his station, the assembly, with
the concurrence of the council, settled on his excellency a
salary of three thousand pounds a year.

Not long after his excellency's arrival, Mr. Cox, the
store-keeper, presented a petition to the assembly, stating
the insufficiency of the tonnage duty to supply the demands for gunpowder, for the use of the forts ; and that
he had been obliged, in obedience to the orders of former
commanders in chief, to make advances to the amount of
three hundred and fifty-four barrels of gunpowder*, and
praying that the house would provide for his reimbursement. An application so extraordinary, from a public
officer, who, if he had not violated his duty, had certainly
exceeded his legal authority, excited no common degree of
popular clamour. The fund, appropriated to this particular
service, was raised by a duty of one pound of gunpowder
per ton on all vessels entering at any port of the island ;
and the storekeeper ought, on no pretence whatever, to
have suffered the disbursements to exceed the receipts of
his office. Should the storekeeper be allowed to comply
with the governor's orders, beyond the limits prescribed by
law, the treasurer might, on the same principle, supply his

---

* Of one hundred and twelve pounds each, valued at nearly 2800l. currency.

excellency's pecuniary demands to an indefinite extent; and thus, by an abuse of the trust reposed in them, the executive power might be rendered independent of the legislative, and a venal despot enabled to convert the people's money to his own use, without the consent of their representatives.

On these grounds, Mr. Cox's petition was strenuously opposed by the speaker. He contended that the storekeeper had no discretionary power, by law, to purchase powder for the use of the forts; that, in the present season of profound peace, the powder had not been required for the service of the country, but had been wasted in firing salutes, either to indulge an idle vanity, or for the no less unwarrantable purpose of enriching some favourite captain gunner. To impose on the people the burthen of paying for powder, thus illegally issued, and profusely expended, by the officers of divisions, during their military feasts, would be contrary to justice, and inconsistent with the trust reposed in the members of that house, as faithful guardians of their constituents' property.

The sense of the house appearing to be in favour of the storekeeper's claim, it was agreed, after a long debate, that the payment of his demand should depend on the future savings of powder. And a memorial was presented to the governor, stating the particulars of Cox's demand, and requesting that his excellency would enforce the orders which he had already given, to prevent the unnecessary firing of cannon, that thus a saving might be made, adequate to the liquidation of the debt in question. His excellency, in reply, assured the assembly of his determination to prevent, as much as lay in his power, any improper expenditure of powder in the forts, and of his cheerful concurrence in any effectual measure for that purpose. Nor was it long before they received a message from his excellency, signifying, that in consequence of his endeavours, a saving of ten thousand weight of powder had already accrued, whence his excellency was induced to hope, that the whole of Mr. Cox's demand might, in a short time, be paid, by the observance of proper economy in that department *. A system fundamentally bad, and an egregious abuse of power, rendered this hope abortive; and, under succeeding administrations, encreased the storekeeper's debt. The tonnage on vessels, and the appropriation of the money arising from that impost, were soon afterwards altered by law; but the door to abuse was still left open.

Towards the latter end of this year, the governor's domestic felicity was interrupted by the death of his amiable consort. She was a niece of the illustrious Earl of Chatham, and a daughter of Thomas Pitt, of Bocconic, who

October 3.

---

* It appears, by a subsequent petition from Mr. Cox to governor Hay, that Mr. Spry's orders for preventing the waste of powder had produced so great a saving in that article, that the demand had been reduced to only eighty-eight barrels and a half.

married a sister of the celebrated Lord Lyttleton. Thus
nobly descended, and elegantly accomplished, her conjugal
attachment impelled her to accompany her husband to
Barbadoes, where her delicate constitution soon sunk
under the influence of an uncongenial climate.

The following year was productive of an extraordinary
dispute between the house of assembly, and the freeholders
of Saint Andrew's parish. By a law of the island, the assembly were restricted from allowing more than two of their
members to be absent from the country at the same time.
The speaker, however, finding his health impaired, was
desirous of trying the effect of a voyage to Europe ; but as
two members were already absent, he was precluded from
obtaining the same indulgence, by the ordinary means. To
remove this obstacle, a bill was introduced by the attorney-
general, Henry Beckles, to empower Sir John Alleyne to
leave the island, without vacating his seat, and to extend
the permission to four members at a time. The bill was
passed unanimously, by both houses; but it appeared to be
a measure of so unusual a nature, that the governor
suspended his assent until the King's pleasure could be
known.

Sir John Alleyne, nevertheless, left the island *; and the

---

* Before the venerable patriot's departure, he made his estate liable to the payment of a perpetual annuity, of forty-five pounds a year, for the support of a charity-
school, in the parish which he represented ; that being the interest of the sum which
he had received on his succeeding, in rotation, to the office of treasurer.

assembly, at their next meeting, addressed the governor to issue a writ for the election of a member in his room. On the day appointed, the freeholders of Saint Andrew's appeared at the poll, but refused to make choice of another representative: and presented an address to Mr. Maycock, the sitting member, explaining the reason of their refusal. They could not be persuaded that Sir John Alleyne had vacated his seat, by his absence; and could not, therefore, with propriety, proceed to another election. It would, in the first place, they said, imply a forgetfulness of his former services, and a willingness to deprive him of the benefit intended him, by two branches of the legislature. Secondly, they affected an apprehension of violating a plain law, since, by electing a new member, they would, in the event of the old one's return, be represented by a greater number than they were legally entitled to. From these considerations, they determined to imitate the governor's example, and await the result of the reference to the crown *.

At the next meeting of the assembly, the governor sent the sheriff's return to the house, and recommended the sub-

October 2.

---

* The act was rejected by the King, on the recommendation of the lords of trade, who reported to his Majesty, that as Sir John Alleyne had already come to England, and vacated his seat, they conceived that the confirmation of the act would involve the legislature in difficulties, in case of the election of another member, without benefiting the person in whose favour it had been proposed; to whose merits Mr. Spry had borne such ample testimony, as to occasion a wish that the indulgence could have been granted, consistently with the constitution of the country.

ject to their serious consideration. The attorney-general immediately rose, and, in an elaborate review of the whole affair, maintained that Sir John Alleyne had vacated his seat, and justified the proceedings of the house. It had been contended, both within and without doors, that the assembly were competent to grant leave of absence to any of its members, without the concurrence of the other branches of the legislature. For, by the law and custom of parliament, whatever matter arises concerning either house of parliament, ought to be examined, discussed, and adjudged in that house to which it relates, and not else-where *. Where, then, it was asked, was the necessity for a law to enable the assembly to indulge its members with occasional leave of absence? The answer was obvious. The privilege in dispute had been surrendered, by the assembly, half a century before †. And, however uncontrollable the house might have been originally, with respect to its members, whatever privileges might have been inherent in them, as representatives of the people; if those, said the learned gentleman, who have gone before us in that capacity, by an acquiescence in a law for that purpose, have abridged the power of the house, until that law is repealed, or the restrictive clause abrogated, it was ridiculous to dispute its validity, or to talk of original privi-

---

* Blacks. Com. vol. 1. p. 158.   † Hall's Laws, No. 148. c. 30.

leges. Though, he admitted, the constitutional maxim on which the law of parliament is founded, he insisted, that no house of commons could pretend to urge a privilege once given up, against a positive law, by which it had been resigned. Nor could any colonial assembly, by an independent act of their own, destroy that which had been established with the concurrence of the other branches of the legislature.

To obviate any doubt that may arise, concerning the legality of their proceedings, under an idea that the representation of the country was incomplete, Mr. Beckles observed, that the house had done all that the law prescribed in such cases; and, as the freeholders had thought proper to give up their birth-right for an idle and fallacious sophistry, the authority of that house could not possibly be affected by their contumacy; all acts of theirs would be as virtual, without another representative for that parish, as if the writ for a new election had been obeyed. This opinion was grounded on the general maxim, that he who disclaims his rights when they are tendered to him in due form of law, can never afterwards complain of a privation of them. He concluded with moving an answer to the governor's message to that effect; which he observed, was all that could be done, unless it should be thought proper to perpetuate their exclusion; but this, for the sake of many worthy men in that parish, he would not recommend, though the obstinacy of those, by whom this ridiculous opposition had been creat-

CHAP. XI.
1770.

Nov. 27.

ed, deserved to suffer the full weight of legislative dis-pleasure.

The attorney-general then complained of an insult which had been offered to the house, no less heinous than that which had occupied their attention. Whilst the members of that assembly were under *a reciprocal implied faith* to keep inviolable the *secrets of the house*; and their clerk was bound by the sacred obligation of an oath; he thought it scandalous to see in a common newspaper a message from the governor, with a *confidential* observation of his own, which had never been entered on their journals till that day. How this had happened, he thought worthy of an inquiry, that the person who had offended may be made to express a due sense of his error. Colonel Ridgeway immediately rose and avowed himself the author of the communication alluded to, unconscious of any impropriety attending the disclosure of what had passed within their walls. With this explanation, Mr. Beckles professed him-self satisfied; and there the business rested until a subse-quent meeting of the assemby, when the rule, which was supposed to have been infringed, was read in these words; that the minutes of the house, taken by the clerk at any of their meetings, should remain with *him* undisclosed till they shall be confirmed by the house at a future meeting.

The question was then put, whether the rule is to be con-sidered binding on the clerk alone, or whether it implies an obligation on the members of the house? and carried in the affirmative. A more extraordinary determination, or a stranger perversion of language perhaps was never known. But admitting the construction to be just, it may be difficult to conceive what *secrets of the house* the representatives of the people are under *a reciprocal implied faith to conceal* from their constituents. Shall the most important public concerns be canvassed and decided upon by a British legislature with the impenetrable secrecy of a Romish inquisition? Shall the free subjects of a British colony remain in silent submission till their fate is determined by an Asiatic divan? or till their delegates condescend, as a matter of grace and favour, to inform them of their proceedings? Nothing should ever pass within the precincts of the town-hall of which the people ought not to have the earliest notice. The inestimable right of proposing laws for their own government is lodged by the constitution in the great body of the people. The inconvenience of tumultuous assemblies first suggested the expediency of delegating the sacred task of legislation to a select number; and those who are appointed to execute the solemn trust are unquestionably accountable to those from whom their authority is derived.

Thus the matter stood till Mr. Henry Duke, impatient of the absurd restraint, objected to the construction which had been put upon the rule, as imposing an obligation of secrecy on the members of that house, equally unnecessary and inconsistent with their duty to their constituents; to whose sentiments they were bound to pay a respectful attention. He, therefore, moved, that the assembly should, by an explicit declaration, confine the rule to the clerk alone. Mr. Beckles, far from wishing to restrain any gentleman from consulting his constituents by an injunction of secrecy, seconded the motion; and what was, if possible, more extraordinary, it was unanimously agreed to.

1772.
The scantiness of our records furnish no further information concerning the administration of Mr. Spry. After the death of his former lady, he married the beautiful relict of Hamlet Fairchild, but he had not long enjoyed the delights of this union before he was removed to another, and more perfect state of felicity.

Sept. 4.
This melancholy event placed the Honourable Samuel Rous a second time in the presidential chair. Still occupied by the two great objects that had long engaged their attention, of preserving their capital from fire, and facilitating its commerce, the assembly passed two acts, one for the establishment of six fire companies ; the other for deepening, cleansing, and improving the mole-head. To provide a fund for effectuating the latter design, the tax on the importation of slaves from Africa was increased; and, in lieu of the former duty of one pound of gunpowder, a duty of two shillings and sixpence a ton was indiscriminately laid on all vessels resorting to the island. Of the produce of this impost, fifteen hundred pounds were annually appropriated to the purchase of gunpowder for the

use of the forts, and the surplus was made applicable to the works at the mole-head.

This bill was hurried through the house with such celerity, that the ship-owners, whose interest was most immediately affected by it, had no opportunity of endeavouring to arrest its progress by any representation of its evil tendency. The merchants of Bridge-town, therefore, presented a petition to the council, in which they stated, that, by a former law, all vessels, owned by the inhabitants, were exempt from the payment of the tonnage-duty; an immunity which they insisted was calculated to promote the interest of the country by encouraging the increase of its shipping. They represented, that the vessels owned by the native traders were employed in an intercourse among the neighbouring colonies, in which they generally made from twelve to fifteen voyages annually; and that such an impost, so frequently repeated, would be an insupportable burthen on the navigation of the country, and, in effect, prohibit a beneficial branch of commerce.

This being a money bill, could not be amended by the council; it was, therefore, returned to the assembly, with a message, proposing, that vessels, owned by the merchants of the island, should be subject to the duty only thrice a year; secondly, that a commission of two and a half per cent. instead of five, would be a sufficient emolument for the storekeeper; thirdly, that the sum of two thousand

pounds annually should be appropriated to the purchase of
gunpowder for the use of the fortifications. The first of
these propositions was agreed to on a division ; the second,
so apt is private interest to prevail over considerations of
public utility, was negatived by a majority of ten to three;
and the third was, with great propriety, unanimously rejected. The bill, thus amended, was again sent up to the
council, and passed. Upon this occasion, the assembly
addressed the president to discontinue the firing of the
morning and evening gun at Needham's, which unnecessary parade, as they termed it, was attended with
and expense of eight hundred pounds a year. This request,
however, militated too strongly against the interest of the
captain-gunner, to be complied with. And it is worthy of
observation, that notwithstanding the considerable saving
of powder during Mr. Spry's administration, under that of
Mr. Rous, the collector, was inadequate to supply the demand, in a season of profound peace.

Both bills, on being transmitted to England, were referred to the consideration of Mr. Jackson, counsel to the
board of trade. On the act for the establishment of fire
companies, he observed, that it had been more than once
reported to be the opinion of their lordships, that the creating of a corporation, being within the power of the Crown,
and its representative, ought not to be exercised by the
provincial legislature, unless it be under singular circumstances, of which the present occasion of incorporating six

bodies of men at once, may possibly be one. But the most material objection to the act was the power given to the commissioners not only to constitute and establish such rules and orders as they should think convenient for the good government of the fire companies ; but also, " to make and establish such other rules and orders as they shall think conducive to the better execution of the act ; which rules and orders, so to be made, shall bind and oblige all and every person or persons, whom they shall or may concern." " This power to be executed by a few members of the council and assembly," said the learned barrister, " is certainly too extensive, and, at least, approaches too near to a delegated legislature, not to want limitation or explanation.

The utility of its object was sufficient, in Mr. Jackson's opinion, to prevail against a manifest objection to the act for improving the mole-head ; namely, that it imposed a duty on the trade and shipping of Great Britain. The act was, in no other respect, faulty, except that the private property which it might be necessary to convert to the public use was directed to be valued by three justices instead of a jury. For these reasons, both bills were disallowed by the King ; and Mr. Hay, who had been recently appointed to the government, was directed, on his arrival, to recommend the passing of others free from the faults imputed to these. This was accordingly done, and his Majesty confirmed them, in consideration of the importance of their object.

Mean time a law was enacted to empower the general assembly to permit any of their members, not exceeding four at a time, to be absent from the island. The propriety of such an indulgence is at best highly questionable. Many members of the house of commons, it is true, are frequently employed on foreign service, without producing any national inconvenience by their absence; but in a colony whose representative body consists of only twenty-two members, the absence of nearly one-fourth of the number may justly be apprehended to impede the progress of public business, and to facilitate the sinister views of a venal

faction. The law, as we have already seen, originated in the partial design of granting a particular indulgence to Sir John G. Alleyne; but, from the failure of that attempt, and the baronet's jealousy of Mr. Spry, the proposal was not revived until after his excellency's death. Nor was this the only innovation introduced for the personal gratification of Sir John Alleyne. It had ever been a standing rule of the assembly, that the speaker, like the speaker of the house of commons, should vote only in case of an equal division of the house. Such a rule did not suit Sir John Alleyne's ardent, active mind. Anxious to distinguish himself upon every question in which the interest of his country was involved, he could not bear to fettered by a rule which confined the exercise of his intellectual powers, and obstructed the rapid flow of patriotic eloquence which he possessed. The restraint was, therefore, removed, and he was permitted to speak, or vote, upon all occasions, as any other member might do.

The day had now arrived when Mr. Rous was to resign, for the last time, the office of chief magistrate. His Majesty had appointed the Honourable Edward Hay, late consul at Lisbon, governor of Barbadoes; and his excellency, accompanied by his lady and two daughters, arrived in Carlisle-bay, on Sunday the sixth of June. On the Tuesday following, his excellency landed in state, and was received on the wharf by the members of both houses of the legislature. He was attended with the usual military parade to St. Michael's church, whence, after divine service, he proceeded to Pilgrim, and, having taken the inaugural oaths, was formally invested with the supreme authority.

Were an opinion formed of Mr. Rous, from the panegyrics bestowed on him by different public bodies, in their respective addresses, during his presidency, we should be induced to esteem him as a modern Trajan, or Antonine. But no dependence can be placed in such fallacious applause. Truth is little regarded in the composition of these eulogies. By his vigilance and assiduity we are told, that Bridge-town was raised from cinders, that elegant structures had risen, Phœnix like, from ashes; and that the same patriotic hand which performed these wonders had fixed the first stone in the head of the new mole; an undertaking that would shed a lustre on his administration. What peculiar merit may belong to the president for the part which he sustained in these transactions, we cannot precisely ascertain. It is probable, that he participated in common with the other orders of the legislature in their zeal to promote these useful works. But, whatever credit may be due to him on this subject, candour must condemn his neglect of the administration of justice; his inattention to the waste of stores on the forts, and the infringement which he committed on the rights of election.

At the general election immediately preceding his loss of power, he interfered very improperly with the matrosses of Speight's and Reid's-bay divisions; several of whom he encouraged to oppose the interest of their colonel, by promising them indemnity at the expense of the adverse party. But in the parish of Saint John, he not only appeared at the poll and voted himself, but influenced others to vote for the candidate whom he supported. Mr. Haynes, the unsuccesful candidate, petitioned the assembly, complaining of an undue return, and praying that he might be permitted to controvert the election. But before the affair could be investigated, he consented to withdraw his petition, on the president's promising him his future support.

Nevertheless, the solicitor-general, Mr. Henry Duke, a man of a strong, active and generous mind, who, in the study and practice of his profession, had acquired a clear and perfect knowledge of the English constitution, brought the matter before the house. He represented the president's conduct as a flagrant violation of the elective franchise of which it was the duty of that house to record their decided disapprobation; and concluded with moving a resolution in these words; That it is against the freedom of elections, and the privileges of this house, that a commander in chief should vote at, or interfere in, the election of representatives. The learned gentleman's design, however, was defeated, by the speaker's moving the previous question; and the original motion was postponed for future consideration, or, more properly speaking, consigned to eternal oblivion.

Twice in the course of Mr. Rous's administration the same enlightened member complained to the assembly of a suspension of justice, in civil cases, owing to the culpable neglect of the persons appointed to preside in the courts of law. He moved for a committee to inquire into these abuses, and to report to the house what was proper to be done in aid of defective laws, or in redress of those which were violated. But his patriotic exertions were rendered ineffectual by the influence of the judges, of whom several had seats in the assembly*.

---

* The house was, at this time, composed of Samson Wood, and H. Duke, *for St. Michael's.* J. Burke and P. Lovell, *Christ Church.* Joseph Wood and Joshua Gittens, *St. Philip.* H. Walker and J. Cogan Cox, *St. George's.* S. Wallcott and J.

CHAP. XI.
1773.

Miller, *St. John's.* George Sanders and W. Gibbes Alleyne, *St. Thomas's.* T. Alleyne and J. Wheeler Ridgeway, *St. James's.* J. Leacock and S. Hinds, *St. Peter's.* Sir John Gay Alleyne and James Maycock, *St. Andrew's.* Hillary Rowe and H. Rowe, *St. Lucy's.* T. Payne and J. Stewart, *St. Joseph's.*

The members of council were Samuel Rous, J. Dotin, A. Cumberbatch, H. Frere, Conrade Adams, Gedney Clarke, Irenæus Moe, R. Brathwaite, W. Senhouse, R. Cobham, W. Bishop and John Best. The two last were added upon Mr. Hay's ararrival.

CHAP. XII.

MR. HAY ASSUMES THE GOVERNMENT—DISTRESSED CONDITION
OF THE INHABITANTS—REPRESENTATION TO THE THRONE—
OPPOSED BY THE GOVERNOR—SUSPENDS THE SOLICITOR-
GENERAL AND THE JUDGE OF THE ADMIRALTY—ITS IMPRO-
PER INTERPOSITION IN FAVOUR OF CAPTAIN DOTIN—WAR
WITH FRANCE—DANGER OF THE COUNTRY—APATHY OF THE
ASSEMBLY—THE GOVERNOR'S DEATH.

ON the first meeting of the provincial parliament after CHAP.XII.
the governor's arrival, his excellency opened the session in 1773.
the usual manner, with a speech from the chair. He ob- June 15.
served, that the trust which his Majesty had reposed in
him, by promoting him to the government of the island,
was, in its nature, very different from any of the former
posts which he had held under the Crown. The administration of the most ancient, most populous, and, in proportion to its extent, the most wealthy of his Majesty's
dominions in the new world, was a charge of the utmost
importance; and he was sensible required a more intimate
knowledge of the laws and constitution of the country than

he possessed. But when he considered the character of the inhabitants from the first settlement of the island, their loyalty to their Sovereign, and attachment to their excellent constitution; and that those principles had been carefully handed down to the present generation, he professed to feel encouraged to the arduous undertaking; happy in the thought that he could confidently rely on their assistance in conducting the business of government. After recommending a proper attention to the defence of the island, for which, he remarked, no time could be more proper than that of peace, his excellency modestly adverted to the King's instructions respecting the usual provision for the support of the commander in chief, observing that it did not become him to enlarge on a subject of so much delicacy.

The addresses of both houses were in the highest degree polite and respectful. They breathed the same sentiments of joy at his excellency's appointment, and of cordial congratulation on his safe arrival. His excellency's amiable character and approved conduct in other official situations were sufficient pledges, they said, for the faithful discharge of the high office with which he was now invested, and of the happiness of the people placed under his care. The scene of business may be new, the post assigned may be more important, and, in such a situation, the ingenuous mind may be led to feel a diffidence of its powers; but in the very principle which suggested those fears, the assembly were confident would be found the true resources of his

excellency's ease and contentment.

This interchange of civilities was followed by a more substantial proof of regard. A settlement of three thousand pounds a year was made on his excellency during the term of his administration. This sum, the speaker remarked on presenting the bill, which in the days of their prosperity would have been but the easy tribute of their benevolence, must, under the pressure of recent calamities, be acknowledged as the utmost effort of their good-will. It cannot escape observation, that through the whole of Sir John Alleyne's political life, his fine imagination was clouded with an idea of colonial poverty. On this topic he was perpetually disclaiming and lamenting the visionary inability of the country to provide for the necessary expenses of government. The bill was received in the most gracious manner by the governor, who professed to consider it as an ample testimony of the public esteem.

Sensible of the importance of a regular administration of justice, Mr. Hay's attention was early turned to the means of redressing the abuses committed in the judicial department. He sent circular letters to the judges, remonstrating against their dilatory proceedings, intimating that the clamours of the people had reached the Royal ear; and referring to his own diligence on the chancery bench as an example for the dispatch of business. The next object of his care was not of less importance. Thoroughly acquaint-

CHAP. XII. ed with the principles of commerce, his excellency readily
1773. perceived the benefit which the island would derive from an
extension of its trade. To this end he recommended that the
assembly should make an immediate application to parliament
for the establishment of a free port in Barbadoes. The proposal diffused the most general satisfaction; and the committee of correspondence directed the agent to pursue the
speediest and most effectual means of attaining this desire-
able object. The minister approved of the application,
and offered to grant a free trade with the Spaniards, on
the same terms as were enjoyed by Jamaica, which Mr.
Walker most unaccountably hesitated to accept till he
could consult his constituents; and, in the interval, the Jamaica bill having past, the opportunity of securing the advantage was lost.

1775.   The extremities to which the fatal disputes between
Great Britain and her North American provinces were approaching, excited the utmost anxiety and alarm throughout the whole West Indian archipelago. The commercial
intercourse between the British islands and the American
continent was deemed the most essential to the prosperity,
nay to the very existence of the sugar colonies; as it was
the only channel through which they could be supplied
with articles of the first necessity. The interruption of
this necessary intercourse was anticipated by the Barbadians with dismal forebodings of the dangers and distresses to which it would expose them. Yet during the

whole progress of the dispute, the legislature of Barbadoes maintained a respectful silence, unwilling to add to the perplexities of the ministry by mingling their complaints with those which were poured in from every other quarter, or conscious that no application of theirs would be regarded when interests of far greater national importance depended on the issue of the contest.

The sword was, at length, unsheathed, and the commencement of actual hostilities produced in Barbadoes the most alarming apprehensions of famine. Early in the present year, an attempt was made to ascertain the quantity of provisions on hand in Bridge-town, which was estimated to be unequal to the ordinary consumption for the short period of six weeks. At this critical moment Captain Payne, an officer in the British service, arrived for the purpose of purchasing provisions and live stock for the use of the troops at Boston, who had endured uncommon distress from the delays and misfortunes experienced by the victualling ships from Europe. The permission which this officer received from the governor to execute his mission, excited a considerable clamour among the people.

On the meeting of the assembly, the solicitor-general complained to the house of this indulgence, as a measure calculated to endanger the safety of the people, by depriving them of the scanty means of subsistence which they possessed. It was the duty of that house, he said, to adopt measures of precaution, to avert, if possible, the impending

Feb. 13.

calamity.   All trade with America was prohibited; our internal resources had failed, and self-preservation, the primary law of human nature, constrained them to husband the remaining stock of provisions, and not to suffer it to be further diminished.   He lamented their inability to supply his Majesty's forces with every accommodation which their situation required; but, under the existing circumstances, a gracious prince would not wish us to become victims to an impotent zeal for his service.   Upon these considerations, Mr. Duke moved an address to the governor, beseeching him to prohibit the exportation of the necessaries of of life until the island was more plentifully supplied.   As this could only produce a temporary advantage, the solicitor-general next proposed an address to the King, professing their loyalty and attachment to his Majesty and the constitution of the mother country, expressing their gratitude for the favours recently bestowed on the colony; representing the misery and distress to which the bulk of the people must inevitably be reduced, unless relieved by the timely assistance of the King and Parliament; and imploring his Majesty's gracious interposition in their favour. Both motions were unanimously agreed to; but, on the suggestion of the speaker, the farther consideration of the throne was deferred to the morrow.

In the meantime the governor went to the speaker's town residence, and declared, that if the assembly persisted in their resolution of addressing the King, as it would answer no other end than that of disturbing his Majesty's peace of mind, he would immediately dissolve the house. But, finding that the speaker and the other members present were not of a temper to be intimidated by menaces, he lowered his tone, and condescended to employ entreaties. They would make him happy, he said, if they would rescind their resolution ; adding that he was actuated by a friendly motive towards the assembly, in wishing to dissuade them from a measure which he was apprehensive would be displeasing to the King. Neither threats nor entreaties could divert the assembly from their purpose. They met pursuant to adjournment, and agreed to both addresses. But, notwithstanding the unanimity of the preceding day, the address to his Majesty was warmly debated. An address proposed by the speaker, and another by Mr. James Maycock, were both rejected; at length the draught of the solicitor-general reconciled all parties, and was unanimously adopted. But Judge Rowe, who professed himself averse from addressing at all, moved that the agent should be instructed to present or suppress it at his own discretion. This extraordinary proposition was opposed by the speaker. He could not think, he said, of committing the dignity of that house to an agent. If the address was improper, it ought to have been rejected; but now, that it had passed the house, the agent had nothing more to do with it than to present it in the usual form. The propriety of this observation was self-evident, yet Mr. Rowe's motion was negatived only by a majority of ten to nine.

Mr. Hay, naturally irritable, was highly exasperated at these proceedings. He transmitted to the secretary of state a representation of the circumstances of the country, wholly different from that which was made by the assembly, whom he accused of exaggerating the distresses of the people. Not satisfied with this expression of resentment, he determined to make Mr. Duke feel the weight of his indignation; and accordingly deprived him of his rank at the bar as his Majesty's solicitor-general. Duke, ever anxious to involve the public in his private quarrels, flew to the assembly for redress. He poured forth his complaints in an elaborate argumentative speech, and endeavoured to persuade the house that his dismissal from office, as it was the consequence of the faithful exercise of his legislative duty, was a direct violation of their privileges. To this conclusion the speaker objected. He lamented that the duty of an upright representative of the people should in any instance be deemed incompatible with that of a faithful servant of the crown; but he denied that the solicitor-general's suspension was a violation of the privileges of the house. On the contrary, considering the abuses committed by patent officers, Sir John Alleyne insisted that the governor's power of suspending them was beneficial to the public, and advantageous to civil liberty. The house concurring in these sentiments, Mr. Duke could obtain no other satisfaction than a resolution, moved by Mr. V. Jones, that his conduct as a member of that house had been such as became a dutiful and loyal subject. Nor was this tribute to his merit obtained without difficulty, several of the members thinking it unnecessary, as his loyalty was not impeached.

The address of the assembly to the King was accompanied by a memorial from Mr. Walker, the agent, to Lord George Germaine, exhibiting a gloomy picture of the condition of the country drawn by the delicate pencil of Sir John Alleyne. According to this pathetic representation, the poor white inhabitants were on the point of perishing with hunger; those in the neighbourhood of the sea-coast came down in crowds to gather the most wretched of all the fruits of the earth for their subsistence; the negroes, destitute of any allowance for their support, were left to plunder or to starve; the cattle had consequently been stolen; the few plantane walks and corn fields, which, from partial showers, had produced an early harvest, had been robbed, and the bloodshed that followed the rapine, opened a dismal prelude to the tragedy that was preparing. These accounts have been accused of exaggeration. The event indeed proved that the apprehensions of famine were providentially relieved. Yet that the condition of the people, especially the lower classes, was faithfully delineated by the pen of the venerable patriot, is still within the recollection of many who were participators in the common calamity. The scarcity of provisions was so alarming, that the governor himself soon after applied to Admiral Young, to facilitate the importation, by granting passports to vessels laden with American produce. The admiral readily assented to the request; but, to guard against any abuse of the indulgence, recommended an association to carry on the business under his license. This proposal was deemed impracticable; and, for the want of a sufficient bond of union among the merchants, the scheme proved abortive.

Mr. Duke's dismission was soon followed by that of Mr. Shepherd, chief baron of the court of exchequer, for having opposed the governor's nomination of a mercantile gentleman to be one of the puisne barons. Mr. Miller, who was appointed to succeed judge Shepherd, did not long enjoy his elevation before he fell under his excellency's displeasure, by declining to preside as chief justice at the court of grand sessions; and, in consequence of some incivilities which he received from the governor, he resigned his situation. Mr. Francis Cawley Boson, an English barrister, was now placed at the head of the court of exchequer. Nor was it long before Mr. Boson had the misfortune to offend the governor by appointing a reputable merchant of Bridge-town to fill the vacancy on the bench. The governor, recollecting the objection formerly made to a person of that character, proposed by himself, peremptorily refused to confirm the chief baron's choice. Boson ventured to urge his recommendation; and, probably, with a view of enforcing the necessity of an early appointment, requested his excellency's permission to leave the island for the benefit of his health. The extreme inflammability of the governor's temper instantly took fire at this importunity. He immediately convoked the council, and having laid before them the judge's letters, proposed his removal from office; the board readily concurred with their irritable chief, and Boson, without the imputation of any crime, was dismissed from his employment.

An injudicious attempt made by the governor to screen a public officer from condign punishment, contributed materially to increase the ill-humour between his excellency and the assembly. R. Reece, a matross at James Fort, near the Hole Town, lodged a formal complaint in writing to Colonel T. Alleyne against W. Dotin, chief-gunner of that division, for having embezzled and sold considerable quantities of gunpowder, and other stores, belonging to the garrison under his command. The colonel, a man of the most inflexible integrity, applied to the chairman of the commissioners of fortifications, who was the captain's own brother, to convene a board for the purpose of inquiring into the truth of the accusation. The chairman, the Honourable John Dotin, afterwards president of the island, having evaded the application, Alleyne determined to lay the matter before the governor; and, as a necessary precaution, wrote to Captain Dotin, informing him of his intention to suspend him, until he had cleared himself of the charges exhibited against him; and desiring him to deliver the keys of the fort to a person whom he had sent to receive them.

With this demand Dotin refused to comply, and accompanied by his brother, repaired to Pilgrim the next day.

He did not deny having sold the powder in question, but endeavoured to justify the act by alledging that it had accumulated from the usual savings to which the captain gunner was justly entitled, as a perquisite of office. To this doctrine the governor readily assented; adding, by way of sanction, that it was a common practice in the navy; and immediately wrote to the colonel, denying his authority to remove the chief-gunner; ordering the keys of the fort to be instantly restored to Dotin; and forbidding the colonel's interfering farther with the gunners and matrosses than to inform him of any misconduct or neglect of duty in the garrison. This was an unprecedented attack on the colonel's authority. For though the appointment, and of course the removal, of the gunners and matrosses is legally vested in the commander in chief, it had ever been delegated to the respective colonels in their several divisions; the governor only reserving to himself the patronage of the captain-gunner at Charles Fort, and of the gunner and matrosses at Pilgrim.

The receipt of this letter hurried Colonel Alleyne to Pilgrim, with the view of entering into some explanation with the governor on the subject; but he found his excellency little disposed to listen to any thing which he could offer for his vindication. Pale with anger and trembling with rage, his excellency accused him of exceeding the bounds of his authority in attempting to displace Captain Dotin, and of a design to destroy a gentleman's reputation and family, in listening to the idle tales of dirty fellows. Alleyne had a spirit too noble to submit to such treatment. He tore the cockade from his hat, and, indignantly thrusting his commission into the governor's hand, retired, saying he disdained to hold it on such terms.

Mr. Alleyne's next care was to submit his complaints to the only tribunal before which they were cognizable. The regular application to the proper authority having been made without success, the only remaining resource was in the assembly's interposition to enforce the claims of justice. The house therefore presented an address to the governor, Judge Rowe alone dissenting, praying that his excellency would order the chairman of the commissioners of fortifications for Saint James's division to convene a board, for the purpose of inquiring into the charges against the chief gunner.

Unwilling to push matters to extremity with the assembly, the governor issued the necessary directions for investigating Captain Dotin's conduct. A board of commissioners was accordingly held at Jame fort, at which General Rowe presided, in the absence of the chairman, and after a minute examination of the witnesses, Captain Dotin was fully convicted of having embezzled the stores entrusted to his care, and was sentenced to be dismissed from the service. The captain's defence rested on the legality of the savings in the

CHAP. XII. disbursements of the powder. These savings accrued by
1776. stinting the guns of one half the customary charge of powder, and were usually disposed of for the chief gunner's
emolument. This was, indeed, the common practice in
every division of the island long after Captain Dotin's disgrace. That economy must be bad, which, by with-hold-
ing the fair reward of service, compels the officer to seek
remuneration in fraud and peculation. Ordinary service,
says a great master of political economy, must be secured
by the motives to ordinary integrity. An honourable and
fair profit is the best security against avarice and rapacity;
as, in all things else, a lawful and regulated enjoyment is
the best security against debauchery and excess*.

The breach between the governor and the assembly was
now widened by the receipt of a letter from the agent, informing the house of his excellency's correspondence with
the secretary of state, concerning their late address to the
Throne; which his excellency had described as a measure
of the assembly alone; and that the distress of the country was not so great as it appeared to them. Mr. Duke
took up the matter with his usual warmth and public spirit,
and concluded an elaborate harangue, with moving three
resolutions. That it is the undoubted right of the general
assembly, on all occasions, either separately or jointly with
the other branches of the legislature, to address the Throne;

---

* Vide Burke's Speech on Economical Reform.

and that whoever opposes or obstructs the exercise of this privilege is an enemy to the country : that it manifestly appears that the governor has, by an application to his Majesty's secretary of state for the colonies, done what lay in his power to intercept his Majesty's relief towards his loyal and distressed subjects of this colony ; That a dutiful memorial be immediately transmitted to his Majesty, in support of their former petition. The first resolution was agreed to unanimously ; and the other two were voted in the affirmative, by a majority of nine to five.

Things were in this state when the expiration of the assembly led to a general election. On the opening of the session, his excellency made a gracious and conciliatory speech to both houses. After expressing the satisfaction which he felt at meeting them again ; and his hopes that their zeal for the good of the colony and their knowledge and experience would be productive of such regulations as would be of lasting advantage to the country, he observed that the present conjuncture of affairs must awaken the attention of his Majesty's subjects in every part of his dominions. All must feel the effects of a suspension of trade with so many of the northern colonies as were then in open rebellion ; nor was it possible that the West Indies could be exempt from a large share of inconvenience from the interruption. But such had been the provident care of the King, and both houses of parliament, that every precaution had been taken for the benefit of his loyal subjects.

Aug. 22.

He congratulated them on the numerous cargoes which had been recently imported, and the continual showers of rain with which the country had been blessed, and which afforded the most pleasing prospect of greater plenty than they had yet enjoyed. Firmly persuaded that the representatives of the people were desirous of promoting the interest and happiness of their constituents, he earnestly recommended prudence, calmness, and moderation in their proceedings, as essentially necessary to the public welfare. He again urged, what he had often ineffectually suggested to their consideration, the revisal and amendment of their militia laws, and the provision of a daily maintenance for the poor prisoners. The speech concluded with an assurance of his cheerful concurrence in every measure which could contribute to the peace, happiness, and prosperity of the country, than which no object was nearer to his heart.

The moderation and good sense contained in every sentence of this speech, produced no corresponding sentiments of amity on the part of the assembly. They entered into an injudicious recapitulation of past grievances, in their address to the governor, and commented, with unseasonable asperity, on his excellency's *malign interposition*, by which they had been disappointed in the hopes of their sovereign's benevolence, in the hour of distress. Whatever might be his excellency's opinion of the provident care of the King and parliament, they denied that the inhabitants of Barbadoes had received the smallest benefit from their attention. Notwithstanding the supplies, of which his excellency had taken notice, they insisted that, from the extravagant prices of articles of the first necessity, many of the poor inhabitants had been reduced to the most bitter distress; and that even the more opulent planters had found great difficulty in procuring the necessary subsistence for their slaves.

They should be happy, they said, in being allowed to exercise that temper, calmness, and moderation, recommended in the speech, though they were not unprepared, upon the occurrence of any just occasion, to shew that sense of injury and spirit of resentment inseparable from the character of faithful, independant representatives of the people. Having, in the course of last session, passed an act for the relief of insolvent debtors, they thought that they had given sufficient proof of their humane attention to the case of the poor prisoners. They unequivocally declared their unwillingness to revise or amend the militia bill, from the difficulties and distrusts that arose in their minds against the undertaking; which, they acknowledged, were rather increased, than lessened, by every fresh impulse to remove them. In the principle of personal attachment, by which the privates were bound to their officers, they conceived that every legal deficiency might be supplied. Nor would they consent to renounce a principle so honourable to society in times propitious to the claims of civil liberty in the

CHAP. XII.
1776.

colonies, and enforce obedience by a power congenial only with the habits of despotic sway.

These were certainly very extraordinary sentiments for a legislative assembly, professing an unshaken loyalty to their Prince, and a generous zeal for the interests of their country. It rather seemed to be a dereliction of every honourable rule of faction, thus to hazard the public safety, by a wilful neglect of the means of defence, from motives of personal resentment to their commander in chief. Were all the faults imputed to Mr. Hay admitted, yet the posture of public affairs was alarming; and the assembly were bound by every moral obligation, resulting from a sense of duty, to guard againt the danger of invasion. To this address his excellency laconically replied, " I have received your address and laid it before the King."

1777.

Mr. Walker had rendered himself highly obnoxious to the governor, by the promptitude with which he presented the assembly's addresses to the King, and still more by the freedom with which he had censured his excellency's conduct. The annual measure of appointing an agent, soon furnished the governor with an opportunity of indulging his resent-

Jan. 21.

ment, by refusing his assent to the bill which had been unanimously passed by both houses, nominating Mr. Walker their agent. His excellency, at the same time informed the assembly, that he was ready to concur in the appointment of any other person. They immediately voted an address, in which, after an eulogium on the superior talents, and faithful services of their agent, they requested his excellency would communicate to them his reasons for disapproving their choice. To which he briefly replied, " that his reasons had been laid before the King."

Upon the receipt of this succinct message, Mr. T. Alleyne moved the house to come to the following resolution; that after their full experience of the uncommon zeal and extraordinary ability of Mr. Walker, in his official capacity, they could not renounce their nomination of him, and proceed to another choice without an act of injustice to so worthy a servant of the public, an injury to the country, and a dishonour to themselves. The motion was opposed by Mr. D. Maycock. He knew of no circumstances, he said, that ought to prevent a discharge of their duty; and as occurrences might happen to make the appointment of an agent absolutely necessary, if Mr. Walker could not be replaced, they must either elect another and violate the resolution; or adhere to the resolution, and have no agent; by which they would, indeed, to use the language of the motion, do injury to the country and dishonour to themselves.

The speaker thought the resolution justifiable in its full extent. The assembly, he said, were bound in justice to Mr. Walker, in duty to their constituents, and in honour to themselves, not to sacrifice an old and valuable servant to private considerations. By a too ready submission to so great a loss, they would appear to make a virtual surrender of the constitutional right of choosing their own agent, or utterly destroy the salutary effects of that indispensible privilege. For should the assembly passively consent to name another agent, should they thus requite the services of one whose fidelity to their interests was his only fault, what return could be expected from his successor, but that he should betray his trust, encouraged by such an example of their treacherous imbecility. These arguments prevailed, and the house agreed to the resolution. But in little more than twelve months they were guilty of the very inconsistency which Mr. Maycock's prudent foresight endeavoured to prevent; and Mr. Samuel Estwick, after some opposition from the friends of Mr. Brathwaite, who was also put in nomination, was appointed agent.

The unnatural contest in which Great Britain was engaged with her revolted colonies, exposed the Barbadians to innumerable dangers and hardships. Their commerce was ruined, and their coasts insulted by rebel privateers. One of these had the temerity, under cover of the night, to venture into Speight's Bay; but, being discovered, and April 28. fired at from Orange Fort, she retired without doing any other injury than carrying off a negro man, who was found sleeping in a boat in the harbour. This attempt was soon followed by another, less daring, but more injurious in the June 12. event. A small American schooner appeared off the north end of the island, and captured several fishing boats, with many valuable slaves on board. The loss was estimated at two thousand pounds, and fell principally on a useful class of people, whose subsistence, and that of their numerous families, depended upon their success in fishing. These alarming attempts excited the apprehensions of the inhabitants of Speight's Town for their safety. They concurred in a petition to the assembly, representing the danger to which they were exposed from the defenceless state of the town, and its vicinity, and praying that the house would take proper measures for their effectual protection.

This irregular mode of proceeding, gave rise to another no less singular and unprecedented. Having taken the prayer of the petition into consideration, together with the state of the public finances, which they deemed inadequate to provide for the defence of their coasts, the assembly adopted the strange resolution of applying, through their speaker, to the naval commander on the station. The governor certainly was the proper person to whom the communication, in the first instance, ought to have been made, and from whom the application to the admiral ought to have proceeded. But, without the smallest attention to his excellency, Sir John Alleyne, who, in pursuit of the public good, lost sight of every other consideration, readily undertook the task of representing to Admiral Young the defenceless state of the country, and the depredations committed on the property of its inhabitants; and concluded a highly complimentary letter, with soliciting his particular attention to the protection of Barbadoes. The admiral's reply was

CHAP. XII.
1777.

polite, and expressed his concern that he had been hindered by the nature of the service in which his squadron had been employed, from preventing the injuries complained of, but promised that he would station a frigate to cruize round the Island for its more effectual security. For this deviation from official routine, Sir John Alleyne was honoured with the thanks of the assembly, unanimously voted in a full house.

1778.

The repeated applications of the assembly to the British ministry for relief, were at last attended with success. By an order of the lords of the privy council, Mr. Atkinson, one of the government contractors, purchased three thousand barrels of flour, three thousand barrels of herrings, and a large quantity of pease and beans, and consigned them to the governor, to be sold under his direction at prime cost; the money to be received, and remitted to the person appointed by their lordships to transact the business*.

Jan. 20.

Upon the receipt of this seasonable supply, for the support of their slaves, the governor, council, and assembly, concurred in an address to the King, expressing the warmest acknowledgments of grateful hearts for this gracious proof of condescending attention to the wants of his faithful subjects in this distant part of the empire; with the most fervid assurances that, however impoverished and en-

---

* To the honour of Mr. Atkinson, let it be remembered, that he refused to accept the usual commissions, on shipping these goods.

feebled by calamity, inclination as well as duty would prompt them to testify their unshaken loyalty to the best of sovereigns, and to oppose all disturbers of the ease and happiness of his government.

Not to be inattentive to the opportunity of profiting still more by his Majesty's paternal tenderness, the council proposed an humble address imploring his Majesty to recommend to his parliament the measure of putting this ancient and loyal colony, now much distressed by unavoidable calamities, on a footing with all the other West Indian Islands, in regard to the duty on their staple products. This proposal was eagerly embraced by the assembly, though it might probably have been more decorous to have laid the effusions of gratitude at the foot of the throne unattended by any solicitations for additional proofs of the royal benevolence.

The supply of provisions was accompanied by a proposal very inconsistent with the benevolent disposposition manifested by that partial relief. Mr. Hay was directed by the secretary of state to demand of the assembly an allowance for the support of such rebel prisoners as should be brought to Barbadoes. Thus, while relief was administered with one hand, an attempt was made, on the other, to exhaust the country still more by an accumulation of its burthens. In obedience to these orders, the governor used every effort to persuade the assembly to assume the charge of providing for the prisoners. But, with a firmness highly commendable, they resisted every solicitation on the subject; and, as no provision had been made by the British government for securing and maintaining prisoners of war, his excellency was obliged to advance considerable sums of money out of his own pocket for their support.

The encouragement openly given by France to the rebellious colonies in North America, having rendered a war between Great Britain and that kingdom inevitable, Mr. Hay summoned a meeting of the general assembly for the purpose of submitting to them the necessity of adopting effectual measures for the security of the country. At the opening of the session he had warned them of the approaching danger; and as the colony was exposed to insults and injury from American pirates, he earnestly recommended, that provision should be made for repairing the forts; and, above all, urged a due attention to the militia as the most constitutional means of defence which they could possess. As these admonitions had made no impression on the assembly, his excellency again exhorted them to exert themselves in the cause of their country, and to strain every nerve in the defence of its territories, navigation and trade. The reparation of their forts, and the organization of their militia, were again recommended in the strongest terms. But arguments and entreaties were equally vain.

The assembly seemed now to have regained their good humour. Their answer to the speech was unusually civil and respectful; but, while they lamented their insecurity, they persisted in asserting their inability to guard against those dangers which threatened them. To put their fortifications in an efficient state of defence would cost more, they said, than the country was able to afford. And although they admitted the utility of a militia, properly organized, and well disciplined, they asserted, that the legislature, after repeated attempts, had found it impracticable to make any material alteration in their military system without increasing the inconveniences and hardships on individuals. After some common-place professions of zeal and loyalty, they calmly informed his excellency, that such was the exhausted state of the public coffers, and the unfortunate circumstances of the people, that their sole reliance must be on his Majesty's goodness for protection. Nor would they consent to increase the public burthens by new taxes, or additional articles of expense, until war should be actually declared against France. These sentiments ill accorded with their late loyal declarations of opposing all disturbers of his Majesty's government.

That a British legislative assembly should be so perfectly insensible of the blessings of civil liberty, as to hazard its enjoyment by a pertinacious adherence to an erroneous system of economy, and to talk of arming only when the enemy should be at their gate, are facts scarcely credible, were they not authenticated by the minutes of their proceedings, published by their own authority. Nor can it fail to excite the astonishment of posterity, that the representatives of a free people should prefer individual conveniency to the public safety, and risk the whole of their property rather than sacrifice a part for the preservation of the rest. That public virtue, says the elegant Gibbon, which, among the ancients, was denominated patriotism, is derived from a strong sense of our own interest in the preservation and prosperity of the free government of which we are members. But among the Barbadians, the only patriotism known, at the period of which we are speaking, seems to have consisted in an opposition to the measures of government, and an endeavour to promote the voluptuous ease of mercenary individuals at the hazard and expense of the country.

The assembly were not, however, left long in a state of uncertainty respecting the hostile designs of France. Credible information was received early in September, that war had been proclaimed at Martinico on the fifteenth day of August. This was soon succeeded by more alarming intelligence. The Marquis de Bouillé, governor-general of Martinico, with a body of two thousand men, transported in four frigates and fifteen sloops, passed over to the valuable island of Dominica, and commenced an immediate attack on its half-manned batteries. The weak and defenceless state of the garrison left Governor Stuart no other alternative than to make the best terms he could with the invaders. The articles of capitulation were easily arranged, and Dominica was surrendered to the arms of his

Sept. 7.

most Christian Majesty, on conditions the most favourable to the capitulants. This important conquest was achieved while Admiral Barrington, with two ships of the line, and some frigates, was lying inactive at Barbadoes, where he had been waiting two months for orders from the lords of the admiralty. But surely the French declaration of war precluded the necessity of orders; and had the admiral, on receiving notice of that event, put to sea with his squadron, and continued to cruise off Martinico, there is not a doubt that he would have frustrated the design on Dominica.

On the meeting of the assembly, the governor informed them of the recent capture of Dominica; and availed himself of that opportunity to enforce his former recommendation concerning the forts and the militia. "Nobody," said his excellency, in his plain blunt manner, " laments the unhappy situation of many of the inhabitants more than I do, but the island is still the same; the lands and possessions are still of importance; and these are the proper objects of the legislature, whose duty it is to use every effort to put the island in such a state of defence as time and local circumstances will admit of; for should they be torn from us then shall we be poor indeed." The proximity of the danger now awakened the fears of the assembly. The moment had now arrived when it confessedly became their interest, as well as their duty, to prepare in the best manner for their defence. Yet, at this alarming crisis, and

after such an acknowledgment, they resolved that the fortifications, in their utmost extent, were unnecessary and irre-
parable; that the guns and matrosses belonging to the
most useless of them, should be removed to places of more
importance; that intrenchments should be thrown up on
the most accessible parts of the coast; and that the sum of
six thousand pounds should be raised to defray the expenses
of these preparations.

The payment of the gunners and matrosses salaries which
was provided for out of this fund, left a small surplus applicable to any other purpose. And of this balance no inconsiderable proportion was consumed in paying the wages
of the supervisors employed in directing the throwing up
of sand-banks on the western part of the island. Such was
the extreme jealousy entertained of the executive power,
that the assembly inserted a clause in the bill which they
framed in these resolutions, enacting that the money should
only be paid on being addressed for by their house. But,
on the council's rejecting the bill on that account, they
waved this unconstitutional claim. Nor did they affect to
dissemble their unwillingness to attempt any innovation in
their military system; "averse," as they expressed it, "even
under the most pressing exigencies, from resolving, after
the deliberation of a few days only, on points essential in
the minds of a free people, to their greatest happiness."
Melancholy indeed, said the speaker, upon presenting the
bill for the governor's assent, are the circumstances of these

times, compared with the flourishing state of the country in the last war; when, upon a requisition from the Crown, the assembly were able to raise a capitation-tax of seven shillings and sixpence upon slaves, to defray the expense of a body of our own forces, sent upon the expedition against Martinico, although we now find a difficulty in raising a levy of fifteen-pence to protect ourselves from invasion.

Sensible of the danger to which the islands in the West Indies were exposed, Sir Henry Clinton, on the approach of winter, detached five thousand troops from New York, under the command of General Grant, for their protection. The transports, with the troops, were convoyed by Commodore Hotham, with five sail of the line, and some frigates. On their arrival at Barbadoes, Admiral Barrington, who Dec. 10. assumed the command of the fleet, anxious, by some bold, successful stroke, to compensate for the loss of Dominica, determined, without suffering the troops to land, to proceed immediately to Saint Lucia, and attempt the reduction of that island : an enterprise of no small difficulty and danger ; but which, from its ultimate success, was productive of no less glory to the naval and military officers, and the forces by whom the conquest was achieved, than advantage to the service, in the ensuing operations of the war in this hemisphere.

On the intelligence of this event reaching Barbadoes, the assembly unanimously voted the thanks of their house to Admiral Barrington and General Grant, for their gallant

services; and, as a more substantial proof of their gratitude and esteem, passed an act for furnishing the army
and navy, at Saint Lucia, with a gratuitous supply of fresh
provisions and live stock. Admiral Barrington, however,
having resigned the command to Byron, politely declined
accepting the generous donative; alleging, that the healthy
condition of the fleet rendered the intended supply unnecessary; and that great difficulty would inevitably attend
the transporting of it. But on the return of the fleet to
Barbadoes, a few months afterwards, Admiral Parker, on
whom the command had devolved, thankfully accepted the
liberal offer, observing to the deputation of the assembly,
by whom it was made, that a supply of fresh provisions
was extremely necessary for the recovery of the many
brave men who were then in a languishing, dying condition; especially as neither soldier nor sailor had eaten a
meal of fresh provisions for nearly eighteen months. It
must be observed, to the honour of the Barbadians, that,
however reluctantly they submit to the expense and inconvenience of defending themselves, they always contribute
cheerfully to the accomodation of those who are employed
in protecting them.

June.   The whole of the trade from the West Indies to England
having been collected at Saint Christopher's, the immense
value of such a numerous fleet induced Admiral Byron to
employ his whole squadron in convoying them a considerable part of their voyage. However wise or prudent the

measure might have been, it was productive of the most fatal consequences. Taking advantage of his absence, a handful of French, scarcely exceeding four hundred men, under the direction of a naval lieutenant, were detached from Martinico, for the purpose of reducing the valuable island of Saint Vincent, garrisoned by seven companies of regular troops, commanded by a lieutenant-colonel, besides a militia far exceeding the invaders in number. To this inadequate, contemptible force, the island was surrendered without the firing of a single shot on either side. Far different was the reception which the enemy experienced at Grenada. With six and twenty ships of the line, twelve frigates, and nearly ten thousand troops, Count D'Estaing made a descent on that island. The whole force which Lord Macartney, the governor, had to oppose to this prodigious armament, consisted of about one hundred and fifty British soldiers, and not quite four hundred militia. The defence, however disproportioned the means, was obstinate. Advantageously posted on an eminence, the brave defenders of their country, repulsed a formidable column of French troops, headed by D'Estaing in person; but the numbers of the assailants prevailed after a well-contested dispute of more than an hour. A capitulation was then proposed; but the governor and the principal inhabitants preferred surrendering at discretion, to submitting to the dishonourable terms dictated to them by the haughty D'Estaing, in the pride and insolence of conquest.

July 2.

These transactions produced a considerable sensation in Barbadoes, and increased the anxiety of the governor for the safety of the colony.   He immediately convoked the legislature, and represented to them, in the most forcible manner, the danger to which the island was exposed by the progress of the enemy in their vicinity ; and particularly from the recent injury sustained by Admiral Byron's fleet, in a partial action with the French off Grenada, after his return from convoying the trade to a certain latitude, which had compelled him to retire to Antigua to refit. With the internal resources which we possessed, his excellency was persuaded, that a vigorous defence might be made, in case of an attack, and that the island might hold out until it should be relieved by the arrival of naval assistance.   As preparatory measures, he recommended providing tents for the men ; raising entrenchments ; building redoubts at proper distances ; and particularly proposed purchasing a spot of land, in some convenient situation, for a grand redoubt and general depôt of ordnance, ammunition, and provisions, to which the whole army might retire in case of necessity. As the militia were raw and inexperienced, he advised, that they should be more frequently assembled and instructed in the use of arms, and submitted to the consideration of the assembly, whether, in the present critical posture of affairs, a temporary enforcement of martial law were not necessary ? To evince the utility of a militia, under proper regulations, he referred to the rebel army in America, composed entirely of militia, and yet successfully fighting behind entrenchments and strong redoubts against veteran troops.

The house were at last awakened to a due sense of the dangers which surrounded them. They immediately resolved to provide tents for the men, to throw up entrenchments, and build redoubts; to arm a proportion of effective negroes, to call out the militia one day in every week for four months; to equip two small vessels to watch the motions of the enemy, to provide an additional stock of gunpowder, and to purchase land for the purpose suggested by his excellency. But they thought that the adoption of these vigorous measures rendered martial law unnecessary. To give effect to these resolutions, they voted the sum of fourteen thousand pounds, one-half the money to be raised in the course of the ensuing year, and the balance the year after*. Bills were immediately prepared agreeable to these resolutions, and were passed with the greatest unanimity by both houses. By the additional levy bill, five members of council, and seven of the assembly, or any five of them, were appointed commissioners to carry the plan of defence into execution, with full power to borrow money, on the public faith, or to contract for such articles as were required

---

* The minutes of the assembly say ten thousand pounds; but the law, which was passed on the occasion, fixes the sum at fourteen thousand.

CHAP. XII. for its completion, until the taxes laid by the act could be
1779.   collected.

A sufficient quantity of land was accordingly purchased,
in the parish of Saint George; and the building of a grand
redoubt, called Fort George, was begun, to serve as a
general depôt, in case of invasion. But his excellency
lived not to see the completion of his patriotic plans. In
the midst of those preparations, which he had so often
stenuously recommended, he was arrested by the hand of
death, and removed from all the grandeur, bustle, and
October 24. contention of this world, to the mansions of eternal peace.
The early partner of his bed, died in Barbadoes, on the
eleventh day of October, one thousand seven hundred and
seventy-five; upon which occasion his daughters returned
to England, and his excellency, soon after, married Miss
Barnwell, a beautiful Barbadian, whose personal accom-
plishments attracted his admiration, and compensated the
want of rank and fortune. It does not appear, that this
lady's sorrows, for the loss of her deceased lord, experienced
any alleviation from those marks of public favour which
have been occasionally shewn to the family of governors,
not more deserving than Mr. Hay. The character of his excellency presents the eye of candour with a tesselated scene
of good and evil. Of a temper irritable, impetuous, implacable, and vindictive; the extreme roughness of his
manners was little calculated to conciliate the esteem of a
proud, high-spirited people. The violence of his passions,

often hurried him into improprieties which justly gave offence, and for which he had neither liberality of mind, nor strength of understanding, to atone. Yet it must be allowed, that he was a man of honest, upright intentions, zealously attached to the interests of his country, faithful to his prince, anxious to promote the happiness of the people, and to provide for the public security.

The period of Mr. Hay's administration is not distinguished by any peculiar traces of legislative wisdom. Of forty-one laws which received his assent, twenty-seven were temporary, and of the remainder six relate to one object, the improvement of the mole-head; and yet the plan is either extremely defective and ineffectual, or, from an entire dereliction of public spirit, which fatally pervades every department of our little state, is miserably neglected and abused in the execution. Of the other laws one only is entitled to particular notice; this is the hucksters', or, as it is sometimes called, the inspector's act. By this law an exclusive tax was laid on the shop-keepers of Bridge-Town, to be proportionably rated by the parochial vestry, and annually paid into the public treasury *. It was also enacted, that any free negro or mulatto who shall buy any live or dead stock, fruits, roots, or vegetables, or other things, to sell again, without a license from the treasurer,

---

* This clause has been since repealed.

shall, besides the goods bought or sold, forfeit ten pounds for every offence. And the treasurer is authorized to grant an annual license to any free negro or mulatto to carry on the business of a huckster, upon receiving a duty of ten pounds, applicable to the uses of the excise act, besides a fee of one pound five shillings for his trouble. The object of this heavy impost was to discourage, and in effect to prohibit, the nefarious traffic carried on by coloured hucksters. Mr. Duke, by whom the bill was introduced, saw early, and endeavoured to avert, the evils with which the rapid encrease of free coloured people was pregnant. To the penetrating eye of that enlightened statesman it was clear, that the encouragement given to that spurious race, would ultimately deprive such of the white inhabitants as were employed in the menial occupations of life, of the means of subsistence, and, by forcing them into exile, exhaust the country of the best portion of its physical strength.

In this state the bill was sent up to the other house for its concurrence; and though it was evidently a money bill*,

---

* Under the denomination of money-bills, are included all those by which money is directed to be raised upon the subject, for any purpose, or in any shape whatsoever; either for the exigencies of government, and collected from the kingdom in general, or for private benefit, and collected in any particular district. *Black. Comm. vol.* 1. *p.* 170. This rule, says *Christian,* in his notes upon *Blackstone,* is now extended to all bills for canals, paving, poor rates, and those in which pecuniary penal-

the council inserted an amendment, extending the clause,
respecting free negroes and mulattoes, to all white hucksters; who, in default of taking out a license, were made liable to a forfeiture of fifty pounds, from which penalty the coloured retailer was exempt. This was undeniably a most unparliamentary interference, but the assembly, taken by surprise, or heedless of their most invaluable privilege, silently submitted to the invasion of its fundamental right, and unanimously acquiesced in the proposed alteration.

The avowed object of this arbitrary, partial and unconstitutional amendment, was to reduce the number of hucksters by the imposition of an oppressive tax, which few of them were able to pay. In support of the measure it was alledged, that the hucksters were receivers of stolen goods, and their shops the asylums of fugitive slaves. The legislature therefore piously determined to destroy those petty retailers, who eked out a scanty subsistence by revending a few articles of the first necessity, and, to preserve their morals, condemned them to hunger and nakedness. Should the

---

ties and fines are imposed for offences. 3 *Hatsel* 110. And the commons have been, at all times, so tenacious of this privilege, that they never suffer the lords even to make any change in the money bills, which they have sent to them; but they must simply and solely, either wholly accept or reject them. *De Lolme on the Constitution,* *p.* 67.

CHAP.XII. hucksters be guilty of the crimes imputed to them, there are
1779. laws sufficient for their punishment, without resorting to a
measure which threatens them with extinction. Far from
being those pests of society which they are represented to
be, they are an useful description of traders. Through their
medium the poor and middling classes of people, and even
the opulent householder, are daily supplied with articles of
domestic accommodation, and the sable labourer obtains the
comforts of his abject condition. Here he barters the crude,
unsavoury, substantial allowance of the plantations for more
palatable and nutritious food; and, no less fond of variety than
his epicurean master, indulges his satiated appetite with a
change of diet; refreshes his drooping spirits; and reno-
vates his almost exhausted vigour. Let not the hapless
slave be denied these needful comforts by an absurd, unnatural policy, which would confine him to feed perpetually
on the productions of the soil.

Were this law enforced with a spirit, congenial to that in
which it originated, its operation must inevitably produce
the most pernicious consequences   Many of those who are
employed in retail shops, are women, aged and infirm persons; and others, who, having been brought up to no profession, or having failed in higher pursuits, are destitute of
every other means of supporting the weary load of life.
The capital thus employed, is in very few instances equal
to the sum required for a license. They depend for subsist-

ence on the small profits accruing on the revendition of a few articles procured on credit, from the credulous merchant, or the humane wholesale dealer. Consequently, if the duty be exacted from them, they must shut up their shops, and remain in idleness and indigence, whilst their helpless offspring become burthensome to their parish*.

There are others again, whose larger stock in trade will enable them to pay the price of a license, and continue their business with encreased advantage. By diminishing the number of retailers, the law tends to lessen, if not to destroy, that competition in the market which is always found beneficial to the bulk of the people. And the opulent huckster, who complies with the exaction, will triumph in the privileged monopoly ; and, by extorting from those who are driven to his shop by necessity, will amply reimburse himself for the expense of the license, and grow rich

---

* Previous to all the laws of society, man had a right to subsist ; and is he to lose that right by the establishment of laws ? To wrest from him, by a tax, the means of preserving life, is, in fact, to affect the very principle of his existence. By extorting the subsistence of the needy, the state takes from him his strength with his food. It reduces the poor man to beggary, the labouring man to idleness, and makes the unfortunate man become a rogue. *Raynal's History of the East and West Indies, vol.* 8. *p.* 270.

on the spoils of the community. Hence, as a regulation of police, the law is absurd, impolitic, and inhuman. Nor is it less objectionable as a financial expedient.

The grand leading principle of taxation is, that every one should be assessed in proportion to his property and income. But, by this law, an annual capitation tax, of all modes the most arbitrary and unjust, is imposed on a particular class of traders, without any regard to their capital, or the profits of their business. To add to its obvious injustice, the tax is confined to persons who, besides their parochial levies, are annually rated for the support of government, by their respective vestries, on oath, in proportion to their trade and ability. But as this impost falls on indigence and industry, while it passes by the door of wealth and indolence, its manifest inequality cannot escape observation. The poor tenant of an humble shed, who earns his daily support by the precarious revendition of a few provisions, is here taxed beyond all reasonable proportion, with the wealthy merchant, or the opulent possessor of an hundred slaves.

The bill was passed with such precipitancy, that the people without doors, ignorant of what was doing within, had no opportunity of deprecating its vengeance. But no sooner was it known, than the door of every huckster's shop in the island was shut, except a few in the metropolis, the owners of which availed themselves of the sanction of

licenses to enhance the value of the common necessaries of
life. The members for St. Michael's were instructed, by
some of their constituents, to move for a repeal of the obnoxious clause; and the most respectable inhabitants of
Speight's Town, concurred in a petition to the assembly
for its abrogation. These applications were ably supported
by Mr. Duke, who, in an excellent argumentative speech,
after obviating every objection on the plea of consistency,
proposed some modifications of the tax in question. But
the house was deaf to his reasoning and his eloquence.
They would not, formally, consent to rescind an act so
recently adopted; but it was hinted, that the penal clause
would never be enforced.

This assurance, though it quieted the apprehensions of
the hucksters, who thereupon resumed their occupations,
affords them no security. They are still liable to be overwhelmed with ruin, by any malicious informer, who, from
personal pique, pecuniary considerations, caprice, or ma-
levolence, may insist upon having the law enforced. The
worst tyranny is that of bad laws suspended over our heads,
by a single hair, which envy or revenge may sever at discretion. It is not enough that such laws should slumber
in oblivion; they should be repealed. While they are extant, they afford the means of oppressing the poor with
facility, and furnish the vindictive with convenient instruments of revenge, whenever he will avail himself of the

opportunity of prosecuting the disaffected person, under some one or other of the many statutes, which, however useless, remain dormant, like unextinguished volcanoes, ready to pour destruction on the head of the devoted traveller.

CHAP. XIII.

THE GOVERNMENT DEVOLVES ON THE HON. JOHN DOTIN—SUCCEED-
ED BY MAJOR GENERAL JAMES CUNNINGHAME—THE GOVER-
NOR DISAPPOINTED IN HIS SALARY—QUARRELS WITH THE
ASSEMBLY—THE COUNCIL SANCTIONS HIS ILLEGAL CLAIM OF
FEES—THE ISLAND ALMOST DESOLATED BY A DREADFUL
HURRICANE.

UPON the demise of Mr. Hay, the council met for the purpose of administering the inauguration oaths to the president. Mr. Rous, who had twice filled the dignified station, was now so enfeebled by age and infirmities, that he prudently preferred the shades of retirement to the hurry and fatigues of public life. In a respectful letter, addressed to the council, he signified his resignation and enclosed his mandamus; which he requested they would transmit to his sovereign. The government of course devolved on the Honourable John Dotin, the member next in succession to the presidential chair; he was accordingly invested with the ensigns of authority, and commenced his administration with an economical reform. He abolished the expense of oil

CHAP. XIII.
1779.
October 26.

for the use of the lamps at Pilgrim; an act which was extolled as a noble proof of his generous regard for the interest of his country.

Nov. 2. The assembly, which was near the period of its dissolution, having met for the purpose of making a suitable provision for supporting the dignity of the presidency, Mr. Duke moved that the sum of one thousand pounds a year should be settled on Mr. Dotin during his administration. He insisted that it would be the highest folly, under the existing circumstances, to give the next governor a salary equal to that which had been hitherto given; and that it would be prudent to begin the retrenchment now, when the executive power was lodged in the hands of a native; no exception could then be taken by his successor at a conduct so free from any appearance of partiality. These arguments were far from producing the desired effect. The motion was rejected by a large majority; and the salary fixed at fifteen hundred pounds.

1780.
Jan. 18.
A general election having taken place, Mr. Duke embraced the earliest opportunity of their meeting to press the reduction of the governor's salary on the attention of the new assembly*. The proper time, he insisted, to agitate

---

* The proceedings of this assembly form such an interesting part of our colonial transactions, that curiosity may naturally enquire their names. These were, Val. Jones and H. Duke, *St. Michael's*; J Burke and T. Burton, *Christchurch*; S. Walcott and R. Haynes, *St. John's*; Jos. Gittins and J. Wood, *St. Philip's*; James C. Cox

the question was before an appointment had been made; the value of the government would then be known at the moment that it was solicited; their proceedings would be free from any suspicion of prejudice; no offence could be taken nor disappointment felt by the gentleman who should be selected to administer the government. As guardians of the public purse, there was an obligation upon the members of that house, he said, to adjust the public expenses to the power and ability of those who were to pay them. The poor man contributed in an equal proportion, with the wealthy, to the support of government; it was their duty to look to the community at large, and to form their judgment upon that comprehensive view. The unfortunate condition of the bulk of the people rendered the strictest frugality necessary. He wished not to dwell upon a detail of distresses and calamities. Every one who heard him must have seen and felt enough to render such a recital superfluous. After some additional observations, Mr. Duke moved three resolutions, in substance as follows: That the people, reduced by a variety of misfortunes, were now unable to pay a governor the same salary as had been for-

and Rob. Burnet Jones, *St. George's*; T. Alleyne and B. Bostock, *St. James's*; W. Gibbes Alleyne and R. Ashford, *St. Thomas's*; S. Hinds and H. Walke, *St. Peter's*; B. Babb and S. Husbands, *St. Lucy's*; Sir John Gay Alleyne, speaker, and A. Cumberbatch, jun. *St. Andrew's*; J. Steward and Edmund Haynes, *St. Joseph's*.

CHAP.XIII. merly allowed; that two thousand pounds were the most
1780. which they could afford to settle on the next governor; and
that a copy of these resolutions should be transmitted to the
agent for the information of the secretary of state for the
colonies. These resolutions were opposed as being premature and inefficient; and, on the previous question being
moved, the house refused to take them into consideration.

Feb. 23. At their next sitting the assembly received a message
from the president, stating, that it being his Majesty's intention to station troops on the island for its protection, the
eighty-ninth regiment had been landed; and that he had
provided them with quarters; not doubting that the assembly would approve of the measure, and defray the expenses
of their accommodation. This called up Mr. Duke. With
the utmost respect for the parent state, he found himself
under a superior obligation to his native country. He was
averse to any new article of expense, which, however small
in the outset, may increase in its progress. Jamaica had
burthened itself with the maintenance of troops under an
idea that it was a temporary provision for a particular
exigency, but the load was fixed upon it and was likely to
remain. Conscious of the inability of the people to bear
any fresh impositions, Mr. Duke opposed the proposal for
quartering the troops, as a measure productive of one certain evil, and of many that were probable, without any pros-

pect of advantage. The house, however, thought differently, and a committee was appointed to provide barracks for the troops at the expense of the colony.

On the next meeting of the assembly the president sent down another message to the house, announcing the appointment of Major General James Cunninghame, to the government of the island, and requesting that they would prepare for his reception. A similar communication was soon afterwards received from the agent, accompanied by the most favourable representations of General Cunninghame's character, his friendly disposition towards the people, and his professed inclination to render his government easy and happy to them. To this was added, an account of the steps taken by the agent himself, to obtain a remission of the four and a half per cent. duty. Mr. Estwick had submitted to Lord North a statement of facts relative to that impost, and proposed, as a commutation of the duty, a general tax of three pence a hundred upon all sugar imported from the West Indies. Lord North appeared to think that the proposal was fair and eligible; and that there could be no reason why the other islands should not contribute to the revenue equally with Barbadoes. His lordship, however, having taken no steps in the business, Mr. Estwick added, that he had intended to bring the matter before the house of commons himself; but that it had been indirectly conveyed to his knowledge that General Cunninghame would carry out full power for the settlement of

CHAP.XIII. the affair on the island. And he understood the terms
1780, were, that the islands subject to this impost, should engage
to raise a fund sufficient for the payment of the pensions
granted upon the duty; that no additional grant should be
made; and that as the pensions dropped off, the fund should
cease. These he observed were considerable, and some of
them for two or three lives.

July 10. While every mind was anxiously anticipating the halcyon
days that were approaching, General Cunninghame arrived,
and the illusion vanished. The hopes which had been
fondly cherished before his arrival, derived a temporary
confirmation from his specious manners. Bred in camps,
he possessed the imposing politeness, the easy dignity, and
condescending affability of the polished gentleman. But
beneath that pleasing exterior lurked a venality of soul
which soon obscured every virtue, and cast a baleful shade
over every accomplishment.

His excellency landed from on board the Thunderer, Commodore Walsingham's flag-ship, on Wednesday the twelfth
of July. He was received at the wharf by the president
and council,* the speaker and the members of the assem-

---

* The members of council were, J. Dotin, A. Cumberbatch, Henry Frere, Ire-
neaus Moe, Rob. Brathwaite, W. Senhouse, W. Bishop, John Best, Joseph Keeling,
and John Ince. There were two vacancies which were not filled up during Cunninghame's administration.

bly, the principal officers of the militia, and most of the clergy, whence they formed a grand procession, escorted by the guards, the royal regiment of militia, and two companies of the king's troops, to Saint Michael's church, where an appropriate sermon was preached on these words, " When the righteous are in authority the people rejoice *." His excellency then proceeded to Pilgrim where the usual oaths were administered, and he was invested with the government in due form.

The assembly having met pursuant to a special summons, his excellency commanded their attendance in the council chamber, and addressed both houses in a speech of considerable length. After professing his sense of the honour done him by his Majesty's appointment to the government of the island, he observed, " the character which your ancestors have successively transmitted to you, of loyalty to the King, and attachment to the constitution, you have uniformly maintained. The preservation of that order and tranquillity which have reigned so long among you, undisturbed by violence and faction, distinguishes the temper and wisdom of your councils. These circumstances, he added, had recommended and endeared them to their sove-

---

† Proverbs, c. xxix. v. 2. His excellency probably thought the sermon a sufficient commentary on the text, and therefore determined that his conduct should be an illustration of the latter part of the verse; *but when the wicked beareth rule the people mourn.*"

reign, whose goodness and attention to their wants had been signally displayed in the ample supply of provisions which had been sent for their relief, without any charge of transport, the royal present of artillery and military stores for their defence, and the large sums granted for the improvement of the mole-head. To this enumeration of the royal favours, his excellency, by way of climax, added another instance of his Majesty's gracious attention to the island, at a time of public danger, in so speedily sending out a successor to the late governor; and he should be happy, he said, if in executing the Royal commands he might contribute to the safety and prosperity of this respectable part of the empire. Nor did he omit to remind them of the zeal and diligence with which, previous to his leaving England, he had urged every measure which he thought conducive to the welfare of the island.

Having an equal confidence in the wisdom and liberality of the assembly, he refrained from representing to them the necessity of preparing for their defence; or to press for such supplies as the works essential to their safety required for their completion. As the public money would always be applied to such purposes as met their approbation, he trusted they would not neglect to raise sums sufficient for that important service. In their consultations upon this subject, he assured them of his readiness to give them all the information and assistance which his professional experience enabled him to do. To the expected settlement he alluded in these words, " Among many instructions which I have received from the King, framed for the good and welfare of the island, there is one which it seems necessary to communicate to you without delay*; I have therefore directed a copy of it to be laid before you. It would be indelicate in me to enlarge upon a subject in which I find myself so personally interested. I shall therefore submit it to your consideration, with the hope, that an appointment sufficient to support the dignity of government and your own honour, may be the result of your deliberations †."

He had the satisfaction, he said, of bringing from his Majesty's ministers, assurances that every attention should be paid to the safety and welfare of the colony which its character and importance deserved. The powerful naval force destined for the protection of this part of the empire promised the most perfect security; but it behoved them, he observed, to reflect that a state of war is ever, in some degree, a state of danger; and that their confidence in their sovereign's attention to their safety ought not to abate their exertions for their internal defence. Though he professed

---

* This was the instruction usually given to every governor, allowing him to accept of any salary which the assembly should think proper to settle upon him, provided the settlement be made for the whole time of his administering the government; and that it be done in the first session of assembly holden after his arrival.

† He had been told before he left England that his salary would be only two thousand pounds.

to entertain no doubt of their attention to their present situation, he could not omit recommending them, in the
strongest manner, to frame such a militia bill as should give
them all the advantages derivable from the extensive population of the country.   Whatever powers might be lodged
in the commander in chief, he pledged himself should be
exercised with all the moderation which the nature of the
service would justify.   He would not, he said, trouble them
with common professions, his conduct alone must determine
the character of his administration; which he felt would
prove honourable to himself only in the degree that he
should make it happy to them.

Conformably to the rules of the house, a committee was
appointed to prepare an answer to the governor's speech
against their next sitting, and the assembly, in the interim,
proceeded to take into consideration the settlement to be
made on his excellency.   The house being in a committee,
Mr. Duke moved a resolution conceived in these words,
" That the circumstances of the people of this island cannot afford a higher settlement upon his excellency, notwithstanding the high sense which we entertain of his merit,
than two thousand pounds per annum, in augmentation of
the home salary."   He prefaced his motion with remarking,
that his excellency's gracious speech deserved every testimony of gratitude which could be given by the assembly,
consistent with their duty to their constituents.   It must be
the wish of every member of that house, he said, to distin-

guish their present commander in chief with a settlement no less liberal than that which had been made on his predecessor; but acting as they were, in a delegated capacity, they were not at liberty to consult their own inclinations. They were bound to consider the strength of those by whom the burthen was to be borne; and from the deplorable state of the country, afflicted by a variety of evils natural and political, the people were now unable to make a provision for the support of government equal to what they had done under happier circumstances. In order, however, to evince a disposition to treat his excellency with becoming munificence, in the event of a more prosperous turn in their affairs, Mr. Duke moved a second resolution, " That in case his Majesty, in consideration of the many distresses and calamities that had for several years past overwhelmed his faithful and loyal subjects of this colony, should be graciously pleased to relieve them from the payment of the four and a half per cent. duty on their exported commodities, the assembly would make an additional provision of one thousand pounds a year for the support of the colonial government."

Both resolutions were strenuously opposed by Mr. R. Burnet Jones, who thought that the annual saving of one thousand pounds in the governor's salary was not an object of sufficient value to induce the house to acquiesce in a measure which might render his excellency indifferent, if not inimical, to the interests of the country; especially at

this particular juncture, when they were critically circumstanced with regard to their application for relief from the
onerous impost on their staple products.   Mr. Jones professed himself an advocate for economy ; but, as the sum in dispute would not exceed three-pence on each slave, or at most
twenty shillings on each plantation, he could not approve
of a proposal by which so trifling a saving was put in competition with an object infinitely more valuable.   He did
not deny that frugality was necessary, but recommended
that a reform should be made in some other department, in
which it might be more productive of advantage, without
the same risk of being prejudicial.*   The salary, he remarked, was given for the express purpose of supporting the
honour and dignity of government, the house ought therefore to consider that, this being a time of war, the expenses
of the governor's establishment must unavoidably be increased, by the hospitality with which his rank and character
made it necessary that he should receive and entertain the
officers of the army and navy on the station.

To these solid arguments was opposed a presumption,
which a very slender knowledge of human nature would
have shewn to have been entirely unfounded.   It was re-

---

* In the expenditure of stores in the different forts a saving might have been made
which, far from being detrimental to the public service, would have reflected credit on
the government.   In Speight's division alone the waste of powder at this very time exceeded the sum in dispute.

plied, that the governor would always perform the duties of his station uninfluenced by pecuniary considerations. Nor could his excellency justly entertain, it was said, any resentment against the members of that house for a conduct evidently proceeding from a sense of public duty. Actuated by that motive, their conduct could neither give offence nor require apology. Were only the opulent possessors of slaves affected by the payment of taxes, Mr. Duke admitted, that the reduction proposed would indeed be trifling and insignificant; but, as the weight of the burthen would fall heaviest on people of middling circumstances, and others of inferior rank, who found it difficult even to maintain their families, he thought that the smallest saving was important, as it was essential, to their means of subsistence.

On a question so interesting to his country, Sir John Alleyne could not content himself with giving a silent vote. Were the committee to be influenced by personal considerations, the amiable character of General Cunninghame, he acknowledged, claimed the utmost exertion of their benevolence; but when the circumstances of the people were adverted to, he thought their accumulated distresses rendered them unable to indulge their native generosity. He took a comprehensive survey of the impoverished state of the island; and, with his usual pathos, expatiated on the lamentable scenes of misery which every where arrested the attention. The failure of crops, the long drought at a critical season, the privation of accustomed supplies from

America, the wretched condition of the slaves, with respect to whom famine might be said to be stalking through the land ; the sale of plantations by decretal orders of the court of chancery for less than two-thirds of their real value, the depopulation of others torn to pieces by executions for debt, were topics insisted upon with great truth and energy, to shew the positive disability of the people to display that liberality in supporting the dignity of their first magistrate, which they had done in more prosperous times.

He remarked that the colonial salary was a free gift of the people ; and that the revenue on the produce of their estates, having been granted to the crown, among other uses, for that of paying the governor's salary, they were under no obligation to raise one shilling for that purpose. In an historical review of the subject, Sir John shewed that, even in years of comparative prosperity, the salary had fluctuated according to the temper of the assembly, from two to six thousand pounds. And, although for the five preceding administrations, the settlement had been stationary at three thousand, the worthy Baronet contended that, upon a fair comparison of the condition of the country at the different periods, what had been formerly given might be likened, as a part of our abundance to the rich man's portion, said, in scripture, to be cast into the treasury; whilst all we have to give in this day of calamity must be thrown in like the poor widow's mite.

In the course of the debate, Sir John Alleyne took occasion to observe, that the proposed commutation of the four and a half per cent. duty would be far more oppressive than the original imposition. For, however grievous the duty might be, as it was proportioned to the annual produce of their plantations, it was preferable to a certain fixed sum which must be raised at all events, and under every disappointment from a failure of crops. Besides, as all sums due to the crown were entitled to a priority over all private contracts, the consequence of a commutation, upon the terms suggested, would be injurious to the credit of the country, and accelerate its ruin. Precluded from every prospect of relief from this burthen, by the interposition of superior authority, he insisted that it was incumbent on the assembly, as faithful guardians of the public interest, to diminish the load for themselves, in every particular under their immediate controul.

On the question being put, the motion for two thousand pounds was carried in the affirmative, by a majority of sixteen to six; and the second resolution was then agreed to, on a division of eighteen to four. A bill was immediately prepared, agreeable to the first resolution, and, being read three times, passed the house. Judge Gittens, who had reserved his sentiments to the last stage of the business, opposed the bill, because the saving intended by it was pitiful and impolitic. His excellency, he remarked, had succeeded to the government under circumstances which must necessarily compel him to live at a greater expense than his predecessor had done. He had brought with him, Mr. Gittens said, a strong disposition to exert his interest for the benefit of the colony; and his connexions were such as to afford the best grounded expectations that his efforts would be successful, if they were not obstructed by the ungracious treatment of that house; which, by a mere parade of economy might stop the genial current of his good intentions, and lose the critical moment of obtaining the Royal favour and indulgence.

The bill having been sent up to the other house for their concurrence, was returned with the following extraordinary message: " The council have passed the bill for the better support of his excellency, and the dignity of the government, as they cannot amend a money bill. But they cannot help expressing their concern at the injudicious saving therein established, as offering an indignity to government, and doing discredit to the island." The speaker, attended by the assembly, waited on the governor, and, after an elegant and respectful speech to his excellency, offered the bill for his assent. He had the honour, he said, of presenting his excellency with a free and voluntary gift of the people, in addition to the usual salary from the Crown, which also arose out of the produce of the lands of this unfortunate country: unfortunate, indeed, when the representative body were obliged to appear before his excellency with an offering so much inferior to their inclination and his merit. But such were the melancholy circumstances of the people, that were a faithful representation of their wretched state exhibited to his excellency's view, it would rather serve to shew, that they had nothing to give than to excuse them for not giving more; especially when the disappointment which they had experienced in the expected relief from the heaviest of their burthens, left them destitute of every resource but that of a rigid and determined frugality in the management of the little that remained. Yet, of that little, they freely presented him with a part, and such a part too as, proportioned to their real circumstances, would abundantly testify their high regard for his character, and the affection which his amiable deportment had already kindled in their bosoms.

These expressions of esteem were unable to soothe the vexation of disappointment, or to soften a heart indurated by avarice. His excellency replied, " I find, gentlemen, that you have begun your economical reform with me. I hope you mean to go on with it, as I am persuaded there is an ample field. I flatter myself you will believe, that I shall endeavour to second you in every measure for the advantage of the island; but I shall not give my immediate assent to this bill; because, by your resolve, I am convinced, that your attempt to force ministers into a measure which they are certainly inclined to adopt, is more likely to retard than to forward their good intentions."

A more indiscreet answer could not have been returned. Had the governor concealed his chagrin, and received the settlement with a courtesy equal to the politeness with which it was offered, there is not the shadow of a doubt, that the assembly would soon have displayed their wonted liberality, by an augmentation of the salary. It was a mere vapour of economy, which the sunshine of court favour would soon have dispelled. But, whatever difference of opinion may exist concerning the propriety of reducing the governor's salary, it cannot be denied, that the motives which influenced the majority were laudable. The condition of the country was deplorable and disastrous in the extreme. For a period of seven years, the soil, exposed to frequent droughts of long continuance, had lost its accustomed fertility; and its produce was destroyed by various species of vermin, not less destructive than the vengeful tribes which afflicted the Egyptian territory.

On the back of these physical ills, a train of moral and political evils ensued. The commerce of the country was almost annihilated by swarms of hostile cruizers, which infested the ocean. The negroes were almost starving; and the business of sugar-boiling was greatly impeded, for want of the necessary supplies of lumber and provisions from America. Many of the finest plantations were desolated by the cupidity of rapacious, relentless creditors; the slaves of the industrious planter were sold at public auction for less than half their value, and transported to the Dutch settlements; their buildings were destroyed; and some of the fairest portions of the earth became a barren waste, to

the utter ruin of their once opulent possessors, and the
no less manifest injury of their junior creditors. In this
lamentable state of things, prudence imperatively enjoined
the most rigid economy, both public and domestic. Yet,
on the other hand, when the insignificant advantage which
accrued to each individual by the reduction of the governor's salary, is contrasted with the benefits resulting from a
harmonious union between the respective branches of the
legislature, it is at least problematical, whether such a
trifling frugality was worthy the attention of an enlightened
legislature.

Both houses having met, after the usual adjournment, August 22.
they embraced the opportunity of addressing the governor
in answer to his speech. The address of the council was a
nervous, well-written composition, abounding with professions of attachment to their country, of loyalty and gratitude to the King, and of the most profound respect for his
excellency. That of the assembly was not less respectful
and conciliatory. It acknowledged, in the most grateful
terms, the many instances of his Majesty's paternal care
and goodness, particularly in the early and judicious appointment of a gentleman, of his excellency's character,
to the government of the island; one, in whom the most
respectable and useful military talents were happily united
with such an amiable disposition, as allowed them to expect the exertion of those peculiar powers for their safety,
without any fear of danger to their civil rights. But while

they avowed their obligations to their Sovereign and regard for his representative, the assembly lamented their unfortunate situation, which deprived them of the means of giving his excellency a more substantial mark of their esteem, in the provisions made for the support of his dignity. Yet they indulged the pleasing hope, that they should be enabled, in some more propitious hour, to testify the warmth of their regard to his entire satisfaction. They acknowleged the propriety of attending, as far as may be efficacious, to their internal defence, and promised, agreeably to his excellency's recommendation, to adopt some more practicable plan of rendering their military force effective. But they peremptorily declared their unalterable determination, after the immense sums which they had already voted for the use of the fortifications, to raise no farther supplies for that service, however fatal the consequences might prove to the very preservation of the people. Upon the wonted goodness of his Majesty, and the courage and prowess of the navy, they should trust, under Providence, for protection. They concluded with the assurance, that whatever benefits they might derive from the mildness and equity of his administration, they were sensible they could be happy only as they should be just in rendering his government, as far as depended upon them, easy and happy to him.

It required not the gift of divination to perceive, from the whole tenor of this address, that the germ of generosity was beginning to expand, and that, by proper culture, it would soon have produced the most grateful fruits. But, unluckily, General Cunninghame possessed not the art of cherishing and maturing the tender plant. His rough, unskilful hand, repressed its delicate growth, and blasted its infantine bloom.

With the illnatured design of vexing and embarrassing the assembly, he interrupted their deliberations with peevish messages, proposing new schemes of expense, and conveying a decided censure on the management of the public concerns. A large body of prisoners of war being at that time confined in the common gaol, he represented to the assembly the necessity of providing a place in the interior of the country to which they might be removed, to relieve the inhabitants of the metropolis from the danger of contagious distempers. The house replied, there was no place of sufficient security in the country to which the prisoners could be removed, nor were the inhabitants able to take upon themselves the charge of providing for them. They requested his excellency, therefore, to prevail on the admiral to send them to Europe in the fleet then ready to sail; but, if they were to remain on the island, the assembly apprehended it to be the duty of the commissary to provide for their accommodation, as he received an ample recompense from the Crown for his expense and trouble.

This message was immediately followed by another, purporting, that his excellency had hired a small vessel to

CHAP.XIII. convey intelligence to the naval commander at Saint Lu-
1780. cia, of the surrender of Charles-town; and desiring that the
assembly would provide for the payment of the charter: it
would be difficult to assign any good reason for this being
done; but as the expense did not exceed forty pounds, the
assembly complied with his request. This produced a fresh
demand to pay the salary of a proper officer to be employed
by his excellency to visit flags of truce, and other foreign
vessels, arriving in Carlisle-bay. A prompt compliance with
this requisition evinced the wish of the assembly to gratify
his excellency in all his reasonable desires: they unanimously voted a salary of fifty pounds a year to the person
employed on this service, who was dignified with the title
of captain of the ports*.

The house had just entered upon the consideration of a
bill to provide for the expenses of government for the current year, when they were summoned to attend his excellency in the council chamber. He informed them that he
saw, with astonishment and concern, this respectable colony left with an empty treasury, a magazine without stores,
and a numerous train of distressed creditors. The unavoidable consequences, he remarked, must be the destruction of public credit, and a stagnation of all business.

To guard against the evils incident to such a state, he
urged the passing of a constitutional levy bill. The house

---

* In later times the salary of this officer has been encreased to eighty pounds.

accordingly got through the bill, before they rose, and sent it up to the council for their concurrence. Finding that the bill was repugnant to the royal instructions, on the very point which had been so frequently canvassed, and decided by superior authority, the council rejected it ; and the governor, anxious to have it passed, consulted the attorney and solicitor-general, whose report, with a copy of the instructions, was sent to the assembly; but they were inflexible; they would pass no other levy bill, though the public creditors had not been paid for sixteen months.

Having gone through the whole of the business before them, the house were called upon by Mr. Duke to express a proper resentment at the unparliamentary message received from the council at their former meeting. The happiness of every government, he said, consisted in the undisturbed enjoyment of the constitutional powers belonging to each department. Where a legal privilege was exercised, if abuse or defamation followed, the tendency must be to encroach, to irritate, and to throw the whole system into disorder and confusion. The constitution had entrusted the popular branch of the legislature with the right of raising and disposing of the public money. The power of determining the sum to be raised, and the services to which it should be applied, belonged exclusively to the representatives of the people. Arguments were rendered unnecessary by the council's admission that they could not amend a money bill. But then they could have rejected it. To consent to a measure and to vilify it too was unprecedented in all legislative proceedings. Mr. Duke proved, from the parliamentary records, that the House of Commons would never suffer any aspersion from a peer, even at a free conference, without shewing a suitable resentment, and bringing the offender to condign punishment. What then, he asked, must be the feelings of that assembly on an attack from the whole council, clearly calculated and deliberately contrived to interrupt the good correspondence which ought to exist between the commander in chief and the representatives of the people?

After offering a variety of arguments, to convince the house that they could not, consistently with their own dignity, enter the message on their journals, unaccompanied by a proper animadversion on its irregular and illiberal contents, Mr. Duke moved a resolution to this effect, that the council's message, at their last meeting, respecting the settlement upon the governor, is extraordinary, indecent, and unparliamentary. Extraordinary, that they should give their assent to a measure which they considered to be an indignity to government, and discreditable to the island; indecent, because it casts an illiberal reflection upon the judgment of the assembly, upon a point where the constitution has fixed the right of judging, in the first instance, for the credit, as well as for the interest of the public; unparliamentary, as tending to interrupt that harmony and good will between the governor and the house of assembly, so essential to the happiness and prosperity of the community* ; upon motives beneath the dignity even of upright individuals, and yet more unbecoming the second branch of the legislature. Upon the question being put, the resolution was agreed to, the members for Christchurch alone dissenting ; and a copy of it was sent to the council, who sustained, in sullen silence, the reproof of their indiscretion.

On their next meeting, the assembly received the governor's reply to their address, in answer to the speech, filled with the most insulting reproaches and illiberal invectives. He affected to consider their professions of confidence and esteem among the greatest honours of his life ; and wished that their favourable opinion of him might induce them to render back, to the proper branch of the constitution, the appointment of the treasurer and storekeeper, of which they had usurped the disposal; and which, he was persuaded, was, in a great measure, the source of that profusion of which they so justly complained. He was sorry to observe, that the misfortunes which they attributed to bad seasons, were principally owing to corruption in their present system of government ; and the

---

* The learned member might have found a better reason in *Black. Comm. v.* 1. *p.* 183. It is a rule of parliament, when the house of lords reject a bill, that no further notice is taken of it, but it passes *sub silentio,* to prevent unbecoming altercations.

continual encroachments which they were making on the
executive power, were, he said, partly the cause of that
waste of the public money, so notorious to every unpreju-
diced observer.

He regretted that the exertions which he had made, before he left England, in promoting measures advantageous
to the island, should have been so illiberally requited by
their prescribing terms respecting the settlement, highly
improper for his acquiescence. When they made a provision for him, as the King's representative, they ought,
he told them, to have remembered the necessary expenses
attending his situation, from the high price of every article
of domestic accommodation; and had their donative been
more liberal, he should have thought it incumbent on him
to support his commission with greater dignity. Their fortifications, he affirmed, were inadequate to their defence;
and, though surrounded with danger, they had declared
that they would raise no farther supplies for their own protection; a declaration which could not fail to inspire the
enemy with joy. He earnestly exhorted them to lay aside
that spirit of contention, which, he said, was but too visible
in their proceedings; to live with proper economy, the
only means of retrieving embarrassed circumstances; and
to employ themselves in framing wise laws, on constitutional principles, which would restore credit to their finances, energy to their government, and that lustre to the

island which formerly upheld it, as a model of order and loyalty, to this part of his Majesty's dominions.

Nothing could have been more inconsistent and imprudent, than this illiberal and unparliamentary message. Six weeks had not elapsed, since the governor had commended the assembly for maintaining the character of loyalty to the King, and attachment to the constitution, which had been transmitted to them from their ancestors; and for the preservation of that good order and tranquillity, which proved the wisdom of their councils, undisturbed by violence and faction. Yet no sooner was their conduct seen with the jaundiced eye of disappointment, than its complexion was changed; the government appeared corrupt in its system, and administered with profusion, the legislature seemed employed in continual encroachments on the executive power, and its proceedings actuated by a spirit of contention. Declarations so opposite, and irreconcileable, involved his excellency in this dilemma; either his panegyric was undeserved, and originated in the unworthy motive of effecting his sinister designs by venal adulation, or his subsequent aspersions, were the angry ebullitions of disappointed avarice. Be this as it may, this imprudent step was seriously condemned by Lord George Germaine. " It was a great concern to me," said his lordship, in a letter to Governor Cunninghame, " to find that your answer to the address contained so much matter for contention and ill humour, and some expressions which might be expected to excite resentment in minds already heated, and disposed for inflammation. The address of the assembly certainly did not call for such severe reprehension, and the introduction of new subjects; and besides censuring past transactions in an answer to an address, was irregular."

This intemperate message, which was immediately published, by his excellency's directions, in a common newspaper, produced an instantaneous flame in the house, and destroyed every hope of an amicable termination of the dispute. Fired with resentment, the assembly immediately appointed a committee to prepare a memorial, vindicating themselves against the indecent aspersions of the governor. But when the memorial was presented, in the usual form, his excellency declined receiving it.

Sept. 19.
This paper was drawn up with great temper, moderation, and firmness. To be silent, under the accumulated charges which his excellency had brought against them, the assembly said, might be construed into an acknowledgment of guilt; and to reply, in a manner suited to their sense of the injurious treatment which they had received, was no inconsiderable difficulty in addressing the representative of a Monarch, for whose person they entertained the most inviolable esteem, and to whose government they were attached, by every principle of duty and affection. Considering the governor's remark on the power which they exercised, respecting the treasurer and storekeeper, as a

formal demand of those appointments, they seriously declared that they would never be persuaded to surrender the
right of appointing those officers, which they had holden
from time immemorial, by the peculiar favour and indulgence of the crown *. Nor could they conceive on what
ground his excellency had formed the opinion, equally injurious and unjust, that the right of the assembly, to the
disposal of those offices, was the source of public profusion.
By the laws of the country, all orders for the payment of
money, or the disbursements of stores, must originate with
the commander in chief, in council, consequently the profusion which was the subject of complaint, could not, with
any appearance of justice, be imputed to the assembly.
Equally inexplicable was the assertion, that the misfortunes
which they imputed to bad seasons, were, in a great measure, owing to corruption in the system of government.
But they assured his excellency of their readiness to join
in the most rigid inquisition into the crime, for the two-fold
purpose of procuring reparation of the wrong, and of in-
flicting the most exemplary punishment on the delinquents.

With regard to the charge, that their encroachments on
the executive power were the causes of the waste of the

---

* The members of the assembly succeed to these offices themselves, in a triennial
rotation, as a reward for their legislative services, and farm them to the persons by
whom they are executed at three hundred pounds a year.

public money, they defied the governor to name a single instance in which they had infringed the prerogative or usurped a power not expressly warranted by law; or in which they had exercised their constitutional rights uninfluenced by motives of the purest benevolence, directed to the attainment of some public good. They lamented that the salary of his excellency should still be a subject of altercation, after all that they had humbly and respectfully offered in vindication of the abridgment. Had they given the full weight to the consideration, mentioned by his excellency, of the advanced price of the necessaries of life, knowing how much the people had suffered, for a series of years, from this very cause, they would have been discouraged from making any settlement at all, instead of that which they had made under every disadvantage.

Respecting the fortifications, they attempted to justify their resolutions on the plea of necessity, contending that in the impoverished state of the country, it would be folly and wickedness to impose additional burthens on a people struggling under a load of taxes, which they were unable to bear. Whether in their future conduct they should be so happy as to exhibit such a model of order and loyalty, as in his excellency's opinion might be deemed worthy of imitation, the memorialists could not determine; but they would, at least, furnish an example of integrity and independence becoming the representatives of a free, yet loyal, colony. And they concluded with the assurance, that there was no civil right given them by the laws and constitution of their country, which they would either cease to hold, or cease to exercise, whenever the public welfare called for its exertion.

Whatever censure the message of the governor might have incurred, for its intemperance and inconsistency, it must be confessed, that some of the charges which it contained, were not altogether groundless. The proceedings of the assembly, for nearly a century, had been distinguished by frequent attempts to encroach on the prerogative of the crown, not in the appointment of public officers only, but by endeavouring to usurp an undue controul over the disposal of the public money. These claims had given rise to frequent disputes between the different branches of the legislature, which had been as frequently decided against the assembly. But with regard to the nomination of the treasurer and storekeeper, the point had been formally conceded to them, full seventy years before, by an order of Queen Anne. Under this sanction, they have successively assumed the right of appointing the comptroller of the excise, the harbour-master, an inspector of weights and measures, a gauger of casks in each of the four towns, and twelve inspectors of cotton. I shall not stop to inquire, whether the government is better administered, in consequence of this assumption of executive authority; it is sufficient that it is contrary to the principles of the English constitution. It is a right unknown to the house of commons.

Of the profusion imputed to the government, the proof might easily have been found in every division of the island. The unbounded waste of stores, particularly of gunpowder, was indeed a grievance of no small magnitude; but here, the remedy was in the governor's own hands. No stores could be obtained but by his excellency's order on the store-keeper. Over this department the assembly had no control. An abuse of power is too often the only means by which men of weak and sordid minds display their authority and consequence. At each convivial meeting of the militia officers, their loyalty and patriotism were celebrated at the public expense by the repeated discharge of cannon, not unfrequently exceeding a hundred in number. On these occasions half the quantity of powder, allotted for the charge of each gun, was reserved for the benefit of the chief-gunner.

Mr. Estwick, the colonial agent, was now doomed to feel the weight of the governor's displeasure. His excellency attributed the abridgment of his salary to that gentleman's letter to the committee of correspondence, intimating that General Cunninghame had received instructions from the crown to commute the four and a half duty. Besides this, the agent, as a member of parliament, had rendered himself obnoxious to the ministry by opposing their measures. For these reasons the governor rejected the bill, which had been unanimously passed by both houses, re-appointing Mr. Estwick to the agency. Nothing is more clear than that the right of electing their own agent should be exercised by the council and assembly, independently of the commander in chief. For as it is the duty of that minister to convey to the royal ear the complaints of the people, suffering under the incapacity, tyranny and injustice of their rulers, the governor's veto, in this case, must necessarily supersede and destroy the very end and object of the office.

As a constituent part of the legislature, the governor, it is true, possesses a negative on all acts of the assembly, but this power is given for the purpose of preserving the King's prerogative from invasion; and the agent's bill being of a particular nature, resulting from the peculiar circumstances of the colonial constitution, the right of negation is, at least, questionable. The inference from analogy is decisively against it. In England no bill, and especially a money bill, not affecting the rights of the crown, which had been passed by both houses of parliament, was ever rejected by the King. But what occasion is there for a particular law to appoint an agent? A vote of the house of assembly would be sufficient; and the payment of his salary might be provided for in the annual levy bill, as in the case of the other officers of the house. In the passage of this bill, the governor is generally too much interested to suffer his personal resentment to obstruct it. To preserve the privilege of electing an agent, in conjunction with the council, the assembly resolved to nominate no other person to that office, and to allow Mr. Estwick the usual salary, as if his appointment had been confirmed by the governor.

Matters having now come to an extremity between his excellency and the assembly, both sides prepared for their justification by an appeal to the secretary of state, in whose department the colonies lay. With this view the speaker, by order of the house, transmitted to Mr. Estwick the minutes of their proceedings from General Cunninghame's arrival to their latest meeting, with directions to lay them before Lord George Germaine. At the same time the governor wrote to the noble secretary, complaining of the little harmony which he found subsisting between the council and the assembly. This disagreement, he imputed to the factious designs of Sir John G. Alleyne and Mr. Duke. The influence which the former derived from his talents, probity and disinterestedness, was invidiously ascribed to other causes. His power, the governor said, arose from his being employed as attorney to a number of absentees; and, with a view to his lordship's interfering to abridge that power, he particularly mentioned that Sir John Alleyne acted in that capacity for the Society for the propagation of the Gospel, and for Captain Reynolds*, of the navy, patentee

---

* Afterwards Lord Duice.

of the marshal's office. Hence his lordship would perceive, that those people who ought to strengthen the hands of a governor were encreasing the power of a popular leader, who constantly opposed the measures of government, and was ready, when thwarted in his purposes, to throw every thing into disorder and confusion.

In this letter his excellency congratulated himself on having the advice of two such able lawyers as the attorney and solicitor general*, the former of whom he particularly recommended to his Majesty, and hinted that his salary ought to be encreased and paid by the crown. All the principal offices being vested in patentees, who farmed them out to the highest bidders, was a circumstance, his excellency remarked, which extremely limited the power of a commander in chief, and disabled him from conducting the business of government with energy and effect†. Either deceived himself, or willing to impose upon the credulity of his patron, his excellency proceeded to state that the memorial which he had refused to receive from the assem-

---

* The Hon. W. Moore, the elder; and Charles Brandford, Esquire.

† Among the causes which contributed to lessen the influence of the crown in America, Mr. Stokes, chief justice of Georgia, mentions as one of the most material the fatal practice of bestowing almost every lucrative office in the provinces, that could be exercised by deputy, on persons residing in England. *Stokes's Const. of the Colonies*, p. 138. Hence it would seem that the number of patent offices in the colonies, executed by deputies, is as unfavourable to the regal authority as it is pernicious to the people.

CHAP. XIII. bly had given great offence to people in general; he was
1780. therefore induced to hope, now their ill-humour had
evaporated, that the assembly would consent to pass a
proper levy bill; if not, it would be expedient to dissolve
them; and as, from their absurd conduct, they had lost
their popularity, he entertained the most sanguine expectations of the advantages to be derived from a new
election.

Nothing could have been more fallacious than this representation of the state of the public mind. Nor is it difficult
to conjecture by whom his excellency was misled. The
council of Barbadoes had ever been remarkable for a com_
pliance with the wishes of government. The two leading
members of this board were Mr. Henry Frere and Mr.
Ireneus Moe. Of these the former was haughty, reserved
and austere. With an understanding more solid than
splendid, he possessed an inordinate ambition, which led him
to support the most arbitrary measures of government. A
strenuous advocate for the authority of the crown, he naturally became the opponent of Sir John G. Alleyne, who
was uniformly the noble, erect and zealous assertor of the
rights of the people. Between these competitors for fame
and power, personal animosity had succeeded to political
controversy; and Mr. Frere was generally anxious to embrace any opportunity of piquing and mortifying his popular rival, by an inconsiderate opposition, too often incompatible with the public welfare.

To a sound judgment, Mr. Moe united a brilliant imagination, and a private worth without a stain. Nor is it easy to reconcile, with his respectable character, the part which he bore in supporting Governor Cunninghame's arbitrary and illegal administration. To the counsels of these men, General Cunninghame seems, in a great measure, to have resigned himself; while actuated by a perverted ambition, and an absurd opposition to the patriotic leaders of the assembly, they scrupled not to recommend or sanction the most unjust and pernicious measures.

Finding the door of reconciliation effectually closed, the governor now turned his thoughts to devise some method of compensating himself for the insufficiency of the salary. With this view he claimed of the deputy-secretary certain fees, which, he asserted, had been usually paid to former governors; and which, of late had been absorbed in the secretary's office. Mr. Workman replied, that he did not mean to dispute his excellency's right to the fees in question, but having farmed his office from the patentee, under the impression of his being entitled to them, he should naturally expect a proportionable abatement of the rent, if the office was rendered less valuable by a different appropriation of any part of the profits. The governor was no stranger to the hazard of attacking the host of placemen, who, by virtue of patents from the crown, drain the colonies of their wealth; he therefore abandoned this project, and adopted a scheme, in the execution of which he thought to enrich himself, with greater security, from the spoils of a half ruined people. Having obtained a table of fees which had been taken by Lord Macartney at Grenada, he submitted it to the consideration of the council. The pliant members of that board readily concurred in the mercenary designs of their despotic chief, and agreed to sanction the demand of fees, as a compensation for the inadequacy of the legal settlement, but ventured to disapprove of those which were then proposed, as being too exorbitant.

To give these proceedings some appearance of legality, the opinion of the attorney-general was demanded on these queries, Whether either, and which, of the laws of this island, respecting the fees of public officers, extend to any fees taken, or to be taken, by and for the governor? And whether the establishment of fees, by the governor, with the advice and consent of the council, is, in any respect, a breach or violation of any law of this island now in force? A noble opportunity was here presented to Mr. Moore, of immortalizing his name, by asserting the indubitable rights of the people; and, by checking the infant struggles of despotism, by a candid and upright performance of his professional duty. But, he reported, that the several laws of this island, relating to fees only, extend to inferior officers, and not to the governor; and that his excellency, notwithstanding those laws, may receive all *such fees as he was legally entitled to.* Nor did he know of any law that *expressly*

prohibits the governor from establishing fees for himself,
with the advice of his council. To say nothing of the
ignorance which this opinion betrays of the constitution,
its disingenuousness and sophistry are too obvious to require
illustration.

This report was laid before the council, at their next
sitting, together with a new regulation of fees, which, being more moderate, was approved of by the members present *, who recommended his excellency to claim and
enforce the payment of them, and the secretary was accordingly directed to receive the fees thus settled for his excellency's use. This was the most arbitrary and illegal violation of the rights of the subject, that had ever been committed in any part of the British dominions, since the memorable and fatal attempt of Charles I. to levy ship-money
on the people of England. It was a palpable violation of
the charter, the colonial magna charta, granted to the
Earl of Carlisle; by which it is expressly stipulated, that
the inhabitants of Barbadoes should possess all the liberties, franchises, and privileges of British subjects; and that
no decrees, nor ordinances, should be made to the hurt or
discommodity of any person or persons, either to the binding, constraining, burthening, or taking away their liberty,

---

* These persons were Henry Frere, Ireneus Moe, Robert Brathwaite, John Best,
Joseph Keeling and John Ince, Esquires.

CHAP.XIII. goods, and chattles, otherwise than by laws made with
1780.   their own consent.   It was evidently contrary to the spirit,
if not the letter, of several local statutes*.   Nor was it less
repugnant to the principles of the English constitution.
As the King, says the learned commentator on the laws of
England, may create new titles, so may he create new
offices; but with this restriction, that he cannot create new
offices with new fees annexed to them, nor annex new fees
to old offices; for this would be a tax upon the subject,
which cannot be imposed but by act of parliament†.

What a field was here opened to the council for the display of patriotism.   Selected as the peculiar advisers of the
representative of the crown, had they performed their duty
with fidelity, they would have remonstrated with decent
firmness against the injustice and illegality of the measure;
they would have cautioned the governor against the fatal
tendency of his arbitrary proceedings; and by a steady,
temperate opposition, they would have protected the rights
of the people, maintained the dignity of the legislature,
and shielded his excellency equally from royal indignation
and popular odium.   On the contrary, it must excite the
contempt and astonishment of every mind, susceptible of
social feelings, to know that a body of men, of the first
rank and fortune in the community, should thus pusillani-

---

* Vide Hall's Laws, No. 6, 14, 44, and 55.   † Black. Comment. vol. 1. p. 272.

mously surrender their most inestimable privilege, subvert the laws of their country, and sacrifice the interest of the people at the shrine of despotism.

Nor were the absent members free from blame. The negative merit of not consenting to an oppressive measure, is lessened, if not destroyed, by neglecting to oppose it. The establishment of fees had been already agitated in council; and, knowing that it was to be determined this day, they ought to have attended and signalized themselves by a spirited opposition to the measure. Such a conduct might have been as fortunate as it would have been honourable. A prospect of success might have encouraged some of the other members, not wholly insensible to the calls of honour and duty, to join in the virtuous opposition to tyranny and oppression. No man should be deterred from performing his duty, by an apprehension that his exertions may be unsuccessful. No inconvenience nor disgrace can result from the attempt; but the evil of the omission is not problematical.

The arbitrary and unconstitutional proceedings of the governor and council diffused a general dissatisfaction throughout the country; and recourse was had to every expedient by which the payment of the illegal fees could be evaded. Even the fair sex suffered their patriotism to prevail over their natural delicacy, and submitted to the publication of the banns of marriage, rather than their lovers should yield to the governor's exactions for a license. A more spirited and manly conduct was adopted by Mr. Duke. Having paid

the new fee on the probate of a will, to which he was appointed executor, that intelligent patriot determined to
strike at the root of the evil. Though the governor was
not immediately amenable to the law, Mr. Workman, as
the minister of his tyranny, was liable to punishment.
Duke therefore lodged an information, in writing, with Mr.
R. Beckles and judge Weekes, two justices of the peace,
against the secretary for extortion; and a day was appointed
for hearing the complaint. Anxious to ingratiate himself
at Pilgrim, Weeks informed the governor of the affair, and,
the next day, positively refused to take cognizance of the
offence. Incensed at such servility, Duke withdrew the
complaint with the design of applying to another magistrate. But the dreadful disaster which occurred a few days
after, the important concerns which pressed for immediate
consideration, and, above all, the subsequent illness and
death of that valuable man, put an end to the prosecution.

Though the Barbadians were sinking under the accumulated weight of a complication of evils natural, moral and
political, the measure of their woes was not yet full. They
were now doomed to suffer a calamity, in comparison with
which all the other ills that afflicted them were light and
inconsiderable. A tremendous hurricane, which, with in-
discriminate fury, continued to rage nearly eight-and-forty
hours, with a violence unparalled in the history of the
world, threatened them with universal ruin. This was one

of those awful visitations of Providence, whose irresistible force humbles the pride of man, and shews him his absolute dependance on the mercy of that God, who " rides in the whirlwind and directs the storm."

On the morning of Tuesday, the fatal tenth of October, the inhabitants were early alarmed by the unusual violence of the wind, accompanied with heavy falls of rain. The winds, which blew from the north-west, continued hourly to increase; and, before noon, many houses in different parts of the island were either blown down or materially injured. By the third hour of the afternoon, all the vessels in Carlisle bay were forced from their moorings and wrecked; or driven to sea to encounter the horrors and perils of that dangerous element, under circumstances of aggravation, that appalled the hearts of the most fearless and experienced mariners. Nor was the situation of those on shore less hazardous and deplorable. The fury of the tempest encreased with the approach of night; and a scene of terror and distress awaited the ruined and dismayed inhabitants in the dread hour of darkness, of which no powers of language can convey an adequate idea. About the ninth hour of the evening the storm had attained its utmost height, and from that time till four the next morning the work of destruction was accomplished. Within that dreadful interval the whole island was devastated, and its unsheltered inhabitants were reduced to the last extremity of misery and despair.

Early in the evening the cattle had, in some places, broken from their folds, and with dismal bellowings sought refuge among the habitations of men. But these, alas! afforded a doubtful shelter to their possessors; who, to save themselves from being crushed to death, or, which was more horrible, from a premature interment under their falling mansions, fled for safety to the open fields. Each, ignorant of the other's fate, thought his neighbour more fortunate than himself; and, flying from certain death beneath his own crumbling walls, sought an asylum, which, in that universal scene of desolation, was no where to be found. The author of this narrative was himself, with his wife grievously contused by the fall of his house, and an infant daughter, only six months old, among the midnight wanderers, who traversed the dreary waste in search of an uncertain place of shelter and repose. The fairest female forms, stripped of their drapery by the ruthless blast, passed the dismal night, exposed, almost in a state of perfect nudity, to the inclemency of contending elements; while their weeping parents and affectionate husbands, in all the agonies of sympathizing tenderness, ineffectually strove to shield them from the pelting of the pitiless storm.

But the towns exhibited, if possible, greater scenes of horror and distress. Here the sufferings of individuals were augmented by a participation in the general calamity; and the cry which assailed the ear, and the havoc which met the eye, contributed to sudue the firmest mind. The howling of the tempest; the noise of descending torrents from clouds surcharged with rain; the incessant flashings of lightning; the roaring of thunder; the continual crash of falling houses; the dismal groans of the wounded and the dying, the shriek of despair, the lamentations of woe; and the screams of women and children calling for help on those whose ears were now closed to the voice of complaint, formed an accumulation of sorrow and of terror, too great for human fortitude, too vast for human conception.

The return of light served but to render visible to the wretched Barbadians the extent of the calamity in which they had been overwhelmed. Far as the eye could reach, one general scene of devastation presented itself to the sight. The face of nature seemed completely changed. That beautiful scenery, which had so recently delighted the admiring traveller with the variegated bloom of perennial spring, had, in the short space of one night, vanished like the illusive vision which mocks the imagination of the unconscious sleeper. Those luxuriant fields, which the day before teemed with nature's most valuable productions, now resembled the dreary, inhospitable regions, which had never yielded to the arts of cultivation. Trees which, from their bulk and strength, seemed to be little less than of antediluvian growth, were torn up by their roots, or stripped of their foliage, and their ponderous limbs scattered

CHAP.XIII. to an incredible distance. But the amazing force of the
1780.   winds and waves was particularly demonstrated at Bridge-
town, in the removal of a cannon of twelve pound ball from
the pier head to the wharf on the opposite side, a distance
of one hundred and forty yards.* The crops of canes and
corn were destroyed; buildings, strong as human art could
make them, were levelled with the earth, and of the few
which were left standing on the plantations none were free
from material injury. To encrease the calamity, the poultry, live stock and horned cattle, so essential to aid the
planter's labour, had perished in considerable numbers; and
many respectable families were left to sustain the unex-
hausted fury of the storm without raiment, food, or shelter. Speight's-town, though materially injured, fortunately
suffered less than any other part of the island. The Hole-
town and Ostin's participated in the general havoc; and
of eleven churches and two chapels only three were left
standing; these were Saint Andrew's and St. Peter's
churches, and All Saints' chapel.

It was in Bridge-town, however, that the destruction of
property, and the distress of the people, exhibited, by their
concentration, the most lively and affecting spectacles of

---

* Annual Register, vol. 24. p. 32, where it is stated on the authority of the governor's letter to the secretary of state.

human misery. That extensive capital which, for splendour and opulence, was inferior to no town in the British West Indies, was converted into a promiscuous mass of ruins. Not more than thirty houses and stores were left standing, and most of these had suffered considerable damage. The mole-head, a work of great utility, which had cost the country more than twenty thousand pounds, was destroyed; and the bason entirely filled up with sand, stones, and pieces of timber. It was owing to the obstruction given by the pier to the progress of the waves, which rushed with impetuous violence against it, that Bridge-town was preserved from total annihilation. The castle, forts, and batteries, the town-hall and prison, were all demolished. The spacious church of Saint Michael's, with its lofty steeple, was tumbled to the foundation in one confused heap of ruins.

The elegant and stately mansion at Pilgrim, the seat of government, escaped not the general destruction. There every precaution had been early adopted, which seemed likely to afford security against the impending danger. But no human strength nor art could avail. The resistless violence of the wind bore down every obstacle; and soon forced its way into every apartment. One wing, and great part of the other, having been blown down, the governor and his family retired to the centre, where, from its circular form, and the thickness of the walls, they expected to find safety.

But they were disappointed; the roof was blown off, and the continual falling of the stones compelled them to fly for shelter to the cellars; hence they were soon dislodged by the irruption of the water which flowed in with an alarming impetuosity. No alternative was now left but to seek a precarious security in the open fields. The governor, and those who had strength to resist the force of the winds, after being frequently thrown down and rolled in the mire, got under the carriages of the cannon on the platform at Pilgrim. In this situation they remained during the continuance of the storm, in continual apprehension that the cannon, which were violently rocked by the wind, would be dismounted, and crush them in their fall.

The superb residence of the commander in chief of his Majesty's forces having been early blown down, General Vaughan and his family experienced a full share of the dangers and disasters of that long night of horror; his secretary's thigh was broken, nor did the general himself escape without receiving several severe contusions. Though the barracks and hospital were destroyed, such were the happy effects of order and discipline, that, the troops sustained no considerable loss; almost the whole of the provisions and stores designed for the use of the army and navy were fortunately preserved from the fury of the elements and the rapine of the negroes.

The loss of human lives was proportioned to the dangers which surrounded the affrighted inhabitants. Even among the whites the number was considerable, and, including the blacks, who were most exposed, the loss was estimated to exceed three thousand. It was impossible, however, to be accurate in the melancholy enumeration. Besides the wretched victims who perished from the violence of the tempest and the inclemency of the weather, many were crushed to death and intombed in the ruins of their houses, many were swept away by the resistless force of the waves, and were seen or heard of no more; and not a few were precipitated into eternity by the rapid course of the rivers and streams of fresh water which poured into the sea. The loss of property sustained on this memorable occasion was more correctly ascertained, and amounted, according to the returns made to the governor by the vestries of the several parishes to the enormous sum of one million eighteen thousand nine hundred and twenty-eight pounds sterling.

Those who had survived the tragic catastrophe were still exposed to dangers scarcely less imminent than those which they had recently escaped. The general devastation had deprived them of their internal resources, and exhibited to their view the terrific prospect of famine. Availing themselves of the consternation which prevailed, the slaves, instead of assisting their owners, or endeavouring to save the effects of the unhappy sufferers, were actively employed in plundering them of the poor remains of property which had been spared by the hurricane. A body of eight hundred prisoners of war had been liberated by the demolition of the gaol, and the most serious apprehensions were entertained that these men, in conjunction with the licentious slaves, would complete what the rage of the elements had left unfinished. But, fortunately for the Barbadians, General Vaughan, with a body of troops, was at hand, ready to repress any disorder, or to check any attempt on the public safety, and probably prevented the consummation of their ruin. From this gallant commander and his veteran corps, the inhabitants received the most effectual protection, and every humane assistance which their forlorn and destitute condition required. And to the immortal honour of Don Pedro de Saint Jago, captain of the regiment of Arragon, and the Spanish prisoners under his direction, let it be remembered with gratitude, that, laying aside all national animosity in that season of calamity, they omitted no service nor labour for the relief of the distressed inhabitants and the preservation of public order.

From the number of dead bodies lying in the streets, and among the ruins, and the quantity of putrid fish thrown up by the sea, no unreasonable apprehensions were entertained that a pestilence would ensue. To avert this evil, among other necessary purposes, the merchants of Bridge-town formed an association, and appointed committees for the interment of the dead, and the distribution of provisions for the re-

lief of their indigent fellow-sufferers. Nor were they un-
mindful of the services rendered them by the troops. They
voted their thanks to General Vaughan and the officers of
the army, and a gratuity of sixpence per diem to the privates, as an acknowledgment for protecting their property
from rapine and plunder.

The humanity of the Marquis de Bouillè should not be
forgotten. The Laurel and Andromeda frigates having
been wrecked on the coast of Martinico, that magnanimous
commander sent thirty-one English sailors, who were all
that were saved out of both crews, under a flag of truce to
Commodore Hotham, at Saint Lucia, with a letter purporting that he could not consider in the light of enemies, men who had escaped in a contention with the
elements; but that they, in common with his own people, having been partakers of the same danger, were, in
like manner, entitled to every comfort and relief which
could be given in a season of such universal calamity and
distress.

What a contrast does this act of generosity in a noble
enemy afford to the conduct of Governor Cunninghame.
Amid the general convulsion of the Caribbean sea, a small   Oct. 12.
Spanish launch, having a few mules on board, sought security from the winds and waves in Maycock's bay. The
matrosses detained her until the governor's pleasure was
known; and his excellency ordered her to be seized as a

CHAP.XIII. droit of admiralty, made the crew prisoners of war, and

1780. converted the vessel and cargo to his own use. Thus what the wretched mariners had saved from the angry elements was torn from them by the rapacity of a human being, insensible of the tender emotions of pity and compassion!

CHAP. XIV.

ADDRESSES FROM THE LEGISLATURE TO THE THRONE.—EXTRA-
ORDINARY PROPOSAL TO SUSPEND THE PROCEEDINGS OF JUS-
TICE.—PETITION TO THE KING FOR THE GOVERNOR'S RE-
MOVAL.—HIS EXCELLENCY PERSEVERES IN HIS ARBITRARY
AND ILLEGAL MEASURES.

THE bitter affliction with which Providence had visited the Barbadians had not softened the obdurate heart of the governor. Suffering under a disaster so general and so fatal to all ranks of people, it was natural for them to expect that his excellency would have taken the earliest opportunity of convoking the legislature, that the public might enjoy the benefit of their collective wisdom, in a case of such uncommon difficulty and distress. But to shew his utter contempt of the assembly, and, perhaps, with the hope of impressing their sovereign with an unfavourable opinion of them at this awful conjuncture, he summoned the council only, for the purpose of framing an address to the king on the late ruinous event. With the strongest assurances of inviolate attachment to his Majesty's person and

CHAP. XIV.

1780.

government, they humbly besought his gracious attention to their wretched condition. After a series of accumulated misfortunes had reduced this once flourishing island to the lowest degree of poverty, a devastating hurricane had now, they feared, completed the destructive work. Destitute of resources to repair their fallen habitations, or even to procure the materials required for reaping their crops, they were left without any prospect of alleviation to their distress, but in the benignity of his Majesty's compassionate disposition, and those endearing feelings which had taught the world, that in the same person may be united the great and powerful monarch with the good and amiable man. They concluded, with imploring such relief as his Majesty in his wisdom and goodness should judge proper to afford them.

This petition was accompanied by a letter from the governor to Lord George Germaine, containing a recital of the particulars of the dreadful calamity in which the country had been involved. Many years, he remarked, must elapse before the injury which the planters had sustained could be repaired; and he was apprehensive that the proprietors of the soil would be unable to rebuild their houses and sugar-works, so deeply were they indebted to the merchants of England. He particularly suggested to his lordship's attention, the necessity of supplying the colony with provisions from Europe, as, without the bounty and generosity of the best of kings, the people would be in the most imminent danger of starving. Nor was General Vaughan silent on this melancholy occasion. In his dispatches to the se- cretary of state, that distinguished officer concluded an affecting representation of the general ruin and distress, with a pathetic appeal to his lordship's feelings on behalf of the inhabitants of this ruined country, assuring him that a famine must inevitably ensue, unless some effectual means were employed, on the part of government, to prevent it.

The assembly having been, at length, permitted to meet, October 31. pursuant to adjournment, the speaker suggested to the house the propriety of embracing that opportunity of addressing the King, and supplicating his Majesty's gracious assistance under their present exigencies. He regretted that they had not been allowed to concur with the council in a joint address to the throne, but that the house might not appear inattentive to their duty, on an occasion so interesting, he submitted to their consideration an address to his Majesty, which he had prepared for the purpose. It was of course unanimously agreed to, and ordered to be transmitted to the agent to be presented. Mr. Estwick was at the same time directed to renew his application to the ministry to relieve the country from the payment of the four and a half per cent. duty; and for the establishment of a free port, as the most probable means of rescuing it from ruin, and restoring it to its former prosperity.

Notwithstanding the governor's just and affecting representation of the deplorable effects of the hurricane, his first proposition to the assembly was the imposition of fresh bur-thens on an afflicted people, who, according to his own account, transmitted to the secretary of state only ten days before, were in a great measure deprived of procuring food or shelter. As soon as the house had sat, he sent down a message, informing them that he had omitted to convene them on the late dreadful calamity, knowing how much every man must be occupied by his domestic concerns. He tauntingly recommended unanimity in their proceedings at this trying conjuncture, to frame a proper levy bill, and to put their fortifications in a suitable posture of defence. Pilgrim house, he told them, was uncovered, the armory destroyed, and that he had been at considerable expense for labourers to preserve the arms, lumber, and materials; and hoped that the assembly would give directions for repairing the buildings at Pilgrim. He concluded with recommending their passing a law to restrain the high price of workmen and labourers, and assured them of his readiness to concur in any measure for the public welfare.

To this message the assembly replied, that, notwithstanding the pressure of their private concerns, they would willingly have attended an earlier call of public duty, especially at the time his excellency summoned the council. Such, they observed, was the melancholy situation of the bulk of the people, that the little property which had been spared by the storm must necessarily be appropriated to their subsistence, and the rebuilding of their fallen habitations. For this reason, the assembly declined passing a levy bill, or incurring any expense for the repairs of the fortifi- cations. They, however, readily consented to put Pilgrim house in as comfortable a state of accommodation as exist- ing circumstances would allow, and to provide for the secu- rity of the arms which had been exposed to injury by the demolition of the armory.

This message was immediately succeeded by another, requiring the assembly to provide for guarding the prison- ers of war, and for preserving the peace of the island, as the troops would shortly be withdrawn. The house replied, that they knew of no place of sufficient security to lodge the prisoners ; nor could they consent to increase the pub- lic burthens, by raising a body of men capable of guard- ing them, in places so open and insecure as all were at that moment. They, therefore, requested, that the prisoners might be sent away with the troops, or that the proper agent would provide flags of truce for their removal.

A bill of a very extraordinary nature was introduced at this sitting by Judge Gittens, for the purpose of suspend- ing the proceedings of the courts of justice, and of the marshal's office, for a limited term of years. From the novelty of the measure, it is but fair to hear the arguments by which it was supported. The learned judge remarked, that the common ruin in which all ranks of people were in- volved, and the complete desolation which overspread the face of the country, called for the interposition of the le-

gislature to alleviate, as much as possible, the miseries of
the inhabitants, and to revive the sinking spirits of those
who had escaped with little more than their lives. Something, he said, ought to be done, to calm the mind, and
assuage the anguish of the desponding debtor, who otherwise must seek some other friendly shore, where he might
reap, in security, the reward of his labour. With this view
he had introduced the bill in his hand, calculated, as he
said, in this hour of calamity, to brighten the clouded
prospect, and give confidence and assurance to the honest
and industrious, to look forward to days of comfort and
times more propitious, when the bread of carefulness should
not be snatched from their mouths by the rapacious claims
of an unfeeling creditor.

From this general view of the subject, the honourable
mover proceeded to an examination of the separate clauses
of the bill, which, he asserted, were self-evident propositions deduced from facts. Nor could the timid creditor,
he insisted, have just cause of alarm at a measure which
would only deprive him of his power, for a while, to be
restored, with redoubled vigour and effect, at a period
when he may exercise it with greater advantage to himself,
than at a season when nothing but a wild waste of ruins
lay before him. To the elder creditor, he concluded, it
would only operate as a renewed defeasance, with the
prospect of better security; and to the junior creditor it
was such an act alone that could give hope, and keep alive

his expectations, which would otherwise sink into a gloomy
despondency.

The second reading of the bill was ably opposed by Sir John Gay Alleyne. He commenced an eloquent, argumentative speech, with observing, that the feelings of compassion, like all other affections of the human soul, ought to be regulated by the principles of natural justice; and that even the love of his country, however ardent, must yield to those superior obligations. He could not consent to countenance a measure which tended to establish an unworthy and an unwarrantable distinction between the landholder and the other classes of society, who were all entitled to the equal protection of wise and equitable laws. No partial regard to the embarrassments of men of landed property should ever influence the deliberations of that house; there were others who ought to be considered with an equal degree of tenderness. The man who had no other property than money lent out at interest, and who, by the late dreadful visitation from heaven, was probably deprived of a place of rest and shelter, ought not to be excluded from the benefit which the law had given him of procuring a habitation, or food for his family. In this class there were many young ladies whose whole fortune consisted in debts and legacies, and who, perhaps, had been left by the storm, with no other cloaths than those on their backs. Shall the condition of these helpless females, he asked, be rendered more destitute by a law, that would deprive them of the means of procuring the decent habiliments of their sex? Neither could the merchants and tradesmen of the several town, sharers in the common calamity, be debarred, without injustice, from recovering what was due to them, for their immediate subsistence, or the support of that credit on which their mercantile existence depended. Still less should those, who, in their several departments and professions, earn their livelihood by their manual labour, their learning, or their mental ingenuity, be denied the legal right of enforcing their just demands to enable them to rebuild their houses, and to furnish themselves with food and raiment.

Nor did Sir John Alleyne think the bill calculated for the real and permanent advantage of those whom it favoured most, unless it were those whose debts exceeded the value of their property. None others could benefit by a suspension of justice. But to pass an act which should afford debtors, of this description, an opportunity of enjoying their plantations a few years longer, to the prejudice of their creditors, would be to establish iniquity by law. To debtors of every other class, the honourable baronet contended, the bill would eventually prove injurious, as it must effectually destroy all confidence in those whose unfortunate circumstances more particularly required credit to enable them to repair their works, and restore their plantations to a proper state of cultivation. Sir John Alleyne offered a variety of arguments to prove, that the operation

of the bill would not only be prejudicial to those for whose
benefit it was intended, but that it would be inconsistent
with the honour of that house, and injurious to the character of the country.

On the resumed consideration of the bill, its principle
was judiciously combated by Mr. Duke. A country, he
observed, in which the course of justice was obstructed by
law, could be no eligible place for the residence of men.
From such a society all confidence, credit and commerce,
must be banished. It must want support from without,
and be destitute of cement within. The venerable speaker
of the assembly again exerted his patriotic eloquence in
supporting the claims of justice; and, rather than suffer
any imputation on his good faith, moved an additional
clause, excluding himself, by name, from any benefit to
be derived from the operation of the law. The integrity of
Mr. Husbands was eminently displayed in his opposition to
this measure. By a train of misfortunes, he had been almost reduced to a state of insolvency; but his liberal mind
was incapable of entertaining a wish to oppugn the claims
of his creditors by an act, palpably inconsistent with every
idea of public faith. Being without a horse, though he
had a considerable property in possession, he walked with
great firmness, a distance of several miles, to attend the assembly, and give his negative to the bill. But finding the
powerful opposition which he had to encounter, Mr. Gittens withdrew the bill without putting it to the vote.

With the view of harassing and irritating the assembly, the governor now had recourse to weekly adjournments, which, as most of the members resided at a distance from Bridge-town, subjected them to much inconvenience and fatigue. The recent calamity had prevented the assembly, at their last meeting, from taking any notice of the governor's unprecedented and illegal demand of fees. Indeed it was supposed, that the universal devastation with which he was surrounded would have softened his heart, and restrained his cupidity from grasping at what even the fury of the elements had spared. But, finding that he persisted in his unconscionable exactions, and that many extravagant fees had been paid for his use, Mr. Duke, in a speech fraught with legal and constitutional knowledge, called upon the house to assert the rights of the people. He lamented that, in a season of no ordinary calamity, he should be obliged to bring forward a subject of altercation; but they owed it to their own dignity; they owed it to posterity, amidst all their distresses, to guard the constitution from invasion. The assembly, he observed, were the guardians of the people, chosen not merely for the purpose of making laws, but to watch over and preserve inviolate the rights and privileges of the commons of Barbadoes. The conduct of all public offices was subject to their cognizance. It was their province to bring to justice all offenders who could not otherwise be made amenable to the common course of law. The records of parliament furnished, he

said, innumerable instances of impeachments and prosecutions by the house of commons, not only against the
highest ministers of state, but extending even to the subordinate officers of the courts of justice.

The principal branch of their jurisdiction, Mr. Duke admitted, was to guard the money of the subject, and to prevent its being taken away without the sanction or authority
of the legislature; and this was the very grievance of which
he was then to complain. The governor and council had,
contrary to law and usage, established a table of fees, to
be taken by the secretary of the island, for his excellency's
use, in all cases throughout the whole circle of business in
which his name was employed. From a review of the history of the mother country, from the reigns of the Stuarts
to the time of the Revolution, Mr. Duke proved, that the
levying of money, without the consent of parliament, had
been repeatedly and solemnly declared illegal. This being
the case with the King, it could not be supposed that the
servants, or ministers of the Crown, should be left at liberty
to oppress the subject by such arbitrary and unwarrantable
means.

In this island the money of the people had ever been the
first and favourite object of legislative care and concern.
Not only taxes for the support of government require the
concurrence of the three estates before they can be levied,
but the fees of the public offices, which are virtually a tax,
had been fixed and prescribed by law, and the penalties

annexed to the demand of higher fees than those established by that authority were sufficient, he asserted, to deter the officer from the commission of the offence. He then proceeded to shew that the commander in chief was not entitled, by law or custom, to the receipt of fees; and that the addition made by the colonial legislature to the salary allowed by the Crown, was granted upon that implied condition. After vindicating the settlement made upon General Cunninghame, by arguments drawn from the impoverished condition of the country, he quoted several local statutes to prove, that no old fees could be altered, nor new ones established, otherwise than by the united authority of the governor, council and assembly. Yet his excellency and the council, in direct contravention of the most positive laws, had presumed, of their own will and pleasure, to arrange and settle a new table of fees, which had been announced by a formal declaration, in writing, at the secretary's office. Embracing a wide extent of public business, these fees affected the administration of justice, and added weight to an expense already too burthensome to admit of augmentation.

Such illegal exactions, Mr. Duke observed, bore harder on the subject, in proportion to the rank and consequence of the oppressors, because the people were discouraged from applying to the law for redress, and every fresh instance of extortion, although but a repetition of iniquity, served to give it a sort of sanction. Hence it would happen, unless the assembly would interpose, that a toleration of a most nefarious practice would soon assume the name of custom, and then of law. When the public welfare was at stake, he thought the assembly should not only be ready to lay down their political existence, but even to sacrifice their natural lives in opposition to fraud and violence. He mentioned the case of Mr. Wilkes and Lord Halifax as an instance of a successful struggle against illegal power, supported by a train of precedents for eighty years; and thence inferred, that the authority given Mr. Workman to demand the fees in dispute, could no more justify his receiving them than the authority of the secretary of state could protect the messengers who executed his warrant against Mr. Wilkes. Indeed it was so much the weaker, because it was unsupported by a shadow of usage; nor could it derive any strength from the nature of the government, nor the policy of the measure, as it was simply a scheme of public plunder and peculation.

" For every wrong," continued Mr. Duke, " there is a remedy, and the immediate instrument of that wrong acts at his peril. Exclusive of the penalties created by the colonial statutes, Mr. Workman, as the governor's agent, can be made to refund every shilling which he had received over and above his lawful fee. If he withhold papers after a legal tender of the established fee, an action lies against him at common law; and, should any special damage arise, a jury cannot fail to make him answerable, by their verdict. He might not only be stripped of his office, but rendered incapable of holding any other; and, by prosecution and conviction at a criminal court, he may be stamped with the ignominious appellation of an extortioner, and undergo such farther punishment as the court may think adequate to his crime." To be a slave or tool, the learned gentleman remarked, was allowed to be no justification. The act of every man was, in the contemplation of the law, deemed to be his own. The governor and council could neither compel nor authorize the secretary to rob and oppress the people. With equal propriety might they direct him to attack their lives as their properties. One was as much under the protection of the law as the other; and the restraints of the law operate as effectually upon the governor and council as upon the meanest member of the community.

It was unnecessary, he said, to demonstrate that the governor and council possessed no dispensing power over the laws; such a power was unknown to the King himself. Neither was it necessary to shew that the new fees would operate as a tax upon the people, and therefore required the united authority of the three branches of the legislature to legalize them; these points were so obvious as to require no illustration. Much, Mr. Duke said, might be urged against the establishment of new fees in any case. The great reason for the repcal of the stamp act was its tendency to obstruct the progress of business, and to impose restraints and fetters on the commerce of the colonies. He would not insist upon the pernicious influence of fees and the multiplication of offices. No policy could be more evident than that the seat of government, the fountain of justice, ought not to be polluted and degraded by that species of traffic. If the governor and council had a right to establish fees, they could occasionally increase them till they became a source of vexation and oppression. If they could raise and appropriate money in one instance, their authority equally extended to all others; the functions of the assembly were rendered useless, and nothing remained that the people could justly call their own.

Mr. Duke referred to a variety of authorities to establish his position, that the Crown had not a right to create new offices with profits annexed to them, to be paid by the people, and cited a case of an office having been granted by letters patent, to one Poley, for measuring worsteads, with a new fee; but the house of commons resolved that it was void, for that the King could erect no offices with fees to be taken of the people, who could not be legally charged but by parliament; and judgment was afterwards given against the patent in the king's bench. The conclusion is invincible. A colonial governor and council could not legally exercise a power, which did not belong to their Sovereign. In the case of conquered countries, it was admitted, that a difference might exist. Over these the King possessed a plenitude of power. But in colonies settled by

Englishmen, neither the Sovereign, nor his representative, could exercise any jurisdiction incompatible with the constitutional birth-rights of the subject.

After a variety of arguments, tending to prove that the governor and Mr. Workman had been guilty of extortion, interspersed with some strictures on the servility of the council, as harsh as they were just, Mr. Duke concluded a luminous display of legal erudition, with moving nine resolutions: 1. That any other demand of fees, than such as have been prescribed by law, is illegal, and subjects the offender to punishment. 2. That no public officer, on the tender of such fees as are conformable to law, can refuse to perform the business, or withhold the papers, for which such fees are directed to be paid, without being guilty of an offence and misdemeanor in the execution of his office. 3. That a requisition to pay fees, on any pretence whatever, without, or contrary to, the establishment of the legislature, is highly injurious to the subject, an arbitrary and illegal levying of money, subversive of the constitutional rights of the people, and a dangerous encroachment on the peculiar privileges of the general assembly. 4. That no new fees can be claimed, nor allowed, without the joint consent of the governor, council and assembly. 5. That the governor and council, in undertaking to settle a new table of fees, to be paid for his excellency's use, had acted illegally and unconstitutionally. 6. That the fees thus established are not obligatory on the inhabitants of the island. 7. That the assembly will aid and assist all persons who may be aggrieved by the novel demand of fees, or who shall be obstructed in a due course of law, to enforce the penalties on all public officers who shall offend against the laws respecting fees. 8. That an humble petition be presented to the King, beseeching his Majesty to remove Major General James Cunninghame from the government of the island, on account of his oppressive conduct in extorting money from the people, contrary to law and the rights of the legislature. 9. That the conduct of such member's of his Majesty's council, as have concurred in the governor's arbitrary and illegal exactions, be represented to his Majesty, and that he be humbly requested to shew such marks of his royal displeasure towards them as the nature of their crime may deserve.

To prevent the house from coming to any decision on the motion, Mr. R. B. Jones moved the previous question, in order that they might have time to search for precedents, as to the legitimacy of the fees. But, his motion being negatived by a large majority, the question was put on each resolution separately, and carried in the affirmative. Mr. Jones having declined giving his vote, the opposition devolved on Judge Gittens, Judge Walcott, Mr. Burke and Mr. Burton, who voted uniformly against all the resolutions. To the eighth and ninth, Mr. W. G. Alleyne gave his negative; and Mr. J. C. Cox shewed his partiality to the council, by confining his vote to the last. A petition,

framed on the two latter resolutions, was accordingly introduced, and, having been agreed to, on a division of eleven
to six, the speaker was directed to sign it, and transmit it
to the agent, to be presented to the King.

The petition began with stating that, with hearts devoted
to his Majesty's interest, and with the strongest attachment
to his person and government, the assembly were constrained, with grief and sorrow, to supplicate the gracious
interposition of the royal authority, to protect the rights
and liberties of the inhabitants of the island, much injured
and affected by an order of the governor and council, establishing new and oppressive fees for his excellency's use; to
which no former governor, however arbitrary and rapacious,
ever formed pretensions in the most prosperous times. But
at this unhappy juncture, when the people were ill able to
bear even the necessary taxes, to impose upon them new
and illegal burthens and exactions, was adding cruelty to
injustice. Nor could they see, without the deepest concern, his Majesty's sacred name and delegated authority,
prostituted to the mean and sordid purpose of raising a revenue for the governor, to the great oppression of his Majesty's dutiful and loyal subjects, contrary to the ancient
laws and statutes of Great Britain, which forbid the taking
any fee, gift or brokage, on the disposal of places and offices; contrary to the ancient charter of liberties, which
provides that justice shall not be sold; contrary to immemorial usage, and subversive of the principles of the Eng-

lish constitution; and in direct opposition to an express law of the land, confirmed by regal authority, which reserves the right of creating fees to the legislative body of the island. Thus circumstanced, the assembly were driven to apply to their beloved Sovereign for redress of these unmerited and unexampled usurpations, tending to take from the legislative body the right of raising taxes and appropriating the public money; and to bestow on the governor and council a suspending power over the laws of the island, and the constitutional rights of the people. The petitioners therefore besought his Majesty, in compassion to his loyal and oppressed colony, to remove General James Cunninghame from the government; and to shew such marks of his royal displeasure towards those counsellors, who had concurred in the governor's proceedings, as his Majesty in his great wisdom and fatherly affection, to his aggrieved and distressed subjects, should deem them to deserve.

Notwithstanding the temper and moderation of this address, the noble secretary for the American department remarked, on receiving it from the agent, that it was written with great heat and anger, and seemed to assume the part of judge, jury, and executioner. The most exceptionable passage was the prayer for the removal of Governor Cunninghame. But the language was perfectly parliamentary; and it had been the fortune of Lord George Germaine himself, not infrequently, to oppose motions, in the

House of Commons, expressed in similar terms, for the removal of his Majesty's ministers from his presence and councils for ever. His lordship, however, in his conversation with Mr. Estwick, very freely condemned the governor's conduct. If, said he, the assembly had given him but five hundred a year, he ought to have accepted it, and instead of keeping his carriage, and living with the splendour of a commander in chief, he might have rode his horse and lived like a planter. Lord George utterly disclaimed the governor's acting under his instructions with respect to fees; and admitted that, if they were taken contrary to the laws of the island, he had done wrong in demanding them. The petition, having been presented to his Majesty, was, by his commands, referred to the consideration of the Lords Commissioners for trade and plantations, by whom a copy of it was sent to the governor, with an order to transmit his vindication.

Though the governor was convinced, from the effects of the late destructive storm, that the country was unable to bear any augmentation of his salary, he determined to make another effort. For this purpose he summoned the assembly to meet on the twenty-eighth day of November, when he laid before them a letter which he had received from the secretary of state, with a copy of his Majesty's instruction concerning the salary, which had been shewn to them on his arrival. The secretary's letter expressed his Majesty's disapprobation of the settlement on his excellency, and his displeasure at the stipulation made by the assembly, in the event of the country being exonerated from the impost on their exportable commodities, and concluded with a hope, that they would now consent to grant his excellency an additional thousand pounds.

The production of these papers gave rise to a warm and animated debate, in the course of which Mr. Husbands insisted that their loyalty on various occasions had been so amply displayed as to require no farther proof. He defined true loyalty to consist in a due obedience to the laws, and a zealous support of the constitution; but a mean compliance with every unreasonable demand of government, he asserted, was not loyalty, but a slavery of the worst kind, a slavery of the mind. He professed himself an enemy to the former resolution respecting the conditional encrease of the governor's salary, and thought that it ought to be rescinded. But he gloried in having voted for the reduction of the salary; he had done so, because the circumstances of the people required the greatest frugality in the public expenditure; and because a reformation could be begun no where with more propriety than at the head. He had given that vote without fearing the displeasure of ministers, nor should he retract it now he knew they were displeased. A minister, whose private fortune and emoluments of office, enabled him to spend more thousands annually than the whole amount of the colonial revenue, and who disposed of millions of the public money in a year, could neither know nor feel the distresses of the inhabit-ants of the island; but the members of that house felt them, and knew that a thousand pounds a year was no in-considerable saving in the public expense. Had Governor Cunninghame answered the character which partial friend-ship, or servile flattery, had given of him on his arrival; and had not the late dreadful calamity befallen the coun-try, they might have been induced, they said, to pay some attention to the present demand for an increase of salary. But after the treatment that house had experienced from his excellency; after the unjust and injurious aspersions which he had cas ton them; after the indignity offered them, in refusing to receive the memorial in their vindication; af-ter his unconstitutional attempt to tax the people by esta-blishing new and oppressive fees, Mr. Husbands contended, that they could not consent to augment the salary without a forfeiture of their honour, and a violation of the trust re-posed in them.

In explanation of their former resolution, the house una-nimously resolved, that it never was intended, as a condition with the minister for the remission of the four and a half per cent. duty, but was merely designed for the considera-tion of the council. A second resolution was also moved by Mr. V. Jones, that in the present situation of the coun-try, afflicted by the hand of God, and subject to illegal fees, recommended by the council and exacted by the governor, the house were unable to make any farther settlement on his excellency. Judge Gittens and Mr. R. B. Jones admitted the inability of the people to bear any encrease of their burthens; but insisted that the assembly ought to yield to those considerations of policy and prudence, which strongly urged their giving his excellency the same salary as had been allowed his predecessors. The motion was, however, agreed to by a majority of ten to six.

The assembly returned a civil answer to the governor's message, communicating to him the result of their deliberations, expressive of their affliction under their Sovereign's displeasure, and observing that the impoverished state of the country absolutely forbad their passing a levy bill; which appeared to them unnecessary, as a large part of the former levy remained uncollected, from the known inability of the people to pay it. The house continued sitting till after sun-set, in expectation of being adjourned in the usual manner by his excellency's order; but receiving no directions they adjourned, of their own authority, to meet at the end of four weeks, at the same hour of the evening.

Disappointed in his grand objects, an augmentation of his salary and the passage of a levy bill, both of which he thought the secretary of state's letter had rendered secure, the governor now gave his assent to the act of settlement, which had passed on his arrival; and, in pursuance of his long Decem. 7. projected scheme, dissolved the assembly by proclamation. In the same malign spirit, which animated all his other actions, he issued writs for a general election, at a distance of more than two months. But, whatever were the advantages which his excellency might have expected from this step, he was again doomed to suffer the vexation of disappointment. All the members of the former assembly were again elected, with only two exceptions, and in those instances he benefited nothing by the change.

One of these changes was unfortunately produced by the death of that illustrious patriot, Mr. Henry Duke. Though liberally endowed by nature with a vigorous understanding, improved by the study of a science the most likely to strengthen and expand the powers of the mind, Mr. Duke was less distinguished by his eminent talents, than the zeal and spirit with which they were exerted in the public service. Firmly attached to the interests of his native country, he was neither intimidated by the frowns of power, nor allured by its seductive smile, from diligently pursuing the paths which he thought would lead to colonial prosperity. The activity of his mind was continually impelling him to attempt the reform of abuses, or to suggest wise and salutary laws for the benefit of the state. Superior to the sordid considerations of personal ease and private emolument, his integrity and public spirit rendered him obnoxious to those drones in the hive, who sought public employments without any intention of performing the duties annexed to them, or who were desirous only of battening on the spoils of the people. Every admirer of genuine patriotism must lament the loss of one, whose firmness and intrepidity marked him the champion of liberty and the asserter of his country's rights.

The effects of the governor's anger were not confined to the assembly; he embraced every opportunity of harassing and distressing the militia, by keeping them out on alarms, without the smallest necessity. They were frequently kept under arms the whole night, without any sufficient precaution having been taken to afford them rest or shelter. This inconvenience, which was more particularly felt by the cavalry, having been represented to the governor, his excellency ordered the Leeward regiment of horse, commanded by Colonel Poyer, to rendezvous at a small fort called Dover, upon the hill above Speight's-town. Leacock, the colonel of that division, thought this an infringement of his authority, and, on the first alarm, detached Captain Jordan with a company of infantry, from Orange fort, to occupy the post. On the approach of evening, Poyer sent to Mr. Jordan, saying, that he had his excellency's orders to take post there, and requested that he would evacuate the fort, that he might put his men under cover for the night. Jordan replied, that he could not quit his station without orders from his commanding officer. Poyer, having previously dismounted his troop, immediately put them in motion, with the view of marching into the fort; but Jordan, faithful to his orders, threw himself, sword in hand, into the gate-way, and opposed their entrance. A rencounter ensued, in which Poyer's impetuosity threw him off his guard, and he lost his sword; Jordan took no advantage of this accident, and the interference of some of the officers present terminated the fracas, and Poyer immediately dispatched his adjutant to Pilgrim with an account of this extraordinary transaction. Jordan was soon after brought to a court-martial, by the governor's order, and dismissed the service; while Colonel Leacock, under whose orders he had acted, retained the command of the division.

Towards the close of the last year Holland had joined her arms to the combination, formed by the other great maritime powers, for reducing the naval strength and national opulence of Great Britain. Governor Cunninghame received early intelligence of this event, accompanied with an assurance that the proper authorities should be speedily forwarded, for granting letters of marque and reprisal against the subjects of the States General; and directing him, in the interim, to inform the owners of private ships of war, that they should be entitled to the king's share of all Dutch property which they should capture. The business of privateering was carried on at that time with great spirit by the merchants of Barbadoes, and frequently relieved the distresses of the inhabitants, occasioned by the privation of their wonted supplies through the regular commercial channels. Attentive to his own interest, Cunninghame concealed the orders he had received, and, unauthorized, proceeded to issue letters of marque against the Dutch; compelling the owners of privateers to pay the most extravagant fees for commissions, which, he was conscious, were of no validity. To add to the injustice, and increase his emoluments by extortion, he refused to issue commissions against the Dutch, unless those who applied for them would take out others, de novo, against the French, Spaniards, and Americans; on which the fees collectively amounted to one hundred and thirteen pounds.

Many valuable Dutch prizes, which had been captured under commissions thus prematurely granted, were either taken from the captors by his Majesty's cruizers, or seized by the governor's orders, after they were brought into port, and condemned as droits of the admiralty. From the decrees of the court of vice-admiralty, the captors appealed to the justice of a benignant prince, and his excellency insisted that the prizes should be sold, and the money deposited in his hands until his Majesty's pleasure was known. Had this been done, there is little reason to believe that the appellants would ever have benefited by any ulterior determination in their favour. But Mr. Weekes, the judge of the vice-admiralty court, acted with the spirit and integrity becoming his high responsible situation. He appointed a proper officer, under bonds, for the faithful execution of the trust, to sell the prizes, and directed him to detain the money for which they were sold, until the appeals were decided by superior authority. Exasperated at this arrangement,

CHAP.XIV. the governor suspended the officer appointed by the court,
1781.   and endeavoured to intimidate the judge into a compliance
           with his sinister designs; but finding his menaces ineffec-
           tual, he once more had recourse to the prerogative: he sus-
           pended the judge, and appointed William Morris his suc-
           cessor. Weekes was not of a temper to submit patiently
           to injuries. He presented a memorial to the King, and was
           re-instated by his Majesty's particular order.

Feb. 14.   Meanwhile the new assembly having met, the usual inter-
           course of civilities was preserved between the governor and
           the house, notwithstanding the ill-humour which prevailed
           between them. In the speech from the chair, the usual topics
           of discussion were renewed and pressed with great earnest-
           ness on the attention of the legislature. Upon the subject
           of their defence, his excellency wished to engage their most
           serious reflection. A powerful armament, he informed
           them, was daily expected from France, and the number of
           their enemies had been increased by the rupture with the
           States General. In the strong reinforcements sent out for
           their protection, they had a fresh instance of his Majesty's
           paternal care; but he cautioned them against trusting en-
           tirely to a naval force for security. A short interval of its
           absence, he justly observed, might be fatal, if they neglect-
           ed to improve their internal strength; and as their numbers
           constituted the principal means of defence, he again re-
           commended a revision of their militia law. In their deli-
           berations on this subject, he trusted they would find that
           the powers necessary to enforce obedience were not incom-

patible with the principles of civil liberty. Whatever powers they might think proper to vest in the commander in chief, he assured them, should be exercised with an equal attention to the ease of the people and the safety of the country.

He particularly represented to the assembly, the injury which the public service had sustained for the want of a levy bill, and exhorted them to take the state of the fortifications into their immediate consideration. The repairs of the Town-hall, Pilgrim house, and the Mole-head were again adverted to, rather as subjects of irritation than of well-grounded complaint. Nor were barracks for the troops and a place of confinement for the prisoners of war forgotten, though they were points wholly unconnected with the colonial establishment. He was particularly commanded by the King, he said, to recommend harmony to the two branches of the legislature; and he wished he had nothing more to suggest for reform and correction; but their internal police certainly required amendment. Their own observation, he thought, would readily suggest to them the mischiefs and inconveniences to which they were exposed, from the remissness of magistrates and inferior officers; and he hoped every gentleman would exert himself, in his own vicinity, for the preservation of peace, order, and decorum, among the different ranks of society. The speech concluded with common place professions of zeal for the welfare of the country and the happiness of the people.

The address of the council was in the usual style of adulation. They extolled his excellency for virtues, which none but themselves had the penetration to discover that he possessed; and declared their willingness, by harmony and unanimity in their proceedings, to give stability to his government. The assembly, without transgressing the rules of decorum, replied to his civilities in terms no less respectful, mingled with the most poignant sarcasms and deserved reproaches. Sensible of the deficiencies of the militia law, and desirous, as they said, of giving energy to a system essential to their safety, they trusted his excellency would pardon them, if, while they observed in him a disposition to exercise extraordinary powers, not warranted by law, they were restrained from investing him with such an increase of authority, as by an arbitrary stretch or interpretation might irretrievably affect the rights and liberties of the subject. They disclaimed all agency in the inconvenience which his excellency attributed to the loss of the levy bill, which had been regularly passed by that house, and rejected by the council. But, under the present circumstances of the country, they considered the failure of the bill a fortunate event for the people; who must have sunk under the weight of their taxes, added to the misfortune inflicted on them by the late direful calamity.

March 20.

Faithful to the true interests of their country, they professed their readiness to concur, with unaffected harmony, in every measure calculated to promote the general welfare;

but, when they reflected on the partial, oppressive system on which the council acted, in support of his excellency's arbitrary measures, no harmony, they were convinced, could exist betwixt bodies of men actuated by such opposite principles. On the defects imputed to their police they remarked, that if the magistrates were remiss or negligent, the blame could only attach to the power by which they were appointed, and which, notwithstanding their neglect, continued them in office. But if the magistrates were really inattentive to their duty, or the police defective, it was a circumstance highly creditable to the people at large, that so few complaints were made, and so few indictments brought before the court of criminal judicature. They received, with pleasure, the assurances of his excellency's disposition to promote the happiness of the people; but, anxious as they were to contribute to that ultimate object of all human legislation, the honour of the act, they declared, must be entirely his own; since, to a free people, it would be in vain to hold out a prospect of happiness, whilst they continued to smart under the rod of despotism.

Hitherto the governor had omitted to demand any unusual fees in Chancery; but, at a meeting of council on the twenty-fifth day of April, he proposed a new table of fees to be established for his use as chancellor. On this occasion, the clerk of the council was excluded, and on the subject of the fees being agitated, President Dotin and

Mr. Cumberbatch, were the only members who had the honest firmness to express their disapprobation of them.   No
question was put to the vote; but his excellency drew up a
minute of their proceedings, conveying the sanction of the
board to his proposal, which, without being shewn to the
members present, was afterwards entered on their journals,
by his directions.

It cannot fail to excite the astonishment of every man of
reflection, that these enormities should not have roused the
spirit of the people to vindicate their violated rights, by
an appeal to the laws of their country.   Unhappily, those
laws afforded but a feeble security.   In all cases, civil and
criminal, an appeal lies from the judgment of the courts of
inferior jurisdiction to the court of error, composed of the
governor and council.   No prospect of success could,
therefore, attend a prosecution, which might be ultimately
determined by judges, who were themselves the authors of
the injustice which was the subject of complaint.   Under
every disadvantage, Mr. Duke, as we have formerly seen,
made an unsuccessful attempt to punish the deputy-secretary, and Dr. Andrew Wade, about this time, lodged an
information against him before Mr. Babb and Mr. Skeete,
two justices of the peace.   But a difference of opinion
arising between them, from the latter's doubting Mr. Workman's responsibility as the fees were not taken for his own
use, Wade, knowing that a want of unanimity on the bench
must prove fatal to the complaint, consented to compro-

mise the matter, on Mr. Workman's engaging to be no far-

ther concerned in the governor's illegal exactions. His excellency, however, was not long at a loss for an agent to
execute his unlawful commands. He erected a new office,
and a Mr. Nicholas Humphrey Walrond, who had at once
the meanness to accept the employment, and the boldness
to defy the popular resentment, became the instrument of
his tyranny and injustice.

CHAP. XV.

MUNIFICENT GRANT OF PARLIAMENT FOR THE RELIEF OF THE SUFFERERS BY THE STORM—DISTRIBUTION DELAYED—MESSAGE FROM THE GOVERNOR—THE ASSEMBLY REFUSE TO RAISE THE SUPPLIES—ALARMING PROSPECT OF AFFAIRS—OBSTINACY OF THE ASSEMBLY—PATRIOTISM OF THE PEOPLE—DISSOLUTION OF THE ASSEMBLY—NEW ELECTION—CONTINUAL ALTERCATIONS BETWEEN THE GOVERNOR AND ASSEMBLY—PLANS FOR THE DISTRIBUTION OF THE PARLIAMENTARY BOUNTY—THE ASSEMBLY PROROGUED—ARRANGEMENTS FOR THE DISTRIBUTION.

CHAP. XV.
1782.

IT is now time that we should take notice of the result of those applications, which, immediately after the late destructive hurricane, had been made to a beneficent monarch, by the ruined inhabitants of a devastated country. No sooner was the direful disaster known in England, than the sympathy of a generous nation was awakened by the sufferings of their unfortunate fellow subjects. In the midst of an unnatural and ruinous foreign and domestic war, in which the national treasure was lavished in a manner unparalleled in any former period, the house of commons seemed,

for a moment, to have forgotten the dangers and difficulties which surrounded them, and to have felt no other
anxiety than to relieve the distresses of others. With a
spirit truly characteristic of British liberality and grandeur,
that august assembly unanimously resolved, on the motion
of Lord North, "That the sum of eighty thousand pounds
be granted to his Majesty, for affording immediate assistance to our unhappy fellow subjects in the island of Barbadoes, and to relieve and support such of them as have
been reduced to distress and necessity by the late dreadful
calamity, which, in the month of October last, ravaged
and laid waste the greatest part of the island." This noble
donative, and humane attention to the sufferings of their
fellow subjects, in this distant part of the empire, will
ever be regarded with gratitude and admiration, while
benignity and generosity are esteemed as virtues among
mankind.

The liberal benefactions of individuals were proportioned
to the public munificence; but the humanity of the generous citizens of Dublin was peculiarly conspicuous. They
were convened at the Tholsel, by Sir Edward Newenham,
lord mayor of the city, to consider on the most effectual
and expeditious method of relieving the wants and necessities of the people of Barbadoes. Twenty thousand pounds
were quickly raised within that opulent city, by subscription, to which the house of Latouche and sons contributed
the princely sum of one thousand pounds. The money was

judiciously invested in the purchase of articles of the first necessity, and shipped to Barbadoes, to be distributed under the direction of the governor, for the relief of the sufferers. And, it is pleasing to add, the generous intentions of the humane donors were literally accomplished by an impartial distribution among the sufferers, in proportion to their losses. Such an instance of exalted generosity failed not to excite the strongest emotions of grateful sensibility. The house of assembly did all that was in their power. By an unanimous vote of thanks, transmitted to Sir Edward Newenham, by their speaker, they expressed their gratitude to that patriotic, civic officer, and his worthy fellow citizens, for their liberal donative. A sense of such refined benevolence cannot be conveyed by words; it will survive the fragile records of political societies, and live for ever in liberal hearts.

The vote of the house of commons was immediately communicated to Mr. Estwick, the colonial agent, by the lords of the treasury; and a committee of the principal merchants and planters of Barbadoes, resident in London, was formed, by their lordship's recommendation, for taking into consideration the most effectual means of carrying the generous intention of parliament into execution. The committee having met, entered into several resolutions, for exporting building materials, coarse cloathing, and provisions for the immediate supply of those who wanted them; and for remitting the sum of twelve thousand pounds in specie, to

purchase such articles as could be most advantageously
procured on the spot. A sub-committee was appointed for
the purpose of furnishing the requisite supplies, free of
commission, or of any emolument whatever; and of corresponding with a board of commissioners, which they advised should be established in Barbadoes, consisting of the
governor, the council, the speaker, and a certain number
of the assemby, for the distribution of the parliamentary
bounty, by such acts or orders as the legislature should
think proper.

Unfortunately, such a diversity of opinions prevailed on
the subject, that many months were permitted to elapse
before the legislature could agree on any specific plan for
the distribution; and the people had well nigh lost the
greater part of the benefit intended for them, from the
want of a proper concert and agreement among those to
whom the disposal of the bounty was intrusted. On being
informed of the proceedings of the committee in England,
the assembly lost no time in appointing a committee to join April 18.
that of the other house; but no corresponding arrangement
having been made by the council, the business remained
neglected for more than six months.

In the mean time, the assembly received a message from May 14.
the governor, expressing his surprise that the passing of a
levy bill, notwithstanding the obvious urgency and necessity of the measure, should have been so long delayed. To
provide for the support of government, was an act so essen-

tial to the peace, safety, and prosperity of the country, that he thought it his duty to give them an early opportunity of accomplishing a business that so materially concerned themselves, as well as those whom they represented. The colonial debt, he reminded them, had already accumulated to an amazing amount, and was daily increasing to such a degree, that unless its growth was anticipated by a tax, proportioned to the public exigencies, it would soon become enormous. Many of the persons employed in the service of the country had been actually driven from their stations and employments by the difficulty of obtaining the reward of their labour. Public credit was almost annihilated; and, whilst the private buildings of individuals were rebuilt or repaired with the most active and laudable industry, those of the public still remained in ruins. These circumstances were not, he said, more honourable to a respectable colony than injurious and distressing to individuals; and the consequence of longer delay in raising the supplies for the public service, must eventually be the imposition of burthens which few of the inhabitants would be able to bear. He, therefore, conjured the house, by every principle of regard for the interest and welfare of their constituents, not to defer making an adequate provision to meet the necessary expenses of government, since the delay was likely to be productive of consequences extremely dangerous, if not absolutely ruinous, to the community.

Whatever were the governor's motives for thus earnestly

and frequently urging the passing of a levy bill, the propriety of the measure cannot be disputed. That the condition of the country, wasted by a series of calamities, was rendered yet more deplorable, by the effects of the recent disaster, is readily admitted ; but there can be no doubt, that the bulk of the people were still able to pay the moderate taxes which were required, to defray the annual expenses of government. Besides, if it were necessary to retain the ancient expensive establishments of the country, it certainly behoved the legislature to afford immediate remuneration to those who were employed in the several departments of the state. And if a system of government were to be supported by taxes, levied on the people, it was a measure of common prudence, that the ways and means should be gradually furnished, in a manner least oppressive to the subject, rather than by a causeless protraction of the evil, to crush them on some future day, by the accumulated weight of their burthens.

These considerations were, however, disregarded by the assembly. Smarting under the rod of oppression, they were only solicitous of mortifying their tyrannical ruler ; and, in the indulgence of their resentment, they sometimes lost sight of the welfare and safety of their country.— Having taken the message of the governor into consideration, the house unanimously resolved, that the distressed circumstances of the people, labouring under the pressure of a great natural calamity, aggravated by his excellency's illegal and unconstitutional exactions, would not admit of their raising any extraordinary supplies, or even to provide the means of their own defence. Such an explicit avowal of determined indifference to public security, cannot be justified. It was sufficient to have encouraged the enemy to embrace the opportunity, presented by intestine discord, of attempting the conquest of the island. Hence, let governors learn this useful lesson, that the most effectual means of attaching a people to their government, and of arming them in its defence, is the unmolested enjoyment of their civil rights and immunities.

The capture of Saint Eustatius, the emporium of the West Indies, had thrown into the hands of the British commanders, employed on that service, such an immense plunder, that they were, for a long time, incapable of attending to any thing, but the sales of the valuable commodities of which it consisted. Many British merchants, both in England and the West Indies, had property to a considerable amount deposited there, for mercantile speculations, which were greatly facilitated by its being a neutral free port, the whole of which was included in the general confiscation. Whilst Sir George Rodney was thus employed, enriching himself on the spoils of friends and foes, the Count de Grasse arrived at Martinico, with twenty-five sail of the line, and six thousand troops, designed to exterminate the British power in the American archipelago. On receiving intelligence of this event, Admiral Rodney has-ened to form a junction with Sir Samuel Hood, whose squadron, consisting of only seventeen sail of the line, had sustained considerable damage, in a gallant attempt to intercept the French fleet going into Martinico. Some time was necessarily spent at Antigua, in refitting those ships which had suffered in the action; but as soon as this business was accomplished, the commander in chief proceeded with his whole fleet, having an immense treasure on board, to Barbadoes.

The indiscriminate confiscation of property at Saint Eustatius, involved Admiral Rodney in some very disagreeable disputes and legal discussions with the British merchants of both hemispheres; and, in a fit of peevish resentment, he asserted, in his official dispatches, that the English West Indian merchants, regardless of their duty to their country, had contracted to supply the enemy of the neighbouring islands with provisions and naval stores; and that his utmost attention should be employed, to prevent their treason from taking effect. A charge so scandalous and dangerous was not to be endured, by men conscious of their innocence and tenacious of their loyalty. The merchants of Barbadoes, from the latitude of the expression, feeling themselves implicated in the false and malicious imputation, immediately drew up a spirited vindication of their character, in which they wholly and explicitly denied the charge as a hasty, pernicious, and infamous misrepresentation of their principles and conduct, and defied the admiral to support what he had so solemnly advanced. This paper was transmitted to the colonial agent, who, conformably to the request of the mercantile body, wrote to Sir George Rodney, demanding, as an act of justice, that he would discriminate between the innocent and the guilty; that those who deserved it might be brought to condign punishment. No answer having been received to this reasonable request, Mr. Estwick repeated his application with no better success. Disappointed in obtaining the reparation which he expected, Mr. Estwick then made a public demand on Sir George, publishing his letters, together with the defence of the Barbadians; but the admiral, probably regretting his having been betrayed into such an impropriety, silently declined to maintain or to retract the charge.

Meanwhile Saint Lucia was close invested by the enemy's whole naval force; whilst a considerable body of troops, led on by an able and experienced general, were exerting every effort on shore to reduce the island. To the immortal honour of the gallant Brigadier General S. Leger, and the troops under his command, this formidable attack was completely defeated. Discouraged by the determined resistance which every where opposed his progress, the Marquis de Bouillè reimbarked his troops and returned to Martinico.

To compensate for this disgrace, the French commanders immediately turned their arms against Tobago. On the very day that Admiral Rodney arrived at Barbadoes, a small French squadron, with a body of land forces, under the orders of M. de Blanchlande appeared off Tobago. Rodney, on the receipt of this intelligence, which was instantly conveyed to him by governor Ferguson, contented himself with dispatching Rear Admiral Drake, with six sail of the line, some frigates, one regiment and two additional companies, for the relief of the place. Upon Drake's coming within sight of Tobago he had the mortification to discover the whole French fleet, consisting of twenty-seven line of battle ships, between him and the land. Finding it impracticable to succour the island, the rear-admiral, after ascertaining the strength and situation of the enemy, hauled his wind and soon appeared in view of Carlisle Bay. Though the proper communication was directly made to the commander in chief, the fleet did not get under weigh until the next day, having in the interim landed the plunder brought from Saint Eustatius, and taken General Vaughan, with a considerable reinforcement of troops on board. But the opportunity of relieving Tobago was lost. After as gallant and obstinate a resistance as is recorded in history, Governor Ferguson had been compelled to capitulate.

The hostile fleets soon came within sight of each other; but, though, as the enemy were to leeward and shewed no disposition to avoid an action, the option of engaging lay with the British Admiral; they separated after various manœuvres, without exchanging a single shot. The protection of Barbadoes seems to have been at this time the grand object of Sir George Rodney's care; and his declining an engagement with the Count de Grasse, whose fleet was only four in number superior to his own, proceeded, as he stated in his public dispatches, from an apprehension that it was the enemy's design, by drawing him within the influence of certain lee currents among the Grenadines, to gain an opportunity of reducing Barbadoes before he could return to its succour.

The loss of Tobago, and the proximity of an hostile naval force of acknowledged superiority, were circumstances which could not fail to excite the most lively alarm in minds not wholly insensible to the apprehensions of danger. At this critical conjuncture, Admiral Rodney wrote to the governor, commenting, with some warmth, on the inattention of the legislature to the safety of the colony; and, after menacing them with a formal complaint to the King, recommended his excellency to lay the country under martial law. This letter was supposed to have been written at Pilgrim, by the governor's desire; but of this fact there is no evidence whatever. Be that, however, as it may, neither threats nor entreaties could soften the inflexibility of the assembly.

Happily the general spirit of the people served to supply the deficiencies of their representatives. They formed themselves into volunteer associations, and, with a zeal and alacrity highly honourable, undertook the reparation of their dismantled fortifications. The example was set by the public spirited inhabitants of Bridge-Town, who, with the gentlemen of their vicinity, united for their defence, and raised a liberal subscription for carrying their patriotic design into execution. The example of the metropolis excited a general emulation. Similar associations were immediately formed in Speight's, Saint James's, Oistin's and Reed's bay divisions. It happened, however, that in some of these places large sums were subscribed with greater facility than they were paid; and of the money, which was collected with difficulty, much was applied in constructing unserviceable batteries, and in removing old rust-eaten cannon from the most assailable points to positions, where, had they been good, they could have given but little opposition to the progress of an invading army.

This laudable conduct furnished the governor with an opportunity of arraigning the loyalty and patriotism of the assembly, which he did not fail to embrace. Imputing their refusal to grant the necessary supplies to factious motives, he dissolved the assembly by proclamation, with- out even consulting the council. His excellency's reasons for taking a step, which was at all times extremely unpopular, were, at least, plausible. The proclamation stated that, at the very moment when the neighbouring island of Saint Lucia, was actually invested by the enemy, the assembly were so utterly regardless of the safety of their constituents, as to resolve not to raise any supply whatsoever for the defence of the country. The ample subscriptions which had been since laudably raised by individuals, for repairing the fortifications, and the facility with which they had been recently put into a state of defence, were convincing proofs, it was asserted, of the inclinations and abilities of the people to secure their country from the attempts of his Majesty's enemies, and of the readiness and willingness with which they would have paid their respective assessments, if they had not been prevented by their representatives declining to pass a levy bill. It was therefore incompatible with his duty, his excellency said, as the king's representative, to suffer the public authority to remain any longer in the hands of men who had so obstinately refused to provide for the public welfare and security; and, in order that the people might have an opportunity of choosing men, who had a greater regard for their interest and safety, to represent them, at this time of public danger, he thought proper to dissolve the present general assembly.

The proclamation occasioned a second meeting of the associated inhabitants of Bridge-Town, by whom several spirited resolutions were agreed to, and afterwards published, as a refutation of the governor's charges against the assembly. These resolutions asserted, that the reasons suggested for the dissolution of the house were founded in deceit and devised by extreme art, to pervert an originally good act, and to gloss over a most unwarrantable exercise of prerogative by a fallacious colouring. That the representatives of the people had acted uprightly, and perfectly agreeable to the wishes of their constituents, in refusing to pass a levy bill; and that they yielded only to the dictates of the soundest judgment and the impulse of the most patriotic zeal, in disregarding his excellency's importunity, for effecting his favourite object. That a subscription was opened for repairing the fortifications, on account of the inability of the people at large to pay any tax for that purpose. The apprehensions of an immediate invasion; the insufficiency of the public funds; and the lamentable poverty of the community in general, operating at one and the same instant, impelled them to the adoption of that useful, but now perverted, expedient: That the extreme disproportion between the number of subscribers to the laudable design of repairing the fortifications and that of persons liable to pay taxes raised by a levy bill; and between the fund acquired by contribution and the sum arising from a regular levy bill, carried in itself the clearest reputation of the opinion of the general opulence, expressed in the proclamation, and completely exonerated the representative body from the heavy charges which his excellency had brought against them. That the assembly, so far from being exposed to the imputation of feeling no regard for the true interests of their constituents, or the safety of the island, had acted upon principles diametrically opposite, and altogether worthy of their warmest approbation. Actuated by the same sentiments, the other patriotic associations adopted similar resolutions, which were so perfectly in unison with those of the metropolis, as to render any particular notice of them unnecessary.

Whatever might have been the governor's motives for resorting a second time to an expedient so unpopular, he was now, as on the former occasion, doomed to experience a disappointment, aggravated by several circumstances which must have rendered it peculiarly mortifying and vexatious. All the old members were re-elected with an unusual degree of cordiality and good-will. In many parishes patriotic dinners were given by the freeholders in honour of their representatives, accompanied by the most flattering testimonials of popular approbation and esteem. They were presented with addresses from the electors, containing the most pointed reflections on the governor's rapacity and tyranny, at the same time applauding the firmness with which they had refused to increase the public burthens by the imposition of fresh taxes, and encouraging them to persevere, with the same independant spirit, in opposing the unconstitutional strides of despotism. Thus the governor's injudicious appeal to the elective body served only to produce the clearest conviction of the unpopularity of his measures, and the detestation in which he was held by all ranks of people, except the few, who, from the worst motives, continued to court his favour.

In this state of irritation, it was natural to expect that

the meeting between the governor and the assembly could not be very amicable. The house having met on the tenth day of July, proceeded to the choice of a speaker, when Sir John Gay Alleyne was again called to the chair. This gentleman had become so personally obnoxious to the governor, that it was apprehended his excellency would not confirm their election; but, though he did not, as usual, declare his approbation of the appointment, he coolly expressed his consent. His excellency's speech was remarkable for its uncommon brevity. The organization of the militia, the repairs of the fortifications, the necessity of guarding the accessible parts of the coast, the passing of a levy bill, providing barracks or quarters for the King's troops, the improvement of the mole-head, and the establishment of a proper market in Bridge-town, were topics suggested for their consideration, with a cold formality and indifference.

On the last meeting of the late assembly, the merchants of Bridge-town had presented a memorial to the house, which they desired might be laid at the feet of their beloved Sovereign, complaining of the governor's arbitrary and unconstitutional establishment of fees, as oppressive as they were unprecedented. They charged him with fraud and duplicity, in issuing letters of marque and reprisal against the Dutch, before he was authorized to do so, and with having, on weak and frivolous pretences, deprived the

CHAP. XV.
1782.

captors of several valuable prizes, which he had contrived to have condemned as droits of the admiralty. It was also alledged, that, in order to apply the value of the prizes to his own use, he had, without any just cause or reason, suspended the officer who had been legally appointed by the court of vice-admiralty to receive the money arising from the sale of the droits. For these, and many other reasons, the memorialists requested, that the governor's abitrary and tyrannical conduct should be represented to the King.

This memorial was followed, on the first day of the session, by a petition from the parishioners of Saint James's, condemning, in the most pointed and unqualified terms, the tyranny of the governor and council, in extorting money from the people, under the denomination of fees; thereby establishing a system of taxation independent of their representatives, impeding the progress of business, obstructing the channels of justice, and subverting the constitution. The petitioners concluded with praying, that their complaints may be carried to the foot of the throne, with an humble supplication to his Majesty, to redress the grievances of his faithful subjects, and to signify his disapprobation of the conduct of those members of council who had voted for the establishment of fees, so as to deter all future members of that board from prostituting the honour of their high station, by obsequious compliances with the arbitrary and avaricious inclinations of the governor.

The forms of the house would not allow the taking of the governor's speech into consideration until the next meeting, when an address was moved for by Mr. James Straker, and agreed to by the house, with the exception of Judge Gittens, who objected to it, as precluding every idea of a revision of the militia law, and the passing of a levy-bill; objects, which, he said, it had ever been his wish to see effected. The assembly embraced this opportunity of addressing the governor, to remonstrate with great spirit and keenness of reproach on the stigma attempted to be thrown on the character of their house, by the proclamation for its dissolution; which they termed a wanton and manifest abuse of the prerogative, with an artful design of misleading his Majesty's ministers in regard to the general temper of the people, and to gratify an inordinate resentment against the members of that assembly. In the unequivocal approbation of the inhabitants of every description, and the united voice of the whole body of freeholders, by whom they had been re-elected, the assembly confided for a complete and unquestionable refutation of the reasons assigned by his excellency for their dissolution. The generous and voluntary contributions of individuals were, they maintained, no proofs of general opulence, nor of the supposed ability of the bulk of the people to sustain the heavy expense of repairing the fortifications. Having taken particular notice of each subject referred to their consideration, they concluded with declaring, in conformity to the wishes of their constituents, openly and freely expressed, that they never would raise any supplies whatever, while they continued liable to be aggrieved by the demand of illegal and unconstitutional fees.

Public bodies, as well as the individuals who compose them, are always ready to discern and censure in others the faults which, from the partiality of human nature, they are incapable of perceiving in themselves. Whilst the assembly were commendably employed in resisting the arbitrary encroachments of the other orders of the legislature, they scrupled not to overstep their constitutional limits, and to assume a dispensing power over a positive law. They directed the treasurer to suspend, for two months, the collection of the taxes remaining due on the levy bill, which was passed on the twenty-sixth day of July, one thousand seven hundred and seventy-nine. The council, who had without hesitation consented to violate the fundamental rights of the commons, now suddenly became the vindicators of that constitution which they so recently endeavoured to subvert. They resolved that the directions given by the assembly for stopping the payment of the taxes was exercising an illegal, unconstitutional power of dispensing with the operation of a positive law, on the authority of one branch of the legislature; and that an order, so partial, could be no justification of the treasurer for neglecting his duty. But as the intention of the assembly was founded on humanity, for the indulgence of the people under their

Sept. 19.

present disastrous circumstances, their honours professed their readiness to concur in passing an act to protract the payment of the taxes to the time proposed by the assembly; the only constitutional method, they observed, of checking or suspending the operation of the law.

The treasurer, having received a copy of this resolution from the clerk of the council, laid it before the assembly at their next meeting. The reading of a paper of this tendency naturally called up the speaker. He observed that the mode of proceeding now objected to, had been practised by that house, merely for the sake of dispatch, for nearly twenty years, without a single objection having been started by either of the other legislative branches. But now, the objection was made, he recommended the house to pass a bill, as the more regular way of obtaining the required indulgence. A bill for that purpose was accordingly passed, and sent up to the council for their concurrence; with a message, apologising for their unintentional infringement on the privileges of that board. Pleased with the council's resolution of adhering to the principles of the constitution, the assembly cheerfully renounced the slightest deviation from the same line of duty in their own proceedings. But they reflected, they added, with no small degree of consolation, under the sense of having erred, that the error had arisen solely from a zeal to lighten the burthens on the shoulders of their fellow subjects, and not from a presumptuous design of increasing their weight. The bill, however, was re-

CHAP. XV. jected by the governor. No substantial reason, he said,

1782. having been given to induce him to believe, that the proposed indulgence to the inhabitants could materially alter their situation at the expiration of two months. And as the levy, to be raised by the bill whose operation was thus meant to be suspended, was the only fund applicable to the defence of the island, and to carry on the works which, from the state of the war, it was absolutely necessary to complete with the utmost expedition, he could not consent to the delay.

Matters were thus verging to a crisis between the governor and the assembly. Their complaints againts his excellency were pressed forward with great zeal and fidelity by the agent, and a day was actually appointed for a final hearing of the charges before the board of trade. In the mean time, his patron, Lord George Germaine, had expressed such an explicit disapprobation of his conduct, that scarcely a hope remained of his being able to retain his government, unless he could compromise the dispute with the assembly. Hence, in his communications with them, he began to assume a milder tone. Before the house adjourned, they received a message from his excellency, containing an extract of a letter from the secretary of state, in these words: " The temper and good disposition which you have shewn in your speech at the opening of the assembly,*

---

* On the 14th February, 1781, previous to their last dissolution.

gives me just grounds to hope that all animosities will cease; and that the council and assembly will be ready to act with you in pursuing the true interests of Barbadoes; by providing for its security by the passing of a proper levy bill, and by repairing the forts and batteries necessary for its defence; his Majesty having no other wish than that of promoting the happiness of all his subjects."

The message contained a profession of his excellency's concern, at finding that the assembly's last address was written in such an intemperate style, that he could not, consistently with his character, and the station which he filled, return an answer to it. But he took that opportunity of declaring to them that, upon their passing a proper levy bill, he was ready, as he had always been, to join with them in every just and reasonable proposition, for the ease and interest, as well as for the security of the people. On the subject of fees, his excellency thus expressed himself: " Although I consider them as part of my just and lawful rights, I can assure you, that, if the assembly had granted me the salary long enjoyed by many of my predecessors, and which, it is well known, their constituents in general were not only willing, but desirous they should grant, it never would have entered into my mind to propose the establishment of fees to the members of his Majesty's council. Nor can I suppose that board would have concurred in the measure, if they had not been fully convinced that the abridged salary granted by the assembly was by no means sufficient to support the dignity of government. And if any subsequent assembly had shewn an inclination to commute the fees established in council, for the usual salary, I should long since have cheerfully made them the proposal. But as, in consequence of the assembly's petition, they have been lately referred by his Majesty to the lords commissioners for trade and plantations, for their consideration and report thereon, that event must now take place, unless by a proposition from the assembly, the matter is compromised and settled before it comes to a hearing." Here the door of reconciliation was thrown open; but unfortunately the assembly could not enter, either with honour to themselves or security to their constituents. A commutation of the fees would have amounted to an acknowledgment of the governor's right to them; and have laid them at the mercy of every future commander in chief.

The message then proceeded to inform the assembly, that General Christie had arrived with a battalion of the sixtieth regiment, which had been lodged, by his excellency's orders, in the forts; and recommended that the house should make some provision for the better accommodation of the troops. The reparation of the forts was urged with great earnestness, as being indispensibly necessary for the security of the country. And, as a proof of his excellency's attention to minor objects of local convenience, he mentioned the decayed state of the two bridges in Bridge-town, with a view to their being immediately repaired, and at the same time suggested the expediency of an act to prevent the removal of those banks of stones which had been fortunately thrown up by the hurricane, and which contributed in no small degree to the safety of the towns.

The assembly's answer breathed nothing of an amicable or conciliatory spirit. The duty and affection, which they held inviolable to his Majesty's person and government, had induced them, they said, to take his excellency's message into their most serious consideration; and after a calm and dispassionate review of the real circumstances of the people, they found themselves confirmed in their former resolution, not to increase the public burthens on any pretence whatever. The interest and prosperity of the community were blessings that depended lesss on their security from external violence, than on the peaceable enjoyment of liberty and property, secured from the encroachments of arbitrary power within. Concerning the fees, to which his excellency had asserted a just and legal right, they challenged him to produce a single law local or general, written or unwritten, which could sanction his claim. On this subject they ran into a tedious discussion, which we willingly avoid. Their objections to the legality of the fees, and the reasons on which the salary was voted, being substantially the same as those of which we have already taken ample notice.

The overture for a commutation of the fees, as a basis of reconciliation, was rejected with the prudence and spirit

CHAP. XV. becoming the representatives of a free people. Thoroughly
1782. convinced of the illegality of the claim, and not less sensible of the unconstitutional authority by which it had been
sanctioned, they should consider it, they said, a dereliction
of their country's cause, were they to make any proposition that might be construed into an acknowledgment of
his right, or that he had any thing to yield on the ground
of a commutation. On the contrary, they declared their
fixed determination that, so long as such a dangerous usurpation of power, as the levying of money without the consent of the general assembly, was exercised, they, who
were the only proper persons to raise supplies for the service of government, would not, by increasing the burthens
of their constituents, become the instruments of adding to
their grievances.

Nov. 27.   Notwithstanding the failure of this attempt, his excellency determined on making another effort to awaken the
assembly to a due sense of the danger to which the country
was exposed, by the proximity of a formidable enemy,
flushed with success. To this end he sent down a message,
intimating that, from intelligence lately received, there was
every reason to believe that the enemy were preparing to
attack Barbadoes. He therefore requested they would enable General Christie to remove the heavy artillery, ammunition and provisions, to Fort George; and recommended
that the militia should be more frequently assembled, and
better disciplined. His excellency, at the same time, com-

municated to the house, on the authority of a letter from the secretary of state, that the application of a part of the parliamentary bounty, to the defence of the island, would be an appropriation perfectly agreeable to his Majesty; and concluded with hoping, that the loyalty of the assembly would induce them to take the alarming and critical state of the island into their most serious consideration, and to adopt such measures as were most essential to its safety and defence.

The assembly readily voted an aid of negro labour for the removal of the cannon and stores; but they would neither consent to the more frequent assembling of the militia, nor to the proposed appropriation of any part of the money granted by parliament to the repairs of the fortifications. While they acknowledged the danger of their situation, they calmly protested, that they would not suffer their apprehensions to betray them into any means of providing for the public defence, not warranted by the principles of justice and humanity. Upon their loyalty, individually and collectively, they affirmed, his excellency might rely with the utmost certainty; but they could not help lamenting, that they should be called to a contest with an inveterate enemy, under a chief, who, having despoiled them of their property, had destroyed that necessary confidence, with which they would have been happy to have followed a faithful representative of the father of his people. Finding every endeavour fruitless, his excellency pro-rogued the assembly to the twenty-sixth day of February.

Meanwhile the council having appointed a committee to join that of the assembly, to arrange a plan for the distribution of the parliamentary bounty, a bill, the production of the joint committee, had been laid before the house on the second day of October. Various amendments were proposed by the speaker, and, being adopted by the house, the bill passed the assembly unanimously on the thirtieth of that month. The whole of the donation was, by this bill, vested in a board of commissioners, composed of his excellency and a certain number of the members of both houses, to be distributed among such persons as had been reduced to distress and necessity by the hurricane; in other words, to the poor and indigent sufferers. The governor was anxious that the money should be applied to the defence of the island, and had actually written to the secretary of state, representing the want of unanimity in the council and assembly, and soliciting an order to throw the whole of the humane benefaction into the public coffers, by which he would have secured the payment of his salary, and been enabled to complete his plans of fortification. With views no less sinister, the council, who were all men of considerable landed estates, were desirous of appropriating the money to the payment of the public debts, and of distributing the provisions generally among the sufferers of every description. The bill sent up by the assembly, being of an opposite tendency, was unanimously rejected by the council; and the prorogation of the assembly prevented their concerting any measures for the disposal of the valuable cargoes sent out by the sub-committee, and which arrived only the day before that event.

The value of the provisions, many of which were of a perishable nature, was of course materially depreciated by the delay, which was productive of an expense of two hundred pounds a month for storage. Meanwhile the council passed a bill, which was delivered to the clerk of the assembly, to be laid before the house after the recess. The design of this bill was to distribute the four cargoes which had been received, while the cash was to remain locked up from those for whose benefit it was intended till the result of the governor's application was known. It proposed the appointment of commissioners, by whom the stores and goods were to be divided into eleven equal parts, one of which was assigned to the vestry of each parish, who were required to distribute them generally in proportion to the loss sustained by each individual.

Notwithstanding the obvious partiality and injustice of this arrangement, it was plausibly and ingeniously supported on the meeting of the assembly by Mr. Straker and Mr. Husbands. The former of these gentlemen, in a long and animated speech, replete with much severity of animadversion on the conduct of the governor and council,

professed himself an advocate for a general distribution
Mr. Husbands thought that the best, the most effectual,
the most general and impartial mode of disposing of the
parliamentary bounty, would have been to have thrown the
whole into the treasury, applicable to the public exigencies.
By such an appropriation of the donative, they might have
paid off the colonial debt, have done justice to the public
creditors, and shewn a due regard to their distressed constituents, by relieving them from a load of taxes; they
might have repaired the mole-head and rebuilt their fallen
sanctuaries. It was not within the sphere of his comprehension to discover how a state could be benefited more
effectually than by the payment of its debts, the reparation
of useful and necessary works, and the establishment of a
fund to meet the expenses of government for a succession
of years. Besides the gift of parliament, he said, was a
public boon, conferred by the public of England on that
of Barbadoes; the public were to be under the obligation,
and consequently ought to receive the benefit. But as he
was now precluded from all hopes of such an appropriation
of the bounty, as he thought most eligible, and as a distribution at all events was to take place, he voted for the
bill, because of the two he preferred a general to a partial
distribution.

On the other hand, the bill experienced an animated opposition from the humane, disinterested, and patriotic
speaker of the assembly, whose generous soul disdained

every personal consideration, when put in competition with the welfare of his country, or the calls of justice and humanity. He commenced an eloquent and argumentative speech with saying, that he could not rise to deliver his sentiments upon that occasion, without yielding to the most painful reflexions, on the melancholy state of his ill-fated country, which could neither relieve itself from its difficulties and afflictions, nor avail itself of the advantages which were held out to its acceptance. He warmly reprobated the mode of distribution proposed by the council, and highly disapproved of the seeming surrender of the money, implied by their silence on that point. He contended with great force of argument, that the whole of the munificent donative ought to be applied, in conformity to the language of the vote of the house of commons, to the relief of such as had been reduced to distress and necessity by the hurricane. He condemned, in the most pointed terms, the scheme of a general distribution among those, of every description, who had sustained any injury by the storm; many of whom, notwithstanding their losses, continued to enjoy, if not the luxuries of affluence, the blessings of competence. Such a plan, he said, was not less inconsistent with the humane intention of the benevolent donors, than injurious to those distressed, necessitous persons, for whose benefit the gift was designed.

With a peculiar felicity of expression and strength of reasoning, the venerable patriot exposed the injustice of liquidating the colonial debt, and exonerating the opulent planter from the payment of taxes, at the expense of the houseless objects of charity, whose small properties had been ravaged by the storm. By such a disposal of the bounty, those who had suffered the least would probably benefit the most; while others, who had been totally ruined, by the destruction of their property, might, in fact, derive no advantage from the benevolent intention of parliament. For as the taxes for the support of government were chiefly laid on slaves, it was demonstrable, that he who had the greater number would benefit by the proposed mode of distribution, not in proportion to his loss, but in an exact ratio to the taxable property which he had saved from the conflict of elements. As an illustration of this part of his argument, Sir John Alleyne mentioned an instance of a planter who had a hundred and fifty slaves, but whose loss was so trifling, that, in the event of the money being thrown into the treasury, he would be a considerable gainer by that calamity, which had involved others in irretrievable ruin. The honourable baronet concluded an elaborate and brilliant display of oratory, with moving several amendments to the bill; which being adopted by the house, it passed without a dissenting voice. But its progress in the council chamber was obstructed, by an occurrence which rendered it unnecessary.

The governor's application to the secretary of state, for an order to appropriate the money to the repairs of the fortifications, had been referred to the lords of the treasury, who immediately called for the opinion of the London committee on the expediency of the measure. Perceiving that the difficulties which impeded the disposal of the bounty, had been purposely contrived by his excellency, the committee, whose patience sems to have been exhausted by the unreasonable protraction of the business, determined to alter the plan, and exclude the governor from any concern in the distribution. They resolved, that the constituting a board of commissioners in Barbadoes, consisting of all the resident members of council, and an equal number of the assembly, of which the speaker should be one, having power to dispose of the parliamentary grant by a majority of voices, is the most expedient method of carrying the benevolent intentions of parliament into execution. This resolution having been approved of by the lords of the treasury, the secretary of state, by his Majesty's orders, wrote to the governor, directing him to recommend to the council and assembly the passing of a bill, in conformity to the mode suggested by the committee.

A board of commissioners was accordingly constituted by an act of the legislature, with full power to make a final distribution of the bounty in any manner they should think proper. On the first meeting of the commissioners, Mr. Bishop, of the council, moved that the sum of forty thousand pounds sterling should be thrown into the public

May 1.

coffers to liquidate the colonial debt. The motion was supported with great earnestness by Mr. Husbands. To him nothing was more clear, from the words of the resolution of the house of commons, than that it was the intention of parliament to afford assistance to all, relief to the distressed, and support to the necessitous.

On the other hand, Sir John G. Alleyne contended, that the proposal was equally inconsistent with the vote of the house of commons, and the minutes of the lords of the treasury, from both of which it was evident, that the donative was designed for the relief of the *indigent sufferers by the storm;* those who, by that dire calamity, *had been reduced to distress and necessity.* All arguments were unavailing: there was no resisting the mute eloquence of numbers; the boon that was intended for the relief of the poor distressed, was applied to lessen the taxes on the opulent possessors of slaves. Out of this fund, the board agreed to provide for the repairs of the town-hall; one thousand pounds was allotted for the rebuilding the new bridge, and nineteen hundred pounds were granted to six parishes for rebuilding their churches. Fifteen hundred pounds sterling had been paid by the London committee to Mr. Estwick, as agent for the island, to conduct the prosecution against Governor Cunninghame. Of the balance, eighteen hundred pounds were allotted to the sufferers in each parish, to be distributed proportionably among those persons whose losses exceeded not fifteen hundred pounds. Great delays were, however, suffered to obstruct the distribution, and five years had elapsed before it was accomplished. It was surely a curious arrangement, to allow the least populous parishes a sum equal to those which had the greater number of families, equal even to that allotted for the metropolis, whose loss of property as far exceeded that of any other district, as its population surpassed the inhabitants of the other parishes. There cannot be a stronger proof of the absurdity and injustice of the plan which was adopted, than the following fact. A gentleman of Bridge-town, who had very few slaves, sustained a loss of more than fifteen hundred pounds, in houses and other personal effects. But those very circumstances, which were in reality aggravations of his misfortune, precluded him from relief: his loss exceeded the limits prescribed by the commissioners; and, having but few slaves on whom he could save the tax, he was left to bear the undiminished weight of his calamity.

For the sake of perspicuity, we have pursued this subject as far as our means of information extended, without much regard to the order of time. And, while it affords the most incontestible evidence of the national beneficence, opulence, and generosity, at the recollection of which, every heart, susceptible of a due sense of benefits, must throb with grateful sensibility, we cannot reflect without humiliation and concern, on the dissensions which it produced; on the obstacles that retarded the distribution of the bounty, and lessened its value to the unfortunate sufferer; and on the application of so large a portion of the munificent donative to *public* purposes.

Whatever traces of genuine loyalty and patriotism may be discovered in the refusal of the assembly to raise the necessary supplies for the support of government, there seems to have been no inconsiderable degree of impolicy in suffering the public debt to accumulate to such an amount, and of injustice in neglecting to provide for the payment of the public creditors, many of whom, though placed in the most indigent circumstances of human life, had been unpaid for three years.   At length, driven to despair, the gunners and matrosses of Reid's Bay, Speight's, and Saint James's divisions could no longer suppress their complaints.   Their petitions to the assembly, stated, that many of them, with large families to support, were reduced to the lowest ebb of fortune; and were frequently indebted to the benevolence of their more fortunate neighbours for their daily subsistence; their wants, however, were unheeded.   The voice of justice and humanity was heard no more, or was listened to only when it forbade the imposition of taxes.   The petitions were ordered to lie on the table, and in all proba-

bility would soon have been forgotten, had not the commissioners for the distribution of the parliamentary bounty
agreed, as we have already seen, to appropriate a considerable part of that donative to the payment of the colonial
debt.

CHAP. XVI.

THE GOVERNOR RECALLED.—MR. DOTIN ASSUMES THE GOVERN-
MENT.—EXTRAORDINARY CONDUCT OF THE COUNCIL.—MR.
ESTWICK'S CONDUCT CENSURED.—MR. DAVID PARRY SUCCEEDS
TO THE GOVERNMENT.—-LEGISLATIVE PROCEEDINGS.—-AN
ATROCIOUS MURDER COMMITTED.

CHAP.XVI. THE day was now approaching, when the Barbadians
1783. were to be relieved from the tyranny of a rapacious ruler,
and restored to the enjoyment of internal tranquillity.
Their complaints had been thus far urged, with indefatigable zeal and perseverance, by their agent; and the thirteenth day of April had been appointed, by the lords of
trade, for a final hearing of the charges against Governor
Cunninghame. But, in consequence of the memorable
change of ministry, which had taken place within the last
week in March, Mr. Estwick suddenly adopted the resolution, not less culpable than strange, of declining the investigation, which he had so ardently and impatiently solicited. When all difficulties were surmounted, and he had
nearly arrived at the end of his journey, he discovered that

the road which he had been diligently pursuing for twelve months was too circuitous to lead to the direct attainment of his object. The board of trade, he found, could form no ultimate decision on the point at issue. They were only a board of inquiry, on whose report the King, in council, was finally to determine. Hence, he pretended to think it better to rely on the wisdom and justice of Lord Shelburne, the new secretary of state, for an immediate, but partial, redress of the grievances which were the subject of complaint, than to bring the matter to a hearing before the board of trade, which being composed, as he said, of persons devoted to the will of Lord George Germaine, the governor's patron, their report might have been eventually unfavourable to the colony. This is the substance of the reasons which, upon being pressed on the subject by the secretary of the board of trade, Mr. Estwick assigned for declining the hearing before the only tribunal, which, from its earliest establishment, had invariably taken cognizance of all colonial complaints, preparatory to a final adjudication. Their lordships, however, in obedience to his Majesty's commands, met at the time and place appointed, and although Mr. Dunning and Mr. Piggott had been retained on the part of the colony, the agent thought proper to refuse the assistance of council, and stated his objections to any farther proceedings on the proposed inquiry. After hearing what the governor's advocates had to offer on the occasion, the board hesitated whether they ought to report

CHAP.XVI. generally on the case as it then stood before them, or spe-
1783. cially, that the agent for the colony had declined the hearing. Mr. Estwick's politeness removed all difficulty, by
declaring his perfect acquiescence in the latter mode.

Happily for Barbadoes, the agent's confidence in Lord
Shelburne was not misplaced. By the first packet which
left England, after the arrangement of the new administration was completed, General Cunninghame received his
June 11. Majesty's orders to resign the government. Thus the removal of the odious and tyrannical chief was entirely an
act of royal clemency, or rather of ministerial patronage, and not the result of any legal nor formal determination of his guilt. The question of mal-administration
was still undecided, and the oppressor escaped the punishment due to his crimes.

The governor spent but little time in preparing for his
departure. Unable to bear the public eye, or apprehensive of personal insults, he privately embarked, under
June 18. cover of the evening, on board the packet, where he remained, unnoticed and unmolested, from Tuesday till the
Thursday following; when, to the inexpressible joy of all
ranks of men, he bad adieu to a country whose government he had administered, without honour or satisfaction
to himself, to the manifest injury of a faithful, and loyal
people.

June 19. In obedience to his Majesty's commands, signified to him
by the secretary of state, the Honourable John Dotin, as-

sumed the reins of government on the day after the governor left Pilgrim, and immediately issued a special summons to convoke the legislature on the second day of July. Both houses having accordingly met, the president addressed them in a speech less remarkable for its elegance than for the patriotic sentiments which it contained. In simple, artless language, he told them, that having been directed by Lord Shelburn, to take charge of the government, his first care had been the removal of those illegal tables of fees which the late governor, without any colour of right, had set up and extorted from his Majesty's loyal and distressed subjects. After an unqualified reprobation of the governor's conduct, he added, that he had been commanded by his Majesty to use his best endeavours to secure and fortify the island, and to rouse the spirit of the people to a vigorous exertion in their own defence. To the repairs of the fortifications he requested their particular attention, and earnestly exhorted them to unanimity and harmony in their proceedings, as the surest means of obtaining the favour and approbation of their Sovereign, of promoting the prosperity of the country, and of doing honour to themselves.

This honest, unstudied harangue drew from the council the following indecent and unprecedented reply : " The manner in which you were called to the command of the island, your honour has been pleased to signify to us with sentiments that do you credit. The trust delegated to you cannot be abused, while you thus honourably bear witness to its importance. We look up to your honour without a shadow of doubt, for that moderation and propriety which will ensure equal applause to this as to your former mild and impartial administration. But, while we thus express ourselves towards you, with that justice which is due for the opening of your speech, we must, at the same time, with indignant freedom, condemn the censure implied on that branch of the legislature of which your honour surely did not, at that time, consider yourself as head. The liberality of your self-denial, respecting the tables of fees, may be applauded by some, yet how to reconcile your present declarations to your former conduct we are at a loss; and confess them to be no less strange than contradictory. Governor Cunninghame's measures, so decisively, if not indelicately, pronounced illegal and oppressive, met the concurrence and confirmation of that board, at which your honour was then sitting as head. Nor can we now acquiesce in these new ideas of extortion and illegality; but rather place them to that wavering of sentiment which sacrifices the steady principles of government and virtuous consistency, to the giddy pleasure of fickle popularity and ductile compliance. The opposition and extortion thus wantonly thrown upon us, it behoves us to oppose in this public address; and, we trust, that your language, on this occasion, is rather inconsiderately, than deliberately, intended to stigmatise that board, of which your honour has been so many years a member. But this is a subject too delicate for the times, and too pointed to be discussed in such a moment. Yet, surely, it may be permitted us to remark, that, however expedient a compliance with the wishes of the people may have become, your honour might have declined the work of recrimination in this your first public declaration.

" We have hitherto done our utmost for the safety of the island, so often recommended by the late governor, whose attention and unwearied perseverance in the discharge of this part of his duty, every member of this board can vouch for. Whatever difference of opinion may have existed, this tribute surely he claims; nor shall the rage of opposition deter us from giving credit where credit is due. A retrospect of the past, will lead us to adopt the happiest unanimity in all measures that shall conduce to our internal tranquillity and defence; and we look, with pleasure, to the concluding sentiment in your honour's speech. May harmony and peace reside among us; may true freedom for ever flourish over every tyrannic delusion, whether among the rulers or the ruled; may there be one contention only in the different parts of our constitution; the contention of promoting the public good."

This address experienced considerable opposition from some gentlemen of the council. Far from concurring in the resentment expressed in the address against the president for his free and candid declaration concerning the illegality of the fees, extorted by Governor Cunninghame, Mr. Bishop adopted the sentiments of the speech, and asserted, that the fees were not only illegal and unconstitutional, but that they were calculated to establish a dangerous precedent, to the encouragement of future avaricious commanders in chief, to trample upon the rights and properties of the people. The address was, however, agreed to, and, being subscribed by Mr. H. Frere, Mr. Moe, Mr. Best, Mr. Keeling, and Mr. Ince, was presented in due form.

It, however, produced a singular protest, signed by the Rev. Mr. R. Brathwaite, in which, after dissenting from so much of the address as censured the president's remarks on the governor's oppressive exactions, he entered into a formal recantation of his own political heresy. " I do heartily condemn myself," said the reverend divine, " for not having protested against the table of fees which Governor Cunninghame laid before the council, and sincerely wish they could be expunged out of the council-book, and annihilated. His excellency having declared that he should not receive more than fifteen hundred a year of the English salary, and would not accept of the two thousand pounds per annum settled on him by the house of assembly, I, ambitious that the King's representative should have the means of supporting the honour and dignity of his station, acquiesced with him in the measure, not having the least suspicion of the delusive purposes and fallacious drift of the man's mind."

The president too was eager to repel the insinuations of duplicity and vacillation thrown out against him by the council. He published a formal vindication of his conduct, in which much was said and more hinted. Upon a review of what had passed in council, when the question concerning the fees was agitated, he fully exculpated himself, as far as his own uncontradicted assertion can be admitted as exculpatory, from any participation in the guilt of those by whom they were sanctioned. But as the facts, to which he appealed, have been already taken notice of in a former chapter of this volume, it is unnecessary to repeat them in this place.

Agreeable to the forms of the assembly, no answer could be returned to the president's speech until their next meeting, and as the house was on the eve of its dissolution, it was proper that the salary should be taken into immediate consideration. The house having, for this purpose, resolved itself into a committee, Mr. W. G. Alleyne moved, that the sum of fifteen hundred pounds a year should be settled on the president during his administration. An amendment was proposed by Mr. Straker, the object of which was to reduce the settlement to one thousand pounds; but on the question being put, the amendment was lost on a division of eleven to eight, and the original motion was carried in the affirmative by the same majority.

CHAP.XVI.   The house being resumed, unanimously resolved, that
1783.   an humble address be presented to the King, to return his
Majesty their most grateful thanks for having been graciously
pleased to remove Major-General James Cunninghame from
the administration of this government: That the thanks of
this house be transmitted to the Right Honourable the Earl
of Shelburne, for his active zeal and ready execution of
his Majesty's orders for the recal of Governor Cunninghame; by which the country had been happily released
from an arbitrary and oppressive system of taxation, and
the assembly joyfully restored to the accustomed exercise
of their constitutional powers: That the thanks of this
house be transmitted to Samuel Estwick, Esquire, for the
zeal and activity which he had manifested for the public
service, by his patriotic exertions in promoting his excellency's removal from the government of this island.

The assembly having sat the ordinary term of one year,
its existence was terminated by a political euthānasia.
Perfectly satisfied with the conduct of their representatives,
the freeholders of the different parishes hesitated not to en-
trust their rights in the hands of the same faithful guardians*.

---

* The members were for *St. Michael's*, J. Mayers and J. Beckles; *Christchurch*,
J. Burke and T. Burton; *St. Philip's*, J. Gittens and L Millington; *St. George's*,
R. B. Jones and A. Frere; *St. John's*, S. Walcott and R. Haynes; *St. James's*, T.
Alleyne and B. Bostock; *St. Thomas's*, W. G. Alleyne and J. Straker; *St. Peter's*,
S. Hinds and H. Walke; *St. Lucy's*, B. Babb and S. Husbands; *St. Andrew's*, Sir J.
G. Alleyne and A. Cumberbatch; *St. Joseph's*, J. Stewart and T. Waterman.

On the meeting of the new assembly, the session was CHAP.XVI.
opened with the usual formalities, and with a speech 1783. Sept. 3.
from the chair, containing a few trite observations on common topics. The state of Fort George was recommended
to their serious consideration; and to their wisdom it was
left to determine, whether they would be at the expense of
the works which had been begun there; or rest satisfied with the loss of the large sum which had been
already expended on them. His honour congratulated the
assembly on the unanimity of the late elections, and urged
the council to a punctual attendance on their duty in the
court of chancery. The economy of his former administration, in saving the expense of oil for the lamps at Pilgrim, was not forgotten; and he pledged himself to a
strict observance of the same frugality, now that the reins
of government were again placed in his hands. And, while
in the former part of his speech he regretted the insufficiency of the guard at Fort George, were there was a considerable depôt of gunpowder, with a strange inconsistency,
he concluded with recommending a reduction of the matrosses at Pilgrim. This seems to have been an awkward
attempt to acquire popularity, by a scheme of frugality not
less injudicious than trifling. The matrosses were entirely
at his disposal; and he ought to have made such an arrangement as might have strengthened the guard at Fort
George, by a detachment from Pilgrim.

The council's address was a sensible, nervous reply, to the topics adverted to in the speech, and concluded with these just and apposite observations: " Economy could never be practised at a season that calls more loudly for the greatest exertion of it, than at present. But even in economy, there may be a point to stop at; nor should the mind be busied in little savings that are hardly distinguishable in the greater and more necessary expenditure of government. The true medium, it is hoped, will be attained, equally avoiding an improper parsimony, and an useless profusion. Yet, in a war so implicated as the present, it surely cannot be deemed an economy, either requisite or prudent, to relinquish any part of the number of matrosses, whose use is obvious, where cannon are intended as a means of defence."

The assembly availed themselves of this opportunity, to congratulate the president on his re-accession to the chair; which, according to their polite declaration, he had, by his first generous act of power, elevated to an eminent pitch of splendour, and rendered it, what it always ought to be, the seat of dignity and honour. His unreserved condemnation of the tables of fees, set up by Governor Cunninghame, however unpleasant to the few who had conspired with that venal chief in his oppressive measures, could not fail, they said, to endear his honour to that house, and insure to him the affection and confidence of the people over whom he presided. As they could neither discover the utility of Fort George, nor the propriety of expending a larger sum on a place incapable of a permanent defence, they were content rather to lose what it had already cost, than to impose fresh burthens on their constituents, for the purpose of perpetuating the senseless ambition of the oppressor, under whose inauspicious administration it was planned and carried on. They thanked his honour for continuing the system of economy so happily begun during his former presidency, and assured him of their cheerful co-operation in following the great example set by their beloved Sovereign, and adopted by his parliament, to restore the neglected virtue of frugality to its proper rank and influence. This was an allusion to Mr. Burke's economical reform in the expenditure of the civil list. But while that great and enlightened statesman rejected every idea of a mean and pitiful saving, our colonial patriots amused themselves with extinguishing a few lamps, and depriving half a dozen matrosses of their salaries.

The address was most graciously received by the president. He returned his warmest thanks, for the honour which the assembly had done him, and hoped that every act of his administration would give them pleasure ; adding this remarkable declaration : " Let the few, or let the many, oppose me, as much as they can, no power in this world shall prevent me from being a patriot."

While the president was thus displaying his patriotism, by retrenching the public expenses, a gentleman of an ancient family, and amiable character, was manifesting his loyalty and attachment to his native country, by means no less honourable. Emulous of the heroic virtues of his great ancestor, whose name he bore, Mr. Timothy Thornhill, without the smallest legislative assistance, raised a respectable company of infantry, consisting of seventy-four rank and file, under the patronage of General Vaughan, for the service of his Sovereign. This corps was of essential service during the remainder of the war, in strengthening the garrison, not only in Barbadoes, but at Saint Lucia and Antigua. *But Mr. Thornhill was not treated by government with the liberality which he deserved.* On the restoration of peace, his company was disbanded; and, though he was reduced to half pay, he was not allowed to retain his rank in the army.

Notwithstanding the unanimity with which the thanks of the assembly had been voted to Mr. Estwick, the first transports of joy, at the governor's removal, had no sooner subsided, than the error which he had committed became visible, and his conduct was censured with equal severity in England and Barbadoes. His declining the hearing, before the board of trade, was imputed, without reserve, to his wish of affording impunity to the members of council, who were participators in General Cunninghame's guilt. Nor did Mr. Estwick altogether deny the charge, but attempted to justify his partiality, by affecting to consider the members of council equally his constituents with those of the other house. He knew them, he said, to be, in general, natives of the island, men of property, who of course were, or ought to be, as much interested as the assembly, in the happiness and prosperity of the country. Hence he inferred, that to take an active part in a remonstrance against the council, was to discover such an absurdity of conduct, as to disqualify him from any pretensions of ever being again the agent for the island.

The fallacy of this reasoning, however, is evident. The bill for his appointment having been rejected by the governor, he was continued in the agency, by a vote of the assembly alone; and Cunninghame, in a letter to Lord George Germaine, expressed his surprise that he should be received by his Majesty's ministers, as the accredited agent of the island. However favourably he might have been inclined to judge of the council's attachment to their native soil, they had given him such unequivocal proofs, as could not be mistaken, of their readiness to support the strong arm of despotism, in burying the liberties of the people under the ruins of their constitution. But, although Mr. Estwick was doubtless very loth to adopt any measures which might have interfered with his pretensions to the agency, there was another reason, which, though kept out of view, had its full weight. The agent had married the sister of Mr. Frere. The public welfare is too often sacrificed to the petty interests of family connexions, and the sordid considerations of retaining an office.

The introduction of a bill, re-appointing Mr. Estwick agent for the island, furnished the assembly with an opportunity of arraigning his conduct, and shewing their resentment, by discarding him from their service. But, strange as it may appear, no direct opposition was given to the appointment of one whom they soon afterwards, without any clearer evidence of his guilt, declared unworthy of their confidence. A sub-agent was proposed by Mr. Straker, and rejected by a large majority. And he then gave notice, that he should, at the next meeting, submit to the consideration of the house, some resolutions respecting the agent's conduct in declining the hearing of the assembly's complaints against Governor Cunninghame, and the members of council who supported his illegal measures.

1784.

The Barbadians were not permitted to continue long under the patriotic administration of Mr. Dotin. The fall of one ministerial favourite only made room for the advancement of another. On the recommendation of the Earl of Shelburne, his Majesty was pleased to bestow the vacant government on Major David Parry, a native of the principality of Wales, who arrived in Carlisle-bay on the eighth day of the new year.* His excellency landed in state on the Friday following; and, after attending divine service, proceeded to Pilgrim; where, having taken the

Jan. 10.

---

* His excellency came alone, but was soon followed by his lady and their two sons who arrived on the fifteenth day of April.

usual oaths, he was formally invested with his high em-
ployment, At the same time the two vacancies at the council board were filled by Mr. R. J. Estwick and Mr. T. Callender; and his excellency soon afterwards reinstated Mr. Weekes, sole judge of the court of vice-admiralty *.

On the meeting of the colonial parliament, governor Parry addressed both houses in a nervous, animated, public spirited speech. He began, however, with a panegyric, which, it is apprehended, a mind less disposed to indulgence may probably think undeserved. Since his appointment to the government, he said, he had studiously examined and investigated the laws and statutes of the island, and found them so excellent in their nature, and so analogous to his own ideas of civil and political liberty, that he congratulated himself upon the pleasure he should receive in ruling over a free and generous people, under so happy a constitution. He assured them that he should never forget that every subject of the British empire, however remote from the seat of government, is equally entitled to all the constitutional rights and privileges that are enjoyed by his fellow citizens of London and Westminster. Nor could freedom, he remarked, ever forsake an Englishman, while he has wisdom and virtue to cherish and support it. He then recommended to them a perseverance in that loyalty and

---

* Mr. Dotin did not survive his retirement long. He died on the tenth day of October of the same year.

CHAP. XVI. attachment to their King and parent state, which had ever
1784. most honourably marked the annals of Barbadoes, to promote the general welfare of the empire by every public spirited exertion, and by harmony and unanimity at home to
establish, and make permanent, the particular happiness
and prosperity of their native country. And he requested
them to rest satisfied that no effort on his part should be
wanting to bring the bud of reconciliation, that he found
growing among them, to maturity, by a strict adherence to
the laws, with every possible attention to preserve the three
branches of the legislature in perfect equilibrio.

The interesting and critical situation of public affairs, he
told them, demanded their utmost attention; for, although
from the advanced stage of the negotiation with America,
a general pacification would probably ensue, the period of
suspence between peace and war was of all others the most
dangerous; diligence and activity being ever on the watch,
whilst sloth and indolence lay sleeping. The respectable
military force which they possessed, was, he said, under
proper regulations, fully equal to their internal defence.
To this subject he wished to direct their immediate attention, because they had close at their door a bold and enterprising enemy; and, however much the apparent lenity and
insidious policy of his conduct towards the captured islands
may dazzle at a distance, the lettres de catchet and the
mandates of a French minister were very bad exchanges
for magna charta and the bill of rights. To make freemen

happy, he observed, all the knowledge and good parts that can be possessed by a legislator must be enlivened and directed by true patriotism, or they will become pernicious to the state and productive of discord.

Turning to the assembly, he proceeded in these words; " It having been represented to his Majesty, that you have been much hurt and aggrieved by certain tables of fees that were lately erected in this island, I am commanded by his Majesty to signify his will and pleasure, that you forth-with prepare a bill that will effectually prevent the possi-bility of such an evil arising in future. I shall, therefore, leave this and another instruction,* which I hold in my hand under your consideration, earnestly recommending to you a particular attention to the great objects of public receipts and expenditure; by which you will be enabled to establish such a system of economy as will for the present

---

* This was the 36th Instruction. " Whereas laws have heretofore been passed in our said island, establishing fees for the services performed by the several officers therein-mentioned, which laws are now in force; and whereas doubts have arisen as to the legality of any fees established by order of our governor and council, to prevent which in future, it is our will and pleasure that on your first meeting the general as-sembly of the said island, you do propose to them to prepare a bill for the future and permanent regulation and establishment of such fees as may be deemed just and equitable in respect to the public officers, and as little burthensome as possible to our good subjects on the said island; a draught of which bill, when prepared, you are to transmit to us through one of our principal secretaries of state, that our pleasure may be signified to you thereon." The other was the usual instruction respecting the salary.

alleviate, and, I hope, in the course of time, effectually re-move all traces of the great calamity that has lately be-fallen you. I therefore most ardently request, that, as I was not fortunate enough to come among you in the days of your opulence, I may not add to your distresses in the hour of your misfortune. Satisfied that whenever Provi-dence shall again extend her bounteous hand over this happy island, the fruits of her beneficence will speedily reach Pilgrim." Nothing could have been more liberal and noble than these sentiments; they failed, however, to pro-duce their proper effect on the assembly.

The addresses in answer to the speech reverberated his excellency's patriotic sentiments. Each house seemed emu-lous to surpass the other in the warmest professions of re-spect and esteem for the person and character of the gover-nor, of profound loyalty and fidelity to the king, inviolable attachment to the constitution, and the most zealous regard for the welfare of their country. From his excellency's constitutional declarations the assembly anticipated, with rapturous exultation, the felicity and prosperity which they should enjoy under the administration of a gentleman who had studiously examined the volume of their laws, in order to make them the rule and principles of his government. Both houses professed equal anxiety for the preservation of harmony and unanimity in their proceedings, and concluded with the most fervent assurances of their cheerful co-operation in every measure essential to the public welfare and safety.

Having returned to their own hall, the assembly resolved themselves into a committee of the whole house, for the purpose of taking the governor's salary into their immediate consideration. The debate was opened by Sir John G. Alleyne's proposing two resolutions, the object of which was to restrain the assembly from raising or granting any money, for any purpose whatever, until their rights and privileges were secured from invasion, by a law declaring that the power of establishing fees existed only in the three branches of the legislature collectively; but that as soon as an act of that kind should pass, the assembly would then proceed to make such a provision for the better support of his excellency's dignity as the state of the public finances would permit.

On these principles he had prepared two separate bills, the first, declaratory of the rights of the assembly; which in the event of its receiving the concurrence of the other orders of the legislature, was to be followed by a second, for the support of government. This mode of proceeding was certainly liable to material objections. It was treating his excellency with a degree of illiberality and distrust, which nothing could justify, after the patriotic sentiments which were yet vibrating in their ears, and the gracious instruction which had been just read. The measure of framing a bill to remove all doubts on the subject of fees, came recommended to them from the throne; to make the passing of such a law, therefore, the condition on which the governor's salary depended, was neither respectful nor decorous. The stipulation was as offensive as the caution in which it originated was unnecessary. After a long and animated debate, in which the resolutions were vehemently opposed by Mr. A. Frere and Mr. Mayers, the speaker said he had not so great a predilection for his plan as to feel any difficulty in withdrawing his motion, if the end in view was likely to be attained more effectually, and with greater unanimity, by other means.

The resolutions having been accordingly withdrawn, Mr. Frere moved, that the two bills which had been prepared by Sir J. G. Alleyne should be blended together, and their titles thus united, " An act declaring the right of establishing fees to be only in the three branches of the legislature in their collective capacity; and for the better support of his excellency and the dignity of the government of this island." This arrangement comprehended all the indelicacy, absurdity, and irregularity of the plan which had been rejected but the instant before, without embracing any of its advantages. Probably the gentleman by whom the motion was made, thought with a popular parliamentary leader, in times less favourable to civil liberty, that the most effectual means of obtaining redress was by making *grievances and supplies go hand in hand together*; but an acquaintance with the more modern usage of the British Parliament would have shewn him the irregularity of his plan; and have taught him that it is a standing order of the House of Lords to reject any bill sent up by the Commons connected with a money bill.*

Composed of these heterogenous materials, the bill was agreed to by the committee; but in filling up the blank, a fresh subject of altercation was started; whether the sum to be settled on his excellency should be two or three thousand pounds annually. This question was canvassed with an unusual degree of warmth and vehemence, and was finally determined in favour of the smaller sum, by a majority of thirteen voices to nine. The declaratory part of the act, relating to the right of establishing fees, formed no impediment to its progress through the council chamber; and his excellency, on its being presented for his assent, generously expressed himself in these words: " I am truly sorry for the causes that oblige you to lessen your donation, but am as well pleased with it as if it was ten times as much."

Pursuant to the notice given at a former meeting, Mr. Straker now brought forward his promised investigation of the agent's conduct. In an able, elegant, and perspicuous speech he proved, from a clear and candid review of the whole transaction, that Mr. Estwick had grossly abused

---

* De Lolme on the Constitution, p. 77. *note.*

the trust reposed in him by the house, and concluded with moving two resolutions. First, that the agent by declining to bring the complaints of the assembly to a hearing before the Lords of Trade, without having obtained a solemn declaration of our rights as a security against any future invasion, acted contrary to his duty. Secondly, that so great a neglect, in a point which so materially concerned the immunities of the commons of Barbadoes, as it must be imputed either to a defect in judgment, or to a wilful desertion of the cause, from partial motives, renders him unworthy of the future confidence of the assembly. The motion was productive of a long and interesting debate, in which the conduct of the agent was canvassed with great acuteness and ingenuity, and commented upon with equal freedom and asperity. His defence was undertaken with great zeal and spirit by his two kinsmen, Mr. Applewhaite Frere and Mr. Jones, who displayed an uncommon share of talents upon the occasion. The debate was rendered more remarkable by the distinguished part taken by Mr. John Beckles, a young member, who, in support of the motion, gave an early specimen of those commanding powers of eloquence which have since secured him a deserved pre-eminence in the senate and at the bar. Notwithstanding the notoriety of the facts on which the resolutions were grounded, and the great abilities exerted in their support, they were rejected by a majority of ten to seven.

The freedom with which the agent's conduct was examined, and the severity with which it was condemned, were sufficient to provoke the resentment of a man less irritable, and less firmly persuaded of his own importance, than Mr. Estwick. It is not to be wondered at, therefore, that the censure which he sustained upon this occasion, should have produced the most violent explosion of anger and indignation. In a printed letter, addressed to the speaker of the assembly, he poured forth a torrent of illiberal invective on those public-spirited members, whose strictures on his misconduct had rendered them obnoxious to his resentment. The intemperate warmth of this letter considerably lessened the number of Mr. Estwick's friends in the assembly. Sensible of the indignity with which he had presumed to treat them, the house agreed to several resolutions, purporting that the agent's indecent and illiberal letter, reflecting on two of their members for exercising the freedom of debate, was an insult on their body: that the reasons which he had assigned for declining the hearing before the board of trade, were no justification of his conduct: and, finally, that he was no longer worthy of their confidence. These resolutions, which were transmitted to Mr. Estwick, by the speaker, produced another acrimonious letter, in which, he affirmed that the loss of the agency could occasion no regret to him who had refused to be their ruler. The candid and upright conduct of the venerable speaker of the assembly, in expressing a just resentment against Mr. Estwick, for his libel on the house, was maliciously imputed to the rage of disappointed ambition, occasioned by the failure of his application for the government of the island. Mr. Estwick said, that Lord Radnor called upon him, soon after General Cunninghame's removal, and inquired if he did not think that Sir John G. Alleyne's succeeding to the government, would reconcile all differences, and put an end to disturbances; to which he replied, that he did not think it would; for there being two interests in the country, either taking the lead of the other would, perhaps, rather increase their animosity than reconcile them. His lordship, afterwards, applied to Lord Shelburne, in behalf of Sir John Alleyne, and was refused. Against this charge, Sir John Alleyne vindicated himself, with his usual ability. He did not entirely disavow the application made by his noble relative, but, with a mind conscious of its purity, appealed to the integrity of his life for the proof of his faithful and disinterested exertions in the public service.

Meanwhile the two-fold act, respecting the right of establishing fees, and the settlement on the governor, having been transmitted to England, for his Majesty's information, was referred to the consideration of a committee of the lords of the privy council. Upon which their lordships reported, " That the act contained clauses relative to matters which had no connexion with each other, one of which was foreign to the import of the title of the act; and that, although no clauses of an incongruous nature should be inserted in the same act, one part of it was intended to operate as a perpetual declaratory law, while the other part was in its nature temporary*. Another, and still more forcible objection against the operation of the act, was deduced from the circumstance of the assembly having preferred the most serious charges against the late Governor Cunninghame, for establishing, by an order of council, certain fees, which they asserted to be illegal; his Majesty was pleased to refer the same to the consideration and opinion of the late board of trade; and, in the very moment when the propriety of General Cunninghame's conduct was at issue before that board, upon whose representation his Majesty would have proceeded to a conclusive determination, the agent of the assembly declined the pursuit."

The assembly were deeply affected at the royal disapprobation of the declaratory law; and even the most sceptical could no longer doubt the impropriety of Mr. Estwick's conduct. Unwilling, however, to admit the irregularity of their own proceedings, they consoled themselves under the disappointment, by imputing the disallowance of the act

---

* Wisdom is not always acquired by experience. Notwithstanding this reproof, the assembly have fallen into a similar error. The act, increasing the fines on jurors required to attend the court of grand sessions, refers for admissable excuses for non-attendance to the exemptions allowed by the *present* militia law, then near expiring, and which does not now exist.—1807.

to the inauspicious change in his Majesty's councils; the coalition ministry of Lord North and Mr. Fox having succeeded to the short-lived administration of Lord Shelburne. That his excellency might sustain no injury, by the rejection of the bill, the assembly unanimously voted him a salary of two thousand pounds a year, to commence from the day on which he assumed the government.

Meanwhile, a general election having taken place, the new assembly met on the eleventh day of September. In the governor's speech, at the commencement of the session, the public spirit, so conspicuous at this season, could not fail, it was said, to produce the most happy effects; for public virtue is ever productive of public benefits; and the unanimity with which the late elections were conducted, would, his excellency trusted, inspire every honest breast with such a share of benevolence, as should divert mens' views from the little disgraceful objects of private interest to the more noble and liberal prospect of the public good. Encouraged by such favourable appearances, and impelled by a particular anxiety for the prosperity of the island, his excellency was induced to suggest a few legislative and economical reforms.

" The spirit of laws," he observed, " is equity, and it might be better for all communities, if they adhered more to the spirit than the bare letter of the law. Laws should be adapted to the circumstances of the times. What might have been very proper, at one period of a state's existence, might be very improper at another, which may, perhaps, lead you to think that what was well calculated for this island, in the zenith of prosperity, may be ill suited to the present hour of distress. Distress, which I feel most poignantly, when I behold the devastation that is made by the too hasty, or injurious, execution of the laws, by which the junior creditors are much hurt, the lands laid waste, or converted into provision fields, your staple products lessened, your trade irreparably injured, and the royal revenue excessively diminished. To these growing evils emigration will succeed, and the strength and safety of the island be affected. Your negroes too, the pillars of the colony, for without them the land will be of little use, are, I see with regret, daily sent off in crowds, under the sanction of a very defective law. I shall, therefore, leave your wisdom and experience to determine whether it will not be prudent and necessary to check the present unlimited power of exporting so valuable a part of your property."

A revisal of the militia law, and the state of the fortifications, those topics of perpetual, unavailing declamation, were next adverted to with great propriety. Nor was the culpable neglect of the commissioners of public accounts passed over without a gentle reprehension. Addressing himself to the assembly, his excellency observed, " As the levying of all public money is the undoubted right of the representatives of the people, so it is their business to look into the expenditure of it when raised. Public accounts cannot be settled too often, or inspected too narrowly; those of this island have been strangely neglected; the laws of the country give you the power of control, and the interest of your constituents should furnish inclination to exercise it."

The addresses of both houses were written in the usual polite and respectful style. The honour reflected on the public, by the unanimity which marked the late elections, was courteously imputed to the mild and disinterested tenor of his excellency's administration, which left them without a subject of contention. Ever querulous and discontented, the assembly lamented, that after all the evils and disasters under which they had been long suffering, the blessings of peace should at last come to them, clogged with the disadvantages of war; a heavy load of duty upon their chief staple, with an uncertain commerce for the supply of their plantations, and the sale of their produce. While they acknowledged and deplored the devastation occasioned by the too rigorous execution of the laws upon the estates of unfortunate debtors, as tending to the removal of slaves to other more flourishing settlements, such was the force of their attachment to an absurd and pernicious system of jurisprudence, that they professed themselves unable to suggest any remedy for the evil, consistent with the long established rights of the fair creditor, and the faithful administration of justice. With regard to the other topics submitted to their consideration, warm professions of zeal for the public good, and of attention to the means by which it may be best promoted, were substituted for those exertions by which the object which they professed to have in view might have been easily accomplished.

A spirit of licentiousness and insubordination among the negroes, about this time, hurried them into the commission of many atrocities. Among these, the murder of Doctor John Horsham, is perhaps unparalleled for sanguinary cruelty and wanton inhumanity. This gentleman was a practitioner of physic, of considerable reputation, of manners mild and inoffensive, and had been absent from the island until within seventeen days of his assassination. In the exercise of his profession, Doctor Horsham had, on the day of his death, visited a plantation, called Tuncks's, whence he was proceeding on his diurnal rounds, when he was unfortunately driven by a shower of rain to seek shelter in a thatched shed, or watch-house, near the road, and within half a mile of the buildings which he had just left. Under this cover, the doctor found several negro-men, one of whom, called Nick, belonging to Tuncks's, he employed to hold his horse. The rain being over, Mr. Horsham proposed to pursue his journey, but, on attempting to quit the shed, he was seized by two of the men, while a third stabbed him on the right side of the neck, dividing the jugular vein, and gave him a wound under the left breast, which pierced his heart. The horse was afterwards given to the ranger of the plantation, with an information that it

CHAP.XVI. was found grazing, and carried to the manager, Mr. F. S.
1784. Bayley, by whom it was ordered to be put into the stable
and taken care of, until the next day, when it was sent to
the house of the deceased. This occasioned an alarm in
the doctor's family, and produced a diligent inquiry into
the cause of his absence. At length some information was
received from a negro girl, who, at a distance, was an eye
witness of the tragic scene ; and the corpse, by her direction, was found buried in a field of canes, about thirty
feet from the road.

After a full and patient investigation of the affair, which
lasted the greater part of three days, the coroner's inquest
pronounced a verdict of wilful murder against four negro
men ; Nick, already mentioned, and Jeffery, Prince, and
Sambo, belonging to the Belle plantation. But, on their
subsequent trial for the murder, Nick and Sambo only
were found guilty. The jury not thinking the evidence
sufficient for the conviction of Prince or Jeffery, they
were of course acquitted ; though, on the sentence being
passed, Sambo exclaimed, " We were all together ;" insinu-
ating that they were all equally guilty. The murderers
were afterwards executed, pursuant to their sentence, without discovering the smallest signs of contrition. At the
place of execution, Nick confessed his having formerly
murdered a youth, in a neighbouring plantation, and accused three others of being accomplices in the crime for
which he was going to suffer. One of these, called Borgia,

on hearing the charge, eluded the punishment of the law, by taking a dose of poison, which he carried about him for the purpose. The second was retained as a witness against the third, who, after a trial of nine hours, was fully convicted, and condemned to suffer death.

Of the motives which led to the perpetration of this horrid murder, it is impossible to speak with certainty, or even probability. From the evidence adduced on the trial, it does not appear that the unfortunate man had given the assassins the smallest provocation; neither could they have been instigated to the fatal act, by a wish to rob him; for not even the most trifling article which he had about him was removed from his person, all was found deposited with him in the place of his interment. To a principle of cruelty, inherent in the nature of these ruffians, we must then refer for the proximate cause of an act of such wanton and deliberate barbarity.

CHAP. XVII.

ALTERCATION BETWEEN THE TWO HOUSES CONCERNING THE EX-
CISE-BILL—APPOINTMENT OF A NEW AGENT—AUGMENTATION
OF THE GOVERNOR'S SALARY—SINGULAR PHÆNOMENON—A
LOTTERY—ARRIVAL OF PRINCE WILLIAM HENRY—COMMER-
CIAL REGULATIONS—LEGISLATIVE PROCEEDINGS—MILITARY
OUTRAGE—THE GOVERNOR RETURNS TO ENGLAND—PRESI-
DENCY OF MR. FRERE—THE GOVERNOR'S RETURN—HE REGU-
LATES THE CURRENCY OF THE GOLD COIN—HIS EXCELLENCY
RESIGNS THE GOVERNMENT TO MR. BISHOP—SUSPENSION OF
JUDGE WEEKES—MILITARY OPERATIONS—THE PRESIDENT'S
EXTRAORDINARY ZEAL FOR THE SERVICE.

CHAP. XVII.
1785.

THE harmony which at this time happily subsisted between the different orders of the legislature, and which each
professed an anxiety to cultivate and render permanent,
without feeling a disposition to make any concessions for its
preservation, soon suffered a temporary interruption, by a
dispute between the council and assembly concerning the
excise-bill. For the perfect comprehension of the nature
of this dispute it is necessary to premise, that the act, lay-

ing a duty on wines and other strong liquors, on importation, commonly called the excise-bill, had been, from its
origin, considered of a temporary nature. Its continuance
was expressly limited *to one year, and from thence till the
expiration of forty days, and from thence forward, until the
island is fully represented by a new assembly, according to
the laws in force.*

The obvious intention of this limitation was to secure to
the assembly the certainty of an annual meeting, if for no
other purpose than to exercise their constitutional right of
voting the supplies for the service of government. But in
the excise act, which passed in the year one thousand seven hundred and seventy-four, the council, ever anxious to
encroach on the privileges of the house of representatives,
or, perhaps, from a motive equally unjustifiable, a petulant
wish to mortify the patriotic speaker, whose peculiar pride
and boast it was to guard the privileges of the assembly,
added these words to the clause of limitation, *and until a
new excise-bill shall pass, and become of full force in this
island.* This interpolation, introduced in a manner unworthy the dignity of a legislative body, escaped the vigilant
eye of the speaker, and the act, thus altered, received the
governor's assent. Thus, instead of an annual supply, re-
newable at the discretion of the assembly, a revenue was
established, which, if not absolutely perpetual, possessed
all the disadvantages of perpetuity.

When it was too late to apply a remedy, the assembly

discovered the unfair advantage which had been taken of their want of circumspection. During the progress of the war, and the contest in which they were involved with the council concerning Governor Cunninghame's illegal fees, they silently submitted to the injury ; but, when the establishment of peace abroad and concord at home seemed to furnish a prospect of success, they attempted to recover the right of which they had been surreptitiously deprived. With this view, they passed an excise-bill in the usual

Feb. 17. form, which was sent back by the council, with a message, contrary to parliamentary usage, assigning their reasons for rejecting it; but, at the same time, expressing their readiness to concur in any bill of the same tenor, provided its existence should be protracted until the passing of another excise-law. Had the assembly complied with this proposal, it is evident that they would have relinquished, as far as respected that branch of the revenue, the power of granting, or withholding the supplies; the only constitutional check on the executive authority, possessed by the representatives of the people.

The answer of the assembly was remarkable for its mildness and moderation. In a calm, dispassionate, but tedious review of the subject, from the origin of the duty to the date of the last excise act, including a period of one hundred and twenty years, they shewed, that it had been invariably an annual measure of finance. Nor could they, consistently with their duty to their constituents, or a just regard to their own inherent privileges, they said, yield to a proposition, which must deliberately and clearly tend to establish a perpetual revenue.

To this the council replied, with an unbecoming degree of warmth and asperity, " It seems useless to agitate any question where the parties have taken decided resolutions. Predilection supersedes the necessity of argument. Foreseeing the mischiefs attending the want of a revenue, when caprice or mistaken resentment may think proper to withhold it, the council are resolved not to lose the power which the disputed clause in the excise-bill gives them of preventing the anarchy and confusion that may arise from a total stoppage of public expenditure. To argue upon a supposition that any constitutional rights are invaded, or that any proposition is made to curtail the privileges of the assembly, is to raise up an hydra-headed monster, which could never have existence, but in the heated imaginations of mistaken minds. The council disdain the idea; they consider the fund raised by the excise act as coming not immediately under the cognizance of the representatives of the people, it being an impost laid, not upon the manufactures or produce of the country, but upon articles of foreign growth, meant to answer the contingencies of government, and which has been wisely permitted by the Crown for such salutary purposes. Bearing this in their minds, the council think it a duty which they owe to the Crown, to adhere to the rejection of any excise-bill that shall come before them, without such a clause as was inserted in the excise-law now in force. This determination experience justifies them in adopting. They see clearly that such a clause as they require in the excise-bill, though at present it gives disturbance to the assembly, may prevent a greater disturbance, by hindering an oppressive measure of accumulating on the people a great and insupportable tax at one period, by the delusive appearance of relief held out for a few preceding years. That the bill by this bug-bear clause is made perpetual is surely a mistake, and a mere play upon words: the perpetuity lies with the assembly. An annual bill may be sent up, with such clauses as, from time to time, may become necessary, and which, it is hoped, the council, not less zealous than the house of assembly, in the service of their country, will adopt, when it appears to them that such alterations are conducive to the public benefit. The prevention of an evil is all that is aimed at; and which, however illiberal the doubts arising thereon may appear to the assembly, the council, by a retrospect of the past, are too well justified in their attempts to preclude."

From the whole tenor of this message it is evident, that the old leaven of discord, notwithstanding the appearance of amity which the council had lately exhibited, was still fermenting in their minds; and that they were determined to retain at their command a disposable revenue, to render future commanders in chief, in some measure, independent of the representatives of the people. This determination was grounded on the firmness with which the assembly withheld the regular supplies during the administration of General Cunninghame; when, however justifiable the motives, the effects were most disastrous, in the accumulation of a debt far exceeding the colonial resources; and which, in all probability, never would have been paid, but for the bounty of parliament. The reasons assigned by the council were specious; but at the period to which they alluded, they had given such a specimen of their zeal for the public service, as to preclude all confidence in their integrity whenever they should be called upon to decide between the wishes of the governor and the interests of the people. The house considering any farther altercation beneath their dignity, prudently declined making any reply to the message. But the appointment of an agent soon furnished a fresh topic for disagreement.

After the criminatory resolutions of the assembly respecting Mr. Estwick, it would have been highly incongruous to have continued him in an employment, in the exercise of which he had added insolence to treachery; insult to injury. They, therefore, passed a bill, nominating Mr. John Brathwaite, a gentleman of the most amiable character, and unblemished reputation, to the office of colonial agent; but the council refused to concur in an appointment so prejudicial to the interests of one whose partiality to their board was his greatest crime.   The assembly, however, persisted in their choice; they appointed a committee to correspond with their newly-elected agent; and, to his immortal honour be it recorded, Mr. Brathwaite generously and disinterestedly executed the office, with equal diligence and fidelity, for several years, without enjoying its emoluments.

As Mr. Estwick, in refusing to bring the charges against General Cunninghame, and the six members of council who had abetted his illegal proceedings, to a hearing before the board of trade, had acted without the consent or previous knowledge of the assembly, the new agent was directed to pursue such measures as he should deem proper to enforce their complaints, and obtain a redress of their injuries, agreeable to their former petition to the King.   But, as the petition had been imprudently, not to say perfidiously abandoned, before the complaints against the governor had been substantiated, Mr. Brathwaite thought that it could not be resumed nor acted upon with any prospect of success.

At the same time the assembly unanimously resolved to instruct their agent to call upon Mr. Estwick to account for the fifteen hundred pounds which had been lodged in his hands by the sub-committee, in London, for the purpose of carrying on the prosecution against Governor Cunninghame.   To this demand Mr. Estwick replied, that he was ready to account for the money whenever he was legally required to do so; but, as that could only be done through the medium of an agent appointed by the law of the island, he should regard this resolution of theirs no more than he would that of " a set of drunken porters." By his explanation of this affair, however, it appeared, that one thousand pounds were due to him for five years salary, and that he had advanced two hundred and seventy pounds of his own money for the public service, besides other charges incident to the office, to a considerable amount. No part of this debt, he asserted, would ever have been paid, but for the dreadful hurricane, which, according to his own observation, had thus verified the old adage; " that it is an ill wind that blows no one any good." The assembly having inconsiderately subjected themselves to these insults, discovered, when it was too late, that they had no authority to make the demand; for as the money placed in his hands was a part of the parliamentary bounty, it was contended by Mr. Beckles, that he was only accountable to the commissioners, to whose disposal it had been entrusted.

Meanwhile, the governor effected a reform in the disbursements of the powder office of far greater consequence to the community than the petty retrenchments for which President Dotin had been so highly commended, or even the saving in General Cunninghame's salary, which had been the source of so much strife and inquietude. The waste of stores in the different garrisons had long been complained of as a serious grievance, without any effectual remedy having been suggested for the evil. But it was in Saint Peter's that the abuse was carried to the most lawless extent. There the officers thought they had a prescriptive right to wanton with the stores committed to their charge to any extremity, to which folly, or vanity should lead. Within the short term of three months after Mr. W. Bishop had been appointed to the command of that division, the consumption of gunpowder, on occasions of private festivity, amounted to near five thousand weight; an expenditure, which, had it been continued, would have drawn two thousand pounds a year out of the molehead fund, for the amusement of the officers of that district alone. Indignant at so flagrant an abuse of power, the author of this volume availed himself of the freedom of the press, to convey to the knowledge of the commander in chief, a fact so injurious to the public revenue. Nor was redress delayed. From that time, the disbursements for each division, except Saint Michael's, have been limited to ten barrels of powder annually, unless it be under very particular circumstances, which make a larger quantity absolutely necessary.

The proceedings of the assembly were now marked by an occurrence, which, however right the measure might appear, abstractedly considered, was rendered dishonourable by the manner in which it was accomplished. On the sixth day of July, when there was a very thin attendance of the members, a motion was made by Mr. R. B. Jones, seconded by Mr. A. Frere, to grant his excellency an additional salary of one thousand pounds a year. The proposal was warmly resisted by the speaker. Though he admitted the governor's extraordinary merit, he did not think that the forms of the house should be dispensed with on that account; and that a motion of such consequence should be made without the smallest previous notice. To carry such a question by surprise, and in so thin a house, he said, would neither be honourable to his excellency, nor creditable to the assembly. Several members concurring in these sentiments, the previous question was moved; but, during the debate, Mr. Mayers, being called from the court of chancery, gave the advocates for the additional salary the advantage of numbers; and the motion was negatived by a majority of one.

The original motion was then put, and carried in the affirmative, on a close division of seven to six. Not to lose the favourable opportunity of accomplishing his design, Mr. Jones immediately introduced a bill, which had been previously prepared, and which having been read three times, was passed by a majority of one voice. Determined to give the measure every opposition in his power, the speaker now resorted to the only expedient which was left. He adverted to the tenth rule of the house, by which it was declared, " that no bill whatever, or order of the house for payment of money, shall pass, or be delivered over by the clerk, unless it be read and voted three distinct times, at two several meetings or sittings, between which one Sunday, at least, shall intervene; or unless extraordinary necessity require more speedy dispatch, and in such case, if twelve members consent, or if the bill, or address, pass nemine contradicente, it shall be good and valid, though read but at one sitting.

Agreeably to this rule, Sir John Alleyne observed, the bill could not pass, as it was supported by only seven members, but must be read for passing at the next meeting. But the friends of the measure, impatient of delay, were not to be restrained by a rule which could be broken with impunity, especially when its infraction would facilitate their views. They insisted that the house had a right to dispense with their rules whenever they thought proper to disregard them; and that the same power by which they were established, could unquestionably alter or annul them. As an abstract proposition, it will not be denied that every society, which has authority to prescribe laws for its own government, is equally competent to annul or repeal them; but the change should be made on a general principle, and not merely to answer a sinister or temporary purpose. The society which occasionally deviates from the rules established to regulate its proceedings, is in fact in a state of vacillation, without any certain guide or principle of action. All the speaker's eloquence was exerted without effect. In vain he insisted on the necessity of a strict observance of their rules, and urged the dishonour which must be reflected on their proceedings, by such wavering and inconsistency. The measure was predetermined; the rule was rescinded, the bill passed both houses, and received the governor's assent the same day. At a subsequent meeting of the assembly, the violated rule was restored to its rank; and to prevent any similar attempt in future, it was resolved, that if any member move to repeal any rule of the house, except on the first meeting of the assembly, or at some other sitting, when every member shall be present, he shall be expelled, and the speaker be at liberty to quit the chair.

Among the various operations of nature, which excite our admiration, alarm our fears, or amuse our imagination, the following singular and extraordinary phenomenon will not probably, be deemed the least curious and interesting. On the eleventh day of October, the inhabitants of a part of Saint Joseph's parish, called Crab-hole, were alarmed at the appearance of several deep fissures in the earth, and their apprehensions were soon augmented, at finding that some small tenements had sunk to a considerable depth. These alarming appearances continuing to increase, many persons were induced to remove their effects to places of greater safety. The plantation, known by the name of Walcott's, was destined to be the melancholy scene of this extraordinary occurrence. Here the manager, perceiving that the mansion house was in danger of being buried under the soil, which was descending in large, connected masses, from a neighbouring hill, fled with his family to one of the negro huts for shelter. In the course of that distressful night, most of the buildings on the plantation fell, or sunk into a deep chasm, which was presently filled up with the mold from the the adjacent heights. The alarm now became general, and the people assembling near the spot were witnesses of a scene truly awful and affecting. The aspect of the whole region from Walcott's to Crabhole, extending upwards of a mile in length, and in breadth about three hundred yards, exhibited a lamentable prospect. The earth, violently torn asunder, was intersected with numerous chasms, whose widely extended jaws seemed ready to ingulph whatever might be precipitated into them; while, in other places it was swelled and inflated with enormous tumours, whose convulsive motions menaced the few remaining buildings with destruction. Nor was it long before they were involved in the general wreck, and, sinking into the yawning gulf, left no traces of their former existence behind them. The face of nature was so completely changed in that district, that few of the inhabitants could ascertain the spot on which many objects, familiar to their remembrance, had been recently placed. A field, planted in Eddoes, occupied the site on which the mansion house stood, and brought with it a long slip of the broad road, as perfect and entire as if it had not been removed.* The

* This is an occurrence that happens, not infrequently, in the parishes of Saint

cocoa-nut trees, which grew about the house, and even the wind-mill, were gradually carried some hundred yards from their original situation, where the latter was completely swallowed up, no part of it remaining visible but the extremity of the upper arm.

It is not easy, perhaps, to explain satisfactorily the cause of this extraordinary phenomenon. Probable conjecture ascribed it to the action of a number of subterraneous springs, in a loamy sandy soil, surrounded with recent excessive falls of rain: these springs, struggling for vent, might possibly have excavated the incumbent earth wherever they endeavoured to force a passage. As these invisible waters glided onwards, the surface behind seems to have fallen in, or, meeting with a substratum of a soapy nature, continued sliding down the adjacent declivities as long as it retained, or acquired, sufficient moisture to facilitate its motion.

Andrew and Saint Joseph, during the rainy season. In that part of the country, which, from its resemblance to the highlands of North Britain, is called Scotland, the earth is composed of various strata obliquely disposed. The super-stratum is generally a rich loamy soil of a saponaceous nature, which, being of no considerable depth, easily separates, when saturated with rain, from the substratum, which is commonly of a slippery chalk, flat stones, or loose, red gravel, and slides in large masses, with its growing produce, into the vallies below. Thus whole fields of sugar canes, corn, and potatoes have sometimes changed masters, and even lofty trees have been removed to a considerable distance without injury. Of this the curious reader may find instances related in Hughes's Nat. Hist. Barb. p. 21.

Among the financial expedients of the present year, the assembly proposed raising the sum of fifty thousand pounds by two lotteries, for the purpose of repairing their fallen sanctuaries, which had not been rebuilt since the hurricane. In the original bill, which had been passed two years before, the whole profit to be produced by the scheme was made applicable to the rebuilding of St. Michael's church, without making any provision for the others, which had suffered by the same calamity. But as the raising of money, in the way proposed, was contrary to the positive instructions of the governor, the bill was transmitted to the secretary of state, to be laid before the King. The partiality of the arrangement did not escape the observation of the privy council, and the bill was consequently disallowed by the King. But, as the object of the measure appeared to be useful, his Majesty was pleased to authorise the governor to give his assent to any bill of a similar tendency, provided one half of the money raised should be applied to the rebuilding the church of Saint Michael, and the other half to the use of those parishes whose churches had been destroyed. An act was accordingly passed, agreeably to his Majesty's gracious directions; but it was not productive of those advantages, which were expected from it. The drawing of only one lottery was effected, nor was this done without difficulty and dishonour. One of the managers, to whom the sale of the tickets was entrusted, embezzled the money which he received, and, though he had given sufficient security for the faithful performance of the trust, the bonds were never enforced.

The state of the public roads had long been a subject of general complaint, and though the inefficiency of the existing laws for their repair and improvement was readily perceived and acknowledged, no attempt had been made to alter or amend a system confessedly inefficacious, burthensome, and expensive. At length a number of the most respectable planters of St. George's, and several of the adjacent parishes, presented a petition to the assembly, representing the evils and inconveniences resulting from that cause; and praying that the house would pass an act for the more effectual repair of the great road leading from Bridge-Town to Saint Philip's church. Agreeably to the prayer of the petition, Mr. A. Frere introduced a bill for the establishment of turnpikes, which, after passing the house, was rejected by the council. Encouraged by the obvious utility of the measure, Mr. Frere brought it forward a second time, with a few alterations, to render it less objectionable above stairs. Having gone through the usual stages below, it was again sent up to the council-chamber; where, although, agreeably to every parliamentary acceptation of the term, it was clearly a money bill, no less than eight amendments were made in it. Heedless of this invasion of their privileges, the assembly quietly acquiesced in most of the amendments. But this was not enough to satisfy the council; not content with a partial adoption of their emendations, they again rejected the bill. Disappointed, but not discouraged, Mr. Frere made a third attempt to effect his purpose, in which he was eventually successful. Turnpikes were established, and the roads were effectually repaired. But the spirit which animated the measure, soon evaporated; it was neglected and forgotten.

During the progress of this bill an act was passed for establishing *regular* courts of quarter sessions, and empowering the justices to appoint constables within their precincts. By this law it is enacted, that courts of quarter sessions shall be *occasionally* held every year in each parish; and that no constable shall be compelled to serve longer than one whole year, commencing from the day of his being sworn, *and until the first meeting of a court of quarter sessions after the expiration of the said year.* These latter words condemn the constables to little less than perpetual servitude. Far from that regularity which is promised by the title of the act, courts of quarter sessions are not holden oftener than once in four or five years; and in one instance the period has been extended to eighteen or twenty. This irregularity in holding the courts, and the consequent uncertainty of obtaining a release from the irksome duties of this office, is a real and substantial grievance.

Notwithstanding the public debt had been so recently and completely liquidated by the appropriation of a large part of the parliamentary bounty, and a considerable surplus remained applicable to the exigencies of government, such was the unwillingness of the assembly to draw the purse-strings of their constituents, that no one belonging to the colonial establishment, except the governor, had been paid for more than two years. Frequently had his excellency warned the assembly of the folly and danger of suffering the public debt to accumulate to any considerable amount. The only notice taken of his judicious admonitions was to assure his excellency that they were restrained from doing justice to the public creditors only by the desire of collecting the money due to the treasury from individuals. During the short time that Mr. T. Rowe administered the revenue of the country, there was a deficiency of two thousand pounds in his accounts; and, though the public creditors, for the greater part of that time were peculiarly distressed, seven years had already elapsed without any effectual attempt having been made to obtain restitution from his representative. But, however, the assembly might have felt the collection of this money as a necessary, though painful duty imposed on them, there seems to have been great injustice in suspending the claims of a numerous train of distressed public creditors on that account. At length the gunners and matrosses of several divisions were compelled by necessity to appeal to the equity and humanity of the assembly. This application produced the desired effect; and a trifling capitation tax of fifteen pence on slaves was found sufficient to restore the credit of the country.

Notwithstanding their inattention to the state of the public finances, the assembly occasionally gave proofs of a liberality as commendable as it was inconsistent with the

parsimony which generally marked their proceedings. The arrival of his Royal Highness Prince William Henry, afterwards Duke of Clarence, commander of the Pegasus frigate, was one of those occasions which called forth the most ardent demonstrations of loyalty and affection. At Pilgrim his royal highness was received with every possible mark of respect, and all ranks of people seemed emulous of manifesting their veneration and esteem for the person and family of their illustrious visitor. The presence of the son of a Monarch revered for his virtues, and justly regarded as the father of his people, inspired every breast with joy and gladness. His arival was greeted with the most affectionate addresses of congratulation from the members of his Majesty's council, the general assembly, the clergy, and the merchants of Bridge-town, and even the Jews, as a distinct body of people, joined in the general acclamation, and expressed their gratitude for the happiness and protection which they enjoyed under the clemency of his royal father.

The short time which the prince remained in Barbadoes was the season of mirth and festivity. Besides the balls and entertainments given by Governor Parry in honour of his illustrious guest, his royal highness was sumptuously entertained by the legislature, at the public expense; and in the plenitude of their zeal the council overstepped their constitutional bounds, and sent a message to the assembly, proposing that a sword should be procured, as soon as possible, and presented to his royal highness as an humble but sincere testimony of their veneration, affection, and respect for a prince who had graciously condescended to visit their island; and who had voluntarily relinquished the elegant enjoyments of a polished court to encounter the dangers and inconveniences of a naval life in the service of his country. The assembly replied, that as it was the established privilege of their house, that all grants of the public money should originate with them, they could not consistently with their ancient rights accede to any proposition for an expenditure of the public money coming from that board. Having thus maintained their privileges, the assembly immediately voted the prince a present of a sword of three hundred guineas value.

After some princely frolics, the remembrance of which often contributes to promote the hilarity of the festive board, his royal highness proceeded on a tour through the other islands of the Caribbean archipelago; the inhabitants of which must ever acknowledge with gratitude, that the royal duke has uniformly manifested a thorough acquaintance with the true interests of the colonies and steadily supported their rights. And, while labouring under a load of unmerited opprobrium, exposed to the scorn and ridicule of witty malice, and the calumnious misrepresentations of misinformed philanthropists, it is highly consolatory to them to reflect, that an intelligent prince of the blood is among the liberal few who have spirit and candour to vindicate the unjustly aspersed West Indians.

The parliament of Great Britain having passed an act for the increase of shipping, and the encouragement of navigation, by which the trade between the English colonies and the United States of America, was confined to British-built vessels, navigated by British seamen, it became necessary to ascertain the tonage of all vessels entitled to registers, according to the new regulations. For this purpose Governor Parry appointed a Mr. Paul to examine and ascertain, by admeasurement, the bulk and dimensions of every vessel for which a certificate of registry was required; and as a compensation for his trouble, Mr. Paul was directed, by his excellency, to demand certain fees, proportioned to the burthen of each vessel. This was certainly an attempt to establish a new office, with new fees annexed to it. An exercise of the prerogative, so evidently unconstitutional, was not suffered to pass without due reprehension. Though it produced no legislative inquiry, the measure was freely and judiciously canvassed, by an ingenious anonymous writer, who so fully explained the illegality of the proceeding, that Paul not only desisted from any further exactions, but voluntarily returned the fees which he had already taken.

The restrictions imposed on the commercial intercourse between the colonies and the United States, were strictly observed, and rigidly enforced by the governor of Barbadoes. An armed brig was equipped, at the expense of government, to cruize round the island, for the purpose of preventing all illicit or contraband trade; and many British ships were seized, under various pretences, of having surreptitiously obtained certificates of registry, or of being navigated contrary to law, and were condemned by Mr. Weeks, the sole judge of the court of vice-admiralty. The commerce of the country suffered materially by these harsh, and in many instances, illegal proceedings, which were openly encouraged by the governor, with a view to his private emolument; and drew on him, as well as on Judge Weekes, no inconsiderable share of obloquy and reproach. Indeed, his excellency appears to have acted so oppressively and unjustly, as to have incurred the censure of a very high authority. Upon an appeal, in the case of the ship Columbus, from the decree of the colonial court, his conduct was animadverted upon by Sir James Marriot, judge of the high court of admiralty, with such pointed severity, that his excellency, who was then returning to England, some time afterwards demanded satisfaction of the learned civilian, in the character of a gentleman. The judge, however, not thinking himself personally responsible for any thing said or done in the exercise of his office, declined the combat, and commenced a prosecution against him in the King's Bench, but, upon his excellency's making a suitable apology, the affair was compromised.

Meanwhile, on the prospect of a rupture with Spain, concerning the right claimed by Great Britain, of participating in the trade to Nootka Sound, the governor convened the legislature, and, by his Majesty's commands, recommended that they would concert proper measures for securing the island against the hostile attempts of the national foe. The state of the militia, and the fortifications, was naturally brought into review upon this occasion; and his excellency strongly urged the enacting of such temporary laws as might give energy to their military system. He further requested that they would provide sufficient funds for carrying into execution a plan formed by Lieutenant D'Arcy of the royal engineers, for fortifying the island. Though the danger was remote, the assembly readily voted the sum of two thousand pounds to defray the expense of guarding the country from invasion; and a bill for that purpose immediately received the concurrence of the other branches of the legislature. Fortunately the dispute was adjusted without an appeal to the sword; but not before some money and much negro labour had been literally wasted in collecting the perishable materials for constructing fascine batteries, which were never erected. Though peace was happily preserved, the governor insisted in strong terms on the propriety of completing the works which had been begun. But his advice was disregarded; the surplus of the money which had been raised for this particular service was applied to other uses, and the fortifications were left to crumble in decay.

A most infamous practice had long prevailed among the unprincipled part of the community, to the manifest injury of the cotton planters, of buying the produce of their fields from the slaves by whom it had been stolen. No endeavour to check this nefarious commerce had hitherto proved successful. The laws generally respecting larceny and the receiving of stolen goods were easily eluded, and the municipal law, which had been passed for the express purpose, was found insufficient to prevent the illicit intercourse between negro felons and the dishonest receivers of their plunder. It was reserved for the comprehensive genius and intellectual acumen of Mr. Beckles to devise an effectual remedy for an evil which menaced the industrious planter with ruin; and, if he had given no other proofs of his talents for legislation, his bill to encourage the planting of cotton is sufficient to establish his fame on the firmest basis. But it cannot be dissembled, that the bill in its original state, was liable to many serious objections; yet, though referred to a committee of the whole house, it underwent very little discussion within doors. This deficiency, however, was amply compensated by the freedom with which it was canvassed through the medium of the press; and the learned framer of the bill, with a candour as commendable as it was uncommon, readily availed himself of these anonymous criticisms to improve his plan and correct its errors.

By this salutary law, the assembly is invested with the power of appointing twelve inspectors, who are to keep an office in each town, not for the purpose of inspecting the quality of the cotton, but to guard against fraud, by ascertaining the property, growth, and produce of it, upon the oath of the person by whom it is brought for examination, previous to its being offered for sale. On being satisfied in these particulars, the inspector, who is entitled to one shilling for each hundred weight of cotton which he inspects, is required to issue a certificate, which entitles the owner to dispose of his produce. Any person swearing to a greater quantity of cotton than his land produced, or, upon a survey, is thought to be capable of producing, is, besides a forfeiture of the surplus, indictable for perjury. The bill, containing a variety of other provisions for the security of this species of property, and the punishment of those by whom it may be invaded, having passed the assembly, was sent up for the concurrence of the other house. Equally inattentive to the privileges of the assembly and the prerogative of the Crown, the council took no notice of the right assumed by the assembly of appointing twelve public officers at once, but sent back the bill with an amendment, limiting its continuance to twelve months instead of three years. Considering this as a money-bill, Mr. Straker opposed the amendment, as a violation of the fundamental rights of that house; but the objection was overruled, and the amendment adopted by a majority of nine to four*, and the governor, without hesitation, assented to the bill, by which he surrendered to the representatives of the people an important branch of the executive government, the right of appointing to public offices.

This law, as had been foreseen, gave rise to many criminal prosecutions, and several persons convicted of perjury were condemned to the pillory. Among these was a poor old woman, whose poverty and ignorance had probably contributed to reduce her to that state of degradation. From motives of compassion, congenial to the character of Barbadians, the magistrates directed the constables, who were directed to attend the execution of the sentence, to use their endeavours, during the hour of exhibition, to protect the unfortunate sufferer from the insults and indignities common upon such occasions. An ensign of the forty-ninth regiment, who happened to be present, not approving of this forbearance, strove to instigate the mob to acts of violence, which produced a warm expostulation from the police-officers. The military gentleman immediately drew his sword and made a thrust at one of the constables, who, no less tenacious of his authority, instantly tripped up his heels, and deprived him of his weapon, which was directly carried and put into the possession of

---

* The reader who is desirous of determining the question may consult Blackstone's Comment. vol. 1. p. 170.

Mr. Errington, a respectable justice of the peace. A disgraceful scene ensued. The grenadier company of the regiment, led on by their serjeant, marched, with bayonets fixed, from their quarters at Constitution-hill, to the house of the magistrate, at the western extremity of the town. They rushed up stairs, where Mr. Errington was sitting with his family at dinner, and with the most horrid imprecations presented their bayonets to his breast, threatening him with instant death if the sword was not delivered. Incapable of resistance, Mr. Errington was compelled to give up the sword, with which they returned, after committing several enormities in the neighbourhood, breaking the windows, knocking down and wounding several of the inhabitants, and throwing the whole town into terror and confusion. I have no authority to add, that any steps were taken by the governor to obtain satisfaction for the insult offered the laws, in the person of a respectable magistrate, or that any punishment was inflicted on any part of the corps who had betrayed such a want of discipline in the commission of so flagrant an outrage.

In pursuance of the Duke of Richmond's scheme of fortifying the British islands in the West Indies, the governor of Barbadoes was directed to require of the assembly a sufficient quantity of land, to be purchased at the expense of the country, for the fortifications intended to be erected agreeably to a plan formed by Colonel Fraser. This demand, with a requisition of negro labour, having been sub-

mitted to the house, they resolved, that the circumstances
of the people would not admit of any considerable increase
of their burthens, for the security of the island, and the
support of government; they could not, therefore, comply with the demand farther than to appropriate to this
service, the labour which the inhabitants were required to
contribute, by the existing laws, for the use of the fortifications, for the term of two years.

The grief and consternation that pervaded the kingdom
on the severe indisposition with which it pleased God to
afflict the King, naturally extended to this distant part of
the empire; and when his Majesty was happily restored to
health and the exercise of regal power, the most lively
emotions of joy animated the public mind. A day of general thanksgiving having been appointed by the governor,
the morning was ushered in with the ringing of bells, to
which succeeded an appropriate service in all the churches
throughout the island; and the grateful thanks of a loyal
people were offered up to the throne of grace, for the divine favour, vouchsafed to the best of Kings. After the
performance of this act of devotion, an ox, roasted whole,
with plenty of ale and punch, was served out to the populace; and, in the evening, Bridge-town was brilliantly il-
luminated. Upon the whole, all ranks of people seemed
to vie with each other in the most splendid demonstrations
of joy. The legislature could not be silent on such an occasion: an address of congratulation was voted by both

houses, and transmitted to the agent to be presented to their beloved Sovereign.

Mr. Parry now began to turn an anxious eye towards his native country, and in a very kind and complimentary speech, signified to the legislature his intention of availing himself of his Majesty's permission to be absent from his government for twelve months. Agreeable to this intimation, his excellency embarked on board the Philippa Harbin, and returned to England. His excellency's departure had been preceded by that of his lady about fifteen months, who had died shortly after her return home.

On the governor's leaving the island, the supreme authority devolved on the Honourable Henry Frere, president of the council. Mr. Frere had now attained the object of his ambition, pursued for thirty years, during which he had sat at the council-board, in anxious expectation of obtaining the government of his native country as the reward of his services. In the usual parliamentary communications between him and the assembly, all former political and personal animosities seem to have been forgotten. He took the first opportunity of addressing the legislature from the chair, to express the satisfaction with which he saw the harmony and good disposition of the people in general. Having the fullest confidence in the good sense, experience and discernment of both houses, he hoped that unanimity, which had been always found necessary to give stability to public happiness. would mark their proceedings. And he reflected with particular pleasure, that linked together as they were in one cause, the prosperity of their country, one common interest ought to unite them, nor should any thing, he said, divide a legislature formed upon one just principle and pointing to one salutary end.

The addresses were, as usual, little more than echoes of the speech. The council would not suffer themselves to doubt that his honour's sound judgment and competent knowledge of the constitution, the result of a liberal education, and a long and faithful attendance on public business, together with his distinguished principles of loyalty and patriotism, would leave his administration to reflect the greatest lustre on his character, whilst it diffused happiness among the people. Nor was the address of the assembly deficient in expressions of respect and congratulation suitable to the occasion.

The business of the settlement was brought forward by Judge Gittens, who moved, that the sum of two thousand pounds per annum be settled on the president during his administering the government. The motion was seconded by Mr. Mayers, and opposed by Mr. John Bishop, by whom an amendment was moved, to omit the words " two thousand," and insert *fifteen hundred.* The amendment was supported, with his accustomed ingenuity, by Mr. Beckles. Disclaiming all personal enmity to the gentleman who then filled the seat of government, he declared, that if the dearest friend he had upon earth were president, he would not vote for an increase of salary. It had been said, upon a former occasion, that the King's example, in allowing the president half the salary allotted by the Crown for its representative, would be a proper rule for the observance of that house; and that, as it had been customary to give the governor three thousand pounds, it would be right to allow the president fifteen hundred. Mr. Beckles approved of this rule, and lamented that it had been departed from in the case of General Cunninghame; but, as it had been adopted in favour of Mr. Parry, he thought it would be prudent to make it the standard by which the salary of both the governor and president should, in future, be regulated. After a long debate, the amendment was negatived, and the original motion carried by a majority of fourteen to five.

The depreciation of the gold coin by the nefarious practices of clippers and importers of light gold, was an evil which did not long escape the president's penetrating eye; nor did he omit any thing within the sphere of a vigilant magistrate to suppress, a crime, so pregnant with the most fatal consequences to the interests of a commercial country. He issued a proclamation, prohibiting the iniquitous practice of clipping, under the severest penalties of the law, and commanding all justices of the peace to use every legal method of detecting the dishonest perpetrators of the act, and of bringing them to condign punishment. On the meeting of the legislature, the president recommended this subject to their most serious consideration; and a committee of the assembly was appointed to inquire what would be proper to be done on the occasion; but, though they made a report to the house, no effectual measures were taken to repress the evil until the following year.

Meanwhile, the council made an attempt to introduce an innovation in the colonial penal code, and to punish the white murderer of a slave with death. To this end, they passed an act for the better security of slaves in life and member; which, in consequence of the imposition of a pecuniary penalty of one hundred pounds on any person convicted of maiming a slave, was rejected by the assembly, under the impression of its being a money-bill.

After an absence of little more than eleven months, Mr. Parry returned to Barbadoes, and resumed the government. Mr. Frere's short administration, far from giving rise to those party dissensions which, from a previous acquaintance with his political principles and conduct, were expected to result from it, was happily a season of the most perfect amity and concord. Undistinguished by the exercise of any particular acts of executive or legislative power, the even tenor of his government was influenced by no consideration distinct from the public welfare. And, whatever might have been his errors in a subordinate character, it was his peculiar felicity to administer the supreme authority of his native country, without increasing the animosity of his political opponents, with honour to himself, and to the entire satisfaction both of whigs and tories*.

His excellency's arrival was accompanied with fresh demands on the assembly to furnish negro labour for the completion of the works carrying on at the castle, and to provide funds for the purchasing of such lands as were still required for extending the fortifications. These requisitions were attempted to be enforced by a threat, that the refusal of such moderate aids must suspend the execution of a design, obviously essential to the safety of the island. But the assembly steadily adhered to their former resolution, not to increase the burthens of their constituents by any pecuniary grants towards the works carrying on by government.

The peace of Bridge-town was frequently disturbed, about this time, by the disorderly and offensive manners of the officers of the army. Indeed it is much to be lamented, that a more amicable intercourse does not subsist between the natives and those gentlemen, among whom there are many respectable and valuable characters. With habits of life so widely different from those of the inhabitants, no principle of assimilation seems to exist between them. This contumelious treatment, at that time, occasioned many quarrels between the officers and the natives

1792.

---

* Mr. Frere, having received some injury in getting out of his carriage, died on the 25th day of May, 1792.

some of which having terminated fatally, an appeal to the
laws of the country became necessary. Of the result of
one of these appeals, it may be proper to take some
notice.

It seems that Mr. Gabriel Weekes, son of the judge of
the admiralty, was involved in a dispute with Mr. Slater,
of the forty-ninth regiment. Each had, at different times,
committed an assault and battery on the other, for which
they were both indicted at the court of grand sessions. In
the event, Weekes was sentenced to six months imprisonment, and fined only ten pounds, in consideration of his
pecuniary embarrassments. Slater, on the other hand, was
sentenced to only three months imprisonment, and to pay
a fine of fifty pounds. The chief justice, Mr. W. Bishop,
immediately applied to the governor, and obtained the
entire remission of Slater's punishment, while Weeks was
permitted to endure the unmitigated rigour of his sentence.
Neither the father nor the son were of a temper to submit
patiently to treatment, which appeared to them so partial
and unjust. The chief justice was attacked with all the
asperity of wit, and the venom of abuse.

The debased and mutilated state of the gold coin had
now become a theme of general complaint. The importation of light foreign coins from Great Britain and America
was carried to an alarming extent by strangers, who, having no interest in the colony, felt no scruples of conscience
at a practice so repugnant to religion and morality, while

the clippers were industriously employed in diminishing those which were of standard weight. Urged by the magnitude of the evil, the governor pressed the matter on the attention of the assembly, and earnestly called for their assistance in suggesting some legislative measures, proportioned to the exigency of the case. The house readily

took the subject into consideration, and a law was enacted, to punish all persons convicted of clipping, counterfeiting, or filing the current gold coin with death ; and the importers of all diminished or debased coin, besides forfeiture of the coin imported, were made liable to a penalty of five hundred pounds. This law was soon found to be inefficacious. Offences, privately committed, could not be punished for the want of legal evidence to convict the offenders. Prevention is better than remedy. The most certain and infallible way of keeping men honest, is to make it their interest to be so. Had the gold coin been made current by weight, the most incorrigible mutilator and importer would have been more effectually restrained from their infamous practices, than by their most sanguinary laws.

The subject was most ably and perspicuously treated by the masterly pen of Mr. Gibbes, W. Jordan, the present valuable agent for the colony, whose superior intelligence penetrates with facility into the most difficult and abstruse branches of human knowledge. From the soundest principles, Mr. Jordan deduced this just conclusion, that the only effectual remedy for the existing evil, was the establishment of a legal currency of the gold coins by weight, at a rate proportioned to the real value of the bullion, excluding the expense of coinage. With this principle partly in view, Judge Gittens, one of the committee appointed to take the subject into consideration, introduced a bill to remedy the inconvenience; but by a strange inconsistency, it was proposed to reduce the standard of all foreign gold coins in circulation about ten per cent. below their real value.

The pernicious tendency of the bill was clearly developed and ably combated by Mr. Husbands and Doctor Hinds. They demonstrated by an irresistible chain of reasoning, that the value of the mutilated coin would be increased in proportion to its mutilation; hence the villain, it was said, would be encouraged in his fraudulent practices, and rewarded for his nefarious industry: that as no regulation nor change was made in the value of silver, all coins of the latter metal would be sent out of the country, in change for debased or depreciated gold, to the great injury of the inferior classes of society, who, deprived of a convenient circulating medium would starve, like Midas, in the midst of gold. The obvious tendency of the measure to enhance the price of every species of merchandise was elucidated with great force and perspicuity; and the proposed innovation in the value of the coin, it was insisted, would operate, like a two edged sword, to the injury of both debtor and creditor. In all insular contracts, the fair honest creditor would be the party injured; as he would be compelled to receive money at a greater value than it was known to possess. On the other hand, to the debtor who had remittances to make, either to Europe or to America, it would prove no less detrimental by enhancing the prices of our staple products, and encreasing the rate of exchange.

The principal arguments urged in support of the bill were, that it would be the means of retaining the money within the island, and of guarding from injury the honest money-holder, who had fairly received the mutilated gold in the course of regular circulation. The apprehension of a scarcity of money is a chimera, which has no existence in nature. Agriculture and commerce will ever supply the means of procuring a sufficient quantity of the precious metals for the purpose of internal circulation. And to the money-holder, whatever might have been his immediate loss, the injury must have been small compared with that sustained by the whole community, in permitting the infamous traffic in debased and diminished coin. But all the arguments and rhetoric of the opposition were employed in vain; the bill passed the house by a majority of nine to seven, and was sent up to the council, by whom it was rejected.

July 5.

The governor having recommended the assembly to resume the consideration of this important subject, Doctor Hinds, whose conduct through the whole of the business reflects infinite credit on his talents and understanding, introduced a bill for regulating the currency of the gold coin.

The bill was framed on the salutary and equitable principle of preserving the standard and giving currency to the depreciated coin at two pence three farthings for each grain of its weight. To every mind free from prejudice and un-biased by sinister motives, it must be matter of astonishment, that any objection could exist to a plan so fair and eligible. It afforded the only effectual remedy for the evil which had been so long the cause of complaint and discredit to the country, and was the most permanent security against the fraudulent practices of diminishing the coin, or of importing depreciated specie. The bill, however, experienced a vigor-ous opposition from the friends of the former measure, in which numbers again prevailed over sound reason and good sense.

Mr. Mayers, was now encouraged to introduce a third July 19. bill, the principle and tendency of which were precisely the same as that which had been already rejected by the council, consequently it experienced a similar fate. Six weeks had elapsed since the assembly had taken this import-ant subject into their consideration. Within that time they had frequently adjourned, de die in diem, without being able to come to any decision on the proper means of correcting the evils and abuses complained of. And, as from the obstinacy of the majority there was little proba-bility of their agreeing upon any plan of restoring the mutilated coin to its real value, his excellency had recourse to his prerogative, and, by proclamation, established the Aug. 4.

value of the several gold coins, in general circulation, at a standard proportionate to the legal coin of Great Britain, with an allowance of two pence three farthings for each grain deficient of their original weight. The currency of these coins has continued ever since, agreeable to this equitable regulation; though it must be evident to every man, who is even but slightly acquainted with the constitution of England, that the proclamation wants the confirmation of an act of the legislature to make it binding. The royal proclamation may enforce the observance or the execution of existing laws; but neither the King, nor his representative, can, by proclamation, make that a law which was not so before*.

The bill formerly sent down by the council for making a better provision for the personal security of slaves having been rejected by the assembly, from a punctilious regard to their privileges, and the popular clamour on the other side of the water still continuing against the Barbadians, for the reputed insufficiency of their laws in this particular, the

Aug. 21. measure was revived, and a bill, making the wilful murder of a slave felony, without benefit of clergy, was introduced by Doctor Hinds, who employed the whole force of his genius and rhetoric in its support. The speaker took a decided part in the debate, and spoke with his usual pathos

---

* See this subject clearly illustrated in Blackstone's Comment. vol. 1. p. 270.

and energy in favour of the measure, which, the learned
member, who introduced the bill, affirmed, could be
opposed only by prejudices or the tyrant's fears, while justice
and humanity pleaded in support of it. To talents so deservedly high in the estimation of the public, were opposed
the nervous eloquence of Husbands and the persuasive ingenuity of Beckles. After a long and animated debate, the
bill was lost in the committee.

The atrocious conduct of the regicides of France, having   1793.
rendered a war between Great Britain and the French republic inevitable, the governor, with that prudence which
distinguished his administration, convened the legislature,
and recommended the putting of their militia into such a
state as to be capable of co-operating with the King's
troops. Sensible of the danger to which the island was
exposed, from the critical posture of affairs in Europe, the
assembly appointed a committee to prepare and bring in a
new militia bill. The principal features of this bill were   April 30.
the dismounting of the cavalry, and the establishment of
parochial regiments. After an ample discussion of its
principle and tendency, and various amendments had been
made by the house, the bill passed; but its progress was
obstructed by the unseasonable expiration of the assembly,
which prevented its being sent up to the council for their
concurrence.

Hostilities having actually commenced between Great
Britain and France, an expedition against Martinico was

undertaken by Admiral Gardner and General Bruce. The inhabitants of that country, participating in the misfortunes which afflicted the parent kingdom, were miserably divided, and distracted by faction and rebellion. In this deplorable situation, the royalists sent a deputation to the commander in chief of the British forces at Barbadoes, requesting his assistance, and stating that they were already in possession of some strong posts. In consequence of this invitation, Admiral Gardner, with seven ships of the line, having General Bruce and a body of land forces on board, proceeded to Martinico, where the troops were immediately landed. But, finding they were likely to encounter a vigorous resistance, without receiving that firm and effective support from the royalists, which they had been taught to expect, the British commanders reimbarked their troops,

June 27.
and returned to Barbadoes. Some hundreds of the wretched inhabitants of Martinico, took the opportunity of flying on board the fleet, from the horrors of democratic rage. The sensibility of the Barbadians was deeply affected at the forlorn situation of these unhappy fugitives, who were thus thrown on their humanity, exposed to misery and want. A liberal subscription was opened for their relief, under the patronage of President Bishop, and a sufficient sum was soon raised to supply their necessities, and convey them among the neighbouring British islands, where most of them had connexions.

The ill state of Mr. Parry's health making a change of

climate necessary, he resigned the government into the hands of the Honourable William Bishop, president of the council, and embarked for Nevis, with the design of proceeding to Halifax; and, in the event of regaining his health, of returning to Barbadoes. Disappointed in this hope, he continued his voyage to England, where, on the twenty-sixth day of December, he paid nature's last debt.

A general election having taken place, a few day's before the governor's departure, his honour, the president, had an early opportunity of receiving the congratulations of the legislature. The assembly having gone through the usual ceremony of appointing a speaker, and presenting him to the president, whose approbation of their choice was expressed in terms the most flattering and polite, entered upon the consideration of the provision to be made, for supporting the dignity of government. The subject was introduced by Mr. B. A. Cox, who moved, that the sum of two thousand pounds annually should be settled on the president, for defraying the expenses of his administration. An amendment was moved by Doctor Hinds, and seconded by Mr. Mayers, the purport of which was to limit the settlement to fifteen hundred pounds. The amendment was rejected, and the original motion, which was supported with great eagerness, by Sir J. G. Alleyne and Mr. Beckles, was carried in the affirmative, by a majority of fifteen to six. Thus the standard, which had been so earnestly recommended on the accession of Mr. Frere, was departed from on the very first occasion that occurred.

The first moments of Mr. Bishop's administration, were necessarily occupied in the disposal of the civil and military offices, which had become vacant by his own promotion. Mr. J. B. Skeete was appointed to the command of Speight's division, and colonel of the Leeward regiment of foot*; and Mr. W. Pinder, an eminent attorney at law, was honoured with the appointment of chief judge of Saint Michael's precinct.

These arrangements were quickly followed by the suspension of the Honourable Nathaniel Weekes, sole judge of the court of vice-admiralty. Previous to Mr. Bishop's exaltation to the presidental chair, the ship La Liberté, French East-Indiaman, had been captured, and brought to Barbadoes for condemnation, by the Pilgrim letter of marque, of Liverpool. The immense value of the ship awakened the cupidity of the judge of the admiralty, who immediately had it intimated to Mr. Barton, a merchant of much respectability, at Bridge-Town, who was agent for the prize, that he should expect a fee of one thousand pounds for expediting the condemnation of the vessel. Anxious to obviate the delays of office, and the difficulties

---

* Mr. Skeete dying soon afterwards, the command of that division was entrusted to Samuel Hinds, Esquire, a man of the most benevolent and irreproachable character.

which were thrown in his way, Mr. Barton submitted to

the extortion. Weekes received the money, and condemned the ship. The act was grossly criminal, and deservedly punished.

The commencement of the year was soon succeeded by the welcome arrival of a squadron, under the command of Sir John Jervis, and a considerable body of troops, under the orders of Sir Charles Grey. From this moment all was hurry and bustle at Pilgrim. The president was not only disposed to grant every facility in his power, to the demands of the veteran commanders of the navy and army, he was eager to anticipate their wishes. Having received a letter from Sir Charles Grey, expressing a desire of being furnished with one thousand negro men, to serve as pioneers on the expedition in which he was about to embark, the president immediately convoked the legislature, and laid before them the general's proposal. At the same time, anxious to manifest his extraordinary zeal for the service, he encouraged the general to expect that a corps of insular troops should be raised, at the expense of the colony, to strengthen his Majesty's forces in the West Indies. In the present state of the population of the country, the scheme was absolutely impracticable; and when the proposition came regularly before the assembly, in a message from his honour, it was treated with neglect.

Sir Charles Grey's requisition was of a very different complexion. He proposed to allow a fair hire for each negro, that should be sent, and to pay the full value of such as should be killed, maimed or missing when their time of service had expired. A proposal so fair and liberal was readily agreed to by a large majority of the assembly; and a bill was accordingly passed to compel the owners of slaves to furnish a contingent proportioned to their whole number, which soon received the concurrent sanction of the other branches of the legislature. But, after all, when the negroes were ready to be sent in, Sir Charles Grey abruptly refused to receive them; upon the very conditions which he had proposed.

To lose no opportunity of manifesting the fervency of his zeal, while the armament lay at Barbadoes, the president generously opened a subscription for the support of the wives and children of the non-commissioned officers and privates of both departments. Four hundred pounds sterling were thus raised for the use of these people, who, though they were not suffered to proceed with the troops to Martinico, were amply provided for by government.

On the third day of February, the expedition left Carlisle Bay, and made a descent on the Island of Martinico. From the good understanding which happily prevailed between the president, the admiral and general, their excellencies condescended to communicate to him the ulterior operations of their combined forces, which were regularly published, by his authority, in the Barbadoes Mercury; a conduct at which the admiral and general were not well pleased. But, as the particulars of the campaign are unconnected with the design of this work, we shall decline entering on a subject which rather falls within the province of the general historian. It may not, however, be improper to observe, that a voluntary subscription was opened for supplying the brave soldiers and sailors employed in the reduction of Martinico with live stock and fresh provisions; and that the quantity furnished was in the highest degree creditable to the liberality and humanity of the donors.*

The president's indiscretion in offering the admiral and general assistance which he had not influence to procure, and which, had his influence been greater, the state of society rendered unattainable, produced a letter from Sir John Jervis, in which his honour and the whole legislature were treated with equal indelicacy and disrespect. The admiral began with remarking, that he had waited with some degree of impatience for the powerful aid which Sir Charles Grey and himself had been taught to expect. But far from receiving any assistance, the crews of his Majesty's

---

* The value of this offering was six hundred and fifty pounds.

CHAP. XVII.   ships had been seduced to desert, while the adjacent seas
1794.   were infested with swarms of pirates, under the sanction of
commissions issued by the governors of the different islands.
For these reasons he desired his honour would convene the
legislature and represent to them the necessity of taking up
all seamen harboured in the island, and sending them on
board his Majesty's fleet.

March 21.   Alarmed at the apprehension of having given offence to
persons whose friendship and esteem he had sedulously endeavoured to cultivate, the president hastened to comply
with the admiral's desire. The assembly having met, pursuant to a special summons, received a message from the
president, with a copy of Sir John Jervis's letter, earnestly
conjuring them, " by every just and tender consideration,
for the honour and credit of this ancient and loyal colony,
to pay the fullest attention to the suggestions of his excellency, the commander in chief of his Majesty's naval forces ;
and as the representatives of the people, to make use of the
power vested in them to mark out that loyalty for which
the country had been at all periods conspicuous." The
message concluded with recommending the passing of an
act to strengthen the hands of the civil power, by enabling
the magistrates to apprehend seamen of all descriptions ;
and that a bounty should be granted to a number of able-
bodied seamen, to assist in manning the fleet.

The message having been read, Mr. Solicitor-General

Beckles, after some just and spirited remarks on the offensive insinuations thrown out by the admiral, expressed his doubts concerning the propriety of the president's first requisition. Willing as that house were, at all times, to afford every necessary aid to his Majesty's forces, they should take care, Mr. Beckles said, not to lose sight of the constitutional rights of the subject. Although the impressing of seamen had been sanctioned by custom, he was not aware of any act of parliament by which it was expressly authorized. To take up vagrant seamen, and, if they were found to be deserters from the fleet, to return them might be very proper; but to take up all seamen, indiscriminately, and to send them on board his Majesty's ships, would be, he said, a most glaring infringement on the liberty of the subject. With respect to a bounty to those seamen who should voluntarily enlist, Mr. Beckles had no objection, as it could not burthen their constituents much, and might be of essential service to the expedition.

Justly indignant at the unmerited reproaches which the admiral had cast upon the colony, and yet more at the levity with which the assembly were treated in being called from their distant homes on so frivolous an occasion, Sir John G. Alleyne moved three resolutions. The purport of the first and second was the rejection of both the president's requisitions; while the third was intended to main-

tain the dignity of the house, by declaring that the assembly would not, in future, obey any summons for their
meeting out of the ordinary course of adjournment, unless
the cause of the special call should be recommended to
them, through the speaker, at the time of their being summoned. These resolutions were opposed by Mr. Mayers
and Mr. Beckles, who particularly objected to the last, as
being unparliamentary; they were, nevertheless, agreed to,
those two gentlemen alone dissenting. It must be confessed, that the last resolution was extremely unconstitutional,
and utterly indefensible upon any principle of parliamentary
usage.

The president's extraordinary attention to Sir Charles
Grey, and Sir John Jervis, and the uncommon earnestness with which he endeavoured to promote their designs,
drew from them such favourable representations of his
conduct and zeal for the service, as produced the most flattering expressions of his Sovereign's approbation. And,
in consequence of a communication between Mr. Secretary
Dundas and Mr. Brathwaite, the colonial agent, to whom
the president was nearly allied by marriage, his honour expected to have been confirmed in the government of the
island. But the policy of the British court not allowing the
appointment of a native to that situation, Mr. Dundas, it
was said, proposed the government of Tobago as a reward
for his services. Without consulting the president, Mr.

Brathwaite, to whom the offer was made, replied, that the government of Tobago would neither be agreeable nor profitable; and these prospects at length terminated in an order from the Crown, to the next governor, to reinstate Mr. Bishop in the office of chief judge of Saint Michael's precinct.

CHAP. XVIII.

GEORGE POINTS RICKETTS, ESQ. APPOINTED GOVERNOR—AUS-
PICIOUS COMMENCEMENT OF HIS ADMINISTRATION—JUDGE
WEEKES CONVICTED OF EXTORTION—MILITIA ESTABLISHED—
A REFORM OF THE COURTS OF LAW ATTEMPTED—THE STORE-
KEEPER'S DEMAND REVIVED—ALARMING STATE OF AFFAIRS
IN THE WEST INDIES—A MURDER COMMITTED BY JOE DENNY
—EXTRAORDINAY INTERPOSITION IN HIS FAVOUR—VIOLENT
COMMOTION IN BRIDGE-TOWN—DENNY TRANSPORTED—MR.
GIBBES SUSPENDED—GOVERNMENT ADOPTS THE DANGEROUS
SCHEME OF EMPLOYING BLACK TROOPS—SIR JOHN GAY AL-
LEYNE RETIRES FROM PUBLIC LIFE—MR. RICKETTS RESIGNS
THE GOVERNMENT—IS SUCCEEDED BY PRESIDENT BISHOP—A
COMPENDIUM OF THE CONSTITUTION.

CHAP. XVIII.
1794.

THE government of Barbadoes was now destined to experience an important change. On the recommendation
of Lord Hawkesbury, his Majesty was pleased to appoint
George Poyntz Ricketts, Esq. to represent his royal person in this colony. This gentleman, who was then employed in a similar character at Tobago, was a native of

Jamaica; and, though born within the tropics, possessed the elegant manners of a courtly education. Fame preceded his arrival, and prepared for Mr. Ricketts the most cordial and flattering reception in Barbadoes, representing him as possessing all those valuable endowments of the mind, which peculiarly qualified him for the arduous and delicate task of governing a people whose fidelity to their Sovereign was inseparably connected with an ardent zeal for the maintenance of their civil rights.

Having arrived and assumed the government, his excellency immediately issued the necessary directions for convoking the legislature. On their meeting he addressed both houses in an elegant and impressive speech. Among the various duties annexed to his situation, which, he said, he had undertaken with a pleasure not unmixed with diffidence, he felt, that in availing himself of the earliest opportunity to meet the legislative body of this ancient colony, he discharged the most welcome and the most important. Whether they reflected on the unavailing efforts of distant nations and remote ages, to maintain a government that should unite freedom, order, and stability; or if their attention be forcibly arrested by those wild and sanguinary theories which had endangered the safety and roused the resentment of Britain, her colonies and her allies, they may, he told them, indulge a fair pride in conscious superiority; and exult in the glorious scene which that day presented, when the representatives of a free and happy people were con-

June 4.

vened to express their unrestrained sentiments, and to exercise their acknowledged rights. This dignified system of
liberty, whilst it taught them to defend their own privileges,
would, he was persuaded, lead them to participate in the
general spirit of grateful loyalty which animated the British
empire. They would feel pleasure, he said, in maintaining
the most affectionate harmony with the mother country, and
in suggesting and promoting such measures as would most
effectually contribute to produce individual happiness and
general prosperity. These sentiments, he remarked, naturally arose in the minds of men who were blessed with a
constitution happily and equally remote from turbulence and
despotism. They were such as he was happy to recognise,
where indeed he had been taught to expect them, in a colony which he hoped long to consider as his home.

In allusion to the settlement, he requested that the assembly would suffer no personal consideration towards him to
have the smallest influence in the discussion of a public
question. He assured them that in attending to the interests of the colony, and the wishes of their constituents, as
their primary objects, they would render any tribute of their
esteem doubly welcome to him. He urged both houses to
a continuance of every possible preparation for their defence, and a co-operation in any plan for general security,
and endeavoured to impress on their minds the propriety of
an unremitted attention to the various and important judicial duties of their situations individually. In the courts of

error and equity they had a right, he said, to expect his personal and impartial assiduity. Nor should they expect it in vain. He anticipated the happiness which would result from mutual friendship and reciprocal confidence, and concluded a loyal, patriotic, and judicious oration, with these words; " Born, as I am happy to reflect, within the tropics, and having occasionally resided in these climates, in a public and private situation, I trust you will not find me wholly unacquainted with the interests, and certainly not inattentive to the welfare of my countrymen. And, however, unable I may feel myself to emulate, in other respects, the royal example, I shall, at all times, make the prosperity of this respectable portion of his Majesty's subjects the object of my warmest exertion, and ever consider their affections my noblest reward."

A suitable provision for supporting the dignity of government was naturally the first object that occupied the attention of the assembly. This necessary business was brought forward by the solicitor-general, Mr. Beckles, who moved that a salary of three thousand pounds per annum should be settled on his excellency, during his administration. No motion that had ever been made within those walls was ever received with greater approbation and unanimity. A bill framed, in conformity to the motion, was accordingly introduced, and, having passed the assembly, immediately received the unanimous consent of the council; and was most graciously assented to by his excellency the same day.

Few men in any age or country ever succeeded to the supreme authority under circumstances more auspicious than those which existed at the time of Mr. Ricketts's accession to the government of Barbadoes. A strong predilection in his favour pervaded the public mind. The politeness of his manners, the affability of his deportment and the suavity of his temper, conciliated all hearts and united all parties in one common sentiment of approbation and esteem. An understanding at least specious, joined to a heart glowing with the genuine feelings of patriotism, afforded the most rational presages of the happiness which the prudence, the mildness, and equity of his administration would diffuse among the people placed under his government. The constitutional maxim, that the king can do no wrong, was willingly extended to his representative; and, as if an axiom, obviously right and expedient in politics, were equally true and just in ethics, his most venial faults were, without hesitation, imputed to others. The early exercise of his functions confirmed the public expectation. A generous disinterested zeal for the welfare of the community seemed to be the only spring that actuated his conduct.

From Tobago the governor brought with him, in the character of his private secretary, Mr. Robert Wimberley, a gentleman of the bar, who seems to have been the Piers Gavaston of Barbadoes, and to have possessed at Pilgrim the same degree of favour and confidence which had been enjoyed by the favourite of Edward II. at the British court. Soon after his excellency's arrival Mr. Wimberly was appointed to the command of Charles Fort, which was followed by the appointment of deputy-secretary, in the room of Val. Jones, Esquire, who had resigned the office on being appointed commissary-general of his Majesty's forces in the West Indies. About the same time Mr. Pinder, chief justice of Saint Michael's precinct, resigned his dignified situation, and the president was satisfied to descend from administering the supreme authority to the subordinate office of administering justice in a court of common pleas.

Sensible of the importance of a steady and faithful distribution of justice, his excellency early manifested the deepest solicitude on this subject. In his anxiety to restore the judicature of the country to its proper rank and value, he wrote circular letters to the judges, insisting on a more sedulous attention than had been given, to their duty; to which they were encouraged by the laudable example of diligence and dispatch exhibited to their view in the courts over which he personally presided.

The colonial constitution unwisely requiring an annual election of representatives, we are frequently reduced to the necessity of repeating, in the space of a few pages, the recurrence of the same events and ceremonies. A general election * having taken place, the governor embraced the opportunity of addressing both houses on the meeting of the colonial parliament, to lay before them several important particulars, which he felt it his duty, he said, to suggest for their consideration. The principle on which the militia was founded, however congenial with the ancient common law of England, experience had shewn to be ineffectual and oppressive. It was their province, he remarked, to make such alterations both in the theory and practice, as may appear most conducive to the public interest, avoiding equally established prejudices and unnecessary innovations.

It was an unpleasant, but, he feared, an acknowledged truth, that the administration of justice in most of the courts of law was, at best, irregular and uncertain. This he ascribed to some radical defect in the system, as he was too well acquainted with the characters of the persons who presided in those courts to impute any blame to them. The ineffective state of the police was, he said, a subject of shame and regret. The effects of this negligence were too

---

* The members were, J. Mayers and J. Beckles for *St Michael's;* E. Welch and J. Sullivan, *Christ Church;* J. Gittens and J. A. Olton, *St. Phillips;* B. A. Cox and H. Trotman, *St. George's;* S. Wallcott and R. Haynes, *St. John's;* G. James and S. Hinds, jun. *St. James's;* S. Forte and T. Williams, *St. Thomas's;* S. Hinds and Harrison Walke, *St. Peter's;* Ben. Babb and S. Husbands, *St. Lucy's;* J. Stewart and W. A. Culpepper, *St. Joseph's;* Sir J. G. Alleyne aud J. Jordan, *St. Andrew's.*

obvious to require his enlarging on so painful a theme.
Their situations, as magistrates, he remarked, opened a wide
field to their exertions in the suppression of immorality and
the protection of the friendless and oppressed. This was
surely, he added, the most enviable privilege of wealth and
power, and rendered the possessors of them blessings as
well as ornaments to society. By the noble reward of an
approving conscience he encouraged their exertions in the
restoration and promotion of a constitutional defence, of
their judicial arrangements, and of a firm and effective police. Unless these were secured and maintained, property
must be precarious, credit must be endangered, and freedom itself but an empty name.

Meanwhile Judge Weekes having been restored by an
order of the Lords of the Admiralty, alleging that he ought
not to have been deprived of his office before he had been
convicted of the crime imputed to him, by the verdict of
the jury, the attorney-general was ordered by the governor
and council to prosecute him for extortion. Mr. Weekes December.
was accordingly indicted at the court of Grand Sessions,
and fully convicted of the offence with which he was charged. In commisseration of his age and family, and considering that he would be sufficiently punished by the loss of
his office, the source whence he principally derived the
means of subsistence, the court humanely sentenced him to
pay a fine of five shillings. Mr. Weekes was now judicially
declared unworthy of confidence; and Jonathan Blenman,

Esquire, a gentleman of unblemished character, was appointed to succeed him as sole judge of the court of vice-admiralty.

Weekes consoled himself in meditating revenge on the person whom he suspected as the author of his ruin. He lodged an information with Mr. Philip Gibbes, one of his Majesty's justices of the peace, against Judge Bishop, for extortion, in having demanded and received a fee of ten pounds on issuing a process, for which he was legally entitled to no more than twenty shillings. Mr. Gibbes, who, among all his eccentricities, was always willing to do equal justice between man and man, regardless of rank or condition, readily issued a summons, commanding Mr. Bishop to appear before him at a certain time and place to answer the charge.

The president immediately collected a large party of his friends, chiefly lawyers, and repaired to the town-hall, whence they dispatched Mr. Wimberley's carriage to fetch the justice. Mr. Gibbes inconsiderately went; and as soon as he arrived, Mr. Bishop offered to give bail for his appearance at the court of Grand Sessions, which the other very properly declined receiving before the day appointed for hearing the complaint. This produced a violent altercation, in the course of which Mr. Gibbes, for the faithful performance of his duty, was most grossly abused and unwarrantably insulted by the whole party. Without seeking that redress and indemnity to which, as a magistrate, he was

particularly entitled, in the execution of his office, he selected the solicitor-general as the object of his resentment,
and sent a friend to him the next day; but as it appeared
that he had misapprehended the particular expression at
which he had taken offence, the affair was settled without
producing any ill consequences. In the event, the charge
against the president not being supported by evidence, Mr.
Gibbes dismissed the complaint; and issued a writ of contempt against one Busby, an attorney, who being a material witness in the cause, had neglected to appear, and confined him several days in the common gaol. Busby, having, at length, procured his discharge, brought an action of
false imprisonment against the justice, and obtained a verdict for one hundred and fifty pounds damages.

The militia bill, which had passed the assembly eighteen
months before, and had been dropped from the expiration
of the house before it was forwarded to the council, was
thought of no more; till, urged by the governor's repeated
calls, the assembly resumed the consideration of a subject
which had been too long neglected. The bill was revived,
and, having undergone an ample discussion, successively
received the sanction of the three orders of the legislature.
By this law the military system was entirely changed; the
two regiments of horse were disbanded; the militia was divided into eleven parochial regiments; and every man from
the age of seventeen to sixty was required to enrol himself
in the parish where he resided; with the exception of the

members of both houses of the colonial parliament, the clergy, and all officers in the civil departments, together with all chief overseers of plantations on which there should be a specified number of slaves. These exemptions, particularly the last, created a general dissatisfaction; but, as the act was temporary and experimental, the people submitted to the measure, in the expectation that upon the revival of the law the subject of their complaints would be removed. An enthusiastic spirit of loyalty and patriotism, which peculiarly distinguished the present period, silenced the murmurs of discontent; and, in a very short time, a respectable military force was created, as it were out of chaos and confusion, and assumed an appearance of order and discipline hitherto unknown in this country.

The governor's active mind was perpetually employed in suggesting new schemes of political reform, and plans for promoting the prosperity of the country. In the execution of the designs, his excellency submitted to the assembly two plans which he had arranged, for effecting a radical reform in the courts of law. Of these plans, the principal object was the final consolidation of the judicature of the island, into one supreme court in Bridge-Town. To anticipate the opposition which might have been elicited by a collision of interests, it was proposed that the five chief judges should, in rotation, exercise the functions of chief justice, until they should be successively removed by death, when the whole judicial authority was to centre in

the hands of one supreme magistrate, with an establishment of fees, or a salary, at the option of the assembly,
sufficiently lucrative to render the situation desirable to
some professional man of character and abilities.

These plans experienced no inconsiderable opposition
without doors. Though the proposition assumed the specious aspect of facilitating the course of justice, it was
represented to be obviously calculated for the indulgence
of the lawyers, who were unwilling to submit to the inconvenience of going the circuits ; and therefore suitors, witnesses, and jurors, were all to be dragged from the most
remote corners of the island, and detained from their families and domestic avocations, at a considerable expense,
that the officers of the court might enjoy their ease. This
was alledged to be contrary to every principle of legislation.
It is a maxim in politics, that the interests and inclination
of individuals should yield to considerations of general welfare ; but here, it was said, is a proposal to sacrifice the
ease and convenience of the whole community, to the gratification and indulgence of a favoured few. The necessity
of a reform was admitted, but the objections to the consolidation were illustrated, and urged with great force, by
an anonymous writer, who proposed, as a modification of
the plan, to reduce the judicial establishment to three precincts, by which justice might have been brought home,
as it were, to every man's own door.

A bill, framed on the principles laid down in the go-

vernor's plan, was introduced by Dr. Hinds, and supported
with his usual spirit and ability. The learned gentleman
found a zealous auxiliary in the solicitor-general, who, with
a specious eloquence, and subtilty of argument, strictly
professional, exerted all his ingenuity in support of the
measure*. The opposition was chiefly maintained by the
venerable speaker of the assembly, who was himself an
host, seconded by Mr. Husbands, the patriotic member
for St. Lucy's. With talents so equally balanced, the
question could only be decided by numbers, influenced by
the prejudices of habit and education ; and the bill, on
the first reading, was rejected, by a majority of fifteen
to four.

Meanwhile, the storekeeper's demand for powder, illegally and unnecessarily delivered to the commanding officers of the forts, which had been lying dormant for more
than twenty years, was again brought forward. Early the
last year, Mr. Cox had presented a petition to the assembly,
in which, after recapitulating the particulars of his debt,
which have been already taken notice of in their proper
place, he stated, that during the administration of Mr.
Spry, his debt, from the economical arrangements made by
that gentleman, had been reduced from three hundred and
forty-four barrels, to ninety-four and a half; that, from the

---

* I regret that I am prevented from giving an abstract of the debates on this interesting occasion ; the minutes which were published having eluded my most diligent
inquiry.

demise of Mr. Spry, to the date of his application, there had been no saving made to liquidate that balance, which, calculated at two shillings for each pound of powder, exceeded the sum of nine hundred and forty-four pounds current money, exclusive of interest. The petition further stated, that there were then in his hands upwards of two thousand pounds belonging to the Mole-head funds, which he prayed might be appropriated to the payment of his demand, with interest from the time that it became due. We have already seen how this debt was contracted, and how the powder was wasted. It is admitted, that Mr. Cox was unconcerned in the abuses which existed in the forts; but then his duty was clearly defined by a positive law, and the advances which he had presumed to make on the sole authority of the commander in chief, were as illegal and unconstitutional as Sir Thomas Robinson's building an armory, without the consent of the assembly, or as General Cunninghame's arbitrary establishment of fees.

Mr. Cox's petition had lain on the table more than twelve months, when Judge Gittens introduced a bill for applying a sum of money arising from the funds established for cleansing the Mole-head, to the payment of his demand. With the integrity of a Roman senator, Doctor Hinds steadily opposed the proposition. But, on the question being called for, it was carried in favour of the store-keeper's demand, by a majority of eleven to three. Upwards of fourteen years had elapsed, since the demolition

Feb. 3.

of the pier, by the memorable hurricane, and, notwith-standing the obvious utility of the work, to which the parliament of Great Britain had contributed ten thousand pounds sterling, not a single stone had been replaced. And now, when the funds established for that particular service were sufficient to commence the needful repairs of a fabric of acknowledged commercial convenience, they were diverted into channels the most foreign to their original design.

Nor was this the only drain on that establishment. The celebrated infuriate democrat, Victor Hughes, having, in the course of the preceding year, with a force comparatively inconsiderable, recovered the possession of Guadaloupe, applied himself, with a diligence and perseverance worthy of a better cause, to injure and annoy the British islands in his neighbourhood. Innumerable swarms of armed boats and privateers, issuing from Guadaloupe, committed the most unparalleled depredations on the commerce of Great Britain. From the singular construction of these small, light vessels, they easily eluded the vigilance of our cruizers, in the open sea, and pursued their predatory excursions with impunity. The only effectual remedy for the evil was to blockade the ports whence they issued, and prevent their putting to sea. But as a sufficient number of vessels for this service could not be spared from the naval force on the station, General Vaughan and Admiral Caldwell applied to the governors of the different islands, requesting that an armed vessel might be furnished, at the expense of each colony, for the protection of their trade. The requisition was complied with, by the assembly of Barbadoes, as soon as it was communicated to them ; and the sum of two thousand pounds of the money belonging to the Mole-head was unanimously voted, for the purpose of hiring the Lord Hawkesbury armed brig, for the service required, for the space of four months.

Callous to every sentiment of religion or morality, the sanguinary republican commissioner, to whom the command of Guadaloupe was entrusted, sought by every practicable means, however inhuman or unjust, to gratify his savage enmity against the English. With this view he contrived to introduce his emissaries into Grenada and Saint Vincent's, in each of which the negroes, assisted by the French inhabitants, were excited to insurrection. The insurgents were supplied with arms and ammunition from Guadaloupe; and, without compunction, committed enormities, at the bare recital of which humanity shudders, slaughtering their prisoners with an indiscriminate fury, which respected neither age, sex, nor condition. Whilst this horrid drama was performing in our neighbourhood, the happy Barbadians enjoyed all the blessings of peace and tranquillity. But sensible of the dangers which surrounded them, they proved themselves worthy of the advantages they possessed, by the cheerfulness and alacrity with which they prepared to defend them. One general sentiment seemed to pervade all ranks of people, and firmly united them in a deliberate determination to resist, to the last extremity, all attempts of the savage enemy of social order. Animated by loyalty to their prince, love for their country, and veneration for its constitution, the militia voluntarily turned out, weekly, for the sake of acquiring a proficiency in martial exercises. To encourage and give energy to the popular spirit and ardour, the assembly, in the course of the present session, passed two supplemental acts, to enforce more full and frequent meetings of the militia, and to make a sufficient provision of arms and military stores for their use.

The extraordinary mortality among the British troops in the West Indies, induced the ministry to adopt the scheme of raising black regiments, who, being inured to the climate, were thought to be better adapted to the service than Europeans. Sir John Vaughan was accordingly authorized to raise and embody two corps, of one thousand negroes each, by contribution among the colonies; and Governor Ricketts was directed, by the Duke of Portland, to recommend the measure to the legislature of Barbadoes, and to request that they would grant a proportionate number of able-bodied negro men for the purpose. But when June 25. the matter was brought before the assembly, on a message from his excellency, the house resolved, on the motion of Sir John Gay Alleyne, that the requisition could not be complied with, at that juncture, without distressing the planters in the management of their estates, depriving the colony of a part of the means intended for its defence; and, in its consequences, endangering the salvation of the community, on the return of the slaves, after the service for which they were to be enlisted was at an end. But the scheme was not abandoned.

The disastrous situation of affairs in the West Indies, demanded the most vigorous exertions for the preservation of the British dependencies in this hemisphere. For this purpose, and, at the same time, to deprive the enemy of their colonial resources, a more powerful armament was sent from England, under the command of Sir Ralph Abercrombie and Admiral Christian, than had ever crossed the Atlantic before. On the expected arrival of this armament, the governor laid before the assembly an extract from the Nov. 25. Duke of Portland's dispatches, demanding, that a body of negroes should be provided to act on duties of labour and fatigue with the troops destined for the attack of the French islands. This requisition was enforced by General Knox, in a letter to the governor, by an invincible chain of arguments. As the extent and objects of this armament were of the most important nature, and clearly evinced his Majesty's paternal regard for his colonies in these seas, the governor was persuaded, he said, that every assistance, on their side, would readily be granted, and particularly, that the island of Barbadoes would maintain her ancient character of being foremost in the public service.

The house having resolved itself into a committee for the purpose of taking the governor's message into consideration, Sir John G. Alleyne, in a speech of considerable length, besides pressing the requisition on the house, as a return of gratitude to the Crown for its attention to the wants and weakness of the people in the hour of natural and political distress, insisted that the true interests of the country enjoined their granting the required assistance; and, therefore, moved, that a number of negroes, not exceeding five hundred, should be raised, to accompany the army as pioneers and labourers. On a point of this kind it would have been in vain to expect unanimity, especially as we find, that even the worthy baronet himself had changed his own opinion, on the same subject, in the short space of five months. The motion experienced a formidable opposition from Doctor Hinds, and was warmly supported by the solicitor-general, who was not present on the former occasion. He commenced a loyal, patriotic speech with declaring, the concern, chagrin, and disappointment which he felt at the probable result of the question before the house. Upon all former occasions, the assembly, he said, had properly distinguished between demands made to gratify the vanity or ambition of a minister, or commander in chief, and such as had been made for the real service of the public. With a laudable spirit, they had rejected the one; with becoming loyalty they had granted the other. Similar requisitions had been made before, under circumstances which weakened the claim for colonial assistance, and yet had never been refused. The expedition, he remarked, was expressly undertaken for the protection of the colonies, to preserve them from the shocking cruelties and horrid massacres committed at Grenada and St. Vincent. We were now contending for our lives with a horde of savages. Should the island be taken, we should, probably, be put to the most cruel and barbarous death; or reserved to suffer what, to a feeling mind was worse than death, to fraternise with our slaves, and to see our wives and daughters polluted by their foul embraces. Mr. Beckles admitted the inconvenience which the planters must feel in parting with any of their negro men during the crop season; but ought they not, he asked, to submit to some inconvenience, to some expense for the general good, nay, for their own preservation? Fortunate, indeed, was their happy lot, to sit in quiet and comfort with their families, enjoying the produce of their estates, whilst the ravages of war were spreading not only over distant but neighbouring countries. This splendid display of eloquent patriotism, served only to reflect additional lustre on the character of the learned member by whom it was delivered. A demand of this kind, enforced by an act of legislature, was represented to be an infringement of the civil rights of the people; and the motion was negatived by a majority of three voices.

It appears that the sentiments of the majority were not in unison with those of their constituents: the contingent of negroes, denied by the assembly, was eagerly furnished by the voluntary contributions of individuals. The negroes, as they were sent in, were put under the care of Captain T. Thornhill, assistant quarter-master-general; a liberal hire was allowed for them, and security given by General Knox, for the value of those who should be killed, disabled, or not returned to their owners.

Meanwhile, the negroes of the different islands, intended for pioneers, were collected and brought to Barbadoes, with a number of emigrants, chiefly people of colour, from Guadaloupe, who had volunteered their services, and were retained as guides. An influx of people of dubious principles and uncertain attachment, at a moment when there were no regular troops at hand to keep them in subjection, naturally awakened the attention of a vigilant administration to the means of preserving the internal tranquillity of the country. In such an emergency, his excellency was compelled to call for the services of the militia; and, with a spirit and promptitude highly honourable, the royal regiment, without the smallest legal compulsion, obeyed the summons, and performed the duties of the garrison, at the Castle, and Constitution-hill, in the absence of the King's troops.

To relieve the militia from this new and irksome duty, in which the more remote regiments must have participated occasionally, the assembly, on the motion of the solicitor-general, unanimously resolved to embody three hundred men, for the service, for one month, with proper officers, to be paid at the public expense. Conformably to this resolution, a bill was introduced the next day, and having passed the house, Mr. R. J. Haynes alone dissenting, immediately received the concurrence of the council and the assent of the governor. Of this corps Mr. Beckles was appointed to the command, with the pay of six dollars a day; and until the number of men could be raised and embodied, the governor was authorized to call out such companies of militia as he should think proper, who were entitled to pay, as follows: each captain four dollars, the lieutenants fifteen shillings, the ensigns two dollars, the serjeants one dollar, and the privates five shillings each a day*.

The act being near expiring, the governor convoked the assembly, to give them, as he said, an opportunity of extending the term of its existence; and, by way of encouragement, informed them, that the expense already incurred for this service, had fallen short of one-half the sum at which it had been estimated. Mr. Mayers concluded a short speech, in which he took due notice of the utility of

---

* At this meeting the assembly passed an act for appropriating one thousand pounds of the Mole-head funds to the rebuilding of the old and new bridges.

CHAP.XVIII. the act, with moving that it should be continued in force
  1796.   three weeks longer; but the arrival of a small body of
troops having rendered the aid of the militia unnecessary,
the motion was rejected, on a division of eleven to four.

The discontents excited by the numerous exemptions
from military duty had been silenced by the hope, that, on
the renewal of the militia-bill, the cause of complaint would
May 11. be removed. But on the passing of a new act, to continue in force for three years, the clamours of the people
were disregarded, and the same partial indulgences, were
again extended to those by whom they had been formerly
enjoyed. Incensed at this proceeding, the inhabitants of
many parts of the island, discovered an uncommon spirit of
insubordination, particularly in the parish of Saint Lucy;
where, almost with one accord, they peremptorily refused
to appear under arms, and conform to a law, which, it was
contended, established an invidious distinction between
the different classes of society. Besides denying the policy
of relinquishing so considerable a portion of the physical
strength of the country, the enemies of the bill insisted that
the public safety was a common cause, to which every man
in the community was bound to contribute his personal
and pecuniary aid; and that, as freemen and loyal subjects, they could not but feel, most sensibly, the palpable
injustice of being obnoxious to a laborious personal service,
when particular bodies of men, and those too whose rank
and fortune were additional claims to the most spirited ex-

ertions in its defence, were privileged from serving in the militia.

To appease the popular clamour, Mr. Hinds, the amiable and respectable member for Saint Peter's, introduced a bill to amend the objectionable clauses of the militia law. The second reading of the bill was opposed by Mr. Mayers, not from any objection to its principle, but, on the ground of its being irregular and unparliamentary, to alter or amend an act during the session in which it had been passed. The objection, however, was overruled, and the bill was agreed to by a majority of eleven to five; but it was rejected by the council. Early the next year, a bill of a similar principle and tendency was introduced by Mr. Naboth Greaves, one of the new representatives of Saint Lucy's. Mr. Greaves explained the object of his bill in a very concise and judicious manner. As all were equally interested in the preservation of the country, he thought all, who were able, ought equally to participate in the fatigue and danger of defending it. Among the exemptions claimed, that of the house of representatives, he said, was too evidently partial to escape the most superficial observation, and too well calculated to diffuse distrust among their constituents. A second, than which nothing could be more repugnant to the dictates of reason and justice, was that of gentlemen of extensive landed property, who sheltered themselves under the act as overseers. That those who had most to be protected should be exempted, whilst others, who had little or nothing to lose, were made liable to serve, was, Mr. Greaves said, totally unfounded in reason, and utterly incompatible with every principle of just and equal government. The bill was warmly opposed by Doctor Hinds, who defended the exemption with great ingenuity; and, on the question being put, it was rejected by a majority of eleven to two.

Thus far the administration of Mr. Ricketts may justly be considered as the happiest and most brilliant era in the annals of Barbadoes, surpassing even the traditional felicity of the golden days of Lord Howe. Whilst the dogs of war were ravaging the most fertile territories, almost within sight of their shores, and the demon of democracy, endeavouring to reduce the most polished societies to the rudest state of savage nature, was extending the miseries of suffering humanity, the inhabitants of this favoured island were enjoying all the blessings of peace. Under the auspices of a chief, who governed by their affections, all party feuds had subsided, every murmur was silenced, and the most perfect concord presided over the public councils. But the day had now arrived when the clouds of distrust and discontent were to obscure the gilded scene, and destroy that confidence between the people and their rulers, which has ever been found essential to public happiness.

Joseph Denny, a free mulatto man, of a bold, turbulent and daring temper, whose life had been more than once forfeited to the violated laws of his country, was indicted, at the court of grand sessions, for the wilful murder of John Stroud, a poor white man, of Speight's-town. The deceased had lived with his mother, whose house and yard were divided from that of the prisoner by a fence so tall and thick as not to admit the passing of any person from one to the other. Having occasion to go into his mother's yard about two o'clock in the morning of the thirteenth of September, Stroud observed Denny, wrapped in his cloak, standing under an apple-tree in his own land; and in the instant that he was returning into the house, Denny, at the distance of twenty-eight feet, fired a gun at him, and mortally wounded him. He immediately fell, exclaiming, that Denny had killed him; and the assassin, after putting away the gun, ran round the front of the house to his assistance, expressing great concern at the accident, declaring that he did not know it was John Stroud, and that he did not mean it for him. No, replied the brother of the wounded man, with whom Denny had previously had a quarrel, you intended it for me; to which the other made no answer. After lingering six-and-thirty hours Stroud died, and Denny was indicted at the ensuing court of grand sessions for the murder, of which the jury, after mature deliberation, found him guilty; and sentence of death was pronounced against him by the Honourable Philip Gibbes, who presided as chief justice on the trial.

The prisoner had every advantage of counsel which could have been desired upon such an occasion. His ad-

vocates were Mr. Coulthurst, the present advocate-general;
and Mr. Gibbes W. Jordan, to whose management the colonial concerns at the court of London are now entrusted;
two men, whose learning and talents would adorn any bar.
During the sessions, no idea of a reprieve was suggested;
but the morning after the court was finally adjourned, these
gentlemen, actuated, no doubt, by the purest motives of
humanity, called upon the chief justice, and requested
him to sanction a petition from the prisoner to the governor, to suspend the execution of the sentence, and recommend him to the clemency of the Crown. Mr. Gibbes
readily complied with their request. But, without discernment to discover the point where discretion should stop,
he proceeded to lengths which drew on him the odium of
the whole community. Not content with joining the prisoner's advocates in an application for mercy, he presented
a long memorial to the governor, recapitulating the evidence on the trial, and, besides stating, " as a lawyer," that
there was no legal proof of malice aforethought to convict
the prisoner of murder, he asserted, that " Denny's being
a man of colour, and, as such, having killed a white man,
had raised such a prejudice against him in the minds of
the jury, as was shewn in a manner too shameful not to be
observed by every impartial person present at the trial."
Yet the chief justice had taken no notice of this flagrant
partiality at the proper time and place; but, without even
hinting the smallest disapprobation of the verdict, had

pronounced sentence of death on a fellow-creature, who
appeared, to him, to have been unjustly convicted by a prejudiced jury.

In consequence of this application, and, perhaps, not perfectly satisfied with the chief justices representation, his excellency demanded the opinion of Denny's council in writing. They affirmed that there was no express malice proved, on the part of the prisoner, against the unfortunate man, or against any other person, and that although there had been a dispute between Denny and the brother of the deceased, they had been reconciled, and were upon good terms at the time of the accident. They alledged in their client's defence, without any evidence of the facts, that his land had been frequently robbed, that he had lost his corn and other articles, without his being able to detect the thief; that being disturbed by the barking of his dog, on the fatal night when the murder was perpetrated, he had taken up his gun, and placed himself under a tree in expectation of discovering the person who had occasioned the disturbance; when, perceiving a man in the adjoining tenement, whom he mistook for the thief, he fired and shot him. Without arraigning the verdict of the jury, Mr. Coulthurst and Mr. Jordan were both of opinion that the evidence was insufficient for the conviction of the prisoner; and that he was, therefore, a proper object of mercy. But the mercy for which Mr. Jordan interceded was conditional, and limited to the removal of the murderer from the country in which he had committed so great an offence.

Wavering and irresolute, as if conscious of being about to do wrong, the governor was anxious to shelter his fault under the authority of others. Hence he applied to the solicitor-general, who had conducted the prosecution on the part of the Crown. With characteristic candour and perspicuity, Mr. Beckles submitted to his excellency a report of the principal facts which had appeared in evidence, and which have been already detailed. He vindicated the jury from the malign aspersions of the chief justice, and declared, that so far from manifesting a shameful prejudice against the prisoner, he had never seen a more respectable and impartial petty jury. In short, he was of opinion, that the prisoner had a fair trial. No question of law had arisen, but the whole rested upon evidence, on which the jury were competent to determine; they had examined the witnesses with a minuteness and attention which shewed an anxiety to discover the truth; and, after an hour and a half spent in mature deliberation, they had found him guilty. Though the verdict was not against evidence, Mr. Beckles concluded with saying, had he been upon the jury he should have had some doubt of the malice, and, having the smallest doubt, he should have acquitted the prisoner. Without involving ourselves in an abstruse inquiry concerning the degree of evidence sufficient to remove the scepticism of every temper and understanding, we must confess our surprise, that these doubts were not suggested to the jury by the learned Crown lawyer, who, as he himself avers, had summed up the evidence, in his reply, with the impartiality of a judge rather than the zeal of a prosecutor.

As this is an affair in which, from the events that succeeded, the character of the country is deeply involved, I must be indulged in a few observations on the point at issue. " It is a general rule," says a great law writer, " that wherever a man, intending one felony happens to commit another, he is as guilty as if he had intended the felony which he actually commits." Now there was the strongest presumption that Denny intended to murder the brother of the unfortunate man who fell a victim to his mistaken revenge. But if any doubt could have been entertained on this point, there is another maxim of law which applied exactly to his case. " Whenever it appears," says Hawkins, " that a man killed another, it shall be intended, *prima facie*, that he did it maliciously, unless he can make out the contrary. No proof was produced by the prisoner to shew, that the homicide with which he was charged, was not the result of deliberate malice : none but his own declaration, that he had gone in pursuit of a thief. But the criminal's *ipse dixit*, unsupported by any evidence whatever, was insufficient to invalidate the testimony of unexceptionable witnesses, strengthened by a train of corroborating circumstances. The malicious design was fairly presumable, from the circumstance of Denny's lying in wait, to watch, as he said, for a thief. But it was proved, that he had nothing growing on his land to be stolen. Admitting, however, the truth of this plea, did his apprehension of thieves justify his shooting the first person he saw? The unfortunate man who was separated from his tenement by an impassable hedge, consequently could have excited no suspicion of his intending to rob him; and was, besides, near enough to have been known, as is evident, by his recognition of Denny. There is another maxim laid down by Lord Hale, the great oracle of English jurisprudence, exactly in point. " Malice implied is in several cases, as when one kills another voluntarily, without any provocation, for in this case the law presumes it to be malicious, and that he is a common enemy to mankind." Hence it would seem, that it is not necessary to prove malice prepense in cases of wanton, unprovoked murder. Among a variety of adjudged cases, that of Captain Porteous cannot be forgotten. No previous malice was imputed to him when he ordered his guard to fire among the mob at Edinburgh, by which many were killed. The illegality of the act was sufficient for his condemnation.

Regardless of the popular clamour, his excellency reprieved the prisoner, and transmitted his petition, with the representations which had been made in his favour, to the Duke of Portland, to be laid before his Majesty. Such an unprecedented interposition in behalf of a convicted felon, excited a considerable ferment in the country; nor was this discontent confined to the lower classes of people, it pervaded every rank in society; neither was it owing to any prejudice arising from local distinctions, but the result of a strict regard to impartial justice. The resentment entertained on this occasion was aggravated by a suspicion, that the intercession employed in behalf of Denny was promoted by the influence of certain coloured courtezans, who were known to be favourites with some men in power. Whether this suspicion were well or ill grounded, the author of this work presumes not to determine: it is his province to state that it existed, and that it made a sensible impression on the public mind.

Unfortunately for the governor, unfortunately for Barbadoes, his excellency had brought with him from Tobago, a mulatto woman, who resided at Pilgrim, and enjoyed all the privileges of a wife, except the honour of publicly presiding at his table. His excellency's extraordinary attachment to this sly insidious female was the greatest blemish in his character, and cast a baleful shade over the lustre of his administration. The influence which she was known to possess, produced a visible change in the manners of the free coloured people, who assumed a rank in the graduated scale of colonial society, to which they had been hitherto strangers; and which the impolicy of subsequent measures and the immorality of the times have contributed to extend and confirm in a degree that cannot be contemplated without fearful apprehension. A woman, of this description, who had been convicted of receiving stolen goods, and condemned to imprisonment, had been lately liberated by the governor's order; and some other offenders, in the very commission of their crimes, had boasted of the impunity which they could obtain through the influence of Betsey Goodwin. A report had circulated, at least, a fortnight before Denny's condemnation, of his having received assurances from her, that, let the event of his trial be what it might, she would protect him.

At length the governor received a letter from the Duke of Portland, in these words, " I am commanded to signify to you his Majesty's approbation of the motives which you have assigned for the determination you took to respite Denny; and to acquaint you, that upon the most serious consideration of all the circumstances which appeared on the trial, and in conformity with the sentiments of the law advisers of the crown, his Majesty is of opinion that *Denny is so far an object of Royal mercy as not to suffer the law to take its course upon him in its full extent.* But such is the nature of the act for which this man was brought to trial, and the crime of which he was convicted, that, independant of his character and conduct, which, from the papers before me, do not seem to entitle him to any greater degree of clemency than is warranted by the state of the evidence, it is his Majesty's pleasure that the pardon which Denny is to receive, shall be granted upon the express condition of his being removed from the island, and that it shall become void and be of no effect should he ever presume to return there upon any pretence whatever."

On the receipt of this letter, all the governor's firmness forsook him. Apprehensive of some dangerous commotion, he adopted those means which were most likely to produce it. Carefully concealing the purport of his dispatches, he privately arranged a plan with General Murray for the removal of the prisoner. In the afternoon of the twenty-fifth day of May, when the inhabitants of the town had retired to dinner, the general, at the head of a corporal's guard, was discovered by Mr. Woodroffe, an English merchant resident at Bridge-town, escorting Denny from prison to the wharf. Mr. Woodroffe stopped the general, and, in a very spirited manner, expostulated with him on his adopting a conduct so inconsistent with the character of a British officer of his rank; to which he replied, that Denny was to be transported from the island, in consequence of the King's pardon. Mr. Woodroffe was incapable of resistance, and the prisoner was conveyed on board a government brig, which immediately got under weigh.

An alarm was instantly spread, that Denny, under the protection of an armed force, had escaped from prison. The effect of this intelligence could not have been greater if the capital had been invaded. The whole town was a scene of uproar and confusion; and men, the most respectable for their fortune, virtue, and talents, joined their inferior

fellow-subjects in resisting this flagrant outrage on the justice of their country.   Knowing of no authority for transporting the cause of this disturbance, several of the most
eminent merchants ran to Ricketts's battery and fired upon
the brig; another party tumultuously assembled round the
house of a respectable gentleman with whom the governor
had dined, and insisted upon the prisoner's being relanded.
In the hope of appeasing the tumult, the Duke of Portland's
letter was now read to the mob; but they were too much
irritated to listen to any thing that was offered in extenua-
tion of the governor's conduct; an armed party manned
several boats, and having boarded the brig, brought the
culprit on shore.   Meanwhile the governor, alarmed at this
violent commotion, hastened out of town, and applied to
the commander in chief of the forces to keep the troops in
readiness to march into town in case of necessity.   This,
however, was unnecessary; the people had no intention to
resist the legitimate exercise of authority; they only meant
to maintain their civil rights; and having obtained his excellency's order, remanding the prisoner to gaol, delivered
him, without injury, to the provost-marshal, and then retired to their peaceful homes.   A body of soldiers was
however sent to remain upon guard at the gaol, and to preserve the peace of the town during the night.

The inhabitants having assembled again the next day,
appointed a committee to consider of some effectual plan
for restoring the public tranquillity, and for preventing a

heinous offender from eluding the punishment due to his crime. The committee entered on the business with temper, firmness, and moderation. After mature deliberation on all the circumstances relating to this extraordinary transaction, they came to several resolutions, of which the principal were, That the governor and his Majesty had been grossly abused by the misrepresentation of facts stated in the application for the pardon of Denny: That, as it was impossible, under the existing circumstances, to execute the sentence upon him, and as they were desirous of paying due obedience to his Majesty's orders, though obtained by misrepresentation, his excellency should be requested to transport him as speedily as possible to the island of Ruatan: That his excellency should be petitioned to remove Philip Gibbes, esquire, from his seat at the council board, and from all other public employments whatever, for his false aspersions on the respectable jury by whom Denny had been tried and convicted, and for his misrepresentation and mistatement of the facts which appeared in evidence upon the trial.

Agreeably to these resolutions, an application was made to the governor for the immediate transportation of Denny. In the most conciliatory terms his excellency replied, that, conscious of having in every instance, during his whole administration, acted with zeal and sincerity for the public good, he was willing to give this additional mark of his desire to promote good order and tranquillity; and he hoped, in return, that the committee would exert their efforts and influence in calming the public mind, and restoring that harmony and good humour which it was the interest of all to re-establish and perpetuate. Denny was accordingly sent to Grenada, to be transported with the traiterous brigands of that place to Ruatan.

Another victim was yet necessary to appease the popular resentment. A petition, subscribed by a great number of the inhabitants of all parts of the island, was prepared to be presented to the house of assembly; in which they prayed that the house would take proper measures to obtain Mr. Gibbes's removal from the council board. But his excellency, who had now become anxious to comply with the wishes of the people, anticipated any application on the subject. He proposed to the council to suspend Mr. Gibbes from the exercise of his functions as a member of that board. Of six members who were present on the occasion, two declined voting; the other four concurred in his excellency's proposal. Thus Mr. Gibbes, who was more culpable only as he was less cautious and less prudent than those with whom he acted, was made the scape-goat to expiate the transgressions of all who were concerned in this affair. He immediately went to England and obtained a royal order for his restoration, grounded principally on the insufficiency of the number of members who had voted for his suspension; but he some time after resigned his mandamus.

For the sake of perspicuity we have, without any regard

to chronological order, brought together all the particulars of an affair, which, at one moment, seemed likely to have produced the most fatal consequences; but which was happily terminated by the prudence and good sense of the committee to whom its final arrangement was entrusted. And we have been the more circumstantial in this detail, from an honest wish to vindicate the character of the country from any imputation on its loyalty and attachment to social order.

Meanwhile, on the meeting of the assembly, his excellency sent a message to the house, informing them that Sir Ralph Abercrombie had been commanded by his Majesty to raise five regiments of black troops, consisting of five hundred men each, to be procured by purchase among the islands, and that these corps were to become a permanent branch of the military establishment for the defence of the colonies. The general requested his excellency would recommend this measure to the serious consideration of the legislature, and expressed his hope of receiving their countenance and assistance in carrying it into effect.

A proposition so dangerous to the future security of the country, naturally called up the speaker of the assembly. His known loyalty to the crown would, he trusted, secure him from any imputation on the motives by which he was actuated in opposing a measure which endangered the lives and fortunes of the inhabitants of the colonies, and even the rights of the crown to the sovereignty of these islands.

Highly as he appreciated the wisdom and rectitude of his
Majesty's ministers, he lamented that their comprehension
of points that most essentially affected these distant parts
of the empire, was inadequate to the forming of a correct
judgment on subjects connected with colonial slavery.   On
these points, he said, the inhabitants were themselves the
best judges of what belonged to their own safety and advantage.   Sir John Alleyne concluded these observations
with moving several resolutions to this effect: That the raising of black troops for the defence of the colonies, as far as
the design is likely to affect this island, will prove rather the
means of its destruction than its preservation: That the
only slaves likely to be sold for such a purpose were those
of the worst characters, villains, habituated to plunder, who,
when formed into regular corps, and disciplined with arms
in their hands, would be enabled the more effectually to
perpetrate every species of mischief to which they were naturally prone: That, should an enemy invade our shores,
the arms of these black troops would be employed in murdering their former owners, destroying their plantations, and
wresting the dominion of the colony out of the hands of the
British government: That, should it be their good fortune
to escape these evils, such an establishment would loosen
the bands of that subordination which so happily subsisted,
not less to the ease and comfort of the negroes than to the
satisfaction of their masters, would spread universal discontent among those who were retained in slavery; and dread

and distrust among the white inhabitants of the country. These resolutions were unanimously agreed to by the house, and a copy of them sent to the governor as an answer to his message.

Notwithstanding this just representation of the evils with which this scheme is evidently pregnant, in which all the other colonies concurred, government persisted in the dangerous design, and has raised ten regiments of Africans by purchase. It requires but little political sagacity to perceive the danger and impolicy of employing troops of this description in countries where the population of whites bears so small a proportion to that of slaves. And without pretending to the gift of prophecy, it may be hazarded, as no improbable conjecture, that, at no distant period of time, these faithless blacks, in conjunction with the national foe, or colonial traitors, will employ the arms, unwisely put into their hands, in murdering their officers; subverting the power of Britain in this hemisphere; and erecting the savage despotism of Africa on the ruins of English liberty.

June 6.

The house was now doomed to sustain the privation of those talents by which it had long been illumined, and of that wisdom which had often guided its deliberations. Worne down by the heavy hand of time and the increase of infirmities, Sir John Gay Alleyne was now compelled to quit the service of his country, whose rights he had vindicated with equal spirit and ability, and whose prosperity he had promoted for nearly forty years with the most disinterested zeal and integrity. Led by that hope which never forsakes us till we die, Sir John Alleyne vainly sought in an European climate, a renovation of that health and vigour which age alone had exhausted. Sir John Alleyne was not permitted to carry into retirement with him any testimonies of public favour or gratitude. Even the poor unsubstantial tribute of a vote of thanks was withholden from the venerable patriot, whose life had been spent in a series of meritorious exertions for the benefit of the happy spot which gave him birth. In other men various passions alternately rule the soul and direct their actions; but one uniform principle governed the whole of Sir John Alleyne's political conduct. The welfare of his country was the primary wish of his heart; and, however mistaken he might sometimes have been as to the means of attaining his object, he ever steadily kept the end in view. The sun, which decorated the horizon, was no sooner withdrawn, than the light and warmth which it afforded were forgotten. No other notice was taken of the speaker's letter of resignation than to appoint a successor. On this occasion Mr. Joshua Gittens was unanimously called to the chair, which he continued to fill upwards of six years.

1798.
Although the assembly felt the necessity of rejecting the overture made by government for raising black troops, they soon gave more convincing proofs of their loyalty to their King and their readiness to contribute by every means in their power to the defence of the empire. The obstinacy

of the French republic in refusing to listen to any reasonable terms of accommodation, convinced the people that they were contending with an implacable foe, not only for their civil and religious rights, but for the preservation of their independance as a nation. Under the expectation of invasion the national spirit had been roused to the most vigorous exertion; and the voluntary contributions raised in every part of the kingdom evinced the zeal with which the people were animated in defence of their King and constitution. The generous flame spread across the Atlantic, and warmed the faithful bosoms of the Barbadians. As a small, though sincere testimony of their attachment to the principles for which they were contending, the assembly voted the sum *May 15.* of two thousand pounds towards enabling his Majesty to prosecute the just and necessary war in which he was engaged. The voluntary contributions of individuals far exceeded the public munificence. Subscriptions were opened in every parish, and upwards of thirteen thousand pounds sterling were collected and remitted to the Bank of England for the service of government.

Having been informed by the governor of the deficiency *July 3.* of gunpowder in the magazine, the assembly passed a bill for appropriating one thousand pounds of the much-abused Mole-head funds to the purpose of procuring a sufficient supply of that necessary article. The facility with which several sums were voted during this administration cannot fail to excite astonishment, when the decayed and ruinous

state of the fortifications at that time, is taken into consideration. Few of the forts contained a gun which could be
fired without endangering the lives of the men upon duty;
and, while an expensive establishment was maintained to
its full extent, the assembly, with a strange inconsistency,
refused to repair a few forts of acknowledged utility, and to
supply them with cannon and ordnance stores.

1800.   The happiness of the Barbadians now suffered a temporary interruption, from the afflicting hand of providence;
in the removal of a governor, under whose mild, benignant
administration, their colonial character had shone with peculiar lustre; and, they had attained an unexampled degree
of prosperity amidst the ravages of war. On the twelfth
day of February his excellency convoked the legislature, for
the purpose of signifying to them his intention of leaving
the island for the benefit of his health. To this necessity,
he said, he was reduced by a long and obstinate illness,
which rendered him unable to fulfil the duties of his station
with that punctuality and attention which were due to the
best of sovereigns, for intrusting him with a command that
would gratify proud ambition, and be esteemed a reward
for merit and talents far superior to those which he possessed. This intelligence produced a deep sensation in the assembly; and, as a mark of their gratitude and esteem, they
unanimously voted him a donative of one thousand pounds
to defray the expenses of his voyage. But, from the nature
of the Royal instructions, prohibiting the representative of

the crown from receiving any gift or present from any person or persons whatever, their intention could not take effect until his Majesty's pleasure was known.*

Two days after this intimation had been given, his excellency, declining all military parade, privately embarked on board the Venerable, merchant ship, for Liverpool. The anguish of separation was soothed by every mark of respectful attention to which he was entitled. The most affectionate and consolatory addresses were presented to him by both branches of the legislature, the clergy, and all the inhabitants who could collectively express their sympathy and concern at the melancholy event. But of all the marks of distinction with which he was honoured on this occasion, none was more singular and unprecedented, than that suggested by the piety of his successor. For six weeks successively public prayers were offered up in every church and chapel throughout the island, for his excellency's speedy and perfect recovery. But the decrees of fate were not to be reversed by an act of devotion, probably more ostentatious than sincere. His excellency barely lived to reach Liverpool, where he died, on the eighth of April, fifteen days after his arrival.

On the governor's departure, the administration once more devolved on the Honourable William Bishop, presi-

Feb. 14.

Feb. 24.

---

* The King readily confirmed the grant; and, his excellency dying in the interim, the assembly, by virtue of a new act, paid the money to the governor's executors.

dent of the council. The early meeting of the legislature furnished his honour with an opportunity of addressing both houses in a speech remarkable only for the occasion on which it was delivered. Proud, he said, of meeting them in the dignified situation which he then filled, he trusted they would, in justice to his feelings, believe, that he had reassumed it with regret on the departure of their excellent governor. The objects material for their consideration, he remarked, had been so recently pointed out to them by his excellency, that it was unnecessary for him to enlarge on them ; and it would spare the delicacy which had ever governed his conduct, could he at that moment omit the suggestion which had been always made to the representatives of the people by persons in his situation, on their first meeting, respecting the provision for the support of government. In their resolution to assist him in maintaining the splendour of his seat, he entreated they would have in view the interest of their country rather than his own. He repeated the assurance, which he had given them on his former accession to the chair, that he had brought with him every sentiment of affection towards his native island ; and, aided by their counsels, it should be his earnest endeavour to carry with him from his command, whenever he should leave it, the same approbation of his King and country which it had been his happiness to obtain in his former administration.

The settlement, to which the president had so modestly

alluded in his speech, was moved for by Dr. Hinds. He felt encouraged, he said, to the motion which he was about to submit to their consideration, by the zeal which had ever been evinced by that house for the honour and prosperity of the country; and although the establishment which he intended to propose was greater than that of former times, he flattered himself, that it would meet the wishes of the house. The considerable decrease in the value of money was a circumstance which alone could justify an alteration in the customary establishment. There were other motives, however, which he was persuaded would influence their determination. The president was no new man. He was not known to that house merely as a member of council. They had already been happy under his government. Having been appointed early in life to a seat at the council board, he had ardently promoted the public welfare. United with the assembly, he had opposed the tyrannical measures of Governor Cunninghame, and, in each succeeding administration, he had been distinguished by a firm attachment to his native land. During the whole progress of the war he had endeavoured to relieve the pressing wants of the people, and to prevent impending famine, by urging the occasional suspension of those commercial regulations which, though founded in the highest wisdom during peace, would starve the colony, and materially injure the empire, if rigidly enforced in the time of war. Doctor Hinds concluded with moving, as a grate-

ful tribute to approved merit, that the sum of three thousand pounds per annum be granted to the Honourabl William Bishop, during his presidency.

The motion was supported by Mr. Cadogan, in a long
encomiastic speech, in which he took a wider range, and
employed a variety of arguments to shew, that a president,
a native, possessing an essential and united interest in the
public welfare and prosperity, is entitled to a provision
for the support of his dignity, no less liberal than is usually
made for a governor, a stranger, of whom they know little
more than can be collected from the voice of flattery.
This called up the new attorney-general, not with a view of
opposing the motion, for that met his hearty approbation,
and, indeed, were the salary to be proportioned to the
president's merits, he thought, it ought to have been greater.
He rose merely to oppose the doctrine advanced by the
gentleman who had spoken last. Mr. Beckles then explained, with his usual clearness and ingenuity, the different claims of a governor and a president, arising chiefly
from local circumstances. He expressed, in the strongest
terms, his dissent from the position attempted to be established, that a president was entitled to the same settlement
as a governor; but concluded with voting for the application of the principle in the present instance. The motion
having been agreed to without a single dissentient, a bill,
to give effect to the resolution, was immediately passed,

with equal unanimity, by the council, and assented to by his honour on the same day.

The uncommon liberality of the legislature seemed to render the president superior to all vulgar considerations of political economy. Disdaining the parsimony of Mr. Dotin's frugal administration, he encreased the expenses of his establishment in an exact ratio to the augmentation of his salary, particularly in the article of oil for the lamps at Pilgrim, which were now replenished with a double quantity. The office of chief judge of St. Michael's court having become vacant by his exaltation to the chief magistracy, the president bestowed the appointment on his son, Henry Bishop, Esq. than whom no one had fairer pretensions to it.

Such was the declining state of the colonial commerce and navigation at this period, that the tonnage duty was found insufficient to supply the demand for gunpowder for the use of the fortifications. This deficiency having been intimated to the assembly in a message from the president, they took the subject into consideration, and, without inquiring into the application of the former grant, or ascertaining the necessity of a further supply, voted the sum of one thousand pounds, to be paid out of the Mole-head funds, for the purchase of powder to answer the public exigencies : this continuing to exhaust the resources of an establishment of the most manifest public utility, whose

June 4.

ruinous condition required the application of the money which was diverted to purposes far less useful.

While the president was anxiously endeavouring to diffuse plenty among the people, by the admission of foreign supplies, in neutral vessels, he was not inattentive to the means of guarding them from the imposition which, he imagined, were practised by the bakers of Bridge-town. The reduced size of the loaf of bread appeared, to his watchful eye, to be an evil of such magnitude, not only to the inhabitants of the metropolis, but to the community at October 28. large, as induced him to make it the subject of a message to the assembly, who very gravely replied, that they would embrace an early opportunity of taking it into consideration.

1801. They turned their attention, however, to a subject much more worthy of it. Being informed of the death of their late valuable agent, Mr. John Brathwaite, they appointed a committee to erect a monument to the memory of that exalted man and faithful representative of the colony, and soon after passed an act to pay the expense of this tribute of their esteem out of the public coffers. This monument may be regarded as a reproach on the assembly for the neglect with which they have treated Sir John Gay Alleyne, who died not long after*, and to whose meritorious services

---

* On the 5th of December, 1801.

Barbadoes was more indebted than to those of any other man. But, though no sculptured marble speaks his country's gratitude, his virtues have embalmed his memory, and will transmit it to the admiration of succeeding generations.

A new assembly having been summoned, the president opened the session with a most gracious speech, in which he congratulated both houses on the favourable change of the weather which had recently taken place. And, although he was not able, he said, to announce to them any immediate prospect of peace, he trusted in the goodness of the great all-wise disposer of events, that this most desirable of all objects was not so far distant, as the distracted state of affairs in Europe might lead them to imagine. Having frequently witnessed how far the wisdom of the assembly had anticipated the suggestions which were usually made from the chair, it was unnecessary for him to propose any particular subjects to their attention. He was, therefore, content to rely on their accustomed liberality to provide for the expenses of the current year. It was his misfortune, he said, to be without any official information with regard to the appointment of a governor; but, apprehending, from private communication, that a nomination had been made, it was his duty to request that they would be prepared for his reception. In retiring from his high situation, he hoped they would believe that the welfare of Barbadoes would be as much uppermost in his heart as

when in the exercise of his fullest command; and he eagerly embraced that opportunity to return them his warmest acknowledgments for the assistance and support which
he had received from them individually and collectively,
in conducting his Majesty's government.

The addresses were, in the usual complimentary style,
echoes of the speech, abounding with professions of re-
March 26. gard. The day had now arrived when the president was
to lay down the government which he had twice administered. The Right Hon. Francis Humberstone Mackenzie,
Baron Seaforth, having been honoured with his Majesty's
commands to take upon himself the government of Barbadoes, arrived in Carlisle-bay on the twenty-sixth day of
March. Within a month after Lord Seaforth's accession,
Mr. Bishop went to England, where he died shortly after
his arrival.

We shall now conclude this work with a compendium
of the government.

The constitution of Barbadoes is an humble imitation of
that great fabric of human wisdom, the constitution of
England. Here, as in the mother country, the power of
establishing laws resides in three distinct orders, who collectively compose the supreme legislature of the country.
The constituent parts of this legislative body are the governor, who represents the Crown; a council, or upper-
house, whose rank in the colonial system corresponds with
that of the peers in Great Britain ; and a general assembly,

whose functions are analogous to those of the English house of commons.

The governor's legislative authority is entirely negative. He may recommend proper subjects to the consideration of the assembly ; and without his concurrence no bill can pass into a law; nor can his assent sanction the existence of any law beyond three years, without its having received the royal confirmation. As the depositary of the executive power, the governor's power is more positive and extensive. He is styled excellency, and his title is captain-general, governor and commander in chief, chancellor, ordinary, and vice-admiral. The provison for his maintenance is a salary of two thousand pounds sterling, paid by the Crown out of the four and a half per centage. Besides which, he is entitled to one-third of all seizures made by the custom-house within his government, for any violation of the laws of trade ; and on the colonial establishment he is generally allowed three thousand pounds a year to support the dignity of his government. This settlement, which is entirely optional with the assembly, must be made in the first session of the house after his arrival; and, under Lord Seaforth's administration, has been encreased to four thousand pounds.

As captain-general he is entitled to appoint the officers of the militia, and to remove them if he find occasion. He seldom exercises the right of appointment beyond the choice of the colonels, who generally claim the privilege of nominating the lieutenant-colonels, majors and captains of their regiments; and these again insist upon being allowed the choice of their subalterns. Lord Seaforth asserted his right to these appointments, allowing the officers commanding regiments only to recommend; but their recommendation was invariably adopted. The appointment of the gunners and matrosses also is legally vested in the captain-general, but it is usually exercised by the colonels of divisions, the governor only reserving to himself the patronage of Charles'-fort.

The governor, with the consent of the council, has power to dissolve the general assembly, and to issue writs for a new election; and, with the concurrence of five members, to suspend any member of council; unless it be on some very extraordinary occasion, requiring secrecy; and then his power is absolute. He is, however, bound, in either case, to transmit his reasons to the King, before whom the suspended member is permitted to make his defence. Should there be at any time less than seven members of council resident on the island, the governor is allowed to appoint a sufficient number, *pro tempore*, for the dispatch of business.*

As chancellor, the governor has the custody of the great seal, and presides in the courts of error and equity. But,

---

* The president possesses the same authority.

as the council are judges in both these courts, his excellency only sits *primus inter pares*, his vote, or opinion, being of no greater consequence than that of any other member. In the capacity of ordinary he collates to all church livings, of which there are eleven within the island. He takes probate of all testamentary writings; and, in case of litigation, establishes or annuls the will; and, in default of executors appointed by the testator, issues letters of administration, according to the rules of law.

The judges of the courts of civil and criminal judicature, and the justice of the peace can neither be appointed nor removed without the concurrence of the council. A new commission of the peace is issued by each governor, as soon as possible after his arrival, composed of persons recommended by the council. The governor appoints the two masters in chancery, the escheator and solicitor-general, the coroners of the several parishes, and a captain of the ports. The attorney-general, the judge of the court of vice-admiralty, the register in chancery, the clerk of the Crown, the secretary and clerk of the council, the prothonotary, provost-marshal, and naval officer, are appointed by patent; and, with the exception of the two first, are all executed by deputy, to the great injury of the colony. The casual receiver and auditor-general receive their commissions from the Crown; and the officers of the customs have their appointments from the lords of the treasury. Over each of these departments the governor possesses a

paramount controul; he suspends, at will, all those officers who have incurred his displeasure, and supplies, *pro
tempore*, all vacancies occasioned by death or suspension.

The governor as vice-admiral, is entitled to the rights of
jetsam, *flotsam*, and *ligan**: and, in time of war, being
himself previously authorized by the King, he issues his
warrant to the judge of the court of vice-admiralty to grant
commissions to privateers.

In case of the death or absence of the governor, the president of the council is directed by his Majesty's instructions to administer the government. To maintain the dignity of his station he is entitled to one-half the salary, and
other emoluments of office, allotted by the Crown for the
support of its representative. But the inadequacy of this
provision is amply compensated by the liberality of the
legislature. It was formerly usual to allow the president
half the governor's colonial salary; but in later times the
establishment has been increased to three thousand pounds.
His power differs in very few particulars from that of the
governor. He cannot dissolve the assembly existing at the
time he assumes the government. Neither can he remove,

---

* *Jetsam*, is where goods are cast into the sea, and remain under water; *flotsam*,
is where they continue swimming; *ligan*, is where they are sunk, but tied to a cork,
or buoy. If no owner appear, these articles belong to the governor, as vice-admiral; but the lawful owner is entitled to recover the possession, on proving his right.

or suspend, any civil or military officer, without the consent of at least seven members of council; nor can he issue a new commisssion of the peace. In all other respects his authority is co-equal, and co-extensive with the governor's.

The council consists of twelve members, whose appointment is an act of the Crown, exercised on the recommendation of the commander in chief. By the courtesy of the colonies they are styled honourable. But holding their seats by the precarious tenure of the royal will and pleasure, and, in some measure, at the caprice of the governor, they are supposed not to possess that independence which is essential to an order of men whose rank, on the political scale of the colonies is equivalent to the peerage of England. Hence they do not, collectively, enjoy that degree of popular favour and confidence which is the exclusive privilege of the representatives of the people. As a distinct branch of the legislature, their concurrence is necessary in the passing of all laws. All bills unconnected with the raising of supplies, or the disposal of the public money, may originate with them. In their legislative capacity, the freedom of discussion is expressly granted to them by the royal instructions, but it is extremely circumscribed by the presence of the commander in chief; an absurd custom, which seems to have originated in the infancy of the colony, before the representative body was

CHAP.XVIII. called into existence; and which is, indisputably, a radical defect in the colonial constitution.

As a council of state they stand in the same relation to the governor as the privy council of Great Britain does to the king; and are bound by the solemn obligation of an oath not to divulge any secret of government communicated to them in that character. As privy counsellors they assist the governor with their advice, and are intended to be a check upon him, if he should attempt to exceed his commission and instructions; a feeble check indeed, since it is easy for him, by virtue of his prerogative, to throw off the rein, and pursue the bent of his own inclinations. For, although, as has been well remarked by the elegant historian of the West Indies, every governor is directed, by his instructions, to advise with his council on most occasions, he is competent to act in all cases, not only without, but even against their concurrence. Answerable only to his Sovereign, his proceedings are legal and efficient to all intents and purposes within the colony.

The house of assembly is composed of twenty-two delegates, or deputies, annually elected, two for each parish, by the body of the people. Of the qualifications of the candidates and the electors due notice has been taken in a former chapter of this work. On the expiration, or dissolution of the assembly, the governor immediately issues writs, directed to the senior counsellor in each parish, or, in the absence of a member of council, to any substantial freeholder, requiring him to summon the freeholders to meet, within fifteen days after notice being given at their parish church, and to make choice of two able and discreet persons of their own body to represent them in the general assembly. The person thus authorised to convene the freeholders, is the sheriff for the occasion, and makes a return of the writ, with a certificate of the election, to the governor, on his next sitting in council, when the representatives also meet, and take the state oaths in his excellency's presence. Having performed this ceremony, which is also repeated on the accession of every new commander in chief, the assembly proceed to the choice of a speaker, whom they present for his excellency's approbation. If the choice is confirmed, the speaker, in due parliamentary form, demands from the representative of the Crown, the usual privileges of the house. This done, they possess, within the colony, the same legislative authority which belongs to the house of commons. All money bills must originate with them; though, as we have had frequent occasion to remark, they have often suffered this invaluable privilege to be encroached upon, by admitting the council to amend their bills of that description. They exercise the right of expelling any of their members who have been guilty of any heinous crime, and may grant leave of absence to any of them, not exceeding four at a time, for the term of six months. In case of the death, or expulsion of a member, the house addresses the governor to issue a writ for the elec-

CHAP. XVIII. tion of a person to supply the vacancy. They determine all controverted elections, and can adjourn themselves from day to day; but no longer adjournments are valid bu^t such as are made by the commander in chief; who has power to convene them whenever he thinks proper.

Besides the choice of their chaplain, clerk and marshal, the Assembly have successively assumed the appointment of an agent, treasurer, store-keeper of the magazine, comptroller of the excise, a guager of wine in each of the four towns, a harbour-master, an inspector of weights and measures, and twelve inspectors of cotton. To the offices of treasurer, store keeper and comptroller of the excise, the members of the assembly succeed in triennial rotation and farm them at an annual rent, to the person by whom they are executed; who enters into recognizances before the commander in chief for the faithful performance of their duty. No money can be issued from the treasury, nor stores from the magazine, but in consequence of orders under the governor's sign manual. Nor can the treasurer appropriate the public money to any use whatever not expressly warranted by law.

Four members of council, nominated by the commander in chief, and six of the assembly, chosen by the speaker constitute a committee for the examination and settlement of the treasurer's accounts and of all others relating to the public expenditure. A committee of correspondence consisting of three counsellors and four assemblymen, are appointed to correspond with the agent in England. The commissioners of fortifications are composed of the members of council, the members of the assembly and the field officers of the militia resident in each division. They possess extensive powers, in ordering whatever repairs they may deem necessary to the forts. Nine members of council and twelve of the assembly compose the mole-head committee. From the ruined state in which the pier has been suffered to remain for more than twenty six years, with ample funds to commence its reparation, it would seem that the members of this board have forgotten that they have a duty to perform.

The judicature of the island consists of five courts of common pleas, each composed of a chief judge and four assistants, appointed by the governor's commission under the great seal. They commence their sittings on the last Monday in January and continue them, by adjournments, every four weeks, until September. Appeals in all causes above ten pounds value may be had to the courts of error and equity; and thence, in every case of litigation exceeding five hundred pounds, an ulterior appeal lies to the king in council. The court of exchequer is held by a chief baron and four puisne barons, of whom, as in the other courts, three are competent to hear and determine all matters at issue. The court of chancery composed, as has been already observed, of the government and council, of whom five make a quorum, sits monthly, except

CHAP. XVIII. on particular, occasions which require greater dispatch, or will admit of longer delay.

A court of grand sessions of oyer and terminer, general gaol delivery, and general sessions of the peace, is held twice a year. It is formed by a chief justice, appointed by the governor and council, assisted by at least five justices of the peace. The chief justice is generally a member of the council, or a judge of one of the courts of common pleas. Six freeholders from each parish are summoned to attend the court by virtue of the governor's writ, directed to the senior member of council in each parish; or, in his absence, to any justice of the peace; or should there be no such magistrate in the parish, to any substantial freeholder. From among the persons thus indifferently chosen, the grand inquest and petty juries are selected. This court may continue its session for four days, and possesses a plenitude of power, in all criminal cases, affecting even the life of the offender. In all inferior offences the governor may remit the punishment imposed by the court; and, even in capital cases, such as murder and treason, he may reprieve the convict until the king's pleasure is known.

FINIS.

ERRATA.

For " Barbadoes" read " Barbados" throughout the Work ; a deviation from the Author's orthography, occasioned by the inadvertence of the Printer, and, unfortunately, discovered too late to admit of a general correction.

In the List of Subscribers *for* James Anstie *read* Anstice, and after James Cavan, Esq. *add* 2 Copies.
Page   46 note, *for* Kindall's *read* Kendall's.
         60 note, line 20, *add* ["] after whatever.
         94 line 18, *for* are become *read* had become.
     131...... 9, *for* temperary *read* temporary.
     141......17, *for* goods *read* gods.
     142......19, *for* Lordship's *read* Lordships'.
     218...... 5, *for* wrecking *read* wreaking.
     226 note, *for* but have *read* but I have.
     245 note, line 2, *for* me *read* time.
     313 line 10, *for* brother-in-law *read* brother.
     319 note, *for* compiler *read* compilers.
     320 line 12, *for* generaly *read* general.
     336 last word but one, *for* into *read* in.
     340 line 6, *for* nor *read* or.
         note, *for* pregnant *read* poignant.
     356 line 17, *for* collector *read* collection, and *dele* the comma.
     375......22, *for* Jame *read* James'.
     444 last line, *for* ank *read* rank.
     469......17, *for* nor *read* or.
     473 last line, *for* vote *read* opposition.
     528......12, *for* nor *read* or.
     535......18, *for* were *read* where.
     536......11, *for* implicated *read* complicated.
     586...... 7, *for* agreeable *read* agreeably.
     592......20, *for* their *read* the.
     622......11, *for* Hughes *read* Hugues.
     667 last line but one, *for* government *read* governor.
In the marginal dates, *from* page 490 to page 517 *read* 1781.
             from 517 to 540 *read* 1782.
             from 540 to 558 *read* 1783.
             from 558 to 572 *read* 1784.
             Page 572 *read* 1785.
             from 572 to 578 *read* 1786.
             from 578 to 583 *read* 1787.
             from 583 to 585 *read* 1788.
             from 585 to 589 *read* 1789.
             Pages 589 and 590 *read* 1790.
             from 590 to 597 *read* 1791.